NATIONAL ACADEMIES *Sciences Engineering Medicine*

NATIONAL ACADEMIES PRESS
Washington, DC

Transforming Undergraduate STEM Education

Supporting Equitable and Effective Teaching

Archie Holmes, Kerry Brenner, and Janet Gao, *Editors*

Committee on Equitable and Effective Teaching in Undergraduate STEM Education: A Framework for Institutions, Educators, and Disciplines

Board on Science Education

Division of Behavioral and Social Sciences and Education

Consensus Study Report

NATIONAL ACADEMIES PRESS 500 Fifth Street, NW Washington, DC 20001

This activity was supported by contracts between the National Academy of Sciences and the Gates Foundation (INV-045634), the Howard Hughes Medical Institute (092622), the National Academy of Sciences W. K. Kellogg Foundation Fund, and the National Science Foundation (Award 2309335). Any opinions, findings, conclusions, or recommendations expressed in this publication do not necessarily reflect the views of any organization or agency that provided support for the project.

International Standard Book Number-13: 978-0-309-72998-7
Digital Object Identifier: https://doi.org/10.17226/28268
Library of Congress Control Number: 2025936436

This publication is available from the National Academies Press, 500 Fifth Street, NW, Keck 360, Washington, DC 20001; (800) 624-6242; https://nap.nationalacademies.org.

The manufacturer's authorized representative in the European Union for product safety is Authorised Rep Compliance Ltd., Ground Floor, 71 Lower Baggot Street, Dublin D02 P593 Ireland; www.arccompliance.com.

Printed in the United States of America.

Suggested citation: National Academies of Sciences, Engineering, and Medicine. 2025. *Transforming Undergraduate STEM Education: Supporting Equitable and Effective Teaching*. Washington, DC: National Academies Press. https://doi.org/10.17226/28268.

The **National Academy of Sciences** was established in 1863 by an Act of Congress, signed by President Lincoln, as a private, nongovernmental institution to advise the nation on issues related to science and technology. Members are elected by their peers for outstanding contributions to research. Dr. Marcia McNutt is president.

The **National Academy of Engineering** was established in 1964 under the charter of the National Academy of Sciences to bring the practices of engineering to advising the nation. Members are elected by their peers for extraordinary contributions to engineering. Dr. Tsu-Jae Liu is president.

The **National Academy of Medicine** (formerly the Institute of Medicine) was established in 1970 under the charter of the National Academy of Sciences to advise the nation on medical and health issues. Members are elected by their peers for distinguished contributions to medicine and health. Dr. Victor J. Dzau is president.

The three Academies work together as the National Academies of Sciences, Engineering, and Medicine to provide independent, objective analysis and advice to the nation and conduct other activities to solve complex problems and inform public policy decisions. The National Academies also encourage education and research, recognize outstanding contributions to knowledge, and increase public understanding in matters of science, engineering, and medicine.

Learn more about the National Academies of Sciences, Engineering, and Medicine at **www.nationalacademies.org**.

Consensus Study Reports published by the National Academies of Sciences, Engineering, and Medicine document the evidence-based consensus on the study's statement of task by an authoring committee of experts. Reports typically include findings, conclusions, and recommendations based on information gathered by the committee and the committee's deliberations. Each report has been subjected to a rigorous and independent peer-review process and it represents the position of the National Academies on the statement of task.

Proceedings published by the National Academies of Sciences, Engineering, and Medicine chronicle the presentations and discussions at a workshop, symposium, or other event convened by the National Academies. The statements and opinions contained in proceedings are those of the participants and are not endorsed by other participants, the planning committee, or the National Academies.

Rapid Expert Consultations published by the National Academies of Sciences, Engineering, and Medicine are authored by subject-matter experts on narrowly focused topics that can be supported by a body of evidence. The discussions contained in rapid expert consultations are considered those of the authors and do not contain policy recommendations. Rapid expert consultations are reviewed by the institution before release.

For information about other products and activities of the National Academies, please visit www.nationalacademies.org/about/whatwedo.

COMMITTEE ON EQUITABLE AND EFFECTIVE TEACHING IN UNDERGRADUATE STEM EDUCATION: A FRAMEWORK FOR INSTITUTIONS, EDUCATORS, AND DISCIPLINES

ARCHIE HOLMES (*Chair*), Professor, Chandra Family Department of Electrical and Computer Engineering, The University of Texas at Austin; and Executive Vice Chancellor of Academic Affairs, The University of Texas System

TRACIE ADDY, Founding Director of the Institute for Teaching, Innovation, & Inclusive Pedagogy, Rutgers University, New Brunswick

HILLARY BARRON, Assistant Professor of Biology, Bemidji State University

WILLIAM CLEMONS, Hanisch Memorial Professor of Biochemistry, Division of Chemistry and Chemical Engineering, Caltech[1]

MICHAEL DENNIN, Vice Provost for Teaching and Learning; Dean, Division of Undergraduate Education; Professor of Physics and Astronomy, University of California, Irvine

ERIN DORAN, Associate Professor, Educational Leadership and Foundations, University of Texas, El Paso

ANNE EGGER, Professor, Geological Sciences, Science and Mathematics Education, Central Washington University; and Executive Director, National Association of Geoscience Teachers

MARCO MOLINARO, Executive Director for Educational Effectiveness and Analytics, University of Maryland, College Park

MARY MURPHY, Herman B. Wells Endowed Professor, Indiana University

JOSEPHINE PINO, Instructor of Biology, Portland Community College

MELONIE SEXTON, Professor of Psychology and Undergraduate Research Coordinator, Valencia College

ELLI THEOBALD, Assistant Professor of Biology, University of Washington

CRISTINA VILLALOBOS, Myles and Sylvia Aaronson Endowed Professor, School of Mathematical and Statistical Sciences; Interim Dean of the Honors College, and Founding Director, Center of Excellence in STEM Education, University of Texas Rio Grande Valley

GABRIELA WEAVER, Assistant Vice President for Academic Affairs and Research, University of Massachusetts System; and Professor of Chemistry, University of Massachusetts, Amherst

---

[1] Resigned July 2024.

JOHN WILLIAMS, Associate Professor of Biology, and Chair, Department of Natural Sciences, Albany State University
SEAN YEE, Associate Professor of Mathematics Education, Co-Director of the Center for Science Education, University of South Carolina

Study Staff

KERRY BRENNER, Study Director
JANET GAO, Program Officer
LUCY OLIVEROS, Senior Project Assistant
HEIDI SCHWEINGRUBER, Board Director

Reviewers

This Consensus Study Report was reviewed in draft form by individuals chosen for their diverse perspectives and technical expertise. The purpose of this independent review is to provide candid and critical comments that will assist the National Academies of Sciences, Engineering, and Medicine in making each published report as sound as possible and to ensure that it meets the institutional standards for quality, objectivity, evidence, and responsiveness to the study charge. The review comments and draft manuscript remain confidential to protect the integrity of the deliberative process.

We thank the following individuals for their review of this report:

VICKI L. CHANDLER, Minerva University
ANDREA FOLLMER, University of Kansas
LOGAN E. GIN, Brown University
KELLY HOGAN, Duke University
JAIME LESTER, Johns Hopkins University
COURTNEY NGAI, Colorado State University
CHRISTOPHER RASMUSSEN, San Diego State University
RENATA REVELO, University of Illinois, Chicago
JON-MARC RODRIGUEZ, University of Wisconsin, Milwaukee
BETHANY SANSING-HELTON, Madison Area Technical College
VIJI SANTHY, The University of North Carolina at Chapel Hill
TOM TUBON, Mira Costa Community College

Although the reviewers listed above provided many constructive comments and suggestions, they were not asked to endorse the conclusions or recommendations of this report, nor did they see the final draft before its release. The review of this report was overseen by **MELANIE COOPER**, Michigan State University, and **ANA P. BARROS**, University of Illinois at Urbana-Champaign. They were responsible for making certain that an independent examination of this report was carried out in accordance with the standards of the National Academies and that all review comments were carefully considered. Responsibility for the final content rests entirely with the authoring committee and the National Academies.

This project also included a discussion draft released in fall 2023 to share an initial proposal for the principles of equitable and effective teaching in order to solicit public input. We thank **MELANIE COOPER** for overseeing that review and the following reviewers of that discussion draft for their helpful input during our study process:

MARK BAILLIE, Department of Chemistry, University of Arkansas at Little Rock
KATELYN M. COOPER, School of Life Sciences, Arizona State University
LOGAN E. GIN, Sheridan Center for Teaching and Learning, Brown University
SUZANNE WAKIM, Department of Biology, Butte Community College
ZAKIYA S. WILSON-KENNEDY, Chemistry Education Research and Practice, Louisiana State University

Acknowledgments

The Committee thanks the sponsors of the study, the Gates Foundation, the Howard Hughes Medical Institute, and the National Science Foundation, for providing the funding for this important project on equitable and effective teaching of undergraduate science, technology, engineering, and mathematics (STEM).

Commissioned papers provided great insights into several of the topics of the study. The committee gratefully acknowledges the work of Leslie Gonzales (University of Arizona) and Dawn Culpepper's (University of Maryland) A Framework for Change Agents: Fostering Equity-Minded Change within and across STEM Teaching and Learning Contexts; Xueli Wang's (University of Wisconsin-Madison) Paving Community College Student Pathways for Equitable STEM Education; Michael Brown's (University of Michigan) Toxic Combinations, Content Repetition, and Delayed Momentum: Conceptualizing the Emerging Evidence on Curricular Complexity in Four-Year Institutions as Influence on Equitable and Effective Teaching in Undergraduate STEM Education; Melissa Vito (The University of Texas at San Antonio), Marcela Ramirez (The University of Texas at San Antonio), and Angela Gunder's (University of Arizona) Bridging Innovation and Access: Academic Innovation to Advance Student Success in Undergraduate STEM Education; Milagros Castillo-Montoya (University of Connecticut), Bryan M. Dewsbury (Florida International University), Corbin M. Campbell (American University), and Brian McGowan's (American University) A Response to the National Academies of Sciences, Engineering, and Medicine Draft Report of Equitable and Effective Teaching. The committee thanks the above contributors for preparing the commissioned papers for this study.

We thank all those who asked questions and shared ideas at our public meetings and conference presentations. We are especially grateful to the invited experts who participated in our meetings, including Matthew Hora (University of Wisconsin-Madison); Michelle Smith (Cornell University); Daniel Reinholz (San Diego State University); Ruthmae Sears (University of South Florida); Jayme Dyer (Durham Technical Community College); Cassandra Horii (Stanford University); Corbin Campbell (American University); Brian McGowan (American University); Milagros Castillo-Montoya (University of Connecticut); Bryan Dewsbury (Florida International University); Ebony McGee (Johns Hopkins University); Luis Perez (CAST); Suzanne Wakim (Butte College); Carol Hurney (Colby College); Flower Darby (University of Missouri); Danny Caballero (Michigan State University); Nicole LaDue (Northern Illinois University); Jon-Marc Rodriguez (University of Wisconsin, Milwaukee); Sarah Rodriguez (Virginia Tech); Tatiane Russo-Tait (University of Georgia); April Strom (Chandler-Gilbert Community College); Terrell Morton (University of Illinois, Chicago); Amber Simpson (Binghamton University); Greg Walton (Stanford University); Karen Vignare (Association of Public and Land Grant Universities); Angela Gunder (Online Learning Consortium); Muhammad Hossain (Claflin University); Jim DeKloe (Solano College); Kelly Neiles (St. Mary's College of Maryland); Koari O'Connell (Oregon State University); Linda Powell (Community College of Philadelphia); Adam Fontecchio (Center for the Integration of Research, Teaching and Learning); Francine Glazer (New York Institute of Technology); Susan Bickerstaff (Teachers College, Columbia University); Alison Cook-Sather (Bryn Mawr College); Sarah Whitley (Center for First-Generation Student Success); Steve Dandaneau (Colorado State University and the Association of Undergraduate Education at Research Universities); Anne-Marie Núñez (The University of Texas, El Paso); Gita Bangera (Northwest Commission on Colleges and Universities); Kemi Jona (University of Virginia); Asim Ali (Auburn University); Joseph Dumit (University of California, Davis); Amanda Holloman (University of Florida); Shandy Hauk (San Francisco State University); Hironao Okahana (American Council on Education); Darren Hoffmann (University of Iowa); Edward Watson (American Association of Colleges and Universities); Bennett Goldberg (Northwestern University); Sarah Hokanson (Boston University); Robin Greenler (University of Wisconsin, Madison); and Donald Gillian-Daniel (University of Wisconsin, Madison).

The Committee also wishes to extend our thanks to all who those who provided public input on the discussion draft through the online questionnaire, at our fifth committee meeting, at conference presentations, or by submitting written comments. The Committee thanks the reviewers listed in the previous section and also Carl Wieman (Stanford University) for his very helpful input to the study. In addition, Gregory W. Pearson is appreciated for his assistance with writing and organizing the discussion draft, Heather Kreidler for assistance with fact checking, and Laura Yoder for amazing editing.

The Committee also wishes to extend its gratitude to the staff of the Division of Behavioral and Social Sciences and Education (DBASSE) and in particular the Board on Science Education. They are especially grateful to Kirsten Sampson Snyder of the DBASSE staff for exemplary work in supervising the review of both the discussion draft and this final report.

Contents

Boxes, Figures, and Tables

BOXES

FIGURES

TABLES

Preface

Improvement in post-secondary education will require converting teaching from a solo sport to a community-based research activity.

—Herb Simon

In August 1986, when I stepped onto the campus at the University of Texas at Austin to begin college, I would not have imagined the transformational experience that my studies in electrical engineering would afford me: a faculty career and my current role at the University of Texas System. While there are many factors that have enabled this, an important one was that I was fortunate to be able to successfully navigate the undergraduate curriculum and use it to build upon the talents, skills, and motivation I possessed. Being in the classroom as a faculty member made me realize that what I experienced in my educational journey was not widely experienced. There are many students who also have the talents, skills, and motivation (sometimes more than I had) to complete science, technology, engineering, and mathematics (STEM) majors and are not well served by the status quo. For others, the STEM education they receive through general education, other curricular requirements, or personal interest does not provide them with the knowledge and skills needed to fully participate in an economy and society where science and technology will continue to play a critical role. This has serious implications for our economy and society, and we can and must do better.

For the past two years, I have had the honor of chairing the Committee on Equitable and Effective Teaching in Undergraduate STEM Education: A Framework for Institutions, Educators, and Disciplines. My esteemed colleagues and I have been hard at work discussing how to change the status quo that dominates current undergraduate STEM education. Our approach, outlined in this report, features seven Principles for Equitable and Effective Teaching in undergraduate STEM education. The Principles outlined draw from the research base on what has been demonstrated to lead improved equitable and effective teaching and learning. In order to fully impact the entire undergraduate STEM education ecosystem, we discussed how these Principles would be enacted given variations in modes of teaching (e.g., in-person, online, and hybrid), learning environments (e.g., the classroom, the laboratory, and the field), institutional contexts (e.g., two-year colleges, liberal arts colleges, and research universities), and across multiple levels of the system (e.g., individual instructors, academic units, and institutional leadership). We also contemplated the role that technology (e.g., artificial intelligence, virtual reality) does and will play in support of this effort.

Our development of the seven Principles greatly benefited from a public discussion of a draft of the Principles presented at a Committee meeting in December 2023. At that event, invited panelists and participants (both in-person and virtually) provided us with invaluable feedback which has helped the Committee refine its thinking and these Principles. We are incredibly grateful to those who were able to participate in that discussion and share their ideas.

Through its work, the Committee also recognized that the Principles alone cannot lead to the change needed. As the quotation from Herb Simon states at the beginning of this Preface, change must be a community-based activity. Everyone from instructors to administrators to external partners has an important role to play. To support this, the Committee also had discussions about the importance of institutional infrastructure, academic units and their leaders, and the policies and practices that define the environment in which undergraduate STEM education occurs.

I feel confident that these factors, along with the Principles, will help all institutions achieve equitable and effective teaching and learning for all students. Taken as a whole, this report, its Principles, and the Committee's recommendations provide faculty, academic units, and institutions with a playbook that will help them be successful on this journey.

Probably like all committee chairs that have come before me (and those who will follow), I want to make sure that this report makes a difference. Given the time of this Committee's report (early 2025), there are two challenges worth mentioning here. The first are the conversations around diversity, equity, and inclusion (also known as DEI) in higher education. The evidence presented in this report makes the Committee's position on this issue clear: effective and equitable teaching benefits all students and is intricately linked to excellence. While there are some who do benefit from the status quo, implementation of this report will ensure that students who are currently underserved by higher education benefit as well. The benefits of this implementation do not go just to these students: more equitable learning environments benefit everyone. Given the current climate, there are instructors who are committed to serving all students but do not feel enabled to do this work. Success will require academic unit and institutional leaders along with external partners such as disciplinary organizations to be advocates for equity being a core value and the lens through which effective teaching is enabled.

The second challenge is related to the burnout felt by many in higher education. While much of the focus has been on the mental health of students (and rightly so), instructors and leaders in higher education are also experiencing the same and similar issues. The Committee and I acknowledge that integrating these Principles into learning environments and the policies and practices of academic units and institutions is not easy work; it will take time and focused effort. Having plans for both the short and long terms coupled with appropriate incentives will be critical. Inviting instructors to co-create these plans is important in order to ensure that their needs are appropriately assessed and the timeline to make meaningful change is reasonable. Leaders also need to factor in the workload of those who will do the work and ensure that the work is equitably shared by all (e.g., not tasking an individual such as an instructor of color to do the work that is everyone's responsibility).

In the end, I think that the most important reason for creating equitable and effective learning environments for all students is the impact on them, their families and communities, and our nation. When I think about those who will directly benefit from this work, my thoughts go to my niece's daughter. Currently four, she will be part of the Class of 2043. When she enters the college/university of her choice, what I want for her most of all is to be exposed to STEM in such a way that it is *her* choice on how STEM impacts her life and career and that the system that educated her does not make that decision for her and her classmates.

Archie Holmes, *Chair*
Committee on Equitable and Effective Teaching
in Undergraduate STEM Education: A Framework
for Institutions, Educators, and Disciplines

Acronyms and Abbreviations

AAU	Association of American Universities
AI	artificial intelligence
APLU	Association of Public and Land-Grant Universities
ATE	Advanced Technology Education program of NSF
CBE	competency-based education
CCPI-STEM	Community College Presidents' Initiative in STEM
CIRTL	Center for the Integration of Research, Teaching and Learning
CoP	Community of Practice
CTE	career and technical education
CTL	Center for Teaching and Learning
CURE	course-based undergraduate research experiences
DAT	Departmental Action Team
DBER	discipline-based education research
DFW	D, F, and withdraw
EP3	Effective Practices for Physics Programs
FAITE	Financial Alignment with Inclusive Teaching Effectiveness

HBCUs	Historically Black Colleges and Universities
HHMI	Howard Hughes Medical Institute
HSIs	Hispanic Serving Institutions
ISTP	Inclusive STEM Teaching Project
LGBTQIA+	Lesbian, Gay, Bisexual, Transgender, Queer/Questioning, Intersex, Asexual/Aromantic/Agender, plus other related identities
LMS	Learning Management System
MSI	Minority Serving Institution
NABT	National Association of Biology Teachers
NACUBO	National Association of College and University Business Officers
NIST	National Institute on Scientific Teaching
NSEC	Network of STEM Education Centers
NSF	National Science Foundation
OER	open educational resource
PDSA	Plan-Do-Study-Act
PERTS	Project for Education Research That Scales
PLC	Professional Learning Community
PLD	professional learning and development
PLO	program-level learning outcome
PLTL	peer-led team learning
POGIL	Process Oriented Guided Inquiry Learning
PULSE	Partnership for Undergraduate Life Sciences Education
PWI	Predominantly White Institution
SAGE 2YC	Supporting and Advancing Geoscience Education at Two-Year Colleges
SEISMIC	Sloan Equity & Inclusion in STEM Introductory Courses
SEP	Student Experience Project
SI	supplementary instruction
SoTL	scholarship of teaching and learning
STEM	science, technology, engineering, and mathematics

TA	teaching assistant
TCUs	Tribal Colleges and Universities
UDL	Universal Design for Learning
UERU	Association for Undergraduate Education at Research Universities
UFERN	Undergraduate Field Experiences Research Network
URM	underrepresented minority
VITAL	visiting faculty, instructors, teaching assistants, adjunct faculty, and lecturers

Summary

The science, technology, engineering, and mathematics (STEM) workforce has produced impressive advances in scientific understanding and technology. Colleges and universities deserve enormous credit for their direct (research) and indirect (education) contributions to these advances. STEM education is a wonderful opportunity for people to learn about the world around them; it helps them to become knowledgeable about natural processes, technological innovations, and the built environment in ways that enhance quality of life. It can also prepare them to pursue careers in STEM fields. However, commonly used methods of teaching undergraduate STEM education benefit only a relatively small percentage of learners, leading many to choose not to enroll in STEM courses or pursue STEM careers. This trend severely limits participation in the STEM careers that play a critical role in our nation's prosperity—driving economic growth, seeding innovation, and fostering human well-being. It also means that many students may complete their undergraduate education with a limited understanding of science and of the natural and designed world. Indeed, lack of access to equitable and effective STEM teaching hinders not only the success of individuals and communities, but social and national progress as well.

WHY THE REPORT IS NEEDED

Undergraduate STEM education occurs in many types of institutions of varying sizes, with varying priorities and budgets, but all these types of institutions share a responsibility for providing high-quality STEM learning experiences for students. However, many longstanding policies and practices in undergraduate STEM education have produced, perpetuated, and exacerbated differences in opportunities, experiences, and outcomes among post-secondary STEM students. For example, widespread use of teaching strategies that are not supported by research have contributed to the disparities in opportunity and outcomes for undergraduate STEM students. Students from lower socio-economic backgrounds, students of color, first-generation college goers, women, and students with disabilities have consistently fared worse in post-secondary STEM education. Students from these groups make up much of the current and future undergraduate population. Educating them so that they can contribute to societal efforts to meet the demands of the 21st century requires re-evaluating instructional practices in STEM and improving the learning experiences of undergraduate students in STEM courses and programs.

With this in mind, the Board on Science Education of the National Academies of Sciences, Engineering, and Medicine convened the Committee on Equitable and Effective Teaching in Undergraduate STEM Education: A Framework for Institutions, Educators, and Disciplines to examine research on learning, teaching, and institutional change in order to provide guidance for undergraduate STEM educators and institutions on improving undergraduate instruction and addressing existing disparities in STEM education. This committee brought together individuals from many different kinds of higher education institutions, who represent expertise across the STEM disciplines.

The resulting report is designed to provide a common language and structure for conversations across academia. By anchoring those conversations in a clear understanding of what is known about teaching, learning, and equity, institutions and individuals across disciplines will better understand their important role in changing the system. The report's seven Principles for Equitable and Effective Teaching, conclusions, recommendations, and research agenda together provide a structure by which stakeholders across post-secondary education can converse and plan in order to work toward a system where all students at all institutions of higher education can experience student-centered, equitable, and effective STEM learning experiences. This complex conversation and the resulting actions will require the cooperation and collaboration of all stakeholders, including instructors, leaders of academic units (e.g., departments, programs), institutional leaders, researchers, governing boards, professional societies, funders of STEM education, and students themselves to achieve equitable and effective teaching and learning for all.

TOWARD EQUITABLE AND EFFECTIVE LEARNING EXPERIENCES

Drawing on decades of research on learning and teaching, the committee analyzed the current institutional context for undergraduate STEM education as well as the research literature on teaching, learning, and equity. They used this analysis to develop a set of Principles for Equitable and Effective Teaching: approaches to STEM education that can guide the design and enactment of more equitable pedagogical practices and the creation of inclusive learning experiences in STEM. The Principles are as follows:

1. Students need opportunities to actively engage in disciplinary learning.
2. Students' diverse interests, goals, knowledge and experiences can be leveraged to enhance learning.
3. STEM learning involves affective and social dimensions.
4. Identity and sense of belonging shape STEM teaching and learning.
5. Multiple forms of data can provide evidence to inform improvement.
6. Flexibility and responsiveness to situational and contextual factors support student learning.
7. Intentionality and transparency create more equitable opportunities.

These evidence-based principles reflect key insights from what is known about learning in STEM. Decades of research show that learning involves a set of complex processes and is shaped by the characteristics and experiences of learners, social interactions, and cultural context. Studies are clear that student-centered instructional practices that take students' interests and experiences into account and provide them with authentic opportunities to engage with disciplinary content, practices, and analysis are more effective than instructional practices that rely primarily on lecture, reading, and memorization of content, procedures, and algorithms. While it is important to improve instruction in courses at all levels, experiences in foundational courses are particularly important for student persistence in STEM. Often these courses filter out students rather than deepening their engagement, interest, and understanding of STEM topics. Improving instruction in these courses is an important lever for producing more equitable opportunities and outcomes for undergraduate STEM students.

Equitable undergraduate STEM education systems provide all students with the support they need to succeed, as measured by achievement of clearly communicated learning objectives. In an *effective* undergraduate STEM education system, all students demonstrate learning and have the opportunities and resources to meet desired learning objectives. An equitable and effective undergraduate STEM education does not come at the expense of excellence. The focus is on helping all students learn and understand STEM concepts and be able to use them in practical ways.

A course that is designed around equitable and effective teaching strategies will make the course goals clear to the students, recognize the students' role in their own learning, and give students agency to engage in the course material in ways that welcome and respect their identities. This approach makes student learning the primary driver (e.g., the course is student centered). In contrast, an instructor-centered course usually focuses on covering a certain amount of content, with the volume of content serving as the primary driver of the schedule, course policies, instructional methods, and assessments. Common grading practices generally result in a single letter grade on a transcript for each course. Given the widely varying approaches to assigning these letters they do not fully convey the complexity and extent of student learning and are often assigned in ways that are not equitable. A focus on student learning goals can be one component of addressing these inequities.

Some barriers to students' success emerge from their experiences in individual classrooms or courses, while others arise from the structure of course offerings and requirements for their program, major, or institution. Students are often expected to take a sequence of STEM courses that may not be well coordinated. Focused attention on examining and improving the coherence of learning goals across course sequences, programs, and majors can help educators design pathways that make sense for their students, thereby enabling improvements in individual courses, facilitating alignment to the Principles for Equitable and Effective Teaching, increasing transparency, and improving student outcomes. These changes can therefore help students navigate opportunities for learning STEM and obtaining credentials.

VALUING AND SUPPORTING INSTRUCTORS

Designing, implementing, and improving STEM learning experiences to make them more equitable and effective requires use of a diverse set of instructional practices, attention to the social dynamics in and culture of the classroom, and regular cycles of reflection and innovation by individual or groups of instructors. Making STEM instruction equitable and effective requires academic units and institutions to (a) demonstrate that they value and will reward teaching and (b) provide support and guidance to help instructors achieve high-quality learning experiences in STEM for all students.

Implementation of equitable and effective teaching is a process of continuous improvement that necessitates all instructors engage in reflection about their teaching and work to make it better. Professional learning and development (PLD) is one key tool that instructors can use throughout their careers to learn approaches and engage with colleagues in communities that foster that continuous improvement. This includes everyone who engages with undergraduates in their courses and classrooms: full-time tenured and tenure-track faculty, part-time and contingent faculty, graduate student teaching assistants, postdoctoral fellows, and others. Another important aspect of PLD is its role in the use of digital technologies in the classroom, which have the potential to afford opportunities to enhance equitable and effective teaching in STEM when they are introduced along with PLD opportunities that provide guidance and support for instructors. The PLD can occur on campus or virtually and be conducted in both formal and informal ways.

Institutional support is needed to ensure that ongoing high-quality PLD is available and accessible for all types of instructors. At many institutions, tenure-track faculty are encouraged to prioritize research over teaching and discouraged from spending time on the courses they teach. Some non-tenure-track educators focus more on teaching but may be excluded from professional development opportunities and communities, and sometimes even from faculty or academic unit meetings and functions. The reasons instructors do not engage in PLD vary but include historical precedent, incentives to prioritize other responsibilities, a lack of rewards for attention to teaching, and limitations in funding for time spent on PLD. Exclusion has long-term effects: graduate students and postdoctoral scholars need professional learning and development to prepare for potential roles as future faculty in addition to professional learning and development related to any existing roles as instructors or teaching assistants. Overall, when institutions and academic units do not value teaching and preparing for it via PLD they deprive instructors of appropriate venues for connecting with other instructors to form communities that can advance continuous improvement.

MEASURING AND ADVANCING SYSTEM CHANGE

Using these Principles to improve undergraduate teaching and learning in STEM will require a commitment from, and collaboration of, stakeholders ranging from individual instructors to leaders of STEM academic units and higher education institutions. Academic units hold collective responsibility for ensuring that educators working under their auspices have the resources and supports they need to provide equitable and effective undergraduate STEM learning experiences. Academic units also have responsibility for ensuring that all learning experiences they oversee, including courses, laboratories, field experiences, research experiences, and prerequisite and other requirements for programs and majors, provide equitable and effective STEM learning experiences for students. Academic units play a major role in decisions and policies about teaching assignments, career advancement, rewards, promotion, and tenure, including how teaching is valued, recognized, evaluated, and rewarded, and how teaching assignments are made. Academic unit decisions and policies related to teaching, grading, and other aspects of the culture of the unit can impede or promote the implementation of equitable and effective teaching strategies. For example, in some academic units, instructors teaching courses that are foundational, have large enrollments, or that are designed for non-major learners are not treated with the same respect as those who teach upper-level courses focused on students majoring in the discipline. This culture can be changed; instruction and student learning can become central values.

Policies and procedures at the institutional level can demonstrate instruction is valued and can either impede or promote implementation of the Principles for Equitable and Effective Teaching. Change toward equitable and effective teaching will require coordinated effort from multiple levels of institutional leadership and a culture of growth that is responsive to the needs of students and instructors. Data, both aggregated and disaggregated, are essential to accurately understanding, enacting, and monitoring change. Both quantitative and qualitative data are needed to fully understand what is happening in a system and to provide information to guide change efforts. Reflective analysis of data best guides policy and practice decisions and informs ongoing efforts at improvement. Institutional leaders can analyze and reform policies and practices so that incentives for faculty, instructors, and academic unit leaders are aligned with the goal of equitable and effective teaching and all stakeholders are supported in change efforts. Institutional change at the deepest levels is an ongoing process. Setting up processes for continuous improvement can have a larger long-term impact than seeking quick, dramatic change. Processes for sustained systemic change can include (a) opportunities for institutional stakeholders at all levels to become familiar with the Principles for Equitable and Effective Teaching and why they are important; (b) attention to an academic unit's culture and the challenges of implementing change; (c) both top-down and bottom-up changes with attention to power dynamics in the institution and who holds positional power as well as who holds more informal power and influence; and (d) vigilant and transparent communication among key stakeholders.

RECOMMENDATIONS FOR ACTION

The committee envisions a system in which all undergraduate STEM students have equitable and effective learning experiences, feel welcomed, and have the opportunity to succeed in their STEM courses and programs, regardless of their identity or background. Key to achieving this vision is that all instructors have the knowledge, skills, and motivation to create welcoming, student-centered STEM courses that are built on what is known about how students learn and about the environments in which all students can succeed. Structural changes and collective responsibility within and across institutions are also critical for this vision to be implemented, sustained, and successful. The committee therefore offers recommendations for action that span the range of levels and actors in higher education. Making student-centered learning a central and explicit goal of course design is a necessary, but not sufficient, component of achieving equitable and effective learning experiences. The challenge of defining equitable and effective teaching is also partly a journey in helping the higher education community to redefine what teaching looks like, and in so doing identify the equity-based behaviors missing from our current notion of effective teaching. This challenge involves change at the classroom level in the approaches to teaching and also in the wider system to provide incentives, supports, and structures that influence teaching decisions.

Toward Equitable and Effective Learning Environments

Recommendation 1: Instructors, working independently and collaboratively, should use the Principles for Equitable and Effective Teaching to reflect on and revise their instructional practices, approaches to assessment, course syllabi and grading policies, and the selection and use of instructional resources. They should articulate clear learning goals for courses and use these learning goals to design instruction and assessment for courses in all modalities and settings, including online, in the classroom, in the laboratory, and in the field and continually reflect on and improve instructional practices over time based on student learning data.

Recommendation 2: Members of academic units collectively should take responsibility for reviewing the portfolio of courses offered and the sequencing of courses using the Principles for Equitable and Effective Teaching. They should work collectively to define clear course and program learning outcomes and use them to refine and revise the content and pedagogy of course sequences and individual courses. As part of the review, academic units should use both aggregated and disaggregated data of multiple forms to identify courses or course sequences that appear to be producing systematic, inequitable outcomes and undertake revisions to address them.

Recommendation 3: Developers of instructional materials and resources at institutions of higher education, nonprofits, and companies should work collaboratively with experts in teaching and learning (and

experienced instructors) to develop resources and materials, including educational and instructional technology, using the Principles for Equitable and Effective Teaching as a guide for informing design from the initial stages of conceptualization. If developers attempt to use the Principles to modify a product in a later stage of development it is less likely that the resulting product will be equitable and effective. Developers should also work collaboratively with experts in teaching and learning (and experienced instructors) to create the professional learning, support, and guidance that instructors will need to equitably and effectively use their products.

Valuing and Supporting Instructors

Recommendation 4: Academic unit and institutional leaders should support participation of all instructors in professional learning and development grounded in the Principles for Equitable and Effective Teaching by providing resources, encouragement, and financial compensation. Specifically, they should foster a culture of improvement and change policies to provide incentives and compensation for instructors to engage in professional learning and development as part of their workload so that all instructors receive a base level of preparation before they begin teaching and are provided with, compensated for, and encouraged to participate in ongoing opportunities to continue improving their teaching. Implementation will involve coordinating with academic units to also compensate instructor time (such as course release, salary increase, or funding bonus) for developing or revising courses to align with equitable and effective teaching practices, potentially including changing lesson goals, changing instructional practices, and/or changing instructional tools.

Recommendation 5: Academic unit and institutional leaders should foster a support structure for instructors (e.g., centers for teaching and learning, STEM education centers) that can (a) organize and offer accessible professional learning opportunities (including on campus, virtual, and asynchronous) that are grounded in the Principles for Equitable and Effective Teaching, and (b) support academic unit-level professional learning and development opportunities.

Recommendation 6: Graduate and postdoctoral program leaders should revise programs and expectations to make preparation for teaching an integral learning goal of programs. They should work to change cultures so that all participants are encouraged and supported in meaningful professional learning and development activities focused on teaching, learning, course design, and creating an equitable learning environment that embraces and promotes equitable and effective teaching. When teaching, graduate students and postdoctoral scholars should be supported by a mentor who has expertise in the use of the Principles to support equitable and effective teaching.

Recommendation 7: Academic unit leaders should develop policies and practices that value, recognize, and reward equitable and effective teaching. Steps they can take include

- Providing time in unit meetings to discuss teaching-related topics such as reviewing students' outcomes in courses, discussing the unit's strategy for continuous improvement of teaching, and sharing information about successes and challenges in teaching.
- Supporting individual and groups of instructors as they improve and revise their courses including providing dedicated time to work on course revision or additional financial compensation.
- Encouraging and providing time and resources for collaboration among instructors to work on course and curriculum revision and redesign.
- Designing policies and practices for making teaching assignments that value the teaching of all courses and the contributions of all instructors regardless of their appointment type.
- Identifying and supporting cohorts of instructors who are dedicated to and interested in implementing equitable and effective teaching and providing them with leadership opportunities.
- Facilitating the access and use of relevant data that can help instructors identify and monitor differences and changes in student outcomes.

Recommendation 8: Academic unit leaders should revise practices around hiring and onboarding of new instructors so that teaching is an essential and valued component of the role. In hiring, job candidates should be evaluated by their ability to engage in equitable and effective teaching. Once hired, instructors should receive mentoring related to equitable and effective teaching and be provided with opportunities to engage in ongoing professional learning and development.

Recommendation 9: Academic unit leaders should use the Principles for Equitable and Effective Teaching as professional standards that form the basis of teaching evaluation processes. To achieve this goal, they should use evidence-based approaches to evaluate the entire portfolio of teaching-related activities. This evaluation should go beyond student surveys to include other forms of evidence (e.g., structured teaching observations, analysis of teaching artifacts, course design, instructor reflections) and serve as a formative and holistic evaluation of teaching.

Recommendation 10: Academic unit and institutional leaders should include and value teaching during review processes for advancement and retention such that all instructors are expected and required to provide equitable and effective teaching.

- Determine reappointment, raises, merit, promotion, and tenure in a clear and transparent way that rewards instructor work toward achieving equitable and effective teaching.
- Develop approaches for determining promotion and tenure that include holistic evidence-based evaluation of the faculty member's teaching.
- Develop processes for changes to salaries and titles that consider all different categories of employees who have teaching responsibilities, including visiting faculty, instructors, teaching assistants, adjunct faculty, and lecturers (VITAL instructors).

Measuring and Advancing System Change

Recommendation 11: Institutional leaders should develop and support the infrastructure and approaches needed to collect, use, and monitor data about courses and programs, as well as student outcomes, experiences, belonging, and other affective measures. They should provide access to the system and to the data in a transparent way so that instructors and academic units can use it to improve teaching and learning. This will entail offering guidance to academic units about which metrics to review on a regular basis and multi-level strategies to investigate and decrease any gaps discovered. The systems should include qualitative and quantitative data from both internal and external (from studies or federal agencies) sources and allow for disaggregation of data by students' demographic characteristics so that revised policies and practices can be implemented to decrease disparities.

Recommendation 12: Members of academic units should take into account the complexity of the student undergraduate population and their varied goals and pathways to ensure that all students can equitably and effectively experience and benefit from the unit's courses, programs, and credentials. They should examine data for obstacles and barriers to undergraduate STEM learning and apply the Principles for Equitable and Effective Teaching to smooth the educational journeys of their students. Academic units should analyze transition points, course offerings, student experiences, and student outcomes and use the information to remediate obstacles that limit student learning or student progress toward a credential, especially obstacles that disproportionately impact students who are members of underserved groups.

Recommendation 13: Professional, academic, and disciplinary societies and organizations should publicly endorse and elevate the Principles for Equitable and Effective Teaching and adopt them to guide their work related to undergraduate education. Specifically, they should

- Share clear position statements on and advocate for the importance of equitable and effective teaching with their members, constituents, and the public.
- Coordinate with teaching experts in their discipline to design, offer, or coordinate professional learning and development opportunities to support instructors in their discipline to implement equitable and effective teaching practices.
- Coordinate with teaching experts to develop, curate, and promote resources for addressing discipline-specific teaching needs.
- Offer events that showcase and disseminate practices, tools, data, and research related to implementing equitable and effective teaching.
- Cultivate professional learning and development communities for current and future instructors and encourage academic units to do the same.
- Include experts in equitable and effective teaching in society leadership.
- Review the guidelines for any accreditations that they administer and support academic units to implement these guidelines in ways that maximize equitable and effective teaching and learning.
- Promote comparative studies that help identify approaches that lead to more equitable outcomes, especially for foundational courses.

Recommendation 14: Oversight bodies should endorse and adopt the Principles for Equitable and Effective Teaching to guide their work. Through their oversight, they should require institutional leaders to demonstrate that work at their institution is being done in alignment with the Principles and that policies and procedures have been updated accordingly.

Recommendation 15: Funders should endorse and adopt the use of the Principles for Equitable and Effective Teaching to prioritize evidence-based projects that support both implementation of and research about equitable and effective teaching. Implementation funding should include support for ongoing professional learning and development activities at different types of institutions of higher education, especially those that have fewer resources. Research funding should include some long-term projects that study student experiences and outcomes over time. Implementation projects should include evaluation plans.

1

Introduction

Thousands of post-secondary education institutions exist in the United States. While their missions can differ—sometimes significantly—these institutions share a common aim: to provide an education that affords students the knowledge and skills needed to thrive in their personal and work lives in the present and the future. At its best, the nation's undergraduate science, technology, engineering, and mathematics (STEM) education system can equip all students of all backgrounds to better understand the world around them, make informed decisions as members of society, and meet their individual goals. For some students, a STEM education can provide entry into the STEM workforce, which helps drive American innovation, national security, and economic growth.

For far too long, undergraduate STEM education in the United States has not delivered fully on its promises. Identity plays a role in determining learning experiences and student success. Not all students have been welcomed and supported to enter, pursue, and complete STEM credentials. While there are multiple factors that have contributed to this state of affairs, two overarching issues stand out:

1. The STEM education system as a whole has often not prioritized concerns of equity, and the failure to do so is severely limiting the participation and success of certain groups of students.
2. STEM teaching at the undergraduate level is not as uniformly effective at promoting student learning and engagement as education research shows it could be.

Combined, these two factors have major consequences for individuals and for society as a whole. Currently, commonly used teaching practices in undergraduate STEM education, held in place by related institutional policies and practices, alongside inequities across the system as a whole contribute to a situation in which membership in a marginalized group is frequently predictive of academic performance and educational attainment (Canning et al., 2018; Harris et al., 2020; Holland, 2019; Steele-Johnson & Leas, 2013; Thiele et al., 2014; Weston et al., 2019). For STEM education, the list of marginalized groups is long and can include students who are female; Black; Latina/o; Indigenous; lesbian, gay, bisexual, transgender, queer/questioning, intersex, asexual/aromantic/agender, plus other related identities (LGBTQIA+); veterans; students who are parents; those with both visible and invisible disabilities; as well as those who are from families with low socio-economic status or who are the first in their families to attend college. These inequities have significant costs to the nation: loss of STEM talent, unrealized dreams for individuals, and an overall population that is less able to engage in public discourse about STEM-related issues. In many ways, the nation cannot reach its full potential without doing the critical work of addressing inequity in undergraduate STEM education. Creating equitable and effective learning experiences that promote the success of students from groups that have been and continue to be marginalized in higher education and society is an essential step.

WHY DOES EQUITABLE AND EFFECTIVE TEACHING IN STEM MATTER?

STEM education is a wonderful opportunity for people to learn about the world around them and to become knowledgeable about natural processes, technological innovations, and the built environment. The STEM workforce is an important component of the economy and, more importantly, has produced impressive advances in scientific understanding and technology that have improved the quality of life for millions of people. Colleges and universities deserve enormous credit for the research they have conducted and the education they have provided to their students.

Looking ahead to future needs for innovation to benefit individuals, communities, and society, it is critical to design educational experiences that provide a greater percentage of learners with access to an equitable and effective undergraduate STEM education. Society will not fully benefit from the development and use of future discoveries and innovations if full access and opportunity to effective STEM education is not provided to all, nor will society have the information, tools, and resources needed to address future challenges facing our planet.

While teaching and student learning is one responsibility of all institutions of higher education, ensuring equitable access to high-quality teaching is not always a driving priority. Undergraduate education in the United States, especially in STEM subjects, too frequently relies on a model of passive information transfer, where instructors lecture to students. This approach is not aligned with what is known about how people learn, causing many students to struggle mastering concepts and skills when they are expected to listen passively as opposed to having an opportunity to actively engage with the course material. This mismatch between teaching approach and the complex processes important for learning (see Chapter 3) is quite common in introductory STEM courses and means that many students do not feel welcomed and supported to enter, pursue, complete STEM courses, and go on to earn STEM credentials (certificates, minors, degrees, etc.). In fact, the standard methods of teaching undergraduate STEM education have benefited a relatively small percentage of learners (who are more likely to be male and White or Asian), while many other learners conclude that STEM education is not for them and find other ways to use their talents (Seymour & Hewitt, 1997; Seymour & Hunter, 2019). This second group includes people who are female, non-binary, Black, Latina/o, Indigenous, LGBTQIA+, veterans, multi-lingual learners, students who are parents, those with both visible and invisible disabilities, those who are from families with low socio-economic status, and those who are the first in their families to attend college, among many other identities.

Current inequities in undergraduate STEM education have significant costs to both individuals and to the nation. In their 2024 report Learning and Earning by Degrees: Gains in College Degree Attainment Have Enriched the Nation and Every State, but Racial and Gender Inequality Persists, Georgetown University's Center on Education and the Workforce (CEW) quantified some of the economic and non-economic costs of not fully delivering on this promise for all students (Carnevale et al., 2024). Addressing these equity gaps would have added an additional $11.3 trillion in net lifetime earnings, benefiting both those who receive the credential and society overall.

As one step toward addressing inequities in undergraduate STEM education, this report presents a set of Principles for Equitable and Effective Teaching (listed in Box 1-2; discussed in most detail in Chapter 4) that will enable instructors, with the support of their academic units and institutions, to improve instruction in ways that benefit all students. This report conceives of equitable and effective teaching as the provision of learning experiences that are student centered, where course goals are made clear to the students, the students' role in their own learning is recognized, and students have agency to engage in the course material in ways that respect their identities. These student-centered evidence-based approaches help students best leverage their prior experiences, talents, and skills to complete a STEM education aligned with their aspirations and expectations. Thus, equitable and effective undergraduate STEM teaching can provide learning opportunities to a diverse array of learners who can in turn help to address global and societal challenges, improve the workforce, create a more informed population better prepared to grapple with the complexities of our technological society, and increase opportunities for meaningful life by enhancing connections to the designed and natural world.

THE CHALLENGE OF ADVANCING EQUITABLE AND EFFECTIVE TEACHING

Achieving equitable and effective teaching for all students will require concerted and consistent action by multiple stakeholders, across and beyond the higher education system. One key aspect of making undergraduate STEM education more equitable and effective is to change how teaching is prioritized in academia. In a March 2024 op-ed in Inside Higher Ed, Thorp and Goldstein, authors of Our Higher Calling: Rebuilding the Partnership between America and Its Colleges and Universities (Thorp & Goldstein, 2018), address this challenge as follows (emphasis ours):

> **Myriad analysts have determined where to place the blame for the deprioritization of teaching. The truth is, there is a lot of blame to go around** [...] Administrators are constantly being pressured to grow and do new things that their external and internal stakeholders want. Growing research grants is the simplest way to achieve this in the short run [...] This leads to pressure on faculty to increase their research. They are behaving perfectly rationally when they seek time away from teaching to spend more time generating grants and high-profile publications [...] Meanwhile, trustees like to see positive news coverage and improvement in the rankings, which rewards high-profile faculty research. Trustees also tend to want success in athletics, which comes with significant costs and makes the ability to win grant funding to pay faculty salaries even more important when the bills for athletics come due.
>
> Making teaching a high priority will not happen as long as one set of stakeholders is the only one required to change. **If faculty are simply told to put more emphasis on teaching without changes to the incentives, nothing will happen. Nearly every college president has started off their tenure by saying they are going to emphasize teaching, but usually with no effect. Trustees hear pained testimonials from students and ask for more emphasis on the classroom, but they are unwilling to make the financial tradeoffs necessary to make this happen. All of the groups are going to have to collaborate to get this done.** (Thorp & Goldstein, 2024)

It is clear to the committee that many instructors are committed to providing their students with equitable and effective education and have gone to great lengths to serve all of their students and achieve equitable and effective outcomes. The committee also acknowledges that many academic leaders care deeply about supporting teaching in undergraduate STEM education. All of these efforts are to be commended. However, as Thorp and Goldstein emphasize above, the most significant barriers to widespread application of equitable and effective approaches lie not with the behavior of individuals but in our current system. These barriers result from policies and practices that disincentivize use of and rewards for adopting sound pedagogy. This is not an issue that can be addressed via solutions based in a deficit perspective that calls for "fixing" students or faculty; it is a challenge to be addressed by changing mindsets, approaches, policies, and structures at multiple levels of the system.

Undergraduate learning occurs within a system that undervalues teaching and does not generally prioritize equitable outcomes for students. Many institutions retain policies that do not incentivize spending time, money, and other resources on teaching, leading to instructional approaches that are not aligned with evidence about how people learn and that are only helpful for a small number of students. While many instructors go to great lengths to serve their students, widespread equitable and effective teaching is dependent on changes to the larger system. In the present system, instructors are often unsupported in learning and implementing approaches to instruction that are informed by research and that allow for the creation of learning experiences that engage a wider variety of students and can be applied in the classroom, laboratory, field, and online learning experiences. Instructors cannot be expected to offer equitable and effective teaching if they are not educated in pedagogy, provided with ongoing professional learning and development, and supported with appropriate rewards, recognitions, and resources. Chapters 3, 4, and 5 discuss the research on learning and provide guidance and examples for teaching in an evidence-based manner. Chapter 8 looks at the importance of ongoing professional learning and development in support of equitable and effective teaching.

As a whole, this report examines and explains the systemic changes needed to align incentives in order to facilitate and support better teaching and learning. It discusses multiple levels of the system that could change to work in concert and support instructors, on both the individual and collective levels, so that undergraduate learning experiences (in classrooms and laboratories, both on campus and online) become more equitable and effective. It also acknowledges the challenges and changes that need to be addressed in order to support instructors and administrators in making these crucial changes.

INTERPRETING THE CHARGE AND CONDUCTING THE STUDY

The Committee on Equitable and Effective Teaching in Undergraduate STEM Education was convened by the Board on Science Education, part of the National Academies of Sciences, Engineering, and Medicine (National Academies), to examine efforts to support and improve undergraduate STEM education, and to provide guidance to undergraduate STEM educators and institutions, as well as other stakeholders, on how the interdependent objectives of equity and effectiveness can be achieved in undergraduate STEM teaching. Meeting such objectives is critical to eradicating existing disparities in STEM education and providing rich opportunities for all students to better understand STEM principles, concepts, and practices.

The committee includes members with knowledge and expertise in areas of STEM education research, practice, and leadership relevant to undergraduate STEM education. Committee members represent a diverse set of post-secondary institutions that award certificates, associate's degrees, bachelor's degrees, master's degrees, and doctoral degrees in the STEM disciplines. The institutions are based at urban, suburban, and rural campuses across the United States. Some of the committee members changed institutions during the course of the study, and in these cases, their institution at the time of publication is listed in the front matter. Therefore, the affiliations listed do not represent the full breadth of their experiences in higher education, and more details can be found in the committee bios in Appendix B.

The Charge to the Committee

The project's statement of task (Box 1-1) describes the charge to the committee and guided the development of this report. The study is funded by the Gates Foundation, the Howard Hughes Medical Institute, and the National Science Foundation.

Defining the Scope

In considering their charge, the committee discussed at length the topics and perspectives that they would include within the scope of their work. The charge was specific about some aspects of which populations and institution types should be included, but not prescriptive in other areas. The committee here articulates the inclusive nature of the view they took of the report scope in order to include all types of students, instructors, and institutions involved in undergraduate STEM education in the United States.

BOX 1-1
Study Charge

The National Academies of Sciences, Engineering, and Medicine will convene an ad hoc committee on equitable and effective teaching in undergraduate STEM education. Through examination of successful efforts to improve and support instruction, the committee will develop a framework for equitable and effective teaching in undergraduate STEM and identify policies and practices at the departmental, programmatic, and institutional levels that can facilitate implementation of the principles in the framework.

The committee will conduct a two-phase study. The first phase will produce a discussion draft that outlines a framework for equitable and effective teaching. It will call out practices that may be particularly important for virtual, blended, and hybrid instruction. The discussion draft will serve as a tool to solicit input from stakeholders that will be used to improve the framework. The second phase will revise the framework, call out areas in need of further research, and provide guidance and recommendations for institutions, educators, and disciplines. Specifically, the final report will

1. Present a framework for equitable and effective teaching that includes attention to
   - Approaches to and guidelines for evidence-based, inclusive teaching;
   - Equitable and effective teaching practices for different modes of teaching (e.g., in-person, online, blended and hybrid teaching), and different educational contexts (e.g., two-year colleges, hybrid program, research institutions);
   - The roles that technology does, or can in the future, play in supporting equitable and effective teaching.
2. Discuss the experiences and training opportunities graduate students and postdoctoral students will need in order to be prepared to employ equitable and effective instruction as future faculty members.
3. Examine the institutional infrastructure, policies, and practices needed to encourage and support evidence-based teaching, such as opportunities for professional development, faculty evaluation policies and practices, and reward and advancement systems.
4. Provide actionable recommendations for institutions, disciplinary societies, funders, and policy makers on steps that could support implementation of the framework.

What Is Included as "STEM"?

The committee was inclusive in considering the disciplines of STEM, types of post-secondary institutions, variety of instructors, and all students in their work. We used the National Science Board definition of STEM as including the following areas of study: agricultural sciences and natural resources; biological and biomedical sciences; computer and information sciences; engineering; geosciences, atmospheric sciences, and ocean sciences; mathematics and statistics; multidisciplinary and interdisciplinary sciences; physical sciences; psychology; and social sciences (Deitz & Freyman, 2024; Deitz & Henke, 2023). The committee recognizes that this wide array of disciplines has some commonalities and also that each area has unique challenges and strategies. Throughout the report, we refer both to issues that are STEM-wide and to those that are discipline-specific or more prominent in some disciplines. Similarly, we provide examples of successful strategies and approaches that emerge from specific disciplines, many of which can be applied in others.

The Learners

The committee takes a broad view of who counts as an undergraduate STEM student, and includes those taking a single course, seeking a certificate, or working toward a degree. We included students preparing for careers in fields heavily dependent on STEM knowledge and skills (such as nurses, medical doctors and technicians, biotech workers, scientists, mathematicians, and engineers), as well as those who are taking a course to satisfy a distribution requirement or learn about an interesting topic. STEM students are understood to use STEM knowledge and skills in many different ways, including in jobs that are not traditionally defined as STEM careers; this might range from analyzing data in a spreadsheet in an office to analyzing soil composition on a farm or at a national park. Regardless of whether their STEM courses contribute directly to individuals' careers, the knowledge and skills gained have the potential to prepare all students to be knowledgeable and informed participants in their communities and societies, especially as science and technology play an ever-increasing role in our lives.

For STEM education, the list of marginalized groups is long; as mentioned above, it can include students who are female, non-binary, Black, Latina/o, Indigenous, LGBTQIA+, veterans, multi-lingual learners, students from rural areas, students who are parents or caregivers, those with both visible and invisible disabilities, those who are from families with low socio-economic status, and those who are the first in their families to attend college. The committee also recognizes that the unique circumstances of each student's life outside of academia inform and influence the achievement of their academic goals. For instance, in pursuing their post-secondary education, students frequently do not take all of their courses at a single institution, so issues of transfer credit and simultaneous enrollment complicate student efforts to achieve degrees (National Academies, 2016). Many students have work and caregiving commitments while enrolled. All of these elements of identity impact student learning experiences. Throughout the report we refer to students who belong to one or more of these groups as underserved, in recognition of the ways that people who hold these identities have typically not been the primary audience of STEM education and traditional STEM instructional practices do not leverage the knowledges, backgrounds, experiences, and interests to help them succeed.

The Teaching Workforce

When the committee considers instructors, they include full-time and part-time roles, permanent and contingent employees, adjunct instructors, visiting professors, graduate teaching assistants, and tenured and tenure-track faculty, among others. We make use of the acronym VITAL to encompass the range of non-permanent roles, as discussed by Levy (2019) and emphasized by Lee et al. (2023): VITAL stands for visiting faculty, instructors, teaching assistants, adjunct faculty, and lecturers. The needs and concerns of VITAL educators—and sometimes, more specifically, graduate students and postdoctoral fellows—are addressed at multiple places in the report, as they are often distinct from the needs and concerns of full-time tenure-track faculty. The committee recognizes that these populations frequently have less autonomy to implement new ideas for multiple reasons, including being out of the power structure of the academic unit, operating from a place of contingent employment, or serving as one instructor in a course with multiple sections where curricular choices and decisions about format and assessment are made by others (e.g., curriculum or program committees).

Types of Institutions Included in the Study

Our current system of higher education is a complex one that includes a wide variety of institution types. For the most part, in this report, we discuss all types of institutions together as colleges and universities. In some portions of the report, we use more specific language to discuss institution types. For example, we use the term community college to refer to institutions that offer associate's degrees in addition to multiple other types of certificates and credentials, including those in Career and Technical Education fields. Another aspect of institution type is the population of students served and if the institution is open access or selective in admitting students. While selective colleges and universities receive much of the attention in the press, they make up a small percentage of post-secondary institutions (DeSilver, 2019), Community colleges are generally open-access institutions, and many regional four-year institutions are as well, both are important forces in facilitating education of underserved students. While most colleges and universities in the United States are Predominantly White Institutions, there are multiple types of institutions that serve particular populations, including Historically Black Colleges and Universities, Tribal Colleges and Universities, Hispanic Serving Institutions, and Asian American and Native American Pacific Islander Serving Institutions. While there are many differences across institution type, the Principles for Equitable and Effective Teaching apply to all instructors engaged in teaching undergraduates. The specifics of how the Principles are enacted will differ based on institution type and other factors, such as the discipline of study, the size of the course, and whether it is a course at a foundational level or includes upper-level content.

Defining Equitable and Effective

The committee defines an *equitable* undergraduate STEM education system as one that provides all students with the support they need to succeed, as measured by achievement of clearly communicated learning objectives. In an equitable learning environment, factors such as race, gender, disability status, and socio-economic status do not impact the rate at which students meet the learning objectives. In addition, an equitable system rewards instructors for effective teaching and provides them with the resources they need to successfully educate all of their students.

An *effective* undergraduate STEM education system is one in which all students demonstrate learning and most, if not all, students have the opportunities and the resources to meet desired learning objectives. An equitable and effective undergraduate STEM education does not come at the expense of excellence; the focus is on helping all students learn and understand STEM concepts and be able to use them in practical ways.

The term *inclusive*, which appears in the study charge, is a related concept that the committee considers as a key component of an equitable education. It refers to the opportunity to participate in learning experiences that feel welcoming and cultivate a sense of belonging, and to avoid exclusive or exclusionary environments that limit engagement. These limitations may arise from practical barriers or from expectations that are not student centered.

Information Gathering and Use of Evidence

In developing the report, the committee met eight times, both virtually and in person. They also did significant work between meetings to gather and analyze information and to write and edit drafts. The committee gathered extensive information during the course of the project and specifically considered a wide variety of input on the discussion draft from a diverse array of stakeholders. In particular, the committee gathered input on a discussion draft released for public input in November 2023. More information about the input on the discussion draft and the committee's response can be found in Appendix A. The material from that discussion draft has been revised, and is included here, including a focus on the Principles for Equitable and Effective Instruction in Chapter 4.

Throughout the study, the committee analyzed a large volume of evidence from many sources. They reviewed material that included published peer-reviewed literature, statistical information, conference proceedings, dissertations, and articles in magazines and newspapers, among other documents. After surveying the expertise brought to the table by the members of the committee, we invited experts to present on their work and discuss key issues with us and also commissioned several experts to author papers on key topics where an in-depth analysis would significantly improve understanding of the evidence.

Specifically, as the committee reviewed the literature on pedagogical approaches, we identified principles for improving equity and facilitating effective teaching. We reflected on the extensive work done in these areas and drew on this and our own expertise to identify a set of tenets that delineate equitable and effective teaching approaches for instructors of undergraduates in STEM. These tenets became the seven Principles for Equitable and Effective Teaching (see Box 1-2). While there are many other principles, tenets, and approaches that can and do guide equitable and effective teaching, these capture topics that are foundational to such efforts, and we offer them here as a loose framework that can structure both thought and action.

Similarly, to form the conclusions offered at the end of the chapters in this report, the committee combined qualitative and quantitative evidence from research on pedagogy, professional learning, and system change with members' expertise in the practice of teaching and experiences in higher education, and direct input from researchers and practitioners. The committee considered the strength of the evidence for each topic to determine where they felt the evidence base was sufficient to provide suggestive evidence or to offer robust support. Relatedly, we also directly discuss the "strength of evidence" pyramid in Chapter 3.

In addition, we have included illustrative examples in the text and in boxes throughout the report. These come from a variety of sources, including presentations, websites, and the research literature. These examples serve as a valuable tool for thinking about the strategies and approaches that can be used to improve teaching in a variety of modalities, course sizes, institution types, and other contexts.

Developing a Framework and Guidance on Implementation

The charge calls for the committee to develop a framework for equitable and effective teaching that includes attention to (a) approaches to and guidelines for evidence-based, inclusive teaching; (b) equitable and effective teaching practices for different modes of teaching (e.g., in-person, online, blended, and hybrid teaching), and different educational contexts (e.g., two-year colleges, hybrid programs, and research institutions); and (c) the roles that technology plays, or can play in the future, in supporting equitable and effective teaching. The committee approached this task by considering the multiple lines of evidence related to teaching and learning in undergraduate STEM education that have emerged over the past 30–40 years. There is now a robust body of evidence related to learning in the STEM disciplines that the committee leveraged to develop the set of seven Principles for Equitable and Effective Teaching (see Box 1-2), which reflect key insights from research and can be used to guide the development of individual courses, courses sequences, and disciplinary programs of study. In a sense, these Principles are intended to serve as a kind of "north star" for departments and institutions as they work to improve undergraduate teaching and learning.

The committee was also asked to identify the infrastructure, policy, and practices needed to encourage and support evidence-based teaching (as embodied by the Principles), and to provide guidance to a variety of actors on how to support implementation of the Principles. The committee recognized that this part of the charge could be interpreted as a series of issues related to individual STEM courses; however, we concluded that achieving equitable and effective STEM learning experiences for students requires a broader frame. The committee concluded that to fully address this charge, the report needed to consider the culture and structures of the academic unit and institutions in which teaching and learning occur as well as the wide variety of disciplines, program structures, and course formats in which undergraduate STEM education happens. This insight provides the structure for this final report and its components. The committee analyzed (a) how to move toward more equitable and effective teaching, (b) how to value and support instructors, and (c) how to measure and advance systemic change in order to transform undergraduate STEM education. This focus on systemic change and the need for cross-system collaboration to achieve continuous improvement led to the inclusion of recommendations

BOX 1-2
Principles for Equitable and Effective Teaching

The Principles for Equitable and Effective Teaching (described in detail in Chapter 4) articulate key aspects of pedagogy critical to the student-centered approach to learning necessary to achieve equitable and effective learning experiences. The Principles are

- Principle 1: Students need opportunities to actively engage in disciplinary learning.
- Principle 2: Students' diverse interests, goals, knowledge, and experiences can be leveraged to enhance learning.
- Principle 3: STEM learning involves affective and social dimensions.
- Principle 4: Identity and sense of belonging shape STEM teaching and learning.
- Principle 5: Multiple forms of data can provide evidence to inform improvement.
- Principle 6: Flexibility and responsiveness to situational and contextual factors supports student learning.
- Principle 7: Intentionality and transparency create more equitable opportunities.

Together these Principles serve as a framework that can structure both thought and action by instructors, institutions, and disciplines.

for action for people in many different roles and positions; these include instructors, academic unit and institutional leaders (e.g., department chairs, deans, provosts), and other stakeholders outside of institutions of higher education (e.g., disciplinary and professional associations and funders).

THE COMMITTEE'S VISION FOR EQUITABLE AND EFFECTIVE STEM EDUCATION

The committee envisions a system in which all undergraduate STEM students experience equitable and effective learning experiences, feel welcomed, and have the opportunity to succeed in their STEM courses and programs, regardless of their identity or background. Ideally, through equitable and effective STEM education experiences, all students will learn about STEM disciplines and thereby gain the opportunity to better understand the world around them and use this understanding to better their own lives and careers. Engaging with the process of developing new knowledge and designing new tools as part of the learning experience can foster this understanding. In the committee's vision, the pathways, course schedules, course syllabi, assessments, and other aspects of designing courses and programs build upon the Principles for Equitable and Effective Teaching to create a welcoming and accessible route to STEM learning for all students. We also envision an accessible STEM learning experience that considers the physical, digital, cultural, economic, affective, and sensory needs of students.

Making student-centered learning a central and explicit goal of course design is a necessary component of achieving equitable and effective learning experiences. This approach—which includes making the course goals clear to the students; recognizing the students' role in their own learning; and giving students agency to engage in the course material in ways that welcome and respect their identities—makes learning the primary driver and articulates clearly the desired learning outcomes of each learning experience. In contrast, an instructor-centered course usually focuses on covering a certain amount of content, and the volume of content is the primary driver of the schedule, course policies, instructional methods, and assessments. Disciplinary expectations and historical precedent often drive pressures to focus on covering content as opposed to re-evaluating the learning goals that would be most beneficial to the students' education (Oleson & Hora, 2014; Tripp et al., 2024).

While essential, student-centered learning in itself is not enough to ensure equitable and effective learning experiences. The culture and dynamics of the learning environment and interpersonal interactions are also important. The challenge of achieving equitable and effective teaching is also partly a journey of helping the higher education community redefine the roles and goals of teaching and, in so doing, identify the equity-based behaviors currently missing from common current notions of effective teaching.

Key to achieving this vision is that all instructors have the knowledge, skills, and motivation to create welcoming STEM courses that are built on what is known about how students learn and in which all students can succeed. When the committee considers instructors, they include full-time and part-time roles, permanent and contingent employees, adjunct instructors, visiting professors, teaching assistants (graduate students who are instructors or assistants to instruction), and tenured and tenure-track faculty, among others (more information on the scope of the instructional workforce considered can be found in the section of this chapter on the Charge to the Committee).

Importantly, however, the responsibility for applying the Principles does not rest solely or even primarily with instructors. While making undergraduate STEM education more equitable and effective will likely require many instructors to adjust their practices, doing so will require that their efforts be supported in practical, material, and logistical ways, and that they are encouraged and supported by their colleagues, departments, institutions, and disciplinary organizations and professional societies. The existing challenges require systemic solutions. Structural changes and collective responsibility within and across institutions will be necessary for this vision to be implemented, sustained, and successful. Multiple lines of evidence reveal that we are far from achieving that vision yet also provide guidance for what needs to change for us to make progress and transformative change. Coordination by these diverse stakeholders will contribute to the development of a supportive infrastructure that provides the resources instructors need to develop as educators and to cultivate equitable and effective learning environments for their students. Therefore, this report presents actionable recommendations intended to foster educational transformation on a systemic level across the range of institution types providing undergraduate STEM experiences to students in the United States.

One of the committee's goals for this report is that the seven Principles together with the recommendations for implementation provide a common basis for conversation and action that can help to catalyze more widespread systemic change. Together, the Principles and recommendations can be used by post-secondary education institutions to engage instructors, academic unit leaders, other administrators, and governing boards in aligning policies and procedures to foster and support equitable and effective teaching. The Principles and recommendations can also inform decision making and action outside of post-secondary institutions, at professional societies, at academic associations, and at funders of STEM education and STEM education research. Collaborative and collective efforts across all stakeholder groups can achieve equitable and effective teaching and learning for all students.

REPORT ORGANIZATION

The report includes ten chapters that together explore the context of our system of higher education; explain the Principles for Equitable and Effective Teaching; and describe changes that are needed to the system to make undergraduate education equitable and effective to benefit all students. Chapter 2 presents a brief overview of the institutional context for undergraduate STEM learning in the United States. Chapter 3 discusses scholarship in teaching, learning, and equity. Chapter 4 presents the seven Principles for Equitable and Effective Teaching. Chapter 5 illustrates use of the Principles with examples that instructors can apply to courses to improve learning and equity across a variety of course types and formats. Chapter 6 investigates the roles of departments and academic units in determining who teaches what. Specifically, it considers course sequences and majors in undergraduate STEM education, disciplinary and academic culture, and the role of the instructional workforce. The pathways students actually take in their STEM learning, including some of the obstacles they encounter, are the focus of Chapter 7. Chapter 8 explores ongoing professional learning for the instructors who teach STEM to undergraduates as well as the preparation of future faculty. Chapter 9 discusses the role of institutional-level policies and procedures in supporting action toward system change, including the ways that data can inform decision making and the way that thoughtful policies can support equitable and effective teaching. The final chapter briefly recaps aspects of the conclusions shared in earlier chapters and presents insights the committee has drawn from the evidence and their analysis. Additionally, it provides specific recommendations for action to advance equitable and effective practices in the future, as well as identifying areas in need of further research to advance our knowledge base to allow future improvements.

2

Institutional Context of Post-Secondary STEM Education

Colleges and universities contribute to advances in science, technology, engineering, and mathematics (STEM) and prepare the STEM workforce as well as pursuing their more general mission of educating the population. Many students want to learn STEM at U.S. colleges and universities in particular. This is seen in both the numbers of students who come from abroad to enroll (Institute of International Education, 2024) and the number of domestic students who express an interest in STEM (Main et al., 2023; Walton Family Foundation, 2023). This chapter provides an overview of the types of institutions where undergraduates study STEM and lays out some statistics on the diversity of those students. The chapter concludes with a discussion of how the complex landscape of post-secondary education in the United States has changed over time. Today's undergraduate STEM experiences are rooted in this history, which includes longstanding inequities that profoundly influence teaching and learning. The specific information chosen to be addressed in this chapter is intended to provide context for the reader navigating later chapters of the report, especially those on student pathways, professional learning and development, and the role of institutions in systemic change to support equitable and effective teaching. This context helps in understanding that as the student population has grown and changed over time, policies and structures have not kept pace with the shifts, and this contributes to many students still not having equitable access to STEM learning opportunities.

THE CHANGING LANDSCAPE OF LEARNERS

Students bring with them diverse sets of goals and will follow a variety of different pathways in their undergraduate experiences. Changing demographics require institutions, academic units, and instructors to adjust the learning environment to support all students. If institutions and departments are to meet present and future STEM workforce needs, the system of undergraduate STEM education needs to be broadened and expanded, welcoming and supporting a diverse range of learners through the creation of learning environments that are truly inclusive. This section documents some of the data on the variety of students who make up the undergraduate population that needs to be served by undergraduate STEM instructors and academic units.

Undergraduate Students

Chapter 1 described the broad view the committee takes of who counts as an undergraduate STEM student student—a view that includes those taking a single course, seeking a certificate, or working toward a degree in a STEM major. In the paragraphs below, we share selected statistics on the undergraduate population as a whole, highlighting specific details on undergraduate STEM students where those are available. As is the case throughout the report, statistics reported here use the terminology of the original data source (e.g., Hispanic or Latinx rather than Latina/o).

As of Spring 2024, undergraduate enrollment in bachelors and associates granting institutions totaled 14,683,574 nationwide (National Student Clearinghouse Research Center, 2024). The undergraduate student population in U.S. higher education is diverse, including learners of different ages, races, ethnicities, genders, and religions, as well as veterans, parents, caregivers, students who are the first generation in their families to go to college, undocumented students, and those displaced from jobs looking to upskill or exploring new directions or seeking new career opportunities (Garvey & Dolan, 2021; Jenner, 2017; LeBouef & Dworkin, 2021; National Center for Education Statistics [NCES], 2024c). Students come from different socioeconomic classes, including the approximately 30% who are Pell Grant recipients (NCES, n.d.c) and from rural, suburban, and urban areas and all regions of the United States, as well as many international students. Students who are neurodivergent and those with apparent and non-apparent disabilities are increasingly represented, making up at least 20% of the student population (NCES, 2023e).

In Fall 2023, transfer students accounted for 13% of all undergraduate students (National Student Clearinghouse Research Center, 2023). Transfer is on the rise, especially among underserved groups, including low-income students, Black and Hispanic students, and rural students (National Student Clearinghouse Research Center, 2023). Compared to 2022, the number of students transferred to a new institution increased by 5% in 2023, mainly driven by the upward transfer from two-year to four-year institutions (National Student Clearinghouse Research Center, 2023).

Multiple studies have found that rural students are less likely to enroll in college than nonrural students (Byun et al., 2012; Koricich et al., 2018; Wells et al., 2019). However, it has been suggested that this disparity is also influenced by multiple factors such as family income or socio-economic status, affordability of college, a lack of rural recruitment, lack of college readiness programming, and distance from institutions of higher education (Mowreader, 2024; The Institute for College Access and Success, 2023; Wells et al., 2023).

White students comprised over 52% of the enrolled student population by Fall 2021, compared to Hispanic (22%), Black (13%), Asian (7%), and Native American/Alaskan Native students (1%; NCES, 2023a). In 2021, students identifying as women (58%) outnumbered students identifying as men (42%) across all racial demographics in undergraduate school programs (NCES, 2022). Students who are parents make up nearly a quarter of undergraduate students (Urban Institute, 2024). During the 2019–2020 academic year, students who are military veterans made up approximately 5% of the undergraduate students, with average age of 32 (Melidona & Wright, 2023).

Over half of undergraduate students in the United States are first-generation college students (e.g., students whose parents do not have a bachelor's degree; RTI International, 2023). First-generation college students' parents' median income was $41,000 in 2020 (RTI International, 2023). Nearly three-quarters of Hispanic/Latins/a/o undergraduate students are among this group, as well as approximately two-thirds of Black or African American students (RTI International, 2023).

According to the most current data by NCSES (NCES, 2019b), 19% of undergraduates were identified as having a physical, mental, or learning disability, and 28% of them were enrolled in a science and engineering field. Compared with undergraduates without disabilities, students with disabilities were less likely to receive financial aid and were less likely to be enrolled full time for a full year at one institution (NCES, 2019a).

According to the most current data published in Women, Minorities, and Persons with Disabilities in Science and Engineering (NCES, 2019b), out of all the undergraduates enrolled during the 2015–2016 academic year, 28% of students declared a science or engineering major field of study, with close to 8% of those students in life sciences. In academic years 2023–2024, over half of the international students studied in the STEM fields, with math and computer science being the most common disciplines of study (Institute of International Education, 2024). The number of international students in the United States has steadily increased since 1950, with brief declines in the early 1970s, mid-2000s, and in 2020 (Stewart-Rozema & Pratts, 2023). In 2022–2023, about 5.6% of undergraduate students were international (Stewart-Rozema & Pratts, 2023).

Inequities in STEM Degree Attainment and Workforce Participation

STEM students take non-linear journeys through the landscape of higher education. Institutional curricular programming and "pathways" provide formal entry and exit points, but the journey is an experience that is unique to each student. The complexity of these student journeys can combine with the systemic barriers in ways that, for many, cause their educational STEM journey to stop short of STEM degree attainment for those who were seeking a degree (National Academies of Sciences, Engineering, and Medicine [National Academies], 2016). This is evident in the fact that, six years after initial enrollment, about half of the students enrolled in a STEM bachelor's program have not earned their degrees (Eagan et al., 2014; National Academies, 2016; Van Noy & Zeidenberg, 2014).

Though the proportion of science and engineering (S&E) degrees earned by underserved minorities increased between 2011 and 2020, degree attainment saw uneven growth and representation between racial groups. For example, one study reported that 40% of Black and 37% of Latina/o students switch majors before earning a STEM degree, compared with 29% of White STEM students (Riegle-Crumb et al., 2019). White students and Asian students make up a disproportionately large share of S&E degree recipients at the bachelor's level and above (NCSES, 2023a). From 2021 to 2022, White students and Asian students earned over 70% of bachelor's degrees across all STEM fields (NCCES, 2023c, Table 318.45).

Limited research on community college and career and technical education (CTE) students focuses on persistence, completion, or transfer (Soliz, 2023). One of the most robust studies within this small research base is a national survey of CTE and STEM pathways by Van Noy and Zeidenberg (2017). The authors utilized national transcript data to provide a descriptive portrait of students who navigate STEM and technician programs. Their findings suggest that, nationally, 13% of students enrolled in technician programs earned a certificate or associate degree. About 19% of students in technician programs transferred to a four-year institution in STEM within six years. Further, a small percentage of these students (7%) earned a bachelor's degree and 41% left without a credential (Van Noy & Zeidenberg, 2017). An earlier study situated within the state of California with a focus on CTE transfer rates indicated a similar transfer rate, showing that 20.5% of students starting in CTE courses or programs and having finished at least 12 transferrable credits transferred into a four-year program (Karandjeff & Schiorring, 2011).

People who have STEM degrees on average have higher earnings in the workforce, regardless of gender, race, ethnicity, or disability status (NCSES, 2023a). Broadening access to STEM education and removing barriers that make it difficult for underserved populations to attain STEM degrees ultimately leads to the diversification not only of the student population but of the STEM workforce. While the overall employment in the United States has grown by 34% since 1990, STEM employment has grown by 79% (Funk & Parker, 2018). It is estimated that STEM jobs will grow at a faster rate (7% vs. 2%) than non-STEM jobs during the next ten years (Bureau of Labor Statistics, 2022). There are discrepancies between the specific STEM expertise and upcoming work demands, and institutions are struggling to meet current and future demands for STEM majors and professionals, given the technological advances across industries. Improving STEM enrollment and attainment could help meet the need for STEM workers if we consider that identity-based barriers to education and degrees have kept the pool of potential workers artificially small.

Though the U.S. STEM workforce became more diversified in the last decade (NCSES, 2023a), equity gaps persist, and Black, Hispanic, and American Indian/Alaska Native people continue to be underrepresented in the S&E degrees and S&E occupations relative to their shares of the general population (Fry et al., 2021; NCSES, 2023a; Okrent & Burke, 2021). In 2021, underserved minorities (Hispanic, Black, and American Indian/Alaska Native people) made up a higher share of the skilled technical workforce (32%) than those employed in STEM occupations with at least a bachelor's degree (16%; NCSES, 2023a). While the number of women in the STEM workforce increased by 31% between 2011 and 2021(NCSES, 2023a), the gender gap remains significant, with women making up less than one-third of the STEM workforce (Piloto, 2023). In particular, women made up only 26% of computer and mathematical scientists and 16% of engineers in 2019 (Burke et al., 2022).

TODAY'S STEM LEARNING ECOSYSTEM

Institutions vary by type, culture, and mission, with different emphases around aspects of research and scholarship, education, partnerships with industry and governmental agencies, and their communities. All of this comprises institutional context and disciplinary culture that together influence how each department or program unit makes choices about which behaviors are encouraged or rewarded, discouraged or tolerated. As we discuss later in the report (Chapters 6 and 8), this influence extends to teaching and how it is understood within the broader work of the academic unit and institution. While teaching and student learning is one inherent focus of all institutions of higher education, an emphasis on teaching and learning is not always a driving priority. For example, research plays a disproportionate role in decision making at many institutions. Other factors that influence decision making include the available resources, including the revenue from tuition and governmental funding. To help frame the discussions about priorities and decision making in later chapters, we present here some data on the types of institutions where undergraduates study STEM, with a focus on how much the student demographics vary by institution or institution type.

Institution Types and Enrollment Patterns

Our current system of higher education includes a wide variety of institution types—what we in this report usually refer to collectively as *colleges and universities*. This section presents a high-level overview of some of the ways that post-secondary institutions are grouped and described, including some background on the origins of various types, including some minority serving institutions (MSIs).

Undergraduate students today learn in many different types of settings. In 2022, nearly three times the number of students were enrolled at public post-secondary institutions compared to the number that were enrolled at private institutions (13.5 million vs. 5.1 million on average; NCES, 2023c,d). Institutions of higher education vary dramatically in size, with enrollment ranging from under 100 students to many tens of thousands. Some serve primarily local populations, and some attract students from across the country and the world. Budget and endowments also vary dramatically, which influence the policies and practices, as well as the student experiences.

Open-access institutions employ a non-competitive college admissions process where the only criterion for entrance is a high school diploma, certificate of attendance, or General Educational Development certificate. This type of institution includes some regional public institutions and community colleges. Community colleges enrolled 8.9 million students in 2020–2021 and educated a disproportionate share of underserved students, with 7% Asian, 12% Black, and 26% Latinx (Community College Research Center, 2022). In addition, open-access institutions are often under-resourced compared to other institutions (Yuen, 2020). Community colleges often provide a wide variety of workforce development programs that align students' skills with local job market demand.

Selective institutions (sometimes called highly rejective institutions) require students to compete for admission by demonstrating their credentials in academic and other areas. Collectively these institutions enroll larger shares of White and Asian American/Pacific Islander students, while American Indian/Alaska Native, Black/African American, and Hispanic/Latina/o students collectively remain underrepresented. In 2019, this latter group made up only 21% of selective college enrollments, compared to their 37% share of the general college-age population (Strohl et al., 2024). For both groups, over- and underrepresentation looks similar between 2009 and 2019 (Strohl et al., 2024).

Most colleges and universities in the United States began as Predominantly White Institutions (PWIs). However, multiple types of institutions are classified based on their enrollment demographics or historic missions. MSIs are defined by federal guidelines, which are based primarily on the percentage of students enrolled from designated demographic groups. MSIs enroll approximately five million students, nearly 30% of all undergraduates in U.S. higher education (National Academies, 2019c).

Historically Black Colleges and Universities (HBCUs) were established starting in the 19th century to counter the exclusion of Black students from other institutions. Notably, though HBCUs comprise only 3% of all post-secondary institutions, they account for 8% of Black undergraduate enrollment and are responsible for about 13% of all bachelor's degrees earned by Black students (The White House, 2024). Toldson (2019) reports that HBCUs represent 3% of total institutions of higher education, yet from 2002 to 2011, 21 of these institutions have made the top 50 baccalaureate-origin institutions of Black doctorate recipients in science and engineering (Fiegener & Proudfoot, 2013).

Tribal Colleges and Universities (TCUs) were established starting in the 1960s to give more autonomy to Indigenous communities in educating their members (Stein, 1999). TCUs enrolled about 17,000 undergraduate students in 2022 (Postsecondary National Policy Institute, 2024). Grant-funded opportunities and partnerships in recent years have enabled TCUs to expand STEM programming for traditionally underrepresented populations (National Academies, 2019c).

Hispanic Serving Institutions (HSIs) have considerable variability in size and focus. While they represent 20% of institutions nationwide, HSIs enroll almost two-thirds of the Hispanic student population (Hispanic Association of Colleges and Universities, 2024). Effort has been made to enroll and retain more Hispanic students in the STEM fields at HSIs (National Academies, 2019c).

The federal government also now recognizes Asian American and Native American Pacific Islander Serving Institutions, Alaska Native-Serving and Native Hawaiian-Serving Institutions, Predominantly Black Institutions, and Native American-Serving Nontribal Institutions. Together, these colleges and universities help offer broader access to higher education for students (National Academies, 2019c).

THE CHANGING LANDSCAPE OF THE INSTRUCTIONAL WORKFORCE

According to the National Center for Education Statistics (NCES, 2024a), there were 1.5 million faculty employed at degree-granting post-secondary institutions as of Fall 2022, with 63% employed at public institutions and 33% employed at private nonprofit institutions. Among full-time faculty, 72% were White, 13% Asian, 7% Black, and 6% Hispanic (NCES, 2024a). Though faculty who are women increased by 13% from 2009 to 2021, men make up a greater proportion of full-time tenured faculty. In 2022–2023, at institutions with a tenure system, the percentage of full-time faculty with tenure was higher for men than for women (53% vs. 40%; NCES, 2023f; Kezar & Acuna, 2020). White men make up a higher share of tenure-track positions than non-tenure-track positions, with 39% of professor-rank faculty being White men and 33% of non-professor-rank faculty being White men. A similar pattern is seen for Asian men (8% professor rank and 5% non-professor rank) but not for Hispanic females (3% of the professor rank and 4% of the non-professor rank; NCES, 2024a).

American institutions now heavily depend on contingent faculty (Chun & Evans, 2023; Culver & Kezar, 2020; Garcia et al., 2017; Villanueva Alarcón & Muñoz, 2023). Over the past 30 years, the U.S. academic workforce has shifted from mostly full-time tenured or tenure-track faculty to mostly contingent faculty (e.g., full-time non-tenure-track, full-time with no tenure system, and part-time faculty, included in our definition of VITAL educators). Over two-thirds of faculty members at post-secondary institutions in the United States held contingent appointments in Fall 2021, compared to just under half in Fall 1987 (Association of American Universities, n.d.). These instructors typically hold temporary appointments at colleges and universities, with appointments ranging from a single term to a few years without a guarantee the appointment will be renewed when it expires.

Research shows that the instructional workforce is less diverse than the undergraduates they teach and less diverse than the graduate students and postdoctoral scholars working in academia; in 2022, 76% of faculty were White while 52% of undergraduates were White (Hanson, 2024; NCES, n.d.b). For example, while underrepresented minority students earn 26% of STEM bachelor's degrees, only 10% of STEM faculty at four-year institutions come from underrepresented minority backgrounds (Bennet et al., 2020; NSF, 2023). Whereas women's overall representation has increased steadily across all domains of study, they remain underrepresented among new hires in STEM (Wapman et al., 2022). While women earn approximately half of the bachelor's degrees in STEM, only about 30% of tenured STEM professors and associate professors are women (NCSES, 2023a).

Recent studies have addressed the challenges of instructor workload (Griffith & Altinay, 2020; Misra et al., 2021; Taylor & Frechette, 2022). Mental health and morale are a concern for the instructional workforce with many teaching and learning professionals struggling with expectations and workload that put them at higher risk of burnout due to increases in responsibilities without increases in staffing (Hyson et al., 2021; Muscanell, 2024). One aspect of the increased workload is the number of students requesting flexibility or accommodations or needing additional academic or emotional support (Cole & Griffin, 2013; Guzzardo et al., 2021). The ability to take risks and be available to support students differs across instructional roles. For VITAL educators in particular, these challenges, coupled with the existing struggles to keep up, can take a toll on their well-being.

Centers for teaching and learning are one support and resource for the instructional workforce and they have become more common at colleges and universities over the past several decades. While these types of centers can provide instructional support to instructors, the size and scope vary by institution (Campbell, 2023; Wright, 2023). At some institutions, VITAL educators (including graduate student teaching assistants) are a significant component of the undergraduate education workforce, but they are not always the primary audience for programs run by the institution's center for teaching and learning (Culver et al., 2023; Fuller et al., 2023). Opportunities for professional learning and development for these instructor categories is sometimes limited in part due to policies and structures around the pay and labor practices, and this has implications at institutions with a growing and heavy reliance on them for teaching capacity (Baldwin & Wawrzynski, 2011; Hurlburt & McGarrah, 2016; Walling, 2023). These issues are discussed at greater length in Chapter 8.

The Impact of Funding on Higher Education Institutions

Funding provides opportunities and constraints on decision making including decision making about teaching. While funding is not the focus of this report it does impact student learning experiences in ways that range from the increase in VITAL faculty mentioned above to class size and resources for laboratory and field work.

Institutions have varying levels of resources and make different choices about allocating that funding. An institution often has varied funding sources, all of which contribute to its total budget and impact decision making. Some institutions have significant endowments that support their operations; others receive significant research funding from federal and state governments, industry, and foundations, which provide prestige and influence policies and priorities. Other important sources of funding include support from state legislatures for public institutions, tuition revenue, auxiliary activities (e.g., athletics), and giving by alumni and other supporters of the institution.

Public institutions have seen dramatic changes in the percentage of their budget supported by state funding. In 2020, less than 6% of state revenue (nationally) was allocated to higher education (see Figure 2-1). In the most recent ten-year period, no state has increased its effort to support higher education across the following three measures: allocation to higher education, support per capita, and support per $1,000 of personal income (SHEEO, 2022). This lack of increase effectively functions as a decrease in state funding. This has real and profound consequences: research shows that a decrease in state funding results in declining graduation rates at four-year colleges, leading to decreases in statewide bachelor's degree attainment (SHEEO, 2021).

Research reveals different patterns in the responses of various types of institutions to state funding cuts. In general, doctoral institutions respond to funding cuts by raising tuition and other alternative revenue sources. Four-year and two-year institutions, on the other hand, made up the gap by lowering support—cutting expenditures on instruction, academic support, and student services (Mitchell et al., 2019; SHEEO, 2021).

Several studies have demonstrated that when the National Science Foundation (NSF) has provided institutional support to HBCUs, those institutions saw a drastic increase in research capability and productivity, as well as an overall increase in institutional capacities (National Academies, 2022, 2024b). These studies show that funding is directly tied to the education and successful development of underserved students, particularly at HBCUs, and disparities in funding may be linked to lower outcomes in productivity and research capacity that impact students. Toldson (2019) reports funding, particularly at the federal level, impacts overall success at HBCUs, arguing that lower funding at HBCUs contributes to lower outcomes when compared to PWIs.

In order to help institutions make financial decisions in ways that prioritize students, the National Association of College and University Business Officers (2024c) recently created a Student Success Hub, a combination of toolkits and resources that are organized around three focused areas:

1. Data to Inform Decisions: Infrastructure, Analytics, and Usage
2. Financial Resource Optimization for Students Using Enhanced Return on Investment Concept
3. Student-Centered Planning, Processes, and Budgeting.

These tools demonstrate the relationship between strategic financial investments and equitable students' outcomes.

HISTORY CONTINUES TO INFLUENCE TODAY'S APPROACHES TO EDUCATION

Understanding past decisions, agendas, and beliefs is essential in approaching and achieving equitable and effective teaching in present-day undergraduate STEM education. As mentioned in Chapter 1, despite some recent progress, the pathways and outcomes of students can still be predicted by factors such as their race, ethnicity, gender, and family income. Addressing these inequities requires recognizing that the historical legacy of higher education in the United States has produced deep, persistent, systemic inequities in all of post-secondary education that is even more exaggerated in the STEM fields.

Gradual Increases in Access to Higher Education

The default paradigm of science in the United States is Western and Eurocentric, which is rooted in white supremacy and has actively ostracized diverse ways of knowing (Mensah & Jackson, 2018; Morton et al., 2023). Western science positions humans as removed from the natural world and superior in their objectivity, relegating any conversation about culture or positionality to the periphery, effectively creating a power differential in whose voices count and whose knowledge is considered valid (Bang et al., 2012; Carter, 2006; Harding, 2008). The legacy of this Western and Eurocentric paradigm of science as objective and committed to illuminating singular fundamental truths and unifying theories influences the way instructors today interact in teaching and learning settings.

The education system in the United States is built on a historical legacy of slavery, segregation, and exclusion (National Academies, 2024a; Quijano, 2000). Upon invading the Americas, European settlers used violent means to displace and expel Indigenous people in order to settle on their land. This expulsion took many forms: settlers exposed Indigenous people to harmful illnesses that led to death; they disturbed the natural ecosystems and exploited natural food supplies; they used weaponry to murder Indigenous people; and they pushed Indigenous communities off their native land to build colonial communities, which frequently involved building colleges (Dunbar-Ortiz, 2023; Wolfe, 2006). Indigenous people were rarely allowed to remain near colonial settlements, and even more rarely allowed on college campuses (Dunbar-Ortiz, 2023; Wilder, 2013; Wolfe, 2006). They were only allowed access to college grounds to serve as servants or for the purposes of assimilation. In the latter case, Indigenous men were enrolled as a means of spreading Eurocentric norms, beliefs, and practices (e.g., linguistic, religious) to their respective tribes and communities (Beardall, 2022; Wilder, 2013).

The chattel slavery of Black people was likewise central to the European project nation-building, which was undertaken in part through the development of the education system. The Atlantic slave trade, orchestrated by Europeans, forced enslaved Black people to live and work across all of the Americas, including in the British colonies and what would eventually become the early United States. Although Black people were most often enslaved by White people on privately owned estates, many were forced to labor on colonial college campuses. Indeed, Harris et al. (2019) notes that colleges regularly "rented" enslaved Black people to build and maintain the college facilities and grounds, and Wilder (2013) details how college presidents and faculty members who enslaved Black people forced them to work on campus.

Through these actions, Europeans proclaimed themselves superior—deserving of love, respect, education, health, and limitless possibility—while Black and Indigenous people (and later other People of Color) were cast as less than human, intellectually inferior, and thus undeserving of a full life (Dunbar-Ortiz, 2021; Quijano, 2000; Wilder, 2013; Wolfe, 2006). Europeans stereotyped individuals in these groups as intellectually inferior and incapable (González-Stokas, 2023), but at the same time feared that education might embolden or empower them. Black and Indigenous people were systemically excluded from educational institutions through laws and policies that forbade and severely punished individuals and groups who attempted to pursue education (National Academies, 2023).

This worldview provided a foundational logic or assumption about what kind of people were capable of learning and whose knowledges and ways of knowing were legitimate and worthy of shaping society and being included in higher education (González-Stokas, 2023). The ideas that early American scholars used to build academia were drawn from European ideas, which not only impacted the academic profession and the disciplines but created the legacies of exclusions in contemporary STEM teaching and learning (Gonzales & Culpepper, 2024). The principles used to structure the policies and practices of these institutions, such as exclusivity in admission, were in service of the class and racial hierarchies that were entrenched at the time. Many higher education institutions did not admit students of color or women until the mid-20th century (National Academies, 2023). The debates over the renaming of buildings and colleges, such as Calhoun College at Yale (Branch, 2015), are examples of how the individuals in higher education have been identified as racist and/or inequitable in their actions, but fewer institutions have gone so far as to recognize the historical legacies of the entire system (Lee & Ahtone, 2020). While some progress has been made to better include more diverse populations in higher education, that has not always been the goal of reform efforts and has even more rarely been the result.

Even when admission opportunities expanded, students from underserved populations have often remained marginalized. The Morrill Land-Grant Acts, beginning in 1862, facilitated the creation of public institutions for higher education in states which made it more practical for a wider variety of people in a wider variety of locations to access learning (Morrill Act, 1862). While this legislation increased the number of universities and made post-secondary education more available, the main beneficiaries remained relatively prosperous White men. Additionally, the creation of these land-grant institutions was largely carried out by appropriation and sale of Native lands and still excluded many populations from enrolling as students. Furthermore, many institutions were not optimally suited to meet the needs of the diverse students that did attend them.

The second Morrill Act of 1890 recognized and addressed this limitation but primarily did so by creating Black institutions instead of expanding access for Black students to existing institutions. These are some of the institutions the Higher Education Act of 1965 federally recognized as HBCUs. The 1890 Morrill Act therefore was one factor that allowed existing universities to continue as predominately White environments (Second Morrill Act, 1890). Overall access to higher education increased for Black students, but they remained largely excluded from the best-resourced and well-established institutions. Additionally, the creation of these new components of the higher education landscape was influenced by the existing models as structures, policies, practices, and operating principles largely replicated those first established by the colleges founded in colonial America.[1]

In the early 20th century, the formation of junior or community colleges further expanded access, providing additional and often more affordable opportunities for a wider variety of students. These institutions replicated many of the policies and practices of existing institutions and helped maintain the status quo in the United States by diverting students (largely those who are part of underserved populations) from university to an extension of high school (Brint & Karabel, 1989). Undergraduate admissions further expanded in the wake of the Second World War, when many returning service

---

[1] The founding dates of various institutions are one window into this history: The first university (Harvard University, 1636); the first public institutions (the University of Georgia, 1785, and the University of North Carolina, 1789); the first engineering school (United States Military Academy West Point, 1802); the first technical university (Rensselaer Polytechnic Institute, 1824); the first women's college (Wesleyan College, 1836); the first university for African American students (Cheyney University, 1837); the first designated land-grant institutions (Michigan State University, 1962, and Penn State, 1863); the first community college (Joliet Junior College, 1901); and the first Tribal college (Diné College, 1968).

members were able to attend college through the G.I. Bill, introduced as part of the Servicemen's Readjustment Act (Servicemen's Readjustment Act, 1944; Malcom-Piqueux, 2020). However, due to discriminatory practices, many populations (especially Black veterans) were still excluded and not able to equally benefit. This more firmly entrenched racial stratification within higher education and furthered inequality (Turner & Bound, 2002).

The increase in federal funding for research has precipitated another significant change to the higher education landscape. The 1950 creation of NSF (National Science Foundation Act, 1950) and the expansion of the National Institutes of Health extramural grant program in the 1950s provided money that allowed enormous increases in research on campuses and intensified the prestige accorded to faculty and institutions with high levels of research productivity (Malcom-Piqueux, 2020; Mazuzan, 1994). Prompted by the launch of Sputnik in 1957, the Space Race effort in the United States increased federal funding for science in higher education. However, the educational aspect of this increased funding was focused on individuals to whom society accorded the greatest potential for genius-level contributions to technology, and thus once again excluded many and failed to consider ways in which society benefits when large numbers of citizens have an increased understanding of complex technologies. While efforts to improve racial equity were one part of NSF's plan for this money, the social and political realities forced the agency to set these priorities aside (Malcom-Piqueux, 2020).

The 1965 Higher Education Act creating the federal designation of HBCUs and allocating them some dedicated funding also marked a change in overall federal support for higher education by providing grants and access to loans that increased access to higher education for students from a variety of family incomes and zip codes (Higher Education Act, 1965). The year before, the Civil Rights Act of 1964 prohibited exclusion based on race, color, national origin, sex, or religion. This federal legislation also contributed to increased access for students from a wide variety of races and ethnicities to institutions that had previously offered very limited access (Civil Rights Act, 1964). However, many restrictions remained in practice resulting from discrimination, implicit and explicit bias, and financial barriers, among others.

Federal legislation also increased access for other underserved groups. Title IX in 1972 further enabled participation by women (Title IX of the Education Amendments, 1972). The next year the passage of the Rehabilitation Act increased access for people with disabilities through its Section 504 (Rehabilitation Act, 1973). HSIs were established in the 1980s (formally recognized in 1992) with an intention to serve Hispanic students (Espinosa et al., 2017). The Perkins Act series of legislation (Carl D. Perkins Vocational and Technical Education Act, 1984) helped shift vocational education to CTE, providing programs that connect learning experiences with workforce preparation to be more meaningful and relevant to students' needs (Fletcher et al., 2013). While these and other initiatives have dramatically increased the participation of previously underserved populations in higher education, they have not yet led to equitable opportunities and outcomes for students from all populations.

Systemic Inequities in Teaching and Learning Remain

Systemic inequities in teaching and learning have long been embedded in the practices and standards of educational institutions. The dominant teaching approach has long combined class lectures and testing. Over the past century, tutorials and small-group models have grown, innovations that well-resourced institutions were more able to provide (Zimmerman, 2020). In the past few decades, many commitments to instructional improvement have emerged, although not at a widespread level. These include centers for teaching and learning, course evaluation results in promotion dossiers, and increased use of evidence-based instructional practices (Hampel, 2021; Zimmerman, 2020).

The research university continues to set the standard and expectations about teaching and research. While the past 40 years have seen many signs of progress, in some ways, an educational crisis is recurring from one academic generation to the next with teaching continuing to be undervalued by academic units, disciplines, and institutions.

Even outside of research universities, at institutions where the "publish or perish" mindset is less prevalent, aspects of the historical context persist in, for example, the faculty hiring process; these lingering, often outdated standards are barriers to equitable and effective teaching. In a recent study, Wu et al. (2023) examined how applicant characteristics are considered and evaluated in STEM faculty hiring practices. They found that "affinity bias (preference for sameness), confirmation bias (tendency to believe perspectives that are consistent with our preconceived beliefs), and halo bias (tendency to assume an individual who exhibits one positive quality will also outperform overall)" lead to an emphasis on research and postdoctoral reputation over institutional diversity, equitable and inclusive teaching, research, and service (p. 15).

SUMMARY

The complex landscape of post-secondary education in the United States has changed over time to better include more diverse populations of students. However, policies and structures have not kept pace with the changes, and many students still do not have equitable access to STEM learning opportunities. Demographic changes in the undergraduate population in some ways mirror demographic changes in the country as a whole. These changes reflect initiatives to better prepare students for college and to welcome students who do not fit the traditional expectations for undergraduates to enroll. This expansion of who is considered a potential member of the undergraduate student body is necessary to fairly prepare students to navigate the world and to provide opportunities for them to develop knowledge, skills, and competencies that prepare them to join the STEM workforce. Addressing the uneven representation among demographic groups in taking and completing STEM courses and degrees is a key topic that will be further addressed throughout the rest of this report. Today's instructional workforce differs significantly from past decades, as VITAL educators have become more common and tenure-track positions have declined.

Conclusion 2.1: Undergraduate STEM education occurs in many types of institutions with varying missions, goals, resources, and student populations; but all these types of institutions share a responsibility for providing high-quality STEM learning experiences for students.

Conclusion 2.2: Many longstanding policies and practices in undergraduate STEM education have produced, perpetuated, and exacerbated differences in opportunities, experiences, and outcomes among post-secondary STEM students from underserved population groups. This is shown in research that finds that students from lower socioeconomic backgrounds, students of color, first-generation college goers, women, and students with disabilities are among the groups who have consistently fared worse in post-secondary STEM education.

Conclusion 2.3: Recent changes in the demographics of the student population, college costs, and pressures on higher education to meet the demands of the 21st-century STEM workplace underscore the need to re-evaluate instructional practices in STEM and improve the learning experiences of undergraduate students in STEM courses.

3

Understanding Teaching, Learning, and Equity

Experts have developed a significant body of work on how people learn and what teaching strategies are most effective (National Academies of Sciences, Engineering, and Medicine [National Academies], 2018, 2020). In the past few decades, scholarship that explores issues of equity and inequity in teaching and learning, in particular, has increased. The extent of research and scholarship in the fields of psychology, cognitive science, learning science, cognitive psychology, scholarship of teaching and learning, discipline-based education research, and other related fields that contributes to our understanding of how people learn is vast. The previous chapter gives a brief overview of the institutional context for teaching and learning in U.S. undergraduate science, technology, engineering, and mathematics (STEM) education, raising many issues related to the diversity, opportunity, and challenges for institutions teaching undergraduate STEM education. While the diversity of students, instructors, and institutions means that decisions must be made with awareness of local context, extensive research provides strong evidence to help guide understanding and decision making. This chapter therefore provides an overview of what we know about how people learn, evidence for practices that support learning, and practices of particular concern in the STEM disciplines because they lead to inequity. This rich scholarship provides the grounding for this entire report and is drawn upon in Chapter 4 for the development of the Principles for Equitable and Effective Teaching.

LEARNING IS COMPLEX AND WELL STUDIED

Learning is a process of actively constructing knowledge through conceptual reorganization of ideas, not simply the accrual of information (Kober, 2015). The brain is a "dynamic organ;" even a mature brain is structurally altered during learning (National Research Council [NRC], 2000, p. 235). New knowledge is generated when the brain actively connects information to prior knowledge and experience (Kober, 2015; NRC, 2000).

Effective practices are student centered, learner focused, and grounded in research (e.g., with evidence from multiple studies showing student learning gains; NRC, 2012a, 2015). Evidence-based pedagogies are more cognitively engaging for students and show them the relevance of STEM concepts and skills. In particular, scholarship shows the benefits of taking a student-centered approach, where students actively engage in their own learning process (Bligh, 2000; Chi & Wylie, 2014; Theobald et al., 2020). Researchers have found that when students actively engage in learning they are more likely to develop robust conceptual understanding, be able to transfer learning across contexts, and retain ideas (Armbruster et al., 2009; Devlin & Samarawickrema, 2010; Ebert-May et al., 1997; Hogan & Sathy, 2022; Lyle et al., 2020; Watson et al., 2023). Students in large STEM courses that combine pre-class preparatory assignments and in-class active learning activities earn higher grades, have lower failure rates, and report an increased sense of community over courses that use simply lecture (Eddy & Hogan, 2014; Freeman et al., 2014). Studies also show that these approaches can increase the probability of equitable outcomes between underserved students and their peers (Dewsbury et al., 2022; Eddy & Hogan, 2014; Haak et al., 2011; Theobald et al., 2020). The above citations are only selected examples of the large body of the existing empirical research, which employs a range of methods—including randomized control trials, experiments, quasi-experiments, longitudinal, cross-sectional, correlational, and observational studies—to show that student-centered instructional approaches, often referred to as active learning, can have a positive effect on student learning.

However, despite this evidence and calls for reform, STEM instruction at the undergraduate level remains entrenched in ineffective practices, with traditional lecture primary among them (Egger et al., 2019; Harper et al., 2019; Stains et al., 2018). STEM teaching has historically been didactic, unidirectional, and instructor centered with in-person lectures being the dominant approach. While many effective teachers use a mix of techniques that include lecturing and employ approaches that make it possible for students to actively engage with content during traditional lectures, research has shown that relying solely on lectures or memorization is ineffective for and even alienating to many students (Dewsbury et al., 2022).

This approach to knowledge/skill acquisition is not consistent with what research and theories of learning say works best, and can perpetuate existing biases.

Research on Learning

As mentioned above, a great deal is known about how learning happens, with contributions from the fields of psychology, cognitive science, learning science, neuroscience, cognitive psychology, behavioral science, scholarship of teaching and learning (SoTL), discipline-based education research (DBER), and other related fields (e.g., National Academies, 2018). Together these fields provide evidence for teaching approaches that foster learning of particular relevance to this study; they capture information about inequities in STEM learning and provide information about teaching strategies that reduce inequity in STEM learning environments.

As defined in a 2012 National Academies report, "DBER investigates learning and teaching in a discipline using a range of methods with deep grounding in the discipline's priorities, worldview, knowledge, and practices" (NRC, 2012b, p. 9). DBER investigations lead to generalizable findings that can improve teaching, learning, diversity and inclusion, and other aspects of the discipline.

SoTL involves taking a scientific approach to one's own teaching—informed by prior scholarship on teaching and learning—and sharing the results broadly to serve as a model for others. Testing the impact of an intervention in a particular course or curriculum may not always provide generalizable findings, but it does provide evidence for the potential effectiveness of an approach by describing the criteria necessary for the intervention's success.

Learning science is an interdisciplinary research area focused on the systematic study of how learning occurs in different settings, how to improve teaching, and how to help students learn more effectively (Sawyer, 2005). Most fundamentally, this work has established that learning is not a purely cognitive process, but instead is a dynamic, socio-cultural activity that is influenced by social, emotional, cultural, and physical factors (National Academies, 2018).

The strength of evidence produced by the range of methods has been characterized by the strength of evidence pyramid (St. John & McNeal, 2017), among other models. In this model, expert opinion and practitioner wisdom of disciplinary teaching form the base of the pyramid and can provide evidence for promising practices. Case studies and cohort studies build on this foundation to produce higher-quality evidence, and meta-analyses and systematic reviews at the top of the pyramid provide the strongest evidence. In the present report, evidence comes from multiple STEM disciplines and studies within those disciplines, focusing on the higher levels in the strength of evidence pyramid. In some instances, we will also refer to promising practices, which may be supported by evidence from disciplinary and/or cohort studies.

Increased focus on equitable teaching practices and pedagogy—especially in STEM—has grown over the past decade in part driven by an effort to challenge deficit models of learning and cognition and a desire to mitigate educational inequality (Bell et al., 2017; Medin & Bang, 2014; Philip & Azevedo, 2017; Philip et al., 2018; Uttamchandani, 2018). Creating equitable and effective learning environments requires acknowledging and attending to all of the components of learning.

Understanding Mastery and Mindset

As described in *How People Learn II: Learners, Contexts, and Cultures* (National Academies, 2018, p. 117), "Goals—the learner's desired outcomes—are important for learning because they guide decisions about whether to expend effort and how to direct attention, foster planning, influence responses to failure, and promote other behaviors important for learning" (Albaili, 1998; Dweck & Elliot, 1983; Hastings & West, 2011). Goals can be broadly categorized as mastery oriented (e.g., focused on achieving competence and understanding) or performance oriented (e.g., focused on appearing competent in relation to others; National Academies, 2018). A student with a mastery goal is typically working to master a skill or learn the material, either from intrinsic motivation or being able to use the skill or knowledge to accomplish a task, whereas a student with a performance goal is typically working to look good in comparison to others, often leading to a sense of competition. Instructors in the undergraduate STEM classrooms influence students' learning by defining course-level learning goals and incorporating teaching practices and opportunities for students to achieve these learning goals. Instructors can choose goals and practices that focus on mastery of skills rather than performance in order to help students engage in higher-order cognitive skills, persist in the face of failure, and retain knowledge and skills over the long term (Henry et al., 2019; Hernandez et al., 2013).

Mastery goals are often discussed in relation to growth mindset beliefs that all students can learn with effective effort, good strategies, and help from others (Dweck, 1999; Henry et al., 2019; Limeri et al., 2023; National Academies, 2018). When students endorse growth mindset beliefs, they experience a stronger sense of belonging, higher course grades, and greater intent to persist (Limeri et al., 2023). Moreover, interventions employing randomized controlled trials have yielded impressive results including improving grades and persistence in science and closing achievement gaps, though some student-focused growth mindset interventions have shown mixed results (Canning & Limeri, 2023). In addition, the impact of STEM instructors' mindset beliefs and the mindset culture they create through their teaching practices, policies, and interactions with students has been shown to influence students' learning experiences and performance (Muenks et al., 2020), and influenced, too, the magnitude of racial and class-based achievement gaps in STEM classes (Canning et al., 2019, 2024). Helping STEM instructors adopt more growth-minded beliefs and teaching practices—including designing learning goals that provide multiple opportunities for learning and improvement in various different ways, and assessment practices to match the learning goals (Hecht et al., 2022; Kroeper et al., 2020a,b)—is important to support the goals, learning, and achievement of all students in STEM.

ACTIVE LEARNING EXPERIENCES IMPROVE STUDENT UNDERSTANDING

As we will discuss in the section on Principle 1 in the next chapter, active engagement is critical in the learning process. Here we discuss the related concept of "active learning," which has been frequently used in conversations about improving undergraduate STEM education. The phrase has been so well used that it sometimes seems to mean any practice that deviates from traditional lecturing. The approach of Lombardi et al. (2021) uses a "construction-of-understanding ecosystem" model to illustrate the contrast between traditional learning situations and the active learning environment. In the traditional learning environment, direct experiences with phenomena, working with data and models, and engaging in discipline-based practices are all mediated by the instructor and transmitted to the student. In the active learning environment, the students themselves engage in discipline-based practices with their peers to make sense of data and models, which provides direct experience with the practices of the discipline—including the social component. The committee sees ways of applying this way of thinking to a large range of disciplines and modalities. Active learning approaches have been studied in a variety of STEM disciplines (Apkarian et al., 2021; Driessen et al., 2020; Laursen & Rasmussen, 2019). It can be thought of as a commitment by the instructor to intentionally build in time, opportunities, and activities that allow students agency and direct experience with the practice of the relevant STEM discipline. Students can build agency in their own learning in a large lecture, a small seminar, a fully online course, or any other modality, and the specific approaches an instructor chooses will depend on their local context and goals for student learning.

Not all approaches that have been labeled as active learning necessarily engage students actively in their own learning. Strategies such as the use of clicker questions in lectures, laboratory activities, and a "flipped" classroom disrupt traditional lectures and can be aspects of active learning but do not necessarily meet this definition of active learning. Clicker questions can contribute to engaging students with deep concepts or they can focus on recall of obscure facts at regular intervals during a lecture; while both may serve the purpose of keeping students engaged in listening to the lecture, the latter does not help them focus on direct engagement with phenomena and data of the discipline. Similarly, laboratory activities can be confirmatory tests rather than the collection and analysis of new data. The key goal is to help students achieve learning goals by providing opportunities for them to engage repeatedly in the practices of science, technology, engineering, or mathematics within a disciplinary or interdisciplinary framework. This approach parallels the focus of *A Framework for K–12 Science Education: Practices, Crosscutting Concepts, and Core Ideas* (NRC, 2012a), which presents a vision in which students use disciplinary practices together with cross-cutting concepts to deepen their understanding of disciplinary core ideas.

While implementing active learning has been shown to increase student achievement and can reduce achievement gaps in undergraduate STEM courses it is still incumbent on instructors to implement active learning strategies in equitable ways that respect student identity (Dewsbury et al., 2022; Freeman et al., 2014; Theobald et al., 2020). It is also important for instructors to recognize that some active learning strategies, such as group work, can increase students' anxiety (Cooper et al., 2018). Research has shown that some populations of students have encountered challenges in some approaches to active learning, for example LGBTQIA+ students (Cooper & Brownell, 2016; Voigt, 2022, 2024). Therefore, it is important to note that attending to equity is an important aspect of implementing active learning strategies.

SPECIAL CONSIDERATIONS FOR LEARNING IN THE STEM DISCIPLINES

While pedagogical approaches have shifted some in recent years, didactic instruction remains the dominant way that STEM is taught (Stains et al., 2018). The use of ineffective teaching strategies persists in part because individual faculty work within a system that reinforces ineffective teaching practices or makes change difficult (Borrego & Henderson, 2014; Feola et al., 2023; Henderson et al., 2011; Riihimaki & Viskupic, 2019). A variety of individual and contextual factors have been correlated with instructors' lack of adoption of evidence-based teaching practices; these factors include departmental norms and negative attitudes and beliefs (Lund & Stains, 2015); large class sizes (Yik et al., 2022); inadequate learning spaces (Leijon et al., 2022); greater faculty engagement in research (Apkarian et al., 2021); a hiring, reward, and promotion system that focuses on research excellence over teaching (Dennin et al., 2017); fixed-minded beliefs about students' abilities and potential (Canning et al., 2019; Muenks et al., 2020); beliefs that success in STEM disciplines requires natural genius and brilliance, rather than hard work and learning (Leslie et al., 2015); and lack of exposure to active learning as a student (Apkarian et al., 2021; Kraft et al., 2024a).

Furthermore, teaching excellence is often not selected for in the hiring process, nor is it taught systematically or rewarded, and institutions often rely on outdated methods of evaluation (Bradforth et al., 2015; Dennin et al., 2017). As a result, instructors can have little incentive to learn about and implement evidence-based teaching strategies. In some instances, STEM instructors do not employ teaching strategies shown to be effective simply because those strategies are not known to them: few receive preparation in effective and evidence-based teaching strategies prior to entering the college classroom (Austin et al., 2009; Golde & Dore, 2001), much less the role that dominant and privileged identities play in teaching (Duncan et al., 2023). All of these factors mean that instructors are more likely to rely on teaching strategies that are familiar to them even as such strategies are often less effective at supporting student learning (e.g., Stains et al., 2018). This can further marginalize underserved students and cause them to question their ability to succeed in STEM (Seymour & Hewitt, 1997; Seymour & Hunter, 2019; Tanner & Allen, 2007). These issues are discussed further in Chapter 8.

STEM disciplines remain exclusionary spaces, and STEM learning spaces, by extension, have the potential to perpetuate similar experiences for students. The legacy of systemic inequity can be seen, for example, in unidirectional delivery of course content that positions instructors as the sole experts (O'Neill et al., 2023); isolating research questions from their local context (Anthony-Stevens & Matsaw, 2020; McGinty & Bang, 2016; Medin & Bang 2014); framing content as race neutral (Gildersleeve et al., 2011; Haynes & Patton, 2019); conceptualizing success (and designing assessments) in highly individualized ways (Brayboy, 2005; Lopez, 2021); and presenting only White, Western thinkers in syllabi (Gonzales et al., 2024c; Grant, 2021).

Mitigating the impact of systemic inequities in undergraduate STEM classrooms involves challenging the established model of knowing and learning about the world (Bang et al., 2012). This requires instructors to acknowledge the affective dimensions of learning (e.g., beliefs, attitudes, etc.) and the essential role they play in STEM education (Dewsbury, 2020).

It also involves embracing broader paradigmatic shifts toward validating multiple ways of knowing, learning, and teaching STEM (e.g., Barron et al., 2021; Morton & Parsons, 2018). Decolonization and deconstruction of systemic structures of inequity are also critical in the development of more equitable and effective teaching and learning and involve transformative changes at the systemic level (e.g., Morton et al., 2023). The power of this tansformative change can cultivate the next generation of STEM experts to make a meaningful shift in the disciplines, but only if STEM learning spaces are designed appropriately.

Thus, there is substantial evidence that undergraduate STEM teaching has been both ineffective and inequitable in a wide variety of settings. Because of this, it is also important to note that undergraduate STEM education is not a monolith. While some research uncovers broad understandings about STEM learning as a whole and reveals STEM-wide challenges to equity and effectiveness, other studies show that there are differences between disciplines in their cultures, practices, accrediting bodies, and expectations for teaching and learning. In many disciplines, there is a distinction in the teaching that takes place in classes for majors and classes for general education (typically introductory courses). At various points throughout the following discussion, we highlight a few of the critical equity and effectiveness issues within individual disciplines (or subsets of disciplines) that exist as lasting implications of historical legacies of exclusion. Although this is not a comprehensive list, it includes issues that have been raised repeatedly in the committee's work.

Foundational STEM Courses

Every STEM discipline has a foundational, introductory course or course sequence that serves as an entry to a major in the discipline. In addition, most STEM majors and programs have courses that serve as prerequisites for upper-level courses in the major, often year-long sequences of math, chemistry, and/or physics. These have sometimes been referred to as "gateway" courses (e.g., Koch, 2017), in the sense that all students must pass through these gates to progress along STEM pathways; however, we prefer the term "foundational," which indicates that future learning and success will build upon these courses. Across STEM disciplines, systemic disadvantages lead to grade reductions (Castle et al., 2024), particularly in the large chemistry and calculus courses that are prerequisites for several disciplines (Weston et al., 2019). In particular, students' experiences in foundational courses are especially important for their persistence in STEM, because, often, these courses act as gates and filter out students rather than deepen their engagement, interest, and understanding of STEM topics (Canning et al., 2018; Harris et al., 2020; Holland, 2019; Weston et al., 2019).

These courses are critical junctures where students can easily lose motivation to continue in their degrees or to take additional STEM courses if their grade does not reflect their learning or ability to succeed (e.g., Harris et al., 2020; Hunter, 2019). The impact of foundational courses is disproportionately skewed in favor of White male students: a large, multi-institution study showed that White male students who were intending on a career in STEM had a 48% chance of succeeding in that career path when they received a grade of C or better in all foundational courses. However, for women of color, the percentage dropped to 35%, and if at least one foundational course was less than a C, the probability dropped further to 21% (Hatfield et al., 2022).

Instructors in foundational courses across the STEM disciplines are more likely to emphasize content knowledge as the most important outcome for students, and to spend most of class time lecturing (Ferrare, 2019; Stains et al., 2018), including in chemistry (Wang et al., 2024) and the geosciences (Egger, 2019). Assessment practices in these courses typically focus on performance goals that measure lower-level cognitive skills (Momsen et al., 2013), including rote memorization and reliance on math skills that are not taught in the course, which can disadvantage certain students (Ralph et al., 2022). And yet, engaging students in collaborative group work and other interactive strategies in these foundational courses increases their interest, motivation, and persistence (Gasiewski et al., 2012).

So-called "weed-out" courses are a subset of these foundational STEM courses that are identified as such primarily by students. They can vary widely, but share several characteristics as defined by Weston et al. (2019): they are required courses (or course sequences) for a STEM major; they tend to be large, lecture-style courses; passing the course(s) is difficult (e.g., they award a large number of D, F, or incomplete/withdrawal grades [DFW]); and they are a strong predictor of success and persistence in a major. Weston et al. (2019) used these and other criteria, including a >20% DFW rate to identify weed-out courses at six institutions, and found calculus, chemistry, and computer science to be the most common, making up 60% of all weed-out courses identified. Students identify a course as a "weed-out" when they note misalignment between understanding and assessment practices (including curved grading), when the instructor is indifferent to learning, when there is a lack of organization, and/or when they experience a competitive class culture (Kardash & Wallace, 2001; Weston et al., 2019).

These courses have an impact on STEM beyond just poor grades for a large number of students. Students who receive a DFW from one of these classes are more likely to receive a similar grade in a second class, and more likely to switch out of a STEM major—and these students are more likely to be women, women of color, and from a lower socio-economic status

(Seymour & Hunter, 2019). Experiences in weed-out courses lead to a loss of confidence and lack of sense of belonging for students (Weston et al., 2019), and lead to maintenance and reinforcement of the existing structural inequities in the STEM fields. Modifying these critical foundational courses, which often serve programs in multiple departments (e.g., calculus is required for several STEM majors), requires concerted effort by or across academic units to be effective and make lasting change (Matz et al., 2018; see Chapter 6).

Curricula and Course Combinations

The curricular structures that emerge from an academic unit's design of major programs produce a network of interdependent courses connected via prerequisite and corequisite requirements (Brown et al., 2018). The interdependencies create a complex organizational structure that students must navigate on their way to the degree. A strongly interdependent (e.g., complex) curriculum is going to be experienced differently based on a students' background, social position, previous coursework, access to advising, willingness to accrue debt, and their experience of classroom climate (Harrison & Williams, 2023; see Chapter 7 for more).

This complexity can itself be a barrier for students, particularly when it is distinct from the content interests and needs of students and creates barriers to entry, persistence, and successful completion. Coursework in STEM can be relatively linear and sequential, which makes friction toward academic progress a bigger problem than in fields where students have more flexibility in their pathways. A student who finds themself struggling in one STEM course appears much more likely to struggle in related courses, producing a "snowball" effect of academic difficulty that has been observed in engineering and other courses (Brown et al., 2018). In addition, students can experience delays in making progress if courses with dependencies are offered irregularly, or they are encouraged to take courses in combinations that lead to high rates of failure (e.g., "toxic" course combinations). These particular course combinations may be especially problematic for underserved students and together these effects create a problem for momentum and navigation and can lead to students switching out of a STEM major into other degree programs (Brown et al., 2018; Hunter, 2019; Slim et al., 2014).

In addition to the official curriculum, there is also the "hidden" curriculum, which refers to the unwritten rules, values, and belief systems, and behavioral and social expectations that support student success, but are rarely explicitly discussed or taught (Andarvazh et al., 2017; Jackson, 1968; Snyder, 1971). In STEM disciplines, the hidden curriculum includes expectations about how to interact with instructors and teaching assistants in office hours, the value placed on pursuing undergraduate research, knowing how and when to ask for letters of recommendation, and many more components that are discipline specific. Lack of awareness of the norms of a discipline, or of higher education in general, influences how students interact with professors, advisors, and each other. Advice for making the hidden curriculum more explicit often comes from fellow undergraduate students (e.g., Massey et al., 2022). In general, making both the hidden curriculum and the intended curriculum explicit and streamlining students' pathways through both require combined efforts at the individual, departmental, and institutional levels (see Chapters 6 and 9 for more information). Recent efforts to demystify the hidden curriculum in geoscience graduate programs, called for by leaders in the geoscience community, can serve as a model for undergraduate programs more generally (Cooke et al., 2021; Pensky et al., 2021).

Math Course Sequences

While many disciplines require course sequences that can be problematic for students in their majors, students in virtually all STEM majors are required to traverse the mathematics course sequences, which are traditionally organized in a linear and hierarchical fashion (McFarland & Rodan, 2009). Mathematics frequently serve as the foundational courses to STEM majors (Ellis et al., 2016; Moreno & Muller, 1999; Sanabria & Penner, 2017; Weeden et al., 2020). These classes may serve to motivate or discourage students seeking to persist in *any* STEM field in college and beyond (Bressoud, 2014, 2021; Park et al., 2021), and research has shown that performance in mathematics classes is a predictor of student success and persistence in many contexts, and thus shaping students' trajectories in significant ways (Cohen & Kelly, 2020; Evans et al., 2020; Hsu et al., 2008; Park et al., 2021). In particular, race/ethnicity, gender, and the intersection of the two have all been shown to be predictors of math performance and achievement leading up to college (Riegle-Crumb, 2006).

Many students experience misalignment between the courses they have taken in high school and the course they place into in college, with significant negative impacts on their success and persistence (Park et al., 2021). Underserved students often get assigned to remedial mathematics courses (e.g., "below" calculus) in college, and have limited opportunities to enroll in STEM courses within their intended major, significantly delaying their degree progression and/or pushing them to switch to another major (Boatman & Long, 2018; Cohen & Kelly, 2020; Weston et al., 2019). Though many reform efforts in mathematics sequences and developmental math have sought to address this issue, they tend to focus on general progress without attending to the significant equity issues that are often a factor (Brathwaite et al., 2021).

Teaching and Learning in the Field

In some disciplines, notably the geosciences and biological sciences, field courses and experiences are valued by both instructors and students as critical components of undergraduate programs that produce both cognitive and affective gains for learners (Fleischner et al., 2017; Klyce & Ryker, 2023; Mogk & Goodwin, 2012; Mosher & Keane, 2021; O'Connell et al., 2022; Petcovic et al., 2014; Shafer et al., 2023; Stokes & Boyle, 2009). These experiences also have numerous potential barriers to participation and full engagement that produce systemic inequities in access and success with underserved students facing disproportionate financial, cultural, social, and physical barriers (Carabajal et al., 2017; Morales et al., 2020; Posselt & Nuñez, 2022). The geosciences in particular face inclusion challenges, including an emphasis on ableism (Carabajal & Atchison, 2020) and a historical legacy of exclusion and exploitation of marginalized groups (e.g., Marín-Spiotta et al., 2020).

The Principles for Equitable and Effective Teaching in the field are the same as in the classroom, but the circumstances surrounding their application require additional attention. Given the value that instructors, students, and employers all place on field experiences, recent research has focused on reducing barriers to participation, promoting inclusion, and providing equitable experiences. Recommended strategies to increase access include being intentional with the site selection and considering alternatives to traditional choices. Site survey, field activities design, and risk assessment can help to identify whether there are ways to mitigate potential negative physical or mental impacts (Carabajal & Atchison, 2020; Chiarella & Vurro, 2020). This research has led to the development of models and recommendations for designing undergraduate field experiences that are more likely to be inclusive and effective (Atchison et al., 2019; Gilley et al., 2015; Marshall et al., 2022; O'Connell et al., 2022; Stokes et al., 2019).

Learning and Technology: STEM Learning in a High-Tech World

Eight key affordances of learning technologies were identified by a National Academies consensus study: interactivity, adaptivity, feedback, choice, nonlinear access, linked representations, open-ended learner input, and communication with other people (National Academies, 2018, pp. 165–166). These affordances enable growth of learning technologies, online learning platforms, and adaptive testing. However, use of technology alone does not address the intertwined challenges of ineffective teaching and systemic inequity described above. For example, although online courses and degree programs have the potential to broaden access to higher education, they consistently have higher attrition rates than in-person courses and programs (Bawa, 2016). Impacted by an increase in online learning during the COVID-19 pandemic, students reported they did not prefer online modes of instruction (National Academies, 2021). Many students face one or more components of digital inequality: unequal access to the internet and devices, discrepancies in digital skills and engagement, and unequal outcomes of their efforts to use technology (Katz et al., 2021).

Digital inequality means that not all learners can take advantage of the affordances of technology, and it becomes another site of systemic inequity and ineffective teaching (e.g., Laufer et al., 2021). In the wake of the COVID-19 pandemic, Katz et al. (2021) found that connectivity challenges, device challenges, and communication challenges were all associated with lower remote learning proficiency, and that those challenges were experienced more commonly by students whose families were facing financial hardship and economic insecurity. Technology that is designed around accessibility, student-centered design, and effectiveness and equity has the potential to be a significant driver for improving undergraduate STEM education for all students.

PRACTICES COMMONLY USED TODAY CONTRIBUTE TO INEQUITIES IN STUDENT EXPERIENCES

There is substantial evidence for ongoing inequity in undergraduate STEM and hiring into the STEM workforce. This section presents evidence for some of those inequities, focusing on grade penalties, persistence to degree, and sense of belonging. Many datasets, longitudinal studies, and meta-analyses focus on inequitable outcomes where race/ethnicity and gender are the factors studied although a body of work is developing that analyzes demographic factors such as first-generation students and socio-economic status (Ives & Castillo-Montoya, 2020; O'Donnell & Blankenship, 2018; Reynolds & Cruise, 2020). Several recent books have explored equity issues in detail (Addy et al., 2024; Artze-Vega et al., 2023; Equity Based Teaching Collective, 2024). Further study on the full range of identities that students bring to their STEM education is needed. For examples of some potential research questions that emerged from the Committee's study, see Chapter 10.

Grade Penalties

Evidence from across the STEM disciplines indicates that, when grouped by race/ethnicity or gender, students from underrepresented groups receive proportionally more low grades than their overrepresented peers, even when controlling for other factors like academic preparation (Blatt et al., 2020; Denaro et al., 2022; Harris et al., 2020; Matz et al., 2017). Mean course grades in large STEM courses—primarily introductory courses—increase with the number of systemic advantages (gender, race/ethnicity, income, and first-generation status) that students have (Castle et al., 2024). These grade penalties for underserved students persist over time, and the penalties are the greatest in the STEM fields for first-generation, racial-ethnic minority students (Whitcomb et al., 2021).

Findings are similar within individual disciplines. In biology, performance gaps have been documented between underrepresented minorities (URMs) and non-URMs at inclusive and selective four-year institutions (Salehi et al., 2021) and between binary genders (e.g., students who identify as male or female) in upper-level courses (Farrar et al., 2023). In physics, White males show the greatest gains in common assessments in introductory courses, highlighting both gender- and race/ethnicity-based performance gaps that account for differences in pre-test preparation (Van Dusen & Nissen, 2020).

Persistence to Degree

Grades impact student motivation to persist on their pathway to a degree (Hunter, 2019; Thiry, 2019a); grades in foundational, introductory courses—such as mathematics, discussed above—are particularly critical in students' decision processes (Weston et al., 2019). Many studies have found differences in STEM degree persistence, with Black and Latina/o students more likely to leave the STEM fields than their White peers (Chang et al., 2014; Riegle-Crumb et al., 2019), as are high-performing women when compared with high-performing men (Hunter, 2019). There is strong evidence that pre-college factors—such as high school preparation (Bottia et al., 2015; Salehi et al., 2019a)—have a role in persistence. Evidence that is less clear but still suggestive points to the influence of high school math self-efficacy, family income, and parents' education level as other influences on post-secondary persistence in STEM (Evans et al., 2020; Reynolds & Cruise, 2020; Weeden et al., 2020). In addition, a substantial literature points to "within-college" factors—including earned credits in introductory STEM courses, participation in key academic activities, and hostile classroom environments as shaping students' experiences, persistence, and performance (Barbera et al., 2020; Chang et al., 2014; Evans et al., 2020; Martin et al., 2017b). These within-college factors are correlated with higher rates of change of major out of the natural sciences for Black, Latina/o, and multi-racial students than for White and Asian students.

Several other factors can lead to a decline in motivation to pursue STEM. There is significant evidence for the role of stereotype threat (Steele & Aronson, 1995; Steele et al., 2002; Totonchi et al., 2021). Additional studies suggest the perception of instructor care and the level of interactivity in introductory courses (Rainey et al., 2019), and an institutional culture of independence (Stephens et al., 2012) are other factors to consider. Some students who switch out of STEM majors cite discouragement due to low grades, poor teaching, and a competitive, unsupportive culture as top reasons for their leaving a major (Hunter, 2019).

Sense of Belonging

Interviews and cohort studies have demonstrated a lack of sense of belonging in STEM for underserved students (Rainey et al., 2018), including Black women (Dortch & Patel, 2017); Latina students (Rodriguez & Blaney, 2021); lesbian, gay, bisexual, transgender, queer/questioning, intersex, asexual/aromantic/agender, plus other related identities; and People of Color in the geosciences (Marin-Spiotta et al., 2023); and women in engineering (Glisson, 2023), physics (Seyranian et al., 2018), and chemistry (Edwards et al., 2023). A "chilly" and "hostile" climate in STEM classes and overall creates barriers to access (Jorstad et al., 2017; Marín-Spiotta et al., 2020) and leads students—especially, disproportionately, women and women of color—to switch out of STEM majors into other fields (Hunter, 2019). Sense of belonging is correlated with performance (Edwards et al., 2022; Fink et al., 2020; Master & Meltzoff, 2020). Interventions employed in randomized controlled trials to support students' belonging have been shown to increase college students' persistence and performance and reduce achievement gaps (LaCosse et al., 2020; Murphy et al., 2020; Walton & Cohen, 2011); thus, sense of belonging is an important component of persistence to degree. Although these studies are sometimes smaller and focused on a single discipline or demographic group, the consistency of the above findings across groups and disciplines strengthens the nature of the evidence.

Power and Privilege

In addition to the evidence for inequity in STEM courses and programs, there are issues regarding the centering of power and privilege. Many students perceive that the STEM disciplines privilege White males (Dancy et al., 2020), given their significant overrepresentation in the professorate and institutional leadership (NCSES, 2023a). Across higher education institutions in the United States, women are more likely to leave academic jobs and less likely to be promoted than men. Reasons given for leaving also differ by gender: women are more likely to feel pushed out of their jobs, whereas men are more likely to feel pulled toward another job (Spoon et al., 2023). In their literature review, Fox Tree and Vaid (2022) document evidence for disparities between men and women and between White people and People of Color in virtually all factors that are critical to hiring and promotion, including research, teaching, and service factors. These privileges are both self-perpetuating and trickle down into undergraduate STEM as they lead to maintenance and reinforcement of systemic inequities in the hiring and career advancement of faculty and instructors (e.g., Dancy & Hodari, 2023).

Disciplinary and Institutional Norms

Academic units (often departments) are where disciplinary norms are communicated to students. It is the expectation of many STEM disciplines that students will develop a common set of competencies by taking certain required courses that (a) teach a predetermined amount of content and (b) use predetermined assessment strategies in a specific sequence (e.g., Yother et al., 2022). This rigidity limits the ability of instructors and academic units to deviate from these expectations and adopt equitable and effective teaching practices. When norms that underlie curricular decision making are harmful yet perpetuated without critical equity-minded interrogation, inequities are maintained (Posselt et al., 2020). Successful systemic change recognizes that instructors and academic units do not operate in a vacuum, but in contexts that vary in many ways; in addition to discipline, they vary by size, academic mission, location, and, of course, institutional type. Institutional teaching evaluation policies and processes can both propel and stymie change (see Chapters 6 and 9). In most research institutions tenure-system faculty members are not incentivized to invest much effort in improving their teaching (Braxton et al., 1996; Gonzales & Culpepper, 2024; Griffin et al., 2013; Park, 1996), especially in ways that may involve more emotional labor (Castillo-Montoya, 2020). In many university contexts, VITAL educators (who are more likely to be racially minoritized faculty; DiBenedetto et al., 2021; Wingfield, 2024) are doing the bulk of instructional and other student-facing work (Baldwin & Wawrzynski, 2011; Boss et al., 2019). These faculty are often devalued (Boss et al., 2019) and do not have the same autonomy or power that tenured or tenure-track faculty hold. Given this, if institutions do not have in place intentional language, metrics, and processes for supporting and evaluating equitable and effective teaching, instructors who make changes to their courses to support all students may not be given appropriate credit or recognition for their effort. Instructors who advocate for equitable and effective teaching practice on a wide scale may be viewed with skepticism or considered to be wasting their time.

EXISTING WORK TOWARD EQUITABLE AND EFFECTIVE TEACHING

Many individuals and groups have put significant work into improving undergraduate learning experiences and making them more equitable and effective. These efforts deserve to be honored and learned from so that more widespread change can be achieved. It is not possible for this report to include all efforts. The selected examples are provided to illustrate the variety of projects that inform our current knowledge and future efforts.

Groups and initiatives that have recognized and elevated the link between equity and excellence include a diverse set of actors from professional societies, disciplinary societies, and higher education societies. Some have a focus on research universities or preparing graduate students at research universities to teach. These include the Association for Undergraduate Education at Research Universities (AUERU;[1] which grew out of the Reinvention Center that formed after the Boyer 2030 Commission [2022]), the Sloan Equity & Inclusion in STEM Introductory Courses (SEISMIC) collaborative,[2] and the Center for the Integration of Research, Teaching and Learning (CIRTL).[3] Other projects include the Inclusive STEM Teaching Project,[4] and the Association of College and University Educators (ACUE).[5] Project Kaleidoscope,[6] now housed at the American Association of Colleges and Universities (AAC&U)[7] has also focused on improving undergraduate STEM teaching. A recent publication, *Equity-Based Teaching in Higher Education: The Levers that Institutions Can Use for Scaling Improvement*, dives deeply into the meaning of equity-based education and its place in the ecosystem of higher education. The literature review performed for that project explores in great detail the publications on organizational policies, programs, and practices that can support equity-based teaching and makes recommendations for action based on their analysis of the literature and interviews the authors conducted (Equity-Based Teaching Collective, 2024). Forthcoming work from the Association of Public and Land-Grant Universities (APLU) continues the work of their Faculty Success Initiative

---

[1] More information about the AUERU is available at https://www.ueru.org/home

[2] More information about the SEISMIC collaborative is available at https://www.seismicproject.org/

[3] More information about CIRTL is available at https://cirtl.net/

[4] More information about the Inclusive STEM Teaching Project is available at https://www.inclusivestemteaching.org/

[5] More information about ACUE is available at https://acue.org/

[6] More information about the Project Kaleidoscope is available at https://www.aacu.org/initiatives/project-kaleidoscope

[7] More information about the AAC&U is available at https://www.aacu.org/

to explore teaching in the context of other components of instructor responsibilities via a systemic change approach.[8]

Some initiatives have grown out of discipline-focused efforts, including biology's Vision and Change project,[9] the geosciences project on Vision and Change,[10] BioQUEST Curriculum Consortium' QUBES Hub Platform,[11] and Carnegie Math Pathways,[12] whereas others, such as Project Kaleidoscope, cut across STEM disciplines. Initiatives and groups focused on improving equity in undergraduate STEM education include the Equity Based Teaching Collective,[13] and the toolkits developed by the National Association of College and University Business Officers (NACUBO)'s Blueprint for Student-Centered Strategic Finance.[14] Multiple efforts focus specifically on community colleges, including a variety of programs from Achieving the Dream,[15] initiatives that are part of The Aspen Institute College Excellence Program,[16] and the Community College Presidents' Initiative in STEM (CCPI-STEM),[17] as well as other programs. The Supporting and Advancing Geoscience Education at Two-Year Colleges (SAGE 2YC) project focuses specifically on evidence-based instructional practices, broadening participation, and increasing STEM learning at community colleges.[18] The Universal Design for Learning (UDL)[19] approach works to make college and university learning more accessible for students with disabilities (CAST, n.d.). When operationalized proactively and intentionally by the instructors, UDL can lead to more equitable pedagogies due to its role in creating flexible and

[8] More information about the APLU's Faculty Success Initiative is available at https://www.aplu.org/our-work/2-fostering-research-innovation/aplu-aspire/institutional-change-network/

[9] More information about the Vision and Change project in biology is available at https://new.nsf.gov/news/vision-change-undergraduate-biology-initiative

[10] More information about the Vision and Change project in the geosciences is available at https://www.americangeosciences.org/change/

[11] More information about BioQUEST and Qubes is available at https://qubeshub.org/

[12] More information about Carnegie Math Pathways is available at https://carnegiemathpathways.org/

[13] More information about the Equity Based Teaching Collective is available at https://www.everylearnereverywhere.org/blog/new-playbook-outlines-an-ecosystem-approach-to-equity-based-teaching/

[14] More information about NACUBO's Blueprint for Student-Centered Strategic Finance is available at https://www.nacubo.org/Press-Releases/2024/NACUBO-Student-Success-Hub-Highlights-Financial-Links-to-Equitable-Student-Outcomes

[15] More information about the Achieving the Dream program is available at https://achievingthedream.org/

[16] More information about the Aspen Institute College Excellence Program is available at https://highered.aspeninstitute.org/

[17] More information about CCPI-STEM is available at https://www.ccpi-stem.org/

[18] More information about SAGE 2YC is available at https://serc.carleton.edu/sage2yc/index.html

[19] More information about the UDL approach is available at https://udlguidelines.cast.org/

engaging learning environments (Almeqdad et al., 2023; King-Sears et al., 2023). UDL is discussed at greater length in Chapter 5.

These efforts have been organized and funded by a diverse array of actors. Funders include the National Science Foundation (e.g., Improving Undergraduate STEM Education, NSF INCLUDES, Advanced Technological Education, etc.), the Howard Hughes Medical Institution, the Gates Foundation, Ascendium Education Group, College Futures Foundation, Trellis Foundation, and the Alfred P. Sloan Foundation, among others. Organizations, associations, and societies involved in organizing, coordinating, and providing connections for this type of work include APLU, Association of American Universities, American Association of Community Colleges, American Indian Science and Engineering Society, American Society for Engineering Education, National Association of Geoscience Teachers, National Association of Biology Teachers, American Chemical Society, American Geophysical Union, etc. In addition, many recent publications written for college faculty focus on inclusive teaching strategies (Addy et al., 2021a,b; Hogan & Sathy, 2022; McNair, 2016; McNair et al., 2022).

Systemic change by its nature cannot be achieved by an individual. It is clear from these efforts that systemic change requires coordinated effort by multiple actors at colleges and universities and in outside organizations, foundations, and networks; and it is critical to recognize that the responsibility to provide equitable and effective learning experiences is collectively held by instructors and others at all levels of the higher education system.

SUMMARY

Extensive research on learning and teaching is available to inform decisions related to education at colleges and universities. Strong evidence also exists showing inequities in undergraduate experiences when data are disaggregated by factors such as race, ethnicity, and gender identity. There is also strong clear evidence that evidence-based teaching approaches can improve student learning experiences. The evidence is more mixed on the ability of evidence-based teaching approaches to address inequities in student experiences and more research on the best ways to decrease inequities in grading, persistence, belonging, and other areas would be beneficial. The current common approaches to foundational courses, prerequisites, course progressions, and course combinations complicate efforts to provide equitable and effective STEM education and there are several other special considerations that are relevant to students gaining understanding and navigating experiences in these fields, especially those that focus on labwork or fieldwork.

Conclusion 3.1: Learning in STEM involves a set of complex processes that are shaped by the identities, experiences, and backgrounds of learners and instructors, social interactions, and cultural context. Widespread use of teaching strategies that are not supported by research have contributed to the disparities in opportunity and outcomes for undergraduate STEM students.

Conclusion 3.2: Instructional practices that take students' interests and experiences into account and empower them with authentic opportunities to engage with disciplinary content, practices, and analysis are more effective for a wider range of students than instructional practices that rely solely on lecture, reading, and memorization of content, procedures, and algorithms.

Conclusion 3.3: Students' experiences in foundational courses are particularly important for their persistence in STEM. Often these courses filter out students rather than deepening their engagement, interest, and understanding of STEM topics. Improving instruction in these courses is an important lever for producing more equitable opportunities and outcomes for undergraduate STEM students.

4

Principles for Equitable and Effective Teaching of Undergraduate STEM Education

A foundational concept of the seven Principles for Equitable and Effective Teaching presented in this chapter is that *students' learning is the primary goal of teaching*. The Principles outlined in this chapter capture some the major insights from research on learning and teaching over the past 40 years. They offer a lens for examining and reimagining undergraduate teaching in science, technology, engineering, and mathematics (STEM) that the Committee hopes will catalyze and accelerate efforts to implement equitable and effective teaching. Together, the Principles articulate an aspirational and actionable vision that can help guide instructors, academic units, and institutions as they work to enact change.

For each Principle in this chapter, we explain the concept, highlight the key insights from research that fall under each, and describe some examples of related instructional practices. Chapter 5 elaborates on these descriptions to illustrate how the Principles can be used to guide the design of learning experiences, courses, and course sequences. Thus, more detailed descriptions of instruction based on the Principles are provided in Chapter 5. Subsequent chapters describe how academic units and institutions can support this kind of instruction and facilitate implementation of approaches that are based on the Principles.

THE PRINCIPLES

As noted in Chapter 1, a key commitment that informs the committee's vision for equitable and effective teaching is that student learning must be at the center. In other words, a course rooted in equitable and effective teaching is *student centered*: an approach that makes the course goals clear to the students, recognizes the students' role in their own learning, and gives students agency to engage in the course materials in ways that respect their identities. This approach makes learning the primary driver. In contrast, instructor-centered courses often focus primarily on covering a certain amount of content, with the volume of content being the primary driver of the schedule and the assessments.

Thus, the Principles advance a focus on supporting students as they develop knowledge and skills of the STEM disciplines. They call for goals and expectations to be intentionally chosen and transparently communicated to students. They recognize that fostering a sense of belonging, attending to social interactions, connecting to students' interest, and being responsive to student needs play important roles in their learning of STEM concepts and skills. It is important to note that these Principles are not presented in a priority order; as can be seen in Figure 4-1 below, we conceive of them all contributing to the central goal of equitable and effective teaching and learning. We have numbered them only for convenience in keeping track of the concepts. Also of note is that there is no requirement to immediately implement all of the Principles together at first; some instructors may find it more feasible to focus on a couple as an initial entry point and gradually incorporate additional Principles over time.

The seven Principles for Equitable and Effective Teaching are[1]

Principle 1: Students need opportunities to actively engage in disciplinary learning
Principle 2: Students' diverse interests, goals, knowledge, and experiences can be leveraged to enhance learning
Principle 3: STEM learning involves affective and social dimensions
Principle 4: Identity and sense of belonging shape STEM teaching and learning
Principle 5: Multiple forms of data can provide evidence to inform improvement
Principle 6: Flexibility and responsiveness to situational and contextual factors support student learning
Principle 7: Intentionality and transparency create more equitable opportunities

[1] In this and subsequent chapters we often refer back to the Principles presented in this chapter to illustrate how they are relevant to the topics of later chapters. To avoid repeating the long names of each Principle we utilize some shorthand. Table 4-1, below, gives shorthand naming conventions.

Figure 4-1 places the Principles in the context of courses, academic units, and institutions. Equitable and effective teaching appears at the center of the diagram because this represents the heart of students' experiences in STEM, which take place in classrooms and other learning settings. The outer rings highlight the complex contexts within which teaching and learning interactions take place. While the Principles are presented above as seven separate concepts, in reality instructors will use overlapping ideas and approaches from each of these Principles in the design and teaching of their courses. Some of the instructional practices presented as examples can be used in ways that implement multiple Principles at the same time.

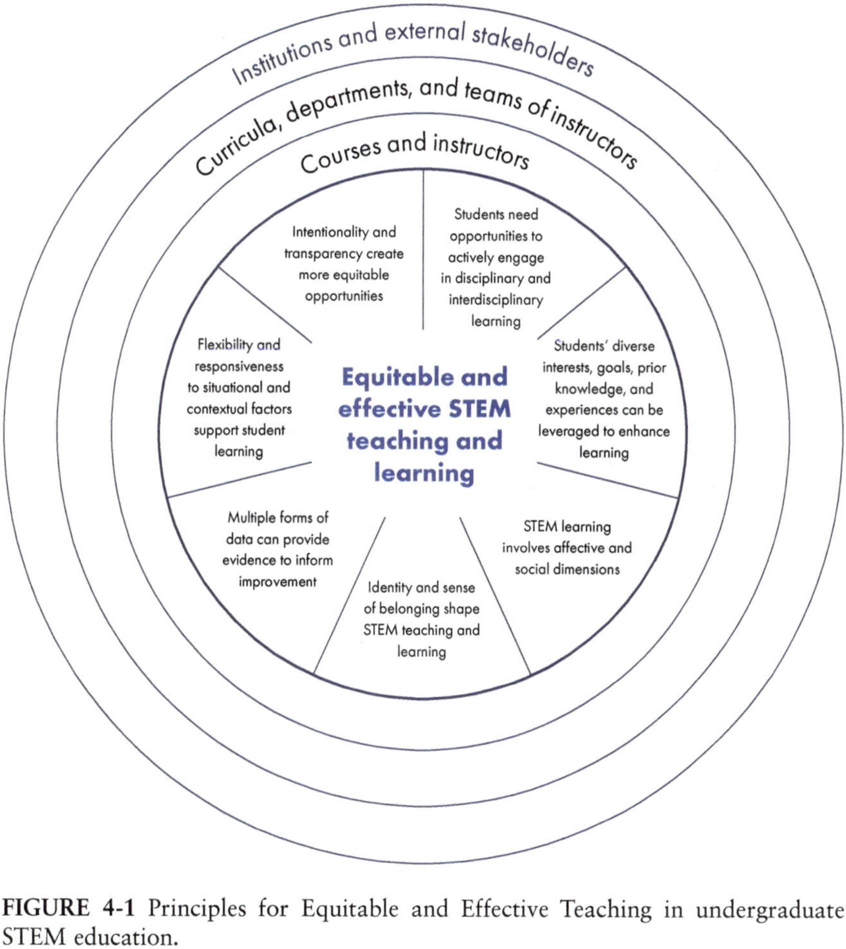

FIGURE 4-1 Principles for Equitable and Effective Teaching in undergraduate STEM education.

Chapter 5 will take up the interconnections between the Principles as they are used to guide design of courses.

The committee also wishes to reiterate a point made throughout the previous chapters: that the responsibility for change that leads to equitable and effective learning experiences is collectively held by instructors and others at all levels of the higher education system. While the seven Principles are focused primarily on the course level, especially those where instructors can improve the student learning experience, it is important to note that they are not presented as the sole responsibility of instructors to individually adopt and implement. Instead, they are presented as standards and goals that instructors, with the support of academic units and institutions, can achieve through course (re)design, changes to instructional practices, and alterations in policies, approaches, and expectations at the systemic level. Structural changes and collective responsibility will be necessary for the committee's vision to be implemented, sustained, and successful. Later chapters of this report will address the systemic issues and the actors responsible for making and sustaining change.

Principle 1: Students Need Opportunities to Actively Engage in Disciplinary Learning

Student learning improves when students are given opportunities to actively engage with the material they are learning, to use disciplinary knowledge and skills in the context of projects and problems, and to reflect on their own knowledge (Borda et al., 2020; Stanberry & Payne, 2018). These kinds of student-centered instructional approaches, often referred to as active learning, engage students in developing and deepening their understanding of disciplinary ideas and practices while they receive guidance from skilled instructors (Benabentos et al., 2021; Capone, 2022; Kressler & Kressler, 2020).

Active learning approaches are more effective than traditional approaches for developing robust conceptual understanding, facilitating transfer of learning across contexts, and promoting long-term retention of knowledge and skill than approaches that rely primarily on lecture or memorization (Armbuster et al., 2009; Devlin & Samarawickrema, 2010; Ebert-May et al., 1997; Hogan & Sathy, 2022; Lyle et al., 2020). Active learning centers students' learning activity, shifting the role of the instructor from simply providing knowledge to skillfully guiding and facilitating students' learning in their role as an expert in the discipline (King, 1993; Morrison, 2014). When students are able to engage in problems and tasks with similarities to those carried out by disciplinary professionals, they develop proficiency with specific skills and practices along with increased agency and greater identification with STEM, a factor shown to increase retention and performance (Marbach-Ad et al., 2019; Starr et al., 2020; Thiry, 2019a). Classroom activities and assignments can provide opportunities to engage with concepts of the discipline and provide opportunities for reflection. These approaches can help students learn what it means to think and reason like a scientist, technologist, engineer, or mathematician.

Intellectual engagement in learning can occur in a variety of ways and in many different kinds of learning experiences. There are many active learning approaches that are feasible to implement during a single class. Active learning can be an effective tool in large, foundational STEM courses as well as in smaller classes. In large, high-structure courses that combine pre-class preparatory assignments with in-class active learning activities, students earn higher grades, have lower failure rates, and report an increased sense of community compared to students enrolled in courses that use lecture only (Eddy & Hogan, 2014; Freeman et al., 2014). In addition, active learning in large classes increases the probability of equitable outcomes between majoritized and minoritized students (Eddy & Hogan, 2014; Haak et al., 2011; Theobald et al., 2020). In order for active learning to be equitable and effective it needs to be carefully designed to ensure that all students have the opportunity to participate and be successful (Dewsbury, 2020; White et al., 2020; see Chapter 5 for further discussion of activities in the classroom and a more in-depth discussion of instructional practices).

In designing active learning opportunities for students that reflect disciplinary ideas and practices, it is important to consider the difficulty of the materials with which students will engage. In order to effectively support learning the material needs to present a challenge for all students, while also being attainable by most[2] (Krim et al., 2019; Nilson, 2015). This requires careful attention to students' prior knowledge and some awareness of the make-up of students in the classroom (see *Principle 2: Leveraging diverse interests, goals, knowledge, and experiences* and *Principle 5: Multiple forms of data*).[3]

There are also longer-term opportunities, such as extended laboratory or field investigations, research experiences, and internships. For example, course-based undergraduate research experiences, project-based learning, independent research, and applied design can all provide students with opportunities to deepen their disciplinary knowledge and skills (Krim et al.,

[2] More information about scaffolding is available at https://pce.sandiego.edu/scaffolding-in-education-examples/#:~:text=Scaffolding%20and%20differentiation%20are%20used,keep%20pace%20with%20their%20peers

[3] In this and subsequent chapters we often refer back to the Principles presented in this chapter to illustrate how they are relevant to the topics of later chapters. To avoid repeating the long names of each Principle we utilize some shorthand. Table 4-1, below, gives shorthand naming conventions.

2019; Kuh, 2016; National Academies, 2018; Ward et al., 2024; Wolniak & Engberg, 2019). Instructors, academic units, and institutions can create authentic and community-engaged learning experiences by integrating formal classroom work with practical experiences in ways that both benefit the community directly and enhance the student learning experience. Opportunities to practice and apply disciplinary skills and knowledge in real-world contexts can come about through service learning, internships, and apprenticeships (National Academies, 2017a; Queiruga-Dios et al., 2021; Salam et al., 2019; Schmidt et al., 2020; Tijsma et al., 2020). Furthermore, the real-world experience gained through internships can help students apply what they have learned in the classroom to professional environments, mirroring the kind of work or approaches to problems seen in the workforce (Rodriguez et al., 2019b; Schweitzer et al., 2016).

Building in opportunities for students to reflect on and revise their thinking is an important component of student-centered learning. Reflection is a component of metacognition that refers to the ability to monitor and regulate one's own cognitive processes and to consciously regulate behavior, and revision is the process of taking action as a result of the reflection (National Academies, 2018). How we understand our own thought processes is particularly vital for learning novel information (McDowell, 2019; Santangelo et al., 2021a). Students who have greater metacognitive capacity are better learners overall (Stanton et al., 2021). Research has shown that students rarely use metacognitive strategies when studying on their own, but they can develop these skills when metacognitive strategies are embedded into instruction (Karpicke et al., 2009; Kober, 2015; Weinstein et al., 2000). These approaches can also contribute to the development of a sense of competency by helping students to recognize, monitor, and strategize about their learning progress. One study found that students who took chemistry laboratory courses designed to prompt metacognitive activity showed significant gains on the Metacognitive Activities Inventory, which measures students' monitoring of their own thinking during problem solving (Sandi-Urena et al., 2011). Chapter 5 considers strategies for promoting reflection and metacognition.

Principle 2: Students' Diverse Interests, Goals, Knowledge, and Experiences Can Be Leveraged to Enhance Learning

The knowledge, skills, and beliefs students bring to their learning influence how they remember, reason, solve problems, and acquire new knowledge (Kober, 2015; Mayer & Alexander, 2011; Renninger & Hidi, 2019; Stanberry & Payne, 2018). Instructional strategies and materials that are designed to recognize, value, and connect to students' interests, goals, knowledge, and life experiences can motivate and engage students in ways that improve their understanding of STEM content, principles, skills, and practices. Such approaches can help students see how STEM is relevant to their daily lives and how STEM can be useful in a variety of careers.

Our understanding of how people learn—based on lessons from research in cognitive psychology and learning sciences—has been summarized in previous National Academies reports (National Academies, 2018; National Research Council, 2000). This research shows that instruction is most effective when it explicitly builds on prior knowledge (Andrews et al., 2022; Lou & Jaeggi, 2020; Stanberry & Payne, 2018; Ziori & Dienes, 2008). In fact, developing expertise in a discipline involves making connections to, reflecting on, and revising existing knowledge in ways that support more sophisticated reasoning and problem solving (Auerbach et al., 2018; Maltese et al., 2015; Peffer & Ramezani, 2019).

Connecting to Students' Knowledge and Interests

Students enter their undergraduate learning experiences with large amounts of existing knowledge, a variety of school experiences, and diverse interest in many topics and activities. Intentionally connecting STEM content to students' interests and providing opportunities for them to connect their familial and community experiences to STEM can increase motivation and engagement, and promote persistence (Kember et al., 2008; Senior et al., 2018). Recognizing the diverse assets that students bring to the learning environment, leveraging them, and helping students see the connections between their everyday lives and STEM concepts and practices promotes more equitable outcomes (Bayles & Morrell, 2018; Booker & Cambell-Whatley, 2018).

Instructors can engage students' interest in STEM concepts, ideas, and practices through in-class activities designed to elicit students' existing knowledge, make connections to current issues, and provide students with choice and autonomy. For example, instructors can assign reflective writings in which students are asked to discuss ways that course material could be useful to their hobbies, interests, or goals to help the students see the value of their learning for their personal and professional goals. These "utility-value" interventions have been shown to increase interest, engagement, and performance (Canning & Harackiewicz, 2015; Canning et al., 2018; Harackiewicz et al., 2016; Hulleman et al., 2010). Some research suggests that assignments that show students how STEM can help to advance communal goals and help others (rather than focusing only on personal goals) can increase students' motivation (Fuesting et al., 2017). Another approach is to incorporate case studies or other real-world examples and give students the opportunity to co-construct reading assignments or research questions (Considine et al., 2017; Mordacq et al., 2017; Scott Coker, 2017; Stenalt &

Lassesen, 2021). To connect their STEM learning to their own backgrounds and experiences, students could be encouraged to study topics that are of personal or cultural relevance (Barnes & Brownell, 2017; Black et al., 2022; Dasgupta, 2023). Making science and engineering research more socially relevant has the potential to engage more diverse learners (Dasgupta, 2023).

Recognizing Cultural Wealth and Funds of Knowledge

While prior knowledge is often used to describe what students know from previous formal education, the concept of funds of knowledge (e.g., Kiyama & Rios-Aguilar, 2017) broadens this idea to recognize the knowledge acquired from informal learning experiences in families, homes, and communities (González et al., 2005; Moll & Diaz, 1987; Vélez-Ibáñez & Greenberg, 1992). Culturally responsive and culturally relevant teaching acknowledges and values the cultural diversity that students bring to the classroom (Aronson & Laughter, 2016; Gay, 2018; Hammond, 2014; Heringer, 2018; Ladson-Billings, 2006, 2014). With these approaches, instructors help students see themselves in STEM topics explored in the classroom (Castillo-Montoya & Ives, 2020; Gay, 2002; Johnson & Elliott, 2020; Ladson-Billings, 1995). Instructors highlight what students already know and help them recognize how that knowledge is relevant to and beneficial for their participation in STEM (Johnson & Elliott, 2020; Mack, 2021; O'Leary et al., 2020; Ortiz-Rodríguez et al., 2021). Instructors could do this by incorporating justice-oriented curricula or humanizing content or by highlighting the accomplishments of STEM professionals from diverse backgrounds, either historical or living (Meuler et al., 2023; Stout et al., 2011; Yao et al., 2023). When students see themselves and their groups in course material, they are more likely to feel a sense of belonging in STEM and increase their STEM self-efficacy (White et al., 2020; see *Principle 4: Identity and a sense of belonging*).

To avoid misusing culturally responsive and culturally relevant teaching pedagogy, it is important for instructors to attend to issues related to power, development of students' critical consciousness, a pedagogy of relationality, and an ethic of care. Recognizing the diversity of experiences students bring to the learning environment, leveraging it, and making connections between students' everyday lives and STEM concepts and practices promotes more equitable outcomes (Bayles & Morrell, 2018; Booker & Campbell-Whatley, 2018).

Universal Design for Learning

The Universal Design for Learning (UDL) framework provides another way of thinking about leveraging student experiences; the motivation for its development was to increase access for students with disabilities (Behling & Tobin, 2018; CAST, 2024; Pérez & Johnston, 2023). UDL employs multiple means of engagement, representation, action, and expression. Fundamental tenets of the UDL framework include recognizing student autonomy; making learning accessible; showing information in multiple ways; and allowing students to demonstrate their learning in various ways (Davies et al., 2013; Izzo & Bauer, 2015; Kumar & Wideman, 2014; Laist et al., 2022; Orndorf et al., 2022; Pérez & Johnston, 2023).

Principle 3: STEM Learning Involves Affective and Social Dimensions

Learning is complex and involves not only cognition, but also affective and social dimensions (Dweck, 1986; Eccles et al., 1998; NRC, 2000; Picard et al., 2004).

Affective Dimensions of Learning

The affective dimension of learning refers to the attitudes, motivation, curiosity, beliefs, and expectations of students (Bureau et al., 2022; Dweck & Leggett, 1988; Mayer & Alexander, 2011; Nasir et al., 2020; Pajares, 1996; Ryan, 2019). These factors are critical to learning because they influence student attention, persistence, and performance (Ames & Archer, 1988; Schunk, 1989; Zimmerman, 2000). Instructors can attend to the affective dimension of learning by recognizing the importance of motivation to learning; providing choice or autonomy in learning; creating learning experiences that students value; and supporting students' sense of control and autonomy (Bureau et al., 2022; Howard et al., 2021). When people are learning material that provides a positive emotional connection, they are willing to work harder to learn the content and skills, especially when those content and skills seem useful and connected to their motivations and future goals (Lim & Richardson, 2021; National Academies, 2018). Emotions like anxiety can undermine learning, deplete cognitive resources, and activate parts of the brain associated with fear and escape rather than with cognitive processes essential for learning (Beilock et al., 2010; Hilliard et al., 2020; Schmader & Johns, 2003). When students do not feel comfortable and safe, their attentional and cognitive processes are less available for engaging with academic content (El Baze et al., 2018; England et al., 2019; Hood et al., 2021). Therefore, it is important for instructors to keep in mind that equitable and effective teaching requires consideration of both the students' cognitive and affective states (Trujillo & Tanner, 2014; Vermunt, 1996; Vogel & Schwabe, 2016).

Historically underserved students, in particular, may experience the learning environment more negatively—resulting in lower levels of belonging, trust, and self-efficacy (Cavanagh et al., 2018; Eddy et al., 2015; Ream et al., 2014; Steele, 1997; Steele et al., 2002; Trujillo & Tanner, 2014). Instructors who recognize and respond to students' cognitive, affective, and physiological states can support enhanced student performance and create emotionally supportive and nonthreatening learning environments where students feel safe and valued (Bernard, 2010; Hen et al., 2022; Turner & Farooqi, 2017; Yee, 2019). The ability of instructors to recognize that their own beliefs, attitudes, and expectations, as well as those of their students, influence the learning environment is crucial to creating and carrying out well-designed learning experiences (Kinnunen et al., 2018; Lytle & Shin, 2023; Meaders et al., 2019).

Being aware of and attending to students' "mindsets" about learning is particularly important (Canning et al., 2019; Dweck & Leggett, 1988; Mangels et al., 2006). Mindsets refer to the beliefs students hold about their own abilities and potential for learning and growth. Students who hold a "growth mindset" believe that their intelligence and ability can be improved through hard work and practice (Dweck, 1999; Dweck & Leggett, 1988). People who adopt a growth mindset embrace challenges, see mistakes as opportunities for improvement, and see effort as the path to mastery (Dweck & Leggett, 1988). In contrast, students who hold a "fixed mindset" believe that their intelligence or ability is fixed and cannot be changed. This can lead to a desire to demonstrate ability or "look smart" (Elliott & Dweck, 1988). People who hold a fixed mindset tend to avoid challenges, avoid mistakes or negative feedback, and give up early (Dweck & Leggett, 1988; Yeager & Dweck, 2012). Students' mindsets are affected by many elements of the learning context including feedback from instructors, the design of activities, and grading practices (Canning et al., 2024; Kroeper et al., 2022a,b; Muenks et al., 2024; Murphy, 2024). Chapter 3 considers mindsets in relation to goal setting, and Chapter 5 further investigates instructional practices and mindsets, including how the mindset beliefs that instructors hold about students' abilities can be predictive of students' experiences and success.

Social Dimensions of Learning

The social dimension of learning includes the activities and interactions students engage in with their peers, instructors, and other individuals in the learning environment (e.g., teaching assistants or undergraduate learning assistants). Learning research over the past 20 years has shown that all learning involves a social component, whether through interactions with others or through use of tools and frameworks developed by other people (such as STEM professionals; National Academies, 2018). There is strong evidence that collaborative activities done in an environment where students feel safe and appreciated can enhance the effectiveness of student-centered learning over traditional instruction (Dennehy & Dasgupta, 2017; Johnson et al., 1998, 2007; Lunn et al., 2021; Rodriguez & Blaney, 2021; Rodriguez et al., 2019a). Opportunities for social interaction can help students reflect on their current understanding, identify areas where they may have misunderstandings, construct shared meaning based on their own experiences, and develop a sense of belonging to the STEM community (Belanger et al., 2020; Li & Singh, 2023; Rodriguez & Blaney, 2021).

Students working together on well-designed learning activities can develop a community of learners that provides cognitive, affective, and social support for the efforts of its individual members (Dasgupta, 2013; Kober, 2015). By working in social groups, students share the responsibility for thinking and doing. They can help each other solve problems by building on each other's knowledge, asking questions, and suggesting ideas that an individual working alone might not have considered (Brown & Campione, 1994). When members of a group are able to safely be explicit about what they mean, challenge each other's thoughts and beliefs, and negotiate conflicts that arise, they can spur each other to engage in metacognition, and this can enhance learning (Stanton et al., 2021). In collaborative two-stage exams, for instance, students complete the task individually then immediately complete the same work again in small groups, where students received feedback from their peers. Analysis showed that students recognize this process as a valuable learning experience and demonstrated greater improvement on subsequent individual testing compared to when only tested as individuals (Gilley & Clarkston, 2014; Nicol & Selvaretnam, 2021; Wieman et al., 2014). Chapter 5 discusses designing effective group work.

Principle 4: Identity and Sense of Belonging Shape STEM Teaching and Learning

Within the undergraduate STEM education system, each individual (e.g., students, instructors, administrators, support staff) has a multi-dimensional identity that influences the way they see the world, are treated, and interact with others. Some aspects of identity, such as skin color or a person's reliance on a guide dog, may be readily apparent. Other identities may be less visible, such as mental health condition; lesbian, gay, bisexual, transgender, queer/questioning, intersex, asexual/aromantic/agender, plus other related identities (LGBTQIA+; veteran or caregiver status; and familial socio-economic status (e.g., Busch et al., 2023). Many other aspects of identity can also influence how students and instructors engage with STEM learning, including, for example, familial experience with STEM or with higher education.

When students are able to leverage features of their identities in STEM learning spaces, they are able to develop agency and ownership of their educational journey (Betz et al., 2021; Espinosa, 2011; Newell & Ulrich, 2022). Further, when their identities are recognized and validated by their instructors, students may develop deeper understanding of STEM concepts as well as build stronger critical thinking skills (Carlone & Johnson, 2007; Upadhyay et al., 2020). For decades, literature on minoritized students' experiences in STEM has examined the ways that students feel marginalized (see, e.g., Berhane et al., 2020; Friedensen et al., 2021; Hatmaker, 2013; Hughes, 2018; Rodriguez et al., 2022). A smaller number of studies (e.g., Morton & Parsons, 2018; Ross et al., 2017; Simpson & Bouhafa, 2020; Wofford & Gutzwa, 2022) have pointed to ways researchers and educators can see students' identities as assets and more intentionally support nondominant (e.g., non-White, nonmale) identities. In a review of over 30 studies looking at student-faculty collaboration in the classroom, Cook-Sather et al. (2023) note that STEM practices often exclude certain voices and limit development of a STEM identity by those students.

Cues About Which Students Are Valued

Two well-studied and related phenomena that can adversely impact student affect are stereotype threat and social identity threat, in which students are reduced to or seen through the lens of negative stereotypes associated with one or more of their social group memberships (Steele, 1997; Steele & Aronson, 1995; Steele et al., 2002). The cognitive and affective experiences of social identity threat can affect anyone, but it has its largest impacts on students from groups historically excluded and negatively stereotyped in educational settings. For example, Latina/o students can underperform on math and spatial ability tasks when reminded of negative ethnic stereotypes (Gonzales et al., 2002); similarly, lower-income students may underperform when stereotypes about their socio-economic background are highlighted (e.g., Croizet & Claire, 1998; Croizet & Millet, 2012).

As students participate in learning environments, they pick up on cues as to whether they are seen as valued and potentially successful participants in the STEM disciplines. Cues that suggest that certain students are less capable, possess less inherent or natural ability, are less motivated, or are less worthy of inclusion in an educational environment than their peers are termed identity-threatening cues, because they threaten students' sense of value and respect based on their social-identity-group membership (Murphy & Taylor, 2012; Murphy et al., 2007; Steele et al., 2002). These cues undermine students' development of identities as successful STEM learners and their sense of belonging in STEM. Conversely, identity-safe cues are equitable and effective teaching practices that signal to people that they are valued and respected based on their social identities. Negative cues about ability that trigger bias and stereotypes often arise in STEM classrooms, and those negative messages can be damaging to developing a positive STEM identity (Harrison & Tanner, 2018; Turochy et al., 2023). In turn, negative STEM identities can discourage students from further study in STEM subjects. In the presence of negative cues, historically excluded and marginalized students (e.g., racial and ethnic minority students, women studying STEM or other fields in which they are numerically underrepresented, students with high levels of financial stress, LGBTQIA+ students) not only experience the learning environment more negatively from an affective perspective—showing lower levels of belonging, trust, and self-efficacy—they also demonstrate lowered motivation, engagement, learning, and performance (e.g., Canning et al., 2019, 2022; Muenks et al., 2020).

There are many studies that show that interventions that address social identity can help underserved students (Bell et al., 2003; Logel et al., 2009; Walton et al., 2015). Studies show that when identity-threatening cues are removed from the environment and replaced with identity-safe cues, these students perform as well as—and in some cases, better than—students from majority groups (McLean et al., 2022; Murphy & Taylor, 2012; Pietri et al., 2019; Spencer et al., 2016; Steele et al., 2002).

Enhancing Sense of Belonging

There is evidence that students' sense of belonging increases when they experience academic and interpersonal validation (Burt et al., 2023; Holland Zahner & Harper, 2022; Rendon, 1994). Students with a higher sense of belonging in STEM are more likely to report having friends in their major, and to socialize with peers and faculty in the field (National Academies, 2017b; Whitehead, 2018). These kinds of interactions can foster a feeling of being an integral part of a community (Hurtado & Carter, 1997; Solanki et al., 2019). When instructors build connections with their students in ways that recognize and validate students as whole people, they increase engagement and learning (Costello et al., 2022; Fries-Britt & White-Lewis, 2020; Thacker et al., 2022). Creating student-instructor partnerships for development of course curricula is another approach (Cook-Sather et al., 2023). Instructors can work to avoid reinforcing cues that suggest to students that not everyone can succeed in STEM by, for example, cultivating a positive STEM learning environment in which they encourage contributions from students. One study of students learning English as a second language showed that interventions promoting belonging improved outcomes (LaCosse et al., 2020).

Students may have increased motivation and sense of belonging during their learning process when they interact with peers who have been through similar experiences, share values and beliefs, and are able to listen and provide support. Such learning approaches have been cited as one critical method for supporting students, especially women and underserved students, within the realms of self-efficacy, interests, skills, and persistence in STEM (Rockinson-Szapkiw & Wendt, 2020). Specifically, interventions that engage students in conversation with peers about overcoming adversity and therefore normalize struggle can raise grades (Binning et al., 2020, 2024).

Another aspect of belonging is the extent to which students develop a positive disciplinary identity and understand the way of thinking of that discipline (Carlone & Johnson, 2007; Hazari et al., 2013). Learning experiences that cultivate this type of disciplinary identity in which students see themselves as capable of accomplishing tasks and achieving goals are key to students' sense of belonging within a discipline (Rainey et al., 2018; Singer et al., 2020; Xu & Lastrapes, 2022). Adopting instructional practices that encourage a growth mindset can be helpful in communicating to students that they are competent in a discipline (Canning et al., 2024; Hecht et al., 2023; Kroeper et al., 2022a,b; Muenks et al., 2024). Instructors can also modify course materials to highlight a range of identities in STEM, rather than only White, male, and cisgender individuals who are overrepresented in many STEM disciplines (Schinske et al., 2016).

Principle 5: Multiple Forms of Data Can Provide Evidence to Inform Improvement

Equitable and effective teaching is an iterative process that requires sustained effort over time to ensure that the best practices and policies are in place. For this reason, the concept of continuous improvement, originally developed in manufacturing, can usefully be applied to this type of STEM education reform (National Academies, 2018; Singh & Singh, 2015). Continuous improvement does not focus on continual change but, rather, on evaluating the outcomes of a change and then using the information to guide actions to improve a process (Jha et al., 1996). Assessments of learning, data on student experiences and student outcomes, data on the progress of change efforts, and self-reflection on these multiple forms of information are all important tools in this regard and can support improved understanding of the challenges students and instructors are encountering and how well students are meeting the learning goals of a course or program (e.g., Grangeat et al., 2021). Below we discuss assessing for student learning, which includes both content knowledge and ability to apply principles and concepts to the practices of the discipline. It is also important to assess the affective and social dimensions that impact student learning experiences. The role of learning goals in course design and teaching is discussed at length in Chapter 5. The role of data at the institutional level is discussed in Chapter 9.

Assessment of Student Learning

Within courses, students and instructors can use data to measure and guide learning. Assessments of learning provide instructors with feedback about what students know, how well they are learning, and where they are having difficulties. Through the frequent use of multiple formats and approaches for assignments, quizzes, tests, and projects, instructors and students generate data that can be used to improve teaching and learning. Disaggregating according to different components of an assignment or assessment can help to identify where students might be excelling versus where they could use more support. When combined with the instructor's observations of the students and the learning environment, decisions about adjustments to course timing or approach can be made to better help students meet defined learning goals. This includes both considering results for individual students and looking at patterns across all students in a course to determine who is and is not being well served.

Effective assessment involves more than just tracking students' grades on exams. Formative and summative assessments are two different types of assessments that give different views of student progress. Formative assessment can be done informally during course sessions to provide the instructors with information on what topics need more attention or more formally to help students determine which topics they need to explore more deeply in order to achieve understanding and meet course learning goals (Kim et al., 2019). Formative assessments focus more on eliciting student thinking and gathering information that allows the instructor to adapt to student needs (Grangeat et al., 2021). They also improve student metacognitive awareness of their own learning (Clark, 2012; Hudesman et al., 2013; Wafubwa & Csikos, 2022). They can help determine if a student is making progress toward their learning goals and therefore give information that allows for improvements in the learning environment. In a student-centered course, formative assessments are not quizzes that simply require memorizing material. Rather, these assessments provide students with opportunities to reflect on, revise, and improve their thinking and help instructors identify areas where students might be struggling. Many of the learning activities described in *Principle 1: Active engagement* are themselves a form of assessment that provides instructors with richer information about students' understanding than they could obtain from traditional assessments and these learning activities themselves support student understanding more than receiving lecture-based instruction.

One of the most important roles for assessment is the provision of timely and informative feedback to students during instruction and learning so that their practice of a skill and its subsequent acquisition will be effective and efficient (NRC, 2001). The addition of frequent and varied opportunities for formative assessment increases students' learning and transfer, and they learn to value opportunities to revise (Lyle et al., 2020; Prince et al., 2020). Some research has shown that using mixed assessment methods can increase performance by underserved students (Cotner & Ballen, 2017; Salehi et al., 2019b). More generally, an overall positive association between formative assessment and student learning has been found and it can generate meaningful feedback about learning to guide choices about next steps in learning and instruction (Andrews et al., 2022; Bennett, 2011; Black & Wiliam, 2009; Graham et al., 2015; Kingston & Nash, 2011).

Summative assessments can include structured projects as well as traditional midterms or final exams. They evaluate students' performance against a standard or benchmark at different times during the course (e.g., at the end of a unit, or at the end of a semester). These assessments indicate how students have progressed in their learning and can be used to determine students' grades (Brownlie et al., 2024). In addition, summative assessments can be used to evaluate the effectiveness of course design and determine which aspects need to be revised in future iterations of the course as well as informing decisions about course sequences and larger issues in a program of major.

Formative and summative assessment can be done in varying ways that support active learning and equitable education experiences; formative assessments with timely feedback from the instructor can help improve student learning (Irons & Elkington, 2021; Morris et al., 2021), while summative assessments that are designed based on the previously shared learning goals for the course can also contribute to equitable and effective learning experiences (Goss, 2022; Osler & Mansaray, 2014). However, the current system, with its focus on grades, does not always allow for such experiences. Research has shown that grades are not always good measures of learning and are based on varying standards; because of this, they can lead to students focusing on grades rather than their own learning (Cain et al., 2022; Lim, 2024; Schwab et al., 2018). Alternately, courses designed in accordance with the science of learning (e.g., the research reviewed in this report) would include summative and formative assessments that are informative to students and integrated through the student learning experience.

Data at the Course, Academic Unit, and Institutional Levels

This type of data analysis can be helpful at the academic unit and institutional level as well as at the course level. When data are appropriately disaggregated according to attributes associated with courses, students, or instructors such information can provide insights into what may or may not be working related to equitable and effective undergraduate STEM teaching. Data can be used to understand the role and impacts of intersectionality, such as between gender and race, or between status as a first-generation college student and socio-economic status. Trends in grades, course completion, and enrollment can illuminate inequities in access to supportive learning contexts and lead to revisions of course design and sequencing. More broadly, data can shine a light on complex interdependencies in STEM education. An approach that is equitable and effective in one classroom, one situation, one institution, or for one group of students may present challenges elsewhere in the system, pointing to the need for a different approach or implementation. Many insights can be gleaned from information about grades and course completion, student and instructor attitudes and beliefs, and usage data from courses and online tools that are independent from or part of learning management systems. This type of data can be combined with other data sources to provide possibilities for institutions of higher education to move beyond a paradigm of course assessment, and more toward the comprehensive analysis of an experience. The latter implies more than student effort (and requisite grades) to determine if outcomes were met, and by definition forces a self-reflection of the other key stakeholders including instructors and beyond to interrogate their role in how the experience transpired. Data are discussed at various points throughout this report as they are relevant to the topic under discussion; Chapter 9 particularly focuses on data and how institutions use data as they relate to teaching.

When multiple types of data are used, one can better understand individual courses, course sequences, programs, majors, and other institutional activities; likewise, multiple types of assessment models can be used to measure student learning. Data on performance outcomes, learning outcomes, and affective outcomes can be combined to guide discussion. Disaggregating these data can inform decisions about structural or policy changes that can improve equitable and effective experiences for students. Careful guidance and support are needed to ensure that data are used to identify students or instructors needing additional support but not to label, exclude, or punish (McNair et al., 2020).

Principle 6: Flexibility and Responsiveness to Situational and Contextual Factors Support Student Learning

Instructors can build flexibility into their courses in order to preserve opportunities to adjust as a term progresses. This allows them to be responsive to formative assessments that reveal students' need for additional guidance with a particular topic by adding material to class meetings or reviewing concepts where students are struggling to understand. Flexibility is also important from the student perspective. When students are given increased autonomy and allowed to make choices it can increase their comfort level and enhance their receptivity to learning new material as well as making courses more responsive to student voice and needs (Chase, 2020; Gube, 2019; Gube & Lajoie, 2020). Instructors can provide guidelines that lay out expectations and provide clear requirements that include options so that students can engage with the course material in ways that facilitate their learning.

When instructors and institutions are flexible and responsive to situational and contextual factors, they are able to make decisions that recognize the individual needs of each student and their circumstances and position them to best meet the course's learning goals. Students have non-academic responsibilities, which can lead to variability in the time and resources they have to be present, prepared, and able to participate fully their coursework (e.g., how secure they are in their basic needs, political situations, social influences, health, disability, geography, etc.). Flexibility and responsiveness to these factors help create an equitable and effective learning environment by recognizing the importance that choice and autonomy play in enhancing learning and promoting motivation and engagement. Furthermore, providing students with flexibility in assignments can give them a sense of autonomy over their own learning (Fujii, 2024; Orakci, 2021; Stenalt & Lassesen, 2021). Being flexible and responsive does not imply a lack of structure. In fact, a course structured around learning goals and assessments that are transparent (as described in *Principle 1: Active engagement* and *Principle 7: Intentionality and transparency*) allows for flexibility in support of those learning goals, without compromising the structures in place to support student achievement.

Assumptions that all students can devote themselves completely to their education exclude those individuals who have other responsibilities or are affected by historic structures or current events. When instructors and institutions are flexible and responsive to situational and contextual factors, they can provide more equitable opportunities for students to engage in STEM learning in productive and supportive environments. Students' lived experiences are important to their learning (see *Principle 2: Leveraging diverse interests, goals, knowledge, and experiences)*. Paying close attention to individuals' lived experiences, and how those experiences have unique relationships to power and inequity, can foster more inclusive learning environments. Studies of STEM education have explored the role of student identity and taken into account the importance of intersectionality where students have more than one marginalized identity (Crenshaw, 1989; Metcalf et al., 2018; Nix & Perez-Felkner, 2019).

When flexibility is designed into courses, instructors can be responsive to events that may impact students' learning. These may be events that are relevant to course content and provide an opportunity to enhance learning; for example, when an event like a major earthquake or volcanic eruption occurs, an Earth science instructor can allow for class time for students to explore data about the event, to ask questions, and to learn more about the impacts of the event on communities and cultures. On the other hand, these events may be upsetting and can impede learning and need to be acknowledged; for example, political or social turmoil or events when members of a particular identity group are targeted may impact students' ability to be present and engaged in a course. Often, a simple acknowledgment of the circumstances can help; at other times, greater flexibility may be needed.

Flexibility can be offered on multiple levels, including potential constraints students have around course scheduling, setting due dates for assignments, and designing assessments. Allowing for options in assignments, which allows students to iterate and improve as their understanding develops, can also make a course more accessible and enhance student learning. Some research suggests that attention to the time periods when classes are offered can increase retention rates and reduce the time to graduation by allowing students to enroll in an increased number of credit hours even as it better accommodates students' extracurricular activities, work, or family obligations (Mintz, 2024). Alternative forms of course grading, like specifications grading, inherently create more student choice and flexibility compared to common grading approaches (Katzman et al., 2021; McKnelly et al., 2021; Villalobos et al., 2024). Not only do students have clear guidance on what to do to achieve a grade, they also have the ability to make informed choices about how and when to complete their assignments.

In a National Academies study on the role of Minority Serving Institutions in promoting success in STEM, institutional responsiveness was identified as a key strategy (National Academies, 2018). Institutional responsiveness included meeting students where they are; that is recognizing STEM students' need for flexibility as well as all students' needs for academic, financial, and social support (National Academies, 2018). A lack of flexibility is frequently seen in the overall suite of courses offered by an academic unit; how the courses are sequenced and structured, the timing with which courses are offered, and whether all students have access to necessary texts and other resources for full participation in courses all impact the ability of students to make progress toward a credential (Bahr et al., 2017, 2023a,b).

Instructors can sometimes be limited in their ability to be responsive and flexible. The academic unit (e.g., department) may control some of these limits through their policies or practices (this is discussed further in Chapter 6). Here, we mention the types of issues that units might consider in their efforts to increase responsiveness and flexibility. In order to decrease barriers to participation, academic units can consider removing certain requirements for prerequisite courses and provide alternative methods for students to demonstrate or acquire the necessary knowledge and skills. They might also consider the cost of textbooks and other course materials. Varied formats that are responsive to student needs allow students to choose the options that will work best for them. Courses that meet virtually can be essential for students who are not able to come to campus due to distance, commuting logistics, caregiving responsibilities, illness, or disability.

Flexibility and situational responsiveness are also crucial for administrators to consider when setting or reviewing expectations for instructors. Recent times have been extremely challenging for students and instructors alike and demands on instructors can be unrealistic and unsustainable. Providing instructors with autonomy to implement equitable and effective approaches in the ways that fit their courses and disciplines is important. Providing professional learning and development about teaching and ensuring support for administrative tasks can go a long way in cultivating an environment conducive to implementation of equitable and effective teaching. This is taken up in more detail in Chapter 8.

Principle 7: Intentionality and Transparency Create More Equitable Opportunities

Intentionality in designing courses, both in terms of careful selection of learning goals and careful design of the course structures and policies, can improve student learning experiences. Transparency in communicating to students about the reasons for these design choices and about priorities, expectations, and norms can help to surmount barriers that arise due to differences in background knowledge about the structures, policies, and expectations of higher education (Sellers & Villanueva, 2021; Villanueva et al., 2018; White & Lowenthal, 2011).

Creating an atmosphere of trust and sustaining it throughout the teaching experience has been shown to help learning (Archer-Kuhn & MacKinnon, 2020; Hartikainen et al., 2022). Winkelmes' (2019) work on the Transparency in Learning and Teaching framework espouses not just an ethos of explaining to students the "why" behind assignments but ensuring that this spirit of openness is present in all pedagogies. For example, an instructor can use the syllabus to make the goals of the class explicit, and they can intentionally state how to be successful in meeting those goals. When the course goals are transparently explained in class and students can see the way that course assignments and projects were intentionally chosen to connect to those learning goals it enhances the opportunities for equitable and effective learning experiences. Topics that might be covered in class and on a syllabus include due dates and times and the process and policies around extensions, an explanation of grading policies, and when students can expect feedback from the instructor. The language can be chosen so that it is easily understood by students and covers a variety of topics including course content, accessibility policies, grading policies, and pedagogical approaches (Gin et al., 2021). When students are to be assessed, instructors can share in advance the criteria they will use to evaluate student work and participation through grading rubrics or other methods.

When instructors are intentional about ensuring that the learning goals in a course are clearly communicated and all elements of the course are intentionally aligned to help students achieve these goals, it is easier to measure if the goals have been reached and students are more likely to be successful (Jensen et al., 2017; Neiles & Arnett, 2021; Reynolds & Kearns, 2017). Giving students information about course and program requirements, expectations, and opportunities provides them agency and empowers them to make decisions about pursuing further study in STEM. Explicitly informing students of policies and priorities can mitigate the negative effects of the "hidden curriculum" that frequently excludes first-generation students and those who are not well connected to campus communities and help students achieve their learning goals (Koutsouris et al., 2021; Rossouw & Frick, 2023; Winter & Cotton, 2012). Course plans and expectations are easier to describe and explain to students when courses are developed around the goals using strategies such as backward design—a process in which instructors start with the end result in mind and ask what they want students to know and be able to do at the end of the course (Wiggins & McTighe, 2005). This type of course design is described in further detail in Chapter 5. It stands in contrast to a content-focused approach, which takes as a starting point a body of knowledge (typically, a textbook). Learning goals can include goals around content, concepts, and practices that students should understand, but can also include skills and affective goals such as increased belonging or self-efficacy. Within courses, open and clear communication about learning goals at the course and assignment level helps students understand the goals and identify the pathway to achieve them (Palmer et al., 2014; Winkelmes et al., 2019). By foregrounding learning goals, and building content and assessments around them, backward design allows instructors to be more intentional in their teaching (Jensen et al., 2017; Neiles & Arnett, 2021; Reynolds & Kearns, 2017).

Likewise, for assessments to be effective, it is crucial for students to understand the goals for learning intended by the instructor and for the assessments to measure the stated learning goals. Students learn more when they understand (and even participate in developing) the criteria by which their work will be evaluated, and when they engage in peer and self-assessment during which they apply those criteria (NRC, 2001). More specifically, developing student assignments in a transparent way can lead to more equitable achievement by first-generation learners and students from underrepresented backgrounds (Palmer et al., 2018; Winkelmes et al., 2019). In general, these practices develop students' metacognitive abilities, which, as emphasized above, are necessary for effective learning.

Learning goals can encompass knowledge of disciplinary skills, concepts, and practices. Some courses, such as those in career and technical education programs, are primarily and intentionally designed to help students gain proficiency in technical applied skills, and they learn about the underlying disciplinary concepts in service of that goal. Other courses and programs may not have such clear career connections, but instructors can intentionally structure learning experiences so that students use skills of the discipline as they design solutions for engineering problems or synthesize molecules in a chemistry laboratory, for example. Students can also learn about careers through assignments that range from interviewing professionals in the field to analyzing data from a government website used by professionals. Career options and career competencies become more transparent when students have direct experience with skills that will be used in a future career and experience class activities and assignments that expose them to aspects of jobs in STEM.

As mentioned above in *Principle 4: Identity and a sense of belonging,* research has found ways that instructors can view students' identities as assets and more intentionally support nondominant (e.g., non-White, nonmale) identities to help overcome ways that students may be feeling marginalized (see, e.g., Berhane et al., 2020; Friedensen et al., 2021; Hatmaker, 2013; Hughes, 2018; Morton & Parsons, 2018; Rodriguez et al., 2022; Ross et al., 2017; Simpson & Bouhafa, 2020; Wofford & Gutzwa, 2022). Some research has found that intentionality is critical to efforts to support academically underprepared students and specifically that those efforts depend upon the intentional implementation of four key features: integrative learning, collaborative classrooms, co-curricular support, and increased faculty-student interaction (Gebauer, 2019). That work also suggested that instructors can create intentional connections across courses by blending remedial or developmental learning into standard courses via purposefully designed assignments that require students to use the developmental-level skills being taught. Transparent and intentional decisions about departmental and institutional policies, including those based on data as described in

Principle 5: Multiple forms of data, can contribute to practices that support students' equitable participation, including intentional inclusion of students from all backgrounds and transparency in major and graduation requirements as well as course offerings, structures, and scheduling.

THE ROLE OF THE PRINCIPLES

Taken together, the Principles provide a lens for examining practices and policies at multiple levels—e.g., in the classroom, the academic unit, and the institution—to identify and enact the changes that need to be made in order to more toward more equitable and effective STEM teaching. They offer a common language and vision that can guide revisions to practice and policy such as re-imagining teaching evaluations, developing guidelines for professional teaching practice, or redesign of course content and course sequencing. Table 4-1 presents some examples of instructional practices that can fit under the Principles laid out in this chapter. The examples shared in the table are illustrative and not comprehensive. Similarly, many practices used in teaching can be classified as falling under more than one Principle and multiple Principles could be used in combination in a given teaching strategy.

While the Principles are envisioned as applying across institution types and different course structures and modalities (such as virtual courses), the specifics of how these Principles appear in practice will vary in different contexts. The following chapters explore how the Principles can inform changes at the classroom, academic unit, and institutional levels.

SUMMARY

This chapter presents a set of Principles for Equitable and Effective Teaching that can be applied across institution types and different course structures and modalities as instructors design equitable and effective learning experiences for students. The Principles are discussed here primarily as seven separate concepts in order to elevate attention to each of them. In the classroom and in other learning settings, instructors use overlapping ideas and approaches from each of these Principles in the design and teaching of their courses. The Principles as a group describe what equitable and effective teaching looks like. Enacting them is the central focus of the journey to equitable and effective learning experiences. Later chapters of this report illustrate in more detail how instructors can use the Principles and how academic unit and institutional leaders can support those instructors. The evidence cited in this chapter is not meant to be exhaustive; rather, it has been selected to illustrate the importance and strength of support and to show that a large body of work underlies these Principles and can be drawn

TABLE 4-1 Instructional Practices Illustrating the Principles for Equitable and Effective Teaching

Principles	Selected Instructional Practices (see Chapter 5 for further elaboration)
Principle 1: Students need opportunities to actively engage in disciplinary learning *Principle 1: Active engagement*	Provide opportunities for students to actively practice and apply disciplinary skills (active learning). Provide opportunities for reflection on learning and consolidation of new ideas.
Principle 2: Connecting to and leveraging students' diverse interests and goals, prior knowledge and experiences enhances learning *Principle 2: Leveraging diverse interests, goals, knowledge, and experiences*	Assess students' prior knowledge and skills and build on them. Validate and build on students' funds of knowledge. Utilize culturally responsive and culturally relevant teaching. Show how STEM is relevant to students' lives and communities.
Principle 3: STEM learning involves affective and social dimensions *Principle 3: Affective and social dimensions*	Design activities with students' attitudes, beliefs, and expectations about learning in mind. Provide opportunities for students to work together and learn from each other. Emphasize students' abilities to learn and improve and engage in growth-minded teaching practices.
Principle 4: Identity and sense of belonging shape STEM learning *Principle 4: Identity and a sense of belonging*	Build meaningful connections between instructors and students. Support approaches that develop community among students. Modify course materials and pedagogical approaches to reflect different identities. Attend to and address cues that send negative messages about who can succeed in STEM.
Principle 5: Multiple forms of data can provide evidence to inform improvement. *Principle 5: Multiple forms of data*	Use formative assessments to elicit student thinking and gather information that allows the instructor to adapt to student needs. Use frequent low-stakes assessments and choose varied formats for the assessments. Use summative assessments to evaluate effectiveness of course design and determine what needs to be adjusted in the future. Use disaggregated student outcome data to gauge the effectiveness of instructional approaches.
Principle 6: Flexibility and responsiveness to situational and contextual factors is important *Principle 6: Flexibility and responsiveness*	Build flexibility into course content and structure. Build flexibility into assessments and grading.

TABLE 4-1 Continued

Principles	Selected Instructional Practices (see Chapter 5 for further elaboration)
Principle 7: Intentionality and transparency support more equitable opportunities *Principle 7: Intentionality and transparency*	Design courses around clear and explicit learning goals for students. Provide a syllabus that makes the goals of the class and how to be successful in it clear. Be clear and explicit with students about the purpose of assignments and how they will be assessed.

NOTE: In this and subsequent chapters we often refer back to the Principles presented in this chapter to illustrate how they are relevant to the topics of later chapters. To avoid repeating the long names of each Principle we utilize some shorthand. The shorthand naming conventions are listed below the full Principle names in the left column of the table. The right-hand column of this table presents sample practices that could be used in an undergraduate STEM course.

upon by scholars and practitioners. The evidence for Principles 1, 2, 3, 4, and 5 is quite strong: these Principles have been well studied in a variety of learning settings for people of diverse ages. The evidence for Principles 6 and 7 is less robust. That said, flexibility, responsiveness, intentionality, transparency, and related topics have been central to conversations about higher education for years, and these concepts underlie many efforts to improve undergraduate STEM education. Increased awareness to these issues and additional research on their use in teaching could help improve student learning experiences.

Conclusion 4.1: A set of Principles for Equitable and Effective Teaching for undergraduate STEM education derived from the evidence on learning and teaching can inform the design and enactment of more equitable and effective pedagogical approaches. Using these Principles to improve undergraduate teaching and learning in STEM will require a commitment from STEM academic units and higher education institutions as well as from individual instructors. The Principles are

- *Principle 1: Students need opportunities to actively engage in disciplinary learning*
- *Principle 2: Students' diverse interests, goals, knowledge, and experiences can be leveraged to enhance learning*
- *Principle 3: STEM learning involves affective and social dimensions*
- *Principle 4: Identity and sense of belonging shape STEM teaching and learning*

- *Principle 5: Multiple forms of data can provide evidence to inform improvement*
- *Principle 6: Flexibility and responsiveness to situational and contextual factors support student learning*
- *Principle 7: Intentionality and transparency create more equitable opportunities*

5

Using the Principles to Improve Learning Experiences

This chapter provides some examples of ways that instructors can put the concepts of the Principles for Effective and Equitable Teaching (described in Chapter 4) into practice. An instructor beginning their journey to becoming a more equitable and effective teacher might initially choose to focus on just one Principle at a time or pick one of the example strategies described below as an entry point. Another might apply multiple Principles in an interconnected way to build upon strategies they have previously incorporated into their teaching. Designing and implementing equitable and effective learning experiences is not a matter of checking off each of the Principles from a list; it is an ongoing process requiring repeated reflection and innovation. This reflection involves getting to know both yourself and your students, including questioning your assumptions about your own expectations and approaches. In order for instructors to teach equitably and effectively, they need to consider the students' point of view and reflect on the planned approach and its implications for equity and student learning in all aspects of course preparation. Engaging in professional learning and development (discussed in Chapter 8) to support course design can be an effective way of learning to create these environments.

The Principles can be a lens for looking at many different aspects of a course, including the content covered, instructional practices, students' tasks, group work, and grading. While the priorities and expectations of disciplinary units and institutions can sometimes be a barrier to transforming teaching, individual faculty who are interested in re-imagining their teaching based on the Principles can consider small changes as starting points. For example, faculty can start by including a few activities for students that reflect the Principles, testing out new approaches to assessment, expanding opportunities for students to get to know each other, or revising the syllabus to provide more transparency.

The chapter is organized into two main sections that reflect major themes captured by the Principles: designing for learning, and cultivating an equitable and effective learning environment. Both sections discuss strategies, approaches, and tools that instructors, either individually or collaboratively, might consider as they reflect on course design and instruction. The section on creating an environment compatible with productive learning explores the need for instructors to reflect on their own assumptions about learning and teaching as well as the need for instructors to get to know their students in order to make design choices that support learning for those students. Implications for disciplinary units and institutions are discussed in subsequent chapters. In this and subsequent chapters we often refer back to the Principles presented in Chapter 4 to illustrate how they are relevant to the topics of later chapters. To avoid repeating the long names of each Principle, we utilize the same shorthand as listed in Table 4-1.

DESIGNING FOR LEARNING

A foundational concept of the Principles for Equitable and Effective Teaching presented in Chapter 4 is that *students' learning is the primary goal of teaching*. Focusing on student learning as the goal of a course has several important components for the instructor, including clearly articulating what they expect students will know and be able to do by the end of a course; making use of assessments that allow them to see students' progress toward those goals; and making use of class time to help students build their skills and be successful on the assessments, thus achieving the learning goals. Designing courses explicitly with learning goals in mind may require a shift in the instructional approaches and classroom activities that instructors use.

Learning is understood by researchers to be an active process that involves both development of an understanding of key concepts in a discipline and the ability to use that knowledge to engage in disciplinary practices (the research basis for this is discussed in greater length in Chapters 3 and 4 and is reflected in the Principles). This means that more traditional instructional approaches that emphasize memorizing decontextualized facts or undertaking decontextualized procedures are not as effective as learning experiences that provide students with opportunities to reflect on and use their developing knowledge (see Chapter 3 for additional discussion of the supporting research). Instructors therefore need to reflect on their own assumptions about teaching and learning as they design courses. In this section, we present guidance and strategies for designing around learning goals.

Applying the Principles has implications for classroom instruction. Table 5-1 presents some of the changes that could increase student learning over "traditional" approaches. The column on the left describes strategies that help to center and support students' learning. The column on the right describes strategies that are common in more "traditional" STEM learning and are less effective for supporting students' learning. Moving away from strategies in the second column to strategies in the first column will help an instructor's teaching become more equitable and effective and have a positive impact on student learning. As discussed in Chapter 3, these strategies reflect multiple lines of research on learning and teaching that have solidified over the past 30–40 years. The following sections elaborate on the approaches in the left column.

The Universal Design for Learning Framework

One tool that can be helpful for developing teaching practices that center student learning is the Universal Design for Learning (UDL) framework, which is grounded in principles of neuroscience and can be utilized to promote equitable learning in science, technology, engineering, and mathematics (STEM; CAST, n.d.). UDL guidelines focus on three major areas, including the design for multiple means of (a) engagement, (b) representation, and (c) action and expression. This framework was developed to account for variability in how people learn, including people with disabilities.

TABLE 5-1 Changes That Can Increase Teaching Strategies Focused on Student Learning

Teaching Focused on Student Learning Includes	
More of...	Less of...
Clear articulation of learning goals and how the work done in the course will help students achieve learning goals	A focus on getting through a set amount of content
Course structures that engage students as active learners	Course structures that maintain students as passive receivers of information
Activities that regularly engage students in using the skills and knowledge of the discipline	Separate laboratory sections focused on skills without clear connections to course content
Being transparent about opportunities and expectations for learning and engagement	Assuming that all students are aware of what they "should" be doing
Grading practices that allow for formative feedback and focus on mastery	Grading practices that focus on a theoretical distribution (a curve) and promote competition in a few high-stakes assessments

CAST updated the UDL guidelines in July 2024 to include components addressing systemic bias and exclusion in learning environments, making the framework even more comprehensive. Figure 5-1 shows the latest version of the UDL guidelines (CAST, 2024). A paper commissioned for the 2023 National Academies event on Disrupting Ableism and Supporting People With Disabilities in the STEM Workforce explored the intersection of UDL with STEM learning in higher education and provides some guidance for making classroom, laboratory, field, and digital spaces inclusive and accessible.[1]

For STEM instructors seeking to implement UDL in their courses, one useful approach is called plus-one, whereby they consider more than one way to represent course concepts, engage students in their learning, and have students demonstrate their learning (Behling & Tobin, 2018). As an example, illustrating a concept in more than one way in a STEM course might involve any of the following: physical or digital models, animations, problem-solving, a case study, descriptive, or oral text. Additional ideas for making courses more accessible are often available from campus centers for teaching and learning or campus disability resource centers as well as national centers such as the DO-IT center at the University of Washington.[2]

UDL has the potential to be integrated to scale within STEM courses to facilitate equitable learning experiences for students with and without disabilities, and to disrupt conceptions of normalcy and traditional approaches to teaching that do not account for learner variability (Fornauf & Erickson, 2020; Schreffler et al., 2019). In a systematic review of 17 articles involving UDL integration in higher education, 15 reported positive outcomes, one had mixed findings, and one did not report outcomes (Seok et al., 2018). Such results highlight the promise of utilizing UDL to support equitable and effective teaching.

Designing Around Clear Learning Goals

When designing for learning, a critical step is to develop clear learning goals for students. These goals then guide selection of course materials, development of tasks and activities for students, and assessments of student learning—an intentional approach to course design that reflects *Principle 7: Intentionality and transparency*. Starting with course goals allows instructors to make good decisions about what to include and exclude from their course by asking, "Will this help my students achieve these learning goals?"

[1] The full version of the paper is available at https://nap.nationalacademies.org/resource/27245/Johnston_and_Perez_Creating_Disability-Friendly_and_Inclusive_Accessible_Spaces_in_Higher_Education.pdf

[2] More information about the University of Washington's DO-IT center is available at https://www.washington.edu/doit/

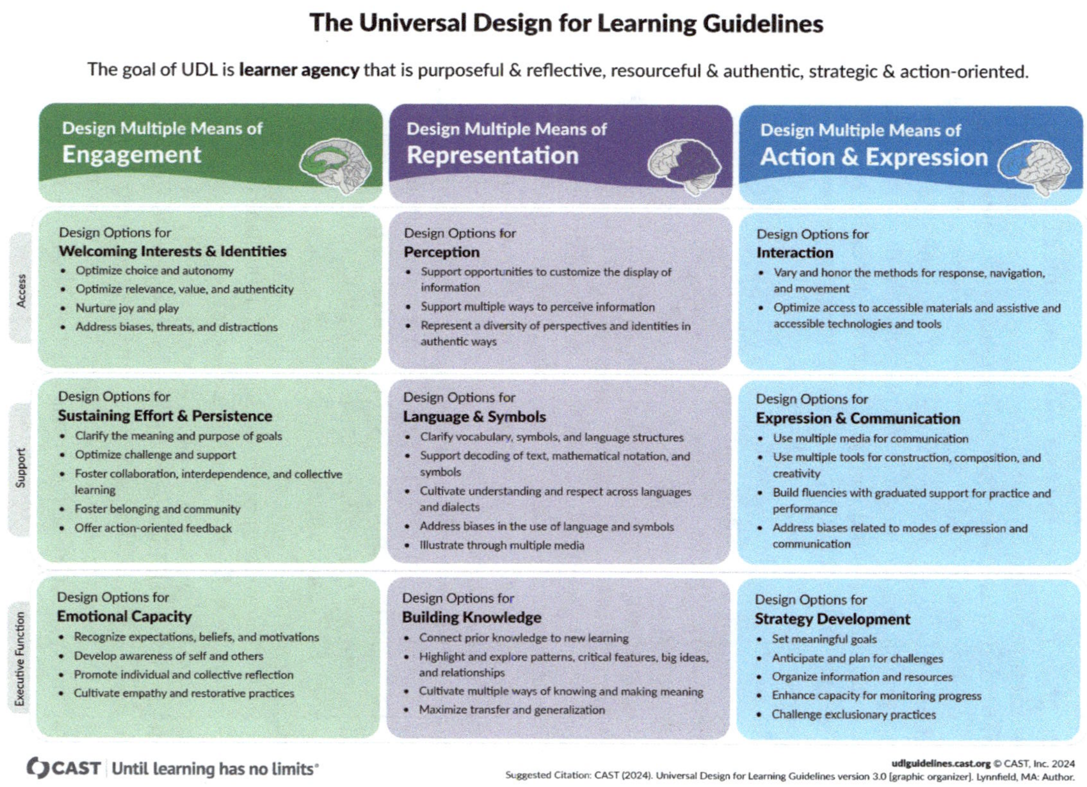

FIGURE 5-1 The Universal Design for Learning guidelines.
SOURCE: CAST (n.d.), retrieved from https://udlguidelines.cast.org

Articulating learning goals for students and designing toward them can be done for an entire course, a sequence of courses, or for a single class session. In some academic units, instructors may have less flexibility in articulating learning goals and redesigning a course accordingly because the course content is laid out by the unit. However, it can still be useful to think through the learning goals related to the established content, or even the goals for a particular class period.

Backward design is one common framework for developing courses based on explicit learning goals (Wiggins & McTighe, 2005). In backward design, the first step is to define course-level learning goals that are substantial, measurable, and achievable (or plausible, in the case of goals in the affective domain). The second step is to develop assessments to determine the extent to which students have met the learning goals. The final step is to design activities that help students develop the knowledge and skills they need to succeed on the assessments. By foregrounding learning goals, and building content and assessments around them, backward design allows instructors to be more intentional and transparent in their teaching (Neiles & Arnett, 2021; Reynolds & Kearns, 2017). This approach differs from approaches to course design that focus mainly on identification of the disciplinary content that needs to be "covered" in a given course. A focus on coverage without articulating goals for what students should learn about the discipline and how they can demonstrate their competence can lead to adoption of less effective instructional approaches, such as heavy reliance on lecture and memorization.

There are tools available to help instructors implement backward design. Neiles and Arnett (2021) provide a primer on using backward design for chemistry laboratory courses to facilitate a more inclusive, scaffolded, and intentional curriculum. Reynolds and Kearns (2017) developed a planning tool that incorporates backward design, active learning, and assessment.

In some STEM disciplines, learning goals have been defined by the community or by outside accrediting bodies, and these can be used as a starting place for designing a course. For example, Vision and Change in Undergraduate Biology Education (American Association for the Advancement of Science, 2009) articulates disciplinary core content and competencies that have been translated into program- and course-level learning outcomes at many institutions (Brownell et al., 2014; Clemmons et al., 2020). The BioSkills Guide is one example that provides a set of measurable learning outcomes for use in the design of individual courses and activities (Clemmons et al., 2020). In the geosciences, the community came together during the COVID-19 pandemic to define learning outcomes for capstone field experiences so that alternatives to in-person field courses could be designed that would meet the needs of students (Burmeister et al., 2020; Rademacher et al., 2021).

Clearly articulated learning goals can help with the careful selection and effective use of instructional resources in the classroom. Instructors may think about a textbook as the primary resource for their course and may choose a textbook based on content and familiarity. However, when choosing textbooks, instructors often need to consider factors such as cost, availability, accessibility, supporting materials for students, and equity and access issues (Marsh et al., 2022). While textbooks from traditional publishers can be unaffordable for low-income students, there are alternatives to each student purchasing a new textbook (older editions, used books, book rentals, library copies, etc.); another alternative is the growing availability of online "open" textbooks, which can be accessed for free, though these may not be available for specific content areas or more advanced courses (Bliss et al., 2013; Cozart et al., 2021; Hilton, 2016; Martin et al., 2017a). It can be useful to choose open educational resource (OER) versions of tools, but they must be properly evaluated first. OER tools might include open-source software and other informal learning materials in the public domain (Diaz Eaton et al., 2022).

Textbooks are not the only instructional resources to consider; digital tools can also support student learning. High-quality instructional resources of other formats (e.g., video recordings, visualizations, simulations) can also support students' active engagement in disciplinary learning (see the next section for further discussion of active engagement which is related to *Principle 1: Active engagement*).

Many publishers offer access to digital learning tools, collectively called "courseware," that are designed to be adaptive platforms that allow students to demonstrate their understanding and allow instructors to monitor their progress. These often contain multimedia lessons, practice problems, and formative assessments and are most commonly available at the introductory level (e.g., Neisler & Means, 2021). While courseware can be expensive, there are ways that institutions can fund access to avoid passing on the cost to students, which may have equity implications. The degree to which courseware aligns with course organization and structure (such as a student-centered adaptive approach) impacts the student experience (O'Sullivan et al., 2020).

Disciplinary and professional societies that focus on teaching sometimes produce curricular materials (e.g. American Association for the Advancement of Science, 2009; Behbahanian et al., 2018; Steer et al., 2019), as do grant-funded efforts (Branchaw et al., 2020; Gosselin et al., 2019; Harlow et al., 2020). Unlike textbooks and courseware produced by publishers, these resources are often free to use due to requirements from their funding sources. They are often based in the research on how people learn (e.g., Steer et al., 2019) and often have been tested in college classrooms for their effectiveness.

Engaging Students Actively

Courses can be designed to develop skills within a particular discipline through the use of inclusive teaching strategies and active learning approaches centered around group work and peer instruction; this incorporation of active learning into STEM courses is the focus of *Principle 1: Active engagement*. To truly develop skills in a discipline, the activities within a course must not only provide active engagement in learning, but must also be aligned with course goals and desired disciplinary outcomes.

As discussed in Chapters 1 and 3, historically, STEM teaching has been didactic and instructor centered, largely featuring in-person lectures; this has shifted some in recent years, but didactic instruction remains the dominant way that STEM is taught (Stains et al., 2018). Research evidence makes clear that this traditional approach is ineffective and even alienating to many students and that active learning approaches are better suited to developing robust conceptual understanding, facilitating transfer of learning across contexts, and promoting long-term retention of ideas (Armbruster et al., 2009; Devlin & Samarawickrema, 2010; Ebert-May et al., 1997; Hogan & Sathy, 2022; Lyle et al., 2020). Evidence suggests that active learning tasks give students an opportunity to construct their own knowledge and understanding, requiring them to do more than simply passively listening to lectures (Freeman et al., 2014).

When implementing active learning approaches, the instructor acts as a guide, facilitator, and expert in the discipline, but is not the focus of the class. Instead, students' tasks and student learning are the focal point. There are many ways to design and implement courses that incorporate active learning, and many strategies have been shown to lead to improved course outcomes for all students. Instructors can learn from the developed approaches or begin on a smaller scale by incorporating a few active learning tasks or group work into a course (Balta et al., 2017; Mazur & Watkins, 2010; Ruder et al., 2020). See Box 5-1 for some established approaches for actively engaging students.

There are many ways that instructors can actively engage students in their learning. One approach is to have students do preparatory work outside of class and then have them participate in deliberate practice facilitated with active learning and groupwork during class. Intentional preparatory

BOX 5-1
Approaches and Resources for Actively Engaging STEM Students in Learning

Process Oriented Guided Inquiry Learning (POGIL)[a] is a teaching approach that focuses on students developing understanding of both disciplinary content and process skills such as critical thinking and problem solving. Students frequently examine a carefully chosen or crafted model (e.g., figure, data) and use it to consider guiding questions provided by the instructor. These models anchor cycles of exploration, concept invention, and application as students work to make sense of the model and integrate it with their existing knowledge. This work is often done in teams with assigned roles (e.g., recorder, presenter, reflector). The instructor guides the students to explore new concepts that are central to the learning goals of the course and the development of disciplinary knowledge. (Balta et al., 2017; Mazur & Watkins, 2010; Ruder et al., 2020; Chapter 5 by Asala in Keith-Le & Morgan, 2020).

Just in Time Teaching[b] is a two-step learning process in which students do an assignment before class that the instructor evaluates in order to determine how to spend class time. The just in time feedback right before class meets allows the instructor to modify the lesson so that it provides information on the topics students most need help to understand instead of preselected content. The idea is that classes become more student centered and that students are encouraged to take responsibility for learning outside of class (Novak et al., 1999).

Peer Instruction[c] is a technique in which conceptual questions are intermixed with instructor-led lecture. The conceptual questions are designed to help student understanding and to address misconceptions. Polling is used as students vote using a flash card or a clicker. The instructor checks to see how many students answer correctly and guides another activity in which students try to convince their neighbors that they have the right answer. Following peer discussion, students are asked to do another poll. The lesson ends with the instructor explaining detailed information about the correct answer (Crouch & Mazur, 2001; Gong et al., 2023; Mazur, 1997).

---

[a]More information about POGIL is available at https://pogil.org/

[b]More information about Just in Time Teaching is available at https://www.vanderbilt.edu/advanced-institute/#:~:text=Just%2Din%2DTime%20Teaching%20

[c]More information about peer instruction is available at https://mazur.harvard.edu/research-areas/peer-instruction

work can include pre-reading (Freeman et al., 2007) or preparatory videos (Casper et al., 2019), and low-stakes knowledge tests. In-class deliberate practice with deliberate group work and individual accountability, can be implemented with peer instruction (Crouch & Mazur, 2001; Smith et al., 2009) and audience response devices such as clickers (Kay & LeSage, 2009). Practice exams provided throughout the term are equally effective and can be graded by peers or by students themselves (Jackson et al., 2018). This approach has been adopted in large, gateway STEM courses with positive outcomes for students (Eddy & Hogan, 2014; Haak et al., 2011; Theobald et al., 2020). Such courses improve student learning (Freeman et al., 2007) and have a disproportionate benefit to students from minoritized groups (Eddy & Hogan, 2014; Haak et al., 2011).

When designing tasks and activities for students it is important to consider which students may or may not benefit from the choices that are made. For active learning to be successful, equitable, and effective it is important that the instructor carefully constructs inclusive assignments, works to create an environment that is welcoming and inclusive, and embraces mistakes as part of the learning process (Dewsbury, 2020; White et al., 2020). Some approaches to active learning and group work can cause increased challenges for women; lesbian, gay, bisexual, transgender, queer/questioning, intersex, asexual/aromantic/agender, plus other related identities; students with anxiety and/or depression; neurodiverse learners; students with disabilities; and other underserved students (Araghi et al., 2023; Cooper & Brownell, 2016; Cooper et al., 2018; Downing et al., 2020; Gin et al., 2020).

Designing Group Work and Opportunities for Collaboration and Cooperation

Group work and opportunities for collaboration are an integral part of active learning. They also reflect *Principle 3: Affective and social dimensions*. Intentionally designing interactive activities and assignments can provide students with opportunities to learn from each other as they solve problems, conduct investigations, and reflect on material presented in lecture or texts. Social interactions can also have a positive effect on motivation when activities foster positive interdependence, and students are able to support the work of others and contribute to a larger effort (Brame & Biel, 2015). These activities can be short components integrated into a lecture format or can serve as the predominant form of instruction. This kind of positive interdependence can also occur across venues, such as courses, living learning residences, workplaces, and in the community.

Group work can take many forms (reviewed in Johnson et al., 1998). For example, groups can be informal or formal (e.g., groups where students turn to their neighbor to discuss vs. are assigned by the instructor), designed to be heterogenous versus homogenous by ability (e.g., Donovan et al., 2018), and permanent or transient during the course (e.g., Connell et al., 2023). It is important to note that equitable experiences within these active or cooperative strategies are not automatic. While social interactions can have positive benefits, they also have the potential to be problematic when instructors are not sensitive to power dynamics, racism, gender oppression, and other related issues. When these issues manifest in the classroom in problematic ways, they negatively affect underserved students. This issue has been most studied in regard to gender (Dasgupta et al., 2014; Dennehy & Dasgupta, 2017). Careful attention to designing activities with student attitudes, beliefs, and expectations about themselves, each other, their instructors, and learning itself is necessary and can mitigate these issues. Engaging students in co-creation of norms for classroom and group behavior can be helpful. Instructors can get started by reflecting on their own experiences and how they are similar to and different from those of their students (these issues are discussed in more depth in the next major section of this chapter). Professional learning and development can also be helpful for instructors to work together to develop and practice strategies (see Chapter 8 for more).

As mentioned above, when instructors ask students to work together, they should consider the features of groups and design instruction to ensure group members know how to work collaboratively (Johnson et al., 1998; Theobald et al., 2017), keeping in mind that the ultimate goal is practicing skills of the discipline vis-à-vis tasks that are enhanced with collaborative efforts (Dyer et al., 2013). It is also important to ensure that all group members are able to contribute by structuring activities in supportive ways and ensuring that students are not excluded from full participation in groups due to physical or sensory disabilities. Some students, especially those with disabilities, may need information to be provided in advance to allow for more processing time on expectations or to be ready to answer poll questions (Gin et al., 2020). Attending to composition of groups and assignment of roles for group tasks is important for fostering environments where students help each other solve problems by building on each other's knowledge, asking each other questions, and suggesting ideas that an individual working alone might not have considered (Brown & Campione, 1994; Dasgupta et al., 2014; Ramsey et al., 2013; Sekaquaptewa & Thompson, 2003). Box 5-2 describes an approach to group work and collaboration that incorporates peer facilitators.

BOX 5-2
Encouraging Collaboration Through Peer-Led Team Learning

STEM-Dawgs Workshops at the University of Washington utilized a supplementary instruction (SI) model in an attempt to support students who are from groups that historically are underrepresented in general chemistry courses. Supplementary instruction means adding support to an existing course structure; in this case the STEM-Dawgs workshop was designed as a "weekly, two-hour, two-credit companion course for Chemistry 142, which is the first in the three-quarter (year-long) general chemistry sequence for majors" (Stanich et al., 2018).

The workshop first started with individual quiz and group work, followed by discussions on a pre-class writing exercise guided by the peer facilitators. Students then worked again in small groups to answer chemistry questions that are relevant to lecture and that required a range of thinking skills. The initiative used the Peer-led Team Learning (PLTL) approach, including sessions designed outside of the classroom with guidance provided by a peer leader. As an extension of the PLTL SI, and in addition to peer-facilitated problem-solving, STEM-Dawgs incorporate two components inspired by learning sciences: (a) research-based study skills, and (b) evidence-based interventions targeting psychological and emotional support. For example, before most workshops or at other specified times, students completed evidence-based writing intervention that addressed the barriers in stereotype threat, mindset, self-regulation, test anxiety, belonging, value of learning, expectancy value, and post-exam metacognition.

This use of supplementary instruction was found to help increase course performance and also other nonacademic outcomes such as sense of belonging for underrepresented minorities, females, low-income students, and first-generation students. Supportive peer-learning environment and relationships with peer facilitators partly contributed to the successes.

Group work of all kinds can also provide the instructor with an opportunity to interact with students to deepen relationships. An instructor can circulate among groups to listen in on conversation or provide real-time answers to questions. Group tasks and discussions also provide an informal assessment opportunity as the students' comments and questions can provide insight into sticking points or areas where students are struggling. (See the section in this chapter on Assessing Learning and Providing Feedback for additional discussion about assessment strategies.)

Help Students Build upon Their Knowledge and Lived Experiences

As articulated in Principle 2, students' prior knowledge and previous experiences set the foundation for new knowledge. Connecting to and leveraging students' prior knowledge and interests can enhance their learning. This includes formal knowledge in the STEM disciplines gained from previous schooling as well as students' experiences outside of formal educational settings that are relevant to STEM learning. Many campus centers for teaching and learning provide guidance for instructors on approaches for activating this student knowledge (e.g., Virginia Tech,[3] University of Texas, Austin[4]) as do the developers of the Universal Design for Learning guidelines discussed in greater detail above.[5]

One example of facilitating use of prior knowledge from a previous lecture involves posing a problem/question to the class at the beginning of lecture or when discussing a case study. Various tools can be used to activate student knowledge and help them to see if it is relevant to the course material (Bransford & Johnson, 1972; Brod, 2021; Hattan et al., 2024; Simonsmeier et al., 2022). Instructors can also implement forecasting, in which they provide a question/problem and ask students to make a prediction or to hypothesize based on their knowledge or past lectures (Byrne et al., 2010; Schwartz & Bransford, 1998). In other instances, understanding students' prior knowledge allows the instructor to help students reflect on any alternative conceptions they may have (Fisher, 2004). There are many strategies instructors can use to activate prior knowledge, including using advanced graphic organizers, anticipation guides, problem solving with case studies, opening questions, and power previewing (skimming text strategically before reading in detail; Center for Excellence in Teaching and Learning, n.d.). In addition, instructors can provide resources to all students by posting supplemental materials or discussing options for obtaining support from peers, tutors, or other campus offices (Vega & Meaders, 2023); such resources may be especially helpful to those who do not have as strong a background in the relevant content area. As the next paragraph discusses, these types of strategies can help compensate for the variety of background and experiences of the students who enter a course and potentially help alleviate equity concerns.

Recognizing the diversity of experiences that students bring to the learning environment, leveraging it, and making connections between students' everyday lives and STEM concepts and practices promotes more equitable outcomes (Bayles & Morrell, 2018; Booker & Campbell-Whatley, 2018). Students enter courses with knowledge from previous educational and life experiences. One way of conceptualizing this is the concept of *funds*

---

[3] More information about guidance for instructors at Virginia Tech is available at https://teaching.vt.edu/teachingresources/adjustinginstruction/priorknowledge.html

[4] More information about guidance for instructors at the University of Texas, Austin, is available at https://ctl.utexas.edu/prior-knowledge

[5] https://udlguidelines.cast.org/representation/building-knowledge/prior-knowledge/

of knowledge, which encompasses the cultural, familial, and household experiences/knowledge/skills that students bring, and which can be leveraged to enhance their abilities to understand academic knowledge relevant to their coursework (González et al., 2005). Textbooks rarely provide these kinds of connections, but instructors can supplement the content of the texts (Meuler et al., 2023). In some studies, instructors provided opportunities for students to draw on the knowledge and skills they have developed within their communities and families, e.g., their existing funds of knowledge (González et al., 2005; Moll, 2019; Moll et al., 1992). Another way to connect students' STEM learning to their experiences outside of the classroom is to provide opportunities for students to choose to study topics that are of personal or cultural relevance (Barnes & Brownell, 2017; Black et al., 2022; Dasgupta, 2023). Showing how science and engineering are socially relevant is also a strategy for connecting with students' interests and has the potential to engage more diverse learners (Dasgupta, 2023). When instructors recognize that students can benefit from drawing on their families, cultural assets, and communities to which they belong, the instructors are better positioned to support deep and critical engagement of students with STEM content in their courses and classrooms (Bang & Medin, 2010; Bang et al., 2010; Covarrubias et al., 2019; Fryberg & Markus, 2007; Solyom et al., 2019). (See Chapter 4's discussion of Principle 2 for additional strategies and approaches that leverage students' cultural knowledge and experiences.)

Deepening Engagement in Disciplinary Knowledge and Work

As discussed above and in Chapter 4, active engagement in disciplinary content is critical for student learning. Several approaches can support this type of learning in and outside of class. The specific approaches may vary for foundational STEM courses versus the often-smaller upper-level courses. In large, high-structure courses pre-class preparatory assignments can be combined with in-class active learning activities such as think-pair-share, polling, and student surveys (Eddy & Hogan, 2014; Freeman et al., 2014; Haak et al., 2011; Theobald et al., 2020). In order for active learning to be equitable and effective it needs to be carefully designed to ensure that all students have the opportunity to participate and be successful and instructors may need support from their academic units or institutions to provide access to learning spaces that are well suited to approaches such as group work[6] or to additional teaching assistants or undergraduate learning

[6] As an example, see additional information about the SCALE-UP model of arranging classrooms for active learning is available at https://www.physport.org/methods/Section.cfm?G=SCALE_UP&S=What

assistants who can provide the workforce to support the implementation of the approaches (Dewsbury, 2020; Talbot et al., 2015; White et al., 2020).

While discipline-based active learning experiences in the classroom can advance students' learning, students also benefit from opportunities to deepen their engagement in a discipline through participation in research (Malachowski et al., 2024; National Academies of Sciences, Engineering, and Medicine, 2017b). Undergraduate research is often cited as an invaluable learning experience for students across all disciplines, even those outside of the STEM field. For example, the High Impact Practices work done by the American Association of Colleges and Universities includes undergraduate research in their list of approaches based on evidence that can provide educational benefits for students.[7] In STEM, engaging in undergraduate research has been shown to benefit diverse students from marginalized populations (Barlow & Villarejo, 2004; Chang et al., 2014; Harsh et al., 2012; Jones et al., 2010; Thiry & Laursen, 2011). Box 5-3 describes reported benefits of a program, Building Infrastructure Learning to Diversity: Promoting Opportunities for Diversity in Education Research (BUILD PODER), for supporting undergraduate research in the sciences that involves partnership between community colleges and a university. BUILD PODER[8] is designed to build power, change campus culture, and nurture research mentoring relationships as it "helps students understand institutional policies and practices that may prevent them from persisting in higher education, learn to become their own advocates, and successfully confront social barriers and instances of inequities and discrimination" (Saetermoe et al., 2017, p. 42). Undergraduate research has been used as a tool for teaching and also a tool for transformation of learning experiences and curriculum. A longitudinal study to explore the role of undergraduate research in changes to institutional culture and student learning is documented in the book *Transforming Academic Culture and Curriculum: Integrating and Scaffolding Research Throughout Undergraduate Education*, which presents guides and toolkits designed to inform change agents (Malachowski et al., 2024).

Course-Based Undergraduate Research Experiences (CUREs)

CUREs offer students the chance to engage in authentic hands-on inquiry as a part of their normal coursework. It has been proposed as a way to expose more students to research as opportunities to work in laboratories are not available to everyone. Students enrolled in classes with CUREs

---

[7] More information about the AAC&U's High Impact Practices is available at https://www.aacu.org/trending-topics/high-impact

[8] https://www.csun.edu/build-poder

BOX 5-3
Building Infrastructure Leading to Diversity: Promoting Opportunities for Diversity in Education and Research

This undergraduate research initiative involved 81 community college students and 41 community college faculty mentors working with California State University, Northridge (CSUN) so that the students could engage in research in STEM and biomedical disciplines. The program Building Infrastructure Leading to Diversity: Promoting Opportunities for Diversity in Education and Research (BUILD PODER) shared some of the benefits of the program reported by the students:

1. Gaining lab experience: A student reported their research experience gained through a summer laboratory experience has been essential in shaping and developing their science identity.
2. Applying academic skills to real-world settings: A student reported through studying the impact of chemicals on plant growth, they learned important research skills such as operating scanning electron microscopes, making posters, and presenting scientific research at conferences.
3. Learning the research process: A student reported enjoying working in the lab and reading research literature, which promoted their interest in biology.
4. Building networking and support system: A student reported that being an undergraduate researcher provided opportunities to meet others and get needed support for transition from a community college to a baccalaureate institution.
5. Developing collaboration skills and preparing future professionals: Students reported summer research experience improved collaborative skills and that mentorship helped inform educational and career paths.

This example demonstrates that baccalaureate-granting universities and community colleges have the capacity to foster interest in undergraduate research (Ashcroft et al., 2021). Additional research studies about the program can be found at https://www.csun.edu/build-poder/build-poder-publications-and-presentations.

learn about the scientific practices and generate new knowledge within their discipline. Over the past few years, CUREs have been used as a tool to improve undergraduate STEM classes while engaging a larger number of students in disciplinary practices (e.g., Werth et al., 2022). These courses have been linked to significantly positive outcomes among the students who participate, including higher levels of career achievement, higher levels of retention in class, in the major, and in college, and deeper comprehension of class material (Fitzsimmons et al., 1990; Hanauer et al., 2016; Lopatto, 2003; Mogk, 1993; Tomovic, 1994; Zydney et al., 2002). These courses also increase access to research experiences for students who may not be aware that these skills are needed to advance in some areas (Bangera & Brownell, 2014).

CUREs can be found at various institutions across the country, although they are more readily supported at doctoral-granting institutions (Wei & Woodin, 2011). Historically, CUREs have been predominantly implemented in upper-level classes. However, in recent years, instructors of large, highly enrolled introductory courses and those at community colleges have begun adopting these practices (Cruz et al., 2020; Sexton & Sharma, 2021; Tomasik et al., 2013; Tuthill & Berestecky, 2017). A major benefit of these efforts is that many students are exposed to the benefits of CUREs as a part of their general education curriculum. In addition to learning valuable STEM skills, students who partake in research report increased confidence, communication, creativity, and collaborative skills (Ahmad & Al-Thani, 2022; National Academies, 2017; Starr et al., 2020). Importantly, they also claim to have a more personal connection to their area of interest. One study found that CUREs students at a Hispanic Serving Institution had significantly higher overall grades in a lecture course directly related to the CURE even after statistically adjusting for demographic and academic characteristics (Ing et al., 2021).

During the COVID-19 pandemic, several instructors and programs had to shift their research agenda to an online learning environment. In doing so, colleges nationwide began to explore alternatives to in-person labs and projects. Though there were concerns about students' long-term transferable skills, studies indicate that students who participate in online research experience still show positive outcomes, such as higher levels in self-efficacy and retention in STEM programs (Erickson et al., 2022; Hess et al., 2023). CUREs are therefore a feasible approach for multiple class modalities (in-person, online, or hybrid).

Field Experiences

Engaging students in making observations and collecting data in the field is a hallmark of some STEM disciplines, including the geosciences (geology, environmental science, and marine sciences) and ecology (O'Connell et al., 2021). Field experiences can provide an opportunity for authentic investigation, in addition to offering a multitude of cognitive, affective, social, and professional benefits. The Undergraduate Field Experiences Research Network (UFERN) developed a model for designing and conducting field experiences that builds on an extensive literature review (O'Connell et al., 2022). As with any activity where learning is the goal, the UFERN model starts with setting intended student outcomes, then incorporates student context factors (e.g., prior knowledge and skills, worldview, identity) and design factors (e.g., timing, orientation, social interactions, choice and control) to create a field experience that supports learning and accommodates all students. The student context and design factors reflect the Principles for Equitable and Effective Teaching and are important whether the field experience is a few hours long or a few weeks.

Virtual field experiences have become more common, in part because of the COVID-19 pandemic, and provide a technology-supported means for broadening access to the field. Recent research suggests that cognitive gains in virtual field experiences can be similar to those seen in real field experiences (e.g., Markowitz et al., 2018; Mead et al., 2019) and can overcome some of the commonly seen gender and race/ethnicity gaps experienced in in-person field experiences (Bitting et al., 2018). However, even as students and instructors hold negative perceptions of the virtual field experience (Bond et al., 2022) and report preferring in-person field experiences (Rader et al., 2021), these promising results provide support for the use of virtual field experiences when an in-person field experience is inaccessible for any reason.

Assessing Learning and Providing Feedback

Designing for learning requires monitoring whether and what students are learning. When assessments are designed to document progress toward carefully chosen learning outcomes, they can provide insights for both the student and instructor on how to improve. Assessment is a major component of *Principle 5: Multiple forms of data*. Assessment practices are a key strategy for supporting and advancing students' progress, so it is essential to reflect on and modify these practices with the principles in mind to ensure that they are being applied in productive and supportive ways (Walvoord & Anderson, 2010).

As described in Chapter 4, assessments can be divided into two major types: (a) formative assessment which focuses on eliciting student thinking and gathering information that allows the instructor to adapt to student needs and (b) summative assessments that document how students have progressed in their learning and are often used to determine students' grades. Summative assessments might also be used to evaluate the effectiveness of a course—that is, to determine whether the structure of the course and the tasks and activities for students have successfully advanced students' learning.

Providing a variety of low-stakes opportunities for students to engage with course content, such as through reflection assignments, breaking large projects into multiple components, peer review of early drafts, or short quizzes, can help students make connections and understand concepts without provoking as much anxiety as midterms and final exams. Frequent assessments can enhance retention of the concepts being covered in class and decrease the weights of each assignment. Including different types of assignments within a course allows students the opportunity to demonstrate their understanding in the formats that might work best for them. These strategies also provide multiple opportunities for feedback so that students and instructors can adapt their approaches during the course (Brame & Biel, 2015; Halamish & Bjork, 2011; Murphy et al., 2024).

Lower-stakes assessments may include laboratory work and reports, written assignments, weekly quizzes, homework, and small-value quizzes, etc. A discipline-based education research study by Cotner and Ballen (2017) describes an example of biology courses in which mixed assessments (not just high-stakes exams) were used and their positive impacts on female-identifying students. The study evaluated gender-based performance trends in nine high-enrollment introductory biology courses in Fall 2016. Course sizes ranged from 90 to 239 students. Grades were categorized as combined grades on midterms and finals, non-exam assessments, and a combination of exam grade and non-exam grade. The study verified that mixed assessment combining different approaches, such as group participation, low-stakes quizzes and assignments, and in-class activities, can minimize the impact of high-stakes exams for underrepresented groups in STEM.

Instructors can also provide varied types of assessments (both formative and summative) within a course or holistically in courses within the degree plan. Types of assessments can include individual/team projects, oral/poster presentations, collaborative group worksheets, individual/team videos along with exams and homework. Assessments may also be designed to build skills such as communication, teamwork, and leadership. Finally, instructors can allow for flexibility in having students show progress in their understanding by allowing students to submit multiple drafts or resubmit corrected work. This kind of flexibility reflects *Principle 6: Flexibility and responsiveness*. This is important for courses such as mathematical proof writing where students are introduced to putting their ideas and mathematics into writing and as such is different from previous computational courses.

Feedback and Messages About Assessments

How an instructor communicates about both the purposes of assessments and what the results of an assessment mean can have a strong impact on students' perceptions of themselves, of the course, and of the discipline. Studies have shown that students' perceptions of their instructors are predictive of engagement and performance (Canning et al., 2024; Muenks et al., 2024).

Messages about whether students' success depends on innate ability (a fixed mindset) or depends on effort and learning (a growth mindset) have been shown to have particular importance for students' motivation and performance (Canning et al., 2024; Muenks et al., 2020, 2024). Researchers have identified teaching behaviors that can foster and communicate to students that intelligence and ability are qualities they can develop through effort, good strategies, and seeking help when stuck (Kroeper et al., 2022a,b). Kroeper et al. identified four categories of teaching behaviors that influence whether students infer that an instructor has a growth mindset about their abilities. Two of these are particularly relevant to assessments. Students perceive instructors as having a growth mindset when

- instructors provide many opportunities for practice and provide frequent feedback to students; and
- instructors respond to students' poor performance, struggles with learning, or confusion by providing support, suggesting strategies, and offering additional opportunities for improvement (rather than with frustration or implying that the student cannot improve).

Designing assessments that are clearly aligned to the stated learning goals for a course and then communicating the goals and expectations to students is critical. This information can be communicated in the course syllabus (see discussion of the syllabus later in this chapter) and in the descriptions of individual assignments. For example, assignments can lay out both the goal or purpose of the assignment and the specific criteria the student needs to include in their response (e.g., as a rubric or a list of points to address). Jonsson and Svingby (2007, p. 130) explain that "the reliable scoring of performance assessments can be enhanced by the use of rubrics" and that "rubrics seem to have the potential of promoting learning and/or improve instruction," given that rubrics make grading criteria more explicit. Some research shows that transparency in teaching can increase students' ability to persist in college and that this impact specifically helps first-generation college students (Winkelmes et al., 2019). This kind of clarity and transparency reflects *Principle 7: Intentionality and transparency.*

Grading Practices

Traditional grading methods typically involve returning a grade or a graded assignment to students (with no or minimal feedback) and continuing on with the next lecture with little or no means to allow students to reassess or improve their understanding of assessed learning objectives. It can be helpful for instructors to reflect on their goals for providing student feedback and how that interacts with their approach to grading (Winstone

& Boud, 2020). There are many alternative approaches to grading that can be adopted in whole or in part to increase the feedback that students and instructors have about learning. Alternative grading methods (including specifications-based grading, standards-based grading, mastery-based grading, and ungrading, among others) are student centered and focus on using learning objectives to permit students to assess their performance in order to improve their understanding and meet the learning objectives (Blum, 2020; Clark & Talbert, 2023; Ferns et al., 2021; Hackerson et al., 2024; Stommel, 2024; Toledo & Dubias, 2017). Alternative grading methods may also help students adopt more of a growth mindset about their skills and abilities (Blum, 2020; Dweck, 2006; Ferns et al., 2021; Stommel, 2024).

Clark and Talbert (2023) discuss the four pillars of alternative grading (clearly defined standards, helpful feedback, grades indicate progress, and re-attempts without penalty), and provide distinctions on various types of alternative grading methods that can be implemented in small-sized and large-sized classes. Mastery-based grading (also called mastery-based testing or MBT) focuses on the student learning process and measuring student understanding of clearly defined learning goals, it has been promoted as a way to improve equity (Alex, 2022; Livers et al., 2024; Perez & Verdin, 2022; Winget & Persky, 2012). Several studies have examined MBT in undergraduate mathematics courses and some preliminary results suggest it may be helpful for decreasing student anxiety and supporting learning (Campbell et al., 2020; Curley & Downey, 2024; Dempsey & Huber, 2020; Harsy et al., 2021; Lewis, 2020). Specifications grading sets out pre-determined criteria that a student knows in advance and works to meet by completing assignments. Graves (2023) provides a brief literature review of implementations of specifications grading in various courses in different disciplines. Katzman et al. (2021) report more positive student attitudes and improved performance on content-related assessment questions in an undergraduate cell biology course using specifications grading. Alternative grading approaches have been explored in chemistry courses as well (Diegelman-Parente, 2011; Noell et al., 2023). These grading approaches have also been reported to motivate students to learn, discourage cheating, give students agency over their own grades, minimize conflicts between student and faculty on grade disagreements, and foster higher-order cognitive development and creativity (Clark & Talbert 2023; Nilson, 2015).

Technology to Support Monitoring of Student Learning

Using technological tools to track real-time data about students can allow instructors to monitor student status and progress through an online interface that displays learning analytics. Instead of traditional grades from summative assessments, robust dashboards can provide real-time information not only on assessment outcomes but also on course activity and other measures of student engagement (Psaromiligkos et al., 2011; Rabelo et al., 2024; Sáiz-Manzanares et al., 2021). For example, an instructor might monitor or track student engagement (e.g., which students watch a particular video) to allow them to follow up with those who did not. These dashboards provide data directly from students and so may help minimize potential implicit bias effects in faculty (Arnold & Pistilli, 2012). The data can also be used by instructors to look at specific student use and assignment outcomes based on student demographic data (see examples of visualizations from data dashboards in Chapter 8). These learning management systems also provide student access, which may provide students with information on their own use relative to the rest of the class.

Technology coupled with learning science has been proposed as a tool that could lead to adaptive learning activities and courseware that might have the potential to improve access and equity by providing personalized learning experiences for students (Gordon et al., 2024). While many examples of courseware have been developed and studies have begun, the promise of the technology has not been conclusively established. A joint project involving four institutions that are members of the Association of Public and Land Grant Universities examined student and faculty perspectives on using adaptive courseware for undergraduate biology courses for non-majors. Results showed some positive impacts on student pass rates and some concerns about aspects of implementation related to both technical challenges and navigating unfamiliar ways of receiving feedback (Buchan et al., 2020; O'Sullivan et al., 2020). Courseware has the potential to include both formative and summative assessments as well as professional learning supports for instructors. The idea is that the approach can pinpoint areas where students are experiencing additional challenges and help guide the instructor in adapting their lessons to support students who may benefit from additional activities or from engaging with the material in a different way. Carnegie Mellon University's Open Learning Initiative[9] has been collecting and interpreting data over time with a goal of improving learning efficiency and overall outcomes mediated both by software-driven support directly to the student as well as faculty evidence-based interventions based on student learning outcome analyses (Bier et al., 2019, 2023).

[9] More information about Carnegie Mellon University's Open Learning Initiative is available at https://oli.cmu.edu/

CULTIVATING AN EQUITABLE AND EFFECTIVE LEARNING ENVIRONMENT

Students' learning and motivation are strongly influenced by many elements of course design that come together to shape students' experiences in a classroom or other learning setting. Indeed, the structure and situational cues in a learning environment—such as what an instructor says and does while teaching and/or the numerical representation of students in the classroom—impact students' attention and their ability to marshal the cognitive and affective resources to engage in the processes essential to learning including encoding, storage, and retrieval of information (e.g., Cohen et al.,1999; Murphy & Taylor, 2012; Murphy et al., 2007; Steele et al., 2002).

In the first part of this chapter, we touched on many of the elements of classroom instruction and organization that shape students' experience including tasks and activities, group work, and assessments. In this section, we turn to other elements of course design that are critical for creating a productive learning environment including the relationships between the instructor and the students, relationships among the students themselves, the cues students receive in the classroom about their own competence and belonging, and students' opportunities for autonomy and choice. These latter elements are related to *Principle 3: Affective and social dimensions*, *Principle 4: Identity and a sense of belonging*, and *Principle 6: Flexibility and responsiveness*. In thinking about how to create a productive learning environment, instructors can use this set of three Principles to reflect on how to implement the many elements described in the first section: tasks and activities for students, organization of group work, engagement in research, and use of assessment. In this way, the Principles are helpful for thinking about both what students should be doing in the classroom *and* how instruction and interactions can be organized to help students feel supported and valued.

Students' perception of and relationship with the instructor is particularly consequential for student learning and motivation. In one study, students in STEM courses and majors identified qualities they valued most in their instructors: a genuine desire for students to succeed, and authentic displays of respect and encouragement (Harper et al., 2019). Research also indicates that students experience greater self-efficacy, sense of belonging, and academic achievement when instructors show care and respect for all students (Christe, 2013; Micari & Pazos, 2012). Effective and equitable teaching is grounded in the approach of mutual respect. Instructors can focus on establishing that respectful culture in order to foster their primary goal of supporting student learning.

One way for instructors to approach how to create a productive learning environment is to consider the students' point of view and reflect on the planned approach and its implications for equity and student learning. This can involve many aspects of course preparation. Reconsidering the syllabus in light of effective and equitable teaching can make it a more useful tool; reviewing choices of instructional resources can lead to materials that are more effective and more equitable; and taking a new approach to getting to know students can help the instructor to make the course more student centered.

Reflecting on Your Own Assumptions

Instructors' knowledge and beliefs about their students influence their teaching and their students' learning. There are multiple frameworks that can help an instructor understand how they perceive students' identities and experiences (Shukla et al., 2022). A commonly used framing to describe an instructor's beliefs is categorizing them as deficit- or asset-based perspectives. A deficit-based perspective is one in which the tendency is "to locate the source of academic problems in deficiencies within students, their families, their communities, or their membership in social categories (such as race and gender)" (Peck, 2020, p. 940). Adopting an asset-based perspective means focusing on the knowledge and skills students have when they arrive in a course and seeing them as important assets to build on, even when that knowledge and experience may not align with educational norms. Through an asset lens, students are seen as bringing rich, diverse backgrounds and experiences with them into their undergraduate STEM classes that can serve as launch points for discussions and opportunities to apply STEM methods to questions of interest (Jaimes, 2021; Johnson, & Bozeman, 2012; Williams, 2021).

Beliefs about learning itself and about learning in a particular discipline are also important for instructors to surface. This can involve instructors reflecting on the *mindset* that guides their instructional practices. As discussed in Chapter 4, numerous studies have explored the differences between fixed mindsets and growth mindsets and the impact they can have on learning (Canning et al., 2019, 2022, 2024; Hecht et al., 2023; Muenks et al., 2020). A growth mindset is the belief that intelligence and abilities can be developed through practice and hard work. In contrast, a fixed mindset is the belief that intelligence is fixed (Dweck, 2006).

This mindset—whether fixed or growth—can profoundly impact an instructor's instructional practices and, in turn, students' experience of learning. The mindset beliefs that instructors hold about students' abilities and how these beliefs are communicated through their teaching practices can be predictive of students' experiences and success (Canning et al., 2019, 2022; Kroeper et al., 2022a,b; Muenks et al., 2020). When instructors hold fixed-mindset beliefs about their students (e.g., that their students' abilities and intelligence cannot change), students become more psychologically vulnerable, more likely to experience imposter syndrome, have negative experiences, and receive lower grades. The impact of these effects is disproportionally greater for underserved students; that is, STEM faculty who believe ability is fixed experience larger racial achievement gaps (Canning et al., 2019; Muenks et al., 2020). In contrast, holding growth-mindset beliefs about students and engaging in growth-minded teaching practices has a positive impact on student motivation, participation, and grades (Canning et al., 2024; Muenks et al., 2024; Murphy, 2024). Students also bring different mindsets to the course, including the beliefs they hold about learning *and* their perceptions of the beliefs their instructors hold. As discussed in *Principle 3: Affective and social dimensions*, feedback from instructors, the design of activities, and grading practices of instructors can impact student mindsets; when instructors are aware of their own assumptions and reflect on the mindsets of their students they are better able to offer equitable and effective instruction.

Getting to Know Students

Getting to know students is an essential part of an instructor's work in teaching and learning, given the important roles of social and affective dimensions (*Principle 3: Affective and social dimensions*). Understanding their students' interests and goals, prior knowledge, experiences, and needs will help instructors create an inclusive classroom environment and design or refine their class activities to create more effective learning experiences by connecting to and leveraging students' identity, sense of belonging, interests, and goals.

In many college classrooms, students come from a range of backgrounds and life experiences which may be very different from the background and experiences of the instructor. The reality is that as the diversity of students in higher education increases (see Chapter 2), so does the variation of students' prior knowledge and experience. Qualitative and quantitative data can help instructors get to know their students. Descriptive data, such as surveys or questionnaires, can be used to ask students about their experiences and potential challenges that they may face academically and personally. Instructors can use surveys to learn about students' backgrounds, characteristics, interests, previous experiences, and any other pieces of information that can assist in the learning process. One example is the PERTS Ascend survey and accompanying tools.[10] This system collects real-time information about how students are experiencing a course and provides the feedback to instructors to allow them to adjust their instruction and is

[10] More information about the PERTS Ascend survey is available at www.perts.net/ascend

based on research from the Student Experience Project (SEP) and Equity Accelerator[11] (Boucher et al., 2021).

Instructors can use disaggregated data about the students they teach coupled with surveys to gain access to information about their students, such as majors, experience with campus, first-generation status, work and family responsibilities outside of school, performance in prerequisite classes, and more, useful to instruction and course design. This can helpfully broaden the instructors' perspective on who is in their classroom. Public universities in California (University of California, Davis, University of California, Irvine, University of California, Santa Barbara, California State University system), Michigan, and Nebraska, among others, have piloted such "Know Your Students" approaches, often coupled with suggestions and materials for faculty to support their students from varied backgrounds. Some of the Know Your Students tools specifically highlight key metrics based on factors such as course grade and completion, bringing in data from all the times an instructor has taught a specific course while putting it in context of course instances and student factors. Most importantly these tools have specifically been designed to support individual faculty reflection on their teaching approaches and student outcomes, not as judgment of teaching effectiveness. The data shared are often only accessible to the individual faculty, further solidifying the non-judgmental focus of the approach. These more robust data gathering approaches may require support from departments or institutions and may be challenging for some instructors to implement. Other more accessible approaches to getting to know students are described in the sections below.

Chapter 8 further discusses ways that data of this sort can be used to inform continuous improvement on the instructor, academic unit, or institution level, and Chapter 9 gives more information on how institutions can support instructors to learn about their students and how the institutions can use data to improve policies and procedures.

Before Classes Begin

Prior to the first day of class, instructors can start the process of getting to know their students by reviewing any campus-provided data and introducing a pre-course survey. This survey can come in many forms, such as an online assessment or quiz, a paper questionnaire, or a private discussion post in the course's learning management system. Instructors can determine

---

[11] More information about the Indiana University Equity Accelerator and its connection to SEP is available at https://accelerateequity.org/resource/case-study-student-experience-project/ and more information about the SEP is available at https://s45004.pcdn.co/wp-content/uploads/Increasing-Equity-in-Student-Experience-Findings-from-a-National-Collaborative.pdf

what students already know or can do through low-stakes assessments, such as assignments that give students the opportunity to bridge their pre-knowledge and skills with what they will learn in a course (Ghanat et al., 2016; Landrum & Mullock, 2007; van Barneveld & DeWaard, 2021). As discussed above in the section "Help Students Build upon Their Knowledge and Lived Experiences," there are many strategies that can build on students' culture and prior experience. These tools can help instructors learn about who their students are, their goals for the course, and their learning needs. Pre-course surveys might include

- A demographic questionnaire with guided questions. The prompts are written to help the instructor get a better sense of the student's background and create a space for the student to share important information that they want their instructor to know. This can be a physical handout for an in-person class or an online activity for a large online class. Prompts can be as broad as "What should I know about you that would help me help you learn better?" or as specific as "What do you prefer to be called? What are your pronouns?"
- Questions about students' goals for the course or their learning preferences: "What do you want to get out of this course?" or "How do you learn best?" This can be done anonymously to encourage honest answers, and it can be incorporated into the first day of class.

Ultimately, the goal is for the instructor to gain a better understanding of who their students are and practice recognizing differences among our students. "Equitable practice and policies are designed to accommodate differences in the contexts of student's learning—not to treat all students the same" (Center for Urban Education, Rossier School of Education, 2015, p. 1). The information gathered from pre-course surveys can help the instructor build connections with students and consider how to better support students during the course.

Engaging with Students in and out of Class

Instructors can learn a great deal about their students just by talking to them. *Principle 2: Leveraging diverse interests, goals, knowledge, and experiences*, emphasizes the importance of developing connections with students. Students who have a working relationship with their instructors are more likely to be successful in class (Bolkan & Goodboy, 2009; Hagenauer & Volet, 2014). This relationship is especially crucial in higher-level classes in STEM (Micari & Pazos, 2012), and in more career-oriented programs such as nursing (Al-Hussami et al., 2011). Using active learning strategies and engaging students in group work can open up additional opportunities for instructors to engage with students informally during class time by circulating and listening in as students work on tasks and participate in small group discussions. Normalizing help-seeking behavior can change students' attitudes about their learning and improve their experiences with STEM courses (Oh, 2020; Won & Chang, 2024).

Office hours provide opportunities for instructors to provide help and to interact with their students as they discuss course material or other related interests in a less formal setting outside of class. Many students do not take advantage of professor office hours, sometimes because they are not familiar with the concept of office hours or are not sure if their presence would be welcomed. An important step in getting students to come to the office hours is to define the purpose of office hours—emphasizing that office hours are there to serve the students. These time blocks act as an extra opportunity for students to engage with professors outside of the main learning environment and can provide a venue for reflection on the course material. One way to make office hours more useful is to improve accessibility, and instructors can try to find creative ways to get students to reduce barriers to attendance. They might hold office hours in a laboratory, at the bookstore or coffee shop, or as a group meetup in a campus lounge (Gao et al., 2022; Guerrero & Rod, 2013; Stephens-Martinez & Railling, 2019). For professors in an online class, office hours typically tend to be held virtually. These too can be tailored to bring more students in. Virtual office hours can offer sessions that go over a fun weekly concept (e.g., review a new article relevant to something that was discussed in class or present a case study for participants to analyze).

A simple change from the name office hours to "student hours" can also help to emphasize who this time is for, and movement has begun to rename and re-envision office hours in this way, so as to better demonstrate their purpose to students (Benaduce & Brinn, 2024; Cafferty, 2021; Mowreader, 2023). It is important to acknowledge that some institutions may not require all faculty to conduct regular office hours or may not compensate them for this time. For instance, part-time or adjunct professors may only be required to teach their class during the assigned hours. Academic units and institutions may consider compensating part-time or adjunct faculty for the work they do outside of class, and that work should include office hours.

Midterm Check-ins

Check-ins can help to catch students who are at risk before too much time passes. A midterm check-in—perhaps using the learning management system with all students or asking a colleague to conduct a small-group evaluation—can help assess what is working and not working. Check-ins, whether midterm or at other times, can be valuable resources to both students and instructors. For students, these check-ins give them an active role in the learning environment. Furthermore, students who may be unaware of their low performance are given the opportunity to turn their grade around before the term is over (Overall & Marsh, 1979). For instructors, check-ins can guide course adjustments to meet students' interests and needs. Incorporating student feedback as a part of the curriculum also empowers students to have a voice and leads to continuous improvement in teaching (Diamond, 2004). Some data suggest that students who identify as first-generation, low-income, and/or underrepresented minoritized college students may benefit from this practice (Kitchen et al., 2020). Educators who implement midterm check-ins create opportunities to address hidden concerns that may be affecting students' learning (Bullock, 2003). Additionally, instructors who use check-ins report receiving more positive course evaluations at the end of the term (Keutzer, 1993). Note that check-ins also provide an opportunity to build relationships between the instructor and students. The importance of the instructor-student relationship is discussed in other sections of the chapter and relates to *Principle 3: Affective and social dimensions*.

Creating a Sense of Community and Belonging

As described in Chapter 4 in the section on *Principle 4: Identity and a sense of belonging*, sense of belonging refers to a student's personal relationships in a given environment and their feelings about being accepted, valued, included, and encouraged (Betz et al., 2021; Espinosa, 2011; Newell & Ulrich, 2022; White et al., 2020). Belonging influences academic motivation, academic achievement, and well-being in students, and has been shown to influence student retention and persistence (Cavanagh et al., 2018; Eddy et al., 2015; Hansen et al., 2023; Ream et al., 2014; Steele, 1997; Steele et al., 2002; Strayhorn, 2018; Trujillo & Tanner, 2014). Instructors can create opportunities for faculty-student and student-student engagements to build interpersonal relationships through class discussions and class group work. To build on students' disciplinary identity in classes, instructors can introduce contributions made by diverse groups of STEM professionals that reflect the demographics of students in the class, along with providing a class environment where students can talk and discuss STEM concepts. Instructors can also provide students with opportunities to share their reasons or personal interests for majoring in STEM especially during beginning-of-the-year class introductions.

Research in multiple disciplines shows that interventions designed to enhance students' sense of belonging can be powerful. Rainey et al. (2018) found four key factors to contribute to a sense of belonging for students (independent of race or gender): interpersonal relationships, perceived competence, personal interest, and science identity. The classroom climate has been shown to be a critical factor in computing disciplines, where students "are exposed to the skills and knowledge, knowledge presentation, and expectations about the kinds of people who belong (or not) in a degree program" (Barker et al., 2014, p. 2). Changing student contexts, such as by increasing cross-gender interactions in class and other approaches that challenge identity-based stereotypes, can improve feelings of belonging and student performance (Binning et al., 2020, 2024). Like normalizing help-seeking behavior as discussed above in the section on getting to know students, short interventions can let students know that it is normal, common, and usually temporary to have social and academic setbacks and challenges as they transition to college and can help them realize that challenges do not mean they should leave the field of STEM or their pursuit of higher education (LaCosse et al., 2020; Walton et al., 2023).

Instructors can also incorporate a sense of belonging and foster community building in class by implementing the use of undergraduate learning assistants (LAs) whose role is to assist students during class or discussion. Clements et al. found that incorporating LAs in a large introductory biology class promoted a "sense of belonging in science, technology, engineering, and mathematics (STEM) by decreasing feelings of isolation, serving as inspirational role models, clarifying progression through the STEM educational system, and helping students become more engaged and confident in their STEM-related knowledge and skills" (Clements et al., 2022, p. 1). Other studies also show increased belonging when courses use undergraduate LAs (Clements et al., 2022).

Highlighting communal values and goals can also affirm students' identities and increase their motivations through assignments that show students how STEM can help them achieve not just their agentic (personal/individual) values (e.g., Harackiewicz et al., 2016), but also their communal values (to help others/their community; Fuesting et al., 2017). Embedding specific practices, such as values-affirmation exercises in assignments or class activities, has also been shown to reduce stress and lift academic achievement—especially for under-resourced students in STEM (Cohen et al., 2006, 2009; Harackiewicz et al., 2014; Miyake et al., 2010; Sherman et al., 2013; Woolf et al., 2009). Values-affirmation activities provide the opportunity for students to reflect on and remind themselves of their core values and the identities and roles that matter most to them. These exercises are grounded in self-affirmation theory which has shown that reminding students of their adequacy, values, and identities helps them gain a sense of self-integrity, which in turn helps them stay motivated and engaged, and frees up mental resources to apply to their learning, boosting their academic achievement (Cohen & Sherman, 2014; Sherman et al., 2021). These effects are seen among all college students and especially women, lower income students, first-generation students, and racial-ethnic minority students (Diekman et al., 2010, 2011; Fuesting et al., 2017; Norman et al., 2022). These low-cost, evidence-based activities can be an explicit part of STEM courses and instructors' teaching practice.

Empowering Students to Take Control of Their Own Learning

When students see how their courses connect to their lives and feel a sense of ownership over their learning, they are able to be more engaged and have better outcomes. Instructors can design courses to increase student empowerment by helping students see the connections and see opportunities for their own agency.

Providing Opportunities for Student Agency

As STEM instructors and academic units engage in creating equitable learning experiences and reflect on their current approaches and future opportunities, it is crucial to give space, attention, and importance to student voices (Cook-Sather et al., 2014; Matthews, 2017; Mercer-Mapstone et al., 2017). Student agency refers to providing students/learners with the agency to contribute to their development by creating an environment where they are empowered to take control of their own learning. According to the Organisation for Economic Co-operation and Development (OECD), students gain an invaluable skill they can use throughout their lives when they have agency in their own learning (OECD, 2019).

To develop student agency, instructors can make students partners in their own learning, allowing them to engage in assignments based on their own interests or make choices between different instructor-designed assessments intended to measure their performance on course learning goals. Research has identified several themes in engaging students as partners in learning including the importance of reciprocity where all (instructors and students) have the ability to contribute equitably, although not necessarily in the same manner (Mercer-Mapstone et al., 2017). Having the ability to make decisions can increase student interest and motivation and can spur students to act as change agents (Brown & Nurser, 2011; Renaissance, n.d.). When instructors ask students to research a STEM topic related to their own identity or to explain how the STEM content affects them or their community personally, this can help shift the power dynamic to one where the student has more agency. This approach requires the instructor to accept that this type of learning is a process with less certain outcomes than they may be used to (Matthews, 2017). Furthermore, instructors can ask students to develop problem-based or case-based inquiries on situations they have encountered in their own lives. Professional learning communities (discussed in Chapter 9) can help instructors create appropriate content based on students' backgrounds that avoids biases and negative cures about social identity. All of these examples tie into *Principle 1: Active engagement* and *Principle 4: Identity and a sense of belonging.*

Metacognition and Self-reflection

Understanding how one's mind thinks and learns is a skill many undergraduate students are still developing. Data show that self-reflection and awareness of one's ability to learn is vital for improving academic performance (Tanner, 2012). However, the concept of metacognition is often one that many undergraduate students have yet to grasp (Stanton et al., 2019; Wang et al., 1990). Many studies have explored the role of metacognition in STEM learning (Avargil et al., 2018; Azevedo et al., 2017; Dori et al., 2018, Santangelo et al., 2021a).

STEM instructors play an important role in helping students recognize strategies that can advance their own learning. Research in chemistry has shown learning benefits of using metacognitive strategies with students (Cook et al., 2013; Lavi et al., 2019). Helping students better understand their own learning can be done in many ways, including (a) demonstrating how the instructors themselves use these strategies in their own practice and (b) providing opportunities for students to reflect on their learning experiences (Mitsea & Drigas, 2019; Tanner, 2012; Van Vliet et al., 2015). For the first idea above, an instructor can apply *Principle 2: Leveraging diverse interests, goals, knowledge, and experiences*, *Principle 3: Affective and social dimensions*, and *Principle 7: Intentionality and transparency* by sharing their academic journey with their students, including struggles, achievements, and ways of perseverance. Being transparent about their own experiences as a scholar can encourage students to be more resilient when challenges arise. Learning about a professional's pathway can help students see their instructors from a new perspective. It is important to remember, however, depending on the circumstances and the story recounted, that some experiences can also further alienate or marginalize students, so it is important for instructors to consider their student population in deciding what to share. Students can also benefit from learning, from near peers in particular, about which study strategies were useful, the mistakes they made, and how they overcame academic pitfalls. These narratives not only allow students to understand their instructors at a deeper level but also encourage students to reflect on their own STEM identities.

The Syllabus as a Useful Tool Throughout the Term

The syllabus is likely the first encounter students have with an instructor and their course, and it plays an important role in setting the tone and framing the experience. A learner-centered syllabus "is supportive and invites students to engage in and take ownership of their own learning" (Palmer et al., 2014, p. 20). In contrast, content-focused syllabi "make clear what the 'course will do' and what 'students will NOT do'" (Palmer et al., 2016, p. 36), and often focus on elements related to performance goals, like grades and late penalties. The extent to which a syllabus is learner centered can impact student engagement and learner outcomes, where more learner-centered syllabi are correlated with more equitable course outcomes (Eslami et al., 2024). Learner-centered syllabi also motivate students and get them excited about engaging in a course with an instructor (Palmer et al., 2016).

A well-crafted syllabus will ensure students have a positive learning experience and may alter how students perceive their instructors (Roberts, 2016). This is particularly true for underserved students (Luke et al., 2012). Socio-historical discrimination of students who are Black and Latina/o resulted in their unjust exclusion from educational opportunities (Ledesma & Fránquiz, 2015; Martin, 2000; Moses & Cobb, 2001). As college access increases for these students (Acevedo-Gil et al., 2015; Bowen & Bok, 1998), they continue to learn the social mores in higher education settings. Effective syllabi are warm and welcoming by including diversity-focused statements that invite students to interact with faculty while affirming students' beliefs that instructors expect them to succeed (Chandar et al., 2023; Eberly et al., 2001; Savaria & Monteiro, 2017; Slattery & Carlson, 2005).

A well-crafted syllabus helps demystify the academy's ambiguous and confusing processes, gives students access to the language of the institution, and improves their chances for success (Collins, 1997). Most students benefit from "full disclosure of the terms of success" (Collins, 1997, p. 2). Items that can be unclear in syllabi include details about effective work and study habits, definitions of terms such as office hours, and locations of important places, such as the bookstore and tutoring center. Content and style choices in a syllabus tell students whether or not instructors expect them to be successful and clarify how they can achieve this success (Collins, 1997; Slattery & Carlson, 2005). A thoughtfully designed syllabus is also inclusive. Bernardi et al.'s (2024) analysis of syllabi and undergraduate student surveys at a STEM institution identified key inclusive practices in course syllabi, including sharing the instructors' pronouns, incorporating readings authored by women and gender minority scholars, and using inclusivity statements. Through incorporating these practices in the syllabus, instructors can help create a more equitable and effective learning environment. The Center for Urban Education offers a syllabus review tool that can help instructors construct syllabi that are equitable and welcoming.[12]

The primary strategies that shift a content-focused syllabus to a learner-centered syllabus are (a) setting a tone that is positive, respectful, inviting, and directly addresses the student as a competent, engaged learner; (b) making the learning goals and outcomes a central, organizing element of the document that makes it clear what students will do to achieve the learning outcomes; and (c) including a schedule that provides transparency on course structure and grading by, for example, using regular due dates/times and describing the reasoning for those due dates and including more information than just course topics for each week/class period. Outlining the reasoning for due dates and feedback timing also provides a structure that facilitates flexibility in the event that the instructor and/or students need it.

SUMMARY

This chapter provides explanations and examples of the Principles presented in Chapter 4, illustrating practical approaches that instructors can use to improve the learning environments in their courses. The discussions in this chapter illustrate that the Principles together identify key elements of the learning environment that need to be attended to, and illustrate how the Principles can be integrated into these elements in ways that ensure that learning is equitable and student centered.

As noted at the start of the chapter, the Principles are interconnected. For example, making progress on *Principle 1: Active engagement* or *Principle 5: Multiple forms of data* will benefit from attention to other Principles such as *Principle 3: Affective and social dimensions* and *Principle 4: Identity and a sense of belonging*. That said, it is possible to start working toward implementing the Principles in small and/or specific ways. An instructor might choose to focus on a single Principle to start or try out some strategies on a small scale before completely redesigning an entire course. Implementing the Principles is best thought of as a continual process of reflection and refinement informed by data, rather than a quick journey to a single destination. The suite of Principles together offers a useful framework for continuing to refine and improve one's teaching over time.

The committee recognizes that instructors may be constrained in how much change they can implement in their courses, depending on their role, the resources and time they have available, the academic unit they are

[12] The Syllabus Review Guide can be downloaded at https://cue-equitytools.usc.edu/

in, and the institution. While most instructors will be able to take up the Principles in at least small ways, a larger transformation of courses may require changes to policies, practices, and priorities in the academic unit or institution within which the instructor sits. The next chapters discuss how academic units and institutions can support the kinds of instruction envisioned through the Principles. However, even before major changes happen at the unit or institution level, instructors may be able to join with like-minded individuals in their units or across units who are interested in using the Principles and support each other as they work to improve their courses. Through these kinds of collaborations, equity-minded instructors may be able to catalyze change not only in their own classrooms, but in their academic units and institutions.

The following conclusions are based on the discussions of the Principles in Chapters 4 and 5.

> *Conclusion 5.1: Designing, implementing, and improving equitable and effective learning experiences require (a) attention to instructional practices, (b) attention to the social dynamics in and culture of the classroom, and (c) repeated cycles of reflection and innovation by individual or groups of instructors.*

> *Conclusion 5.2: Using the Principles to achieve equitable and effective teaching requires careful consideration of how to design courses around desired learning goals and how to develop student-centered productive learning environments.*

6

Role of Academic Units in Achieving Equitable and Effective Teaching

This chapter discusses the critical role of the smallest "organizational unit" that is centered on one or more science, technology, engineering, and mathematics (STEM) disciplines within an institution: the academic unit. Often a department (but not always), these units serve as structures of influence within the institution, which relies on them to coordinate and manage the academic process (Edwards, 1999). They determine course offerings, curricula, and teaching assignments; set major and minor requirements; appoint and promote teaching and administrative staff; and manage essential services for faculty members and students. It has been estimated that 80% of administrative decisions on campuses are made at the unit level (Carroll & Wolverton, 2004). This chapter focuses on how academic units—operating as they do at a structural level—can provide opportunities for effective implementation of the Principles outlined in this document through changes to their cultures, policies, practices, and structures. Where we refer back to specific Principles for Equitable and Effective Teaching to make connections to content in this chapter we use the shorthand names presented in Table 4-1.

The academic unit plays an important role in shaping and understanding the impact of the collection of courses that comprises the curriculum, degree requirements, and other central elements that define the educational experience. This can include establishing a culture that supports inclusivity at all levels. As described in Chapter 5, there are many strategies that individual instructors can enact in their courses to put the Principles into action. An individual instructor enacting these Principles, however, will not address systemic inequities related to persistence in STEM majors and degree completion. Some of these inequities are related to groups of courses and the connections between them—the collective impact of courses that the academic unit is uniquely positioned to oversee and influence. Others of course relate to larger pars of the system, the institution and society.

The unit-designed curriculum that leads to a degree within a discipline is one such group of connected courses; others include prerequisite course sequences and certificate programs. While the academic unit plays an important role in establishing these collections of courses, such clustering is only one aspect of curriculum. Clemmons et al. (2022) developed the "Intended-Enacted-Experienced" curriculum model to name and describe these multiple aspects and show how they relate to one another; the three aspects defined by Clemmons et al. are intended curriculum, enacted curriculum, and experienced, curriculum. When academic units or a group of instructors decide on and develop outcomes for a degree or certificate or program—as in the curriculum defined above—they are defining the intended curriculum. When instructors design and teach courses that are part of that program and are structured to help students achieve the outcomes, they are defining the enacted curriculum. The courses that students take, the conflicts between those courses, and the way they make progress through the set of courses is the experienced curriculum (this is discussed further in Chapter 7). In addition, some refer to another type of curriculum, the "hidden" curriculum of disciplinary norms and behavioral expectations that are implicit and reinforce existing structures (Andarvazh et al., 2017). Addressing challenges at the curricular level requires groups of faculty members to work together within the academic unit to examine the structures that underlie these various aspects of the curriculum, in order to make sure the intended and enacted curricula are based on outcomes that are transparent to students and allow for multiple pathways that accommodate real student needs and situations.

The chapter begins with a section on academic and disciplinary culture to inform analysis and reflection on how decisions are made about what is taught, who teaches it, and what the expectations are for student learning and instructor behavior.

The second section in this chapter considers the Principles as a whole and the ways to use them, as described in Chapter 5, to articulate how academic units might productively reflect on their courses and curriculum with a lens toward the desired goals for student learning. Specifically, it discusses approaches academic units can take to consider their intended curriculum, how it is being enacted now, and how students are experiencing it today. These kinds of approaches can help illuminate choices that can have significant implications for equitable and effective teaching. The way that CTE programs are often designed to help students reach specific learning outcomes is presented as a model that might be more broadly applicable.

The third section of the chapter focuses on certain aspects of the experienced curriculum, including how sequences of courses interact and the problematic role of toxic course combinations and how foundational courses often function as weed-out courses. The chapter ends with a discussion of incentive and rewards, especially highlighting the ways that the departmental and academic cultures discussed at the start of the chapter influence the value placed on instruction, the supports the unit does or does not provide for instructors, and the ways that teaching is measured and rewarded.

Program-level learning outcomes can be both a central tenet of the intended curriculum (e.g., the outcome or degree defined by instructors) that ensures active engagement in disciplinary knowledge and a means for improving flexibility and transparency (related to *Principle 6: Flexibility and responsiveness* and *Principle 7: Intentionality and transparency*) of the enacted curriculum (e.g., the design and structure of the courses that are actually taught).

ACADEMIC UNITS AND THEIR ROLE IN EQUITABLE TEACHING

For the purpose of the discussion that follows, the following characteristics are considered to be essential functions of the academic unit:

- Control over a set of courses intended to be experienced by students as an integrated curriculum or program that contributes to a degree, certificate, or other terminal certification from the institution.
- Some level of curricular and/or budgetary responsibility, even if it is often located in a single administrator (department chair, division head, etc.).
- A role in the hiring, review, promotion, and tenure of faculty.

Other characteristics may include (depending on institution type)

- Responsibility for STEM courses that serve students enrolled predominantly in other units in the institution (either degree requirements or general education requirements).
- Responsibility for determining which courses are acceptable to receive transfer credit for majors.
- Responsibility for graduate student education in a related discipline or interdisciplinary field, with the goal of a postgraduate terminal degree.
- Shared research interests.

These academic units can be departments or divisions or schools; they can be associated with a single major, house multiple majors, or represent interdisciplinary STEM programs. In many colleges and universities, the academic unit is the department, which consists of a group of faculty members within a particular discipline (e.g., biology, physics, geoscience) led by a department head or chair. Another common academic unit is an interdisciplinary program, which brings together faculty from many different departments (e.g., environmental science, data science), and is typically led by a program director. Both departments and programs in these settings offer undergraduate majors and may offer graduate degrees. Community colleges often have academic units that are broad (e.g., a science department), or may have divisions or other functional units that perform the functions described above.

Regardless of the name and composition, academic units hold a unique position with regard to undergraduate education. The Commission on the Future of Undergraduate Education, as part of its examination of the current state of American undergraduate education, recommended that institutions must collaborate with academic units to make a systemic commitment to the improvement of undergraduate teaching (American Academy of Arts and Sciences, 2017). The planning, evaluation, and oversight of a disciplinary unit's collections of courses is naturally the responsibility of academic units, yet at many institutions, courses and how they are taught is not the top priority. While connected by a single or related disciplines, the faculty of academic units possess diverse interests, backgrounds, strengths, and experiences and each member has their own perspective on teaching.

In many cases, instructors are able to make decisions about their own courses and at most institutions teaching is evaluated at the level of individual faculty. However, students do not experience individual courses in a vacuum, but as a collection of courses within a curriculum designed by an academic unit. The ability to truly achieve both an equitable and effective learning experience requires understanding the interactions between the courses students take both simultaneously and sequentially, an understanding that the academic unit is particularly well positioned to achieve. As long as evaluations are focused exclusively on the single instructor and course, collective impacts will be overlooked. Yet the academic unit is well positioned to oversee the collection of courses experienced by students as a collective body that has the potential to achieve a culture of inclusivity and equity that could extend to individual classrooms. With the appropriate structures and culture, academic units could define learning goals and pedagogical approaches to improve the overall quality of the undergraduate learning experience.

The leader of the academic unit (e.g., department chair or program director) may play a leadership role within the university. In the case of department chairs, the position lies at a pivotal junction between the administration and the faculty and serves as a key connection between institutional priorities and faculty work by translating messages from senior institutional leaders, and interpreting questions, issues, and concerns expressed by faculty members (Austin, 2011; Bensimon et al., 2000; Chu, 2006). The role includes considerable duties and responsibilities to maintain the department as well as to meet the needs of the institution (Seagren et al., 1993). Department chairs can also deliberately work to create cultures in their units where equitable and effective teaching is valued and rewarded (Austin, 2011; Fairweather, 2008).

In the context of undergraduate teaching reform, while the policies and practices of academic units can have an immediate and lasting impact, research on their role as a lever for impacting equitable and effective teaching is an emerging area. The need to focus on this structural level is supported by the challenges inherent in sustaining change at the individual instructor level. Despite decades of scholarship to re-envision faculty roles and to develop rich, multisource systems for documenting teaching, these methods have not been broadly implemented into practice (Bernstein & Ginsberg, 2009; Bernstein & Huber, 2006; Glassick et al., 1997; Hutchings, 1996; Hutchings et al., 2011). Stated policies may not be reflected in actual practice, nor can they alone shift institutional structures and cultures to value teaching more highly. A richer, more complete process for transforming the assessment of effective and equitable teaching for tenure, promotion, and merit is necessary for systemic improvement of undergraduate education (Durodoye et al., 2020; Fairweather, 2002; Finkelstein et al., 2020; Heffernan, 2022; Huber, 2002; Kreitzer & Sweet-Cushman, 2021; National Academies of Sciences, Engineering, and Medicine [National Academies], 2020; Weaver et al., 2020). To promote more systemic change, there has been a shift away from funding isolated efforts within individual courses that do not require long-lasting reforms within academic institutions (Fairweather, 2008). Today many funders are designing solicitations with expectations for innovations to occur at scale and result in sustained institutional change (e.g., the National Science Foundation's solicitations through the Improving Undergraduate STEM Education IUSE: EDU program[1] and Howard Hughes Medical Institute's Inclusive Excellence Initiative[2]).

[1] More information about IUSE is available at https://new.nsf.gov/funding/opportunities/iuse-edu-improving-undergraduate-stem-education-directorate-stem

[2] More information about the Inclusive Excellence Initiative is available at https://www.hhmi.org/programs/inclusive-excellence-3

THE ROLE OF ACADEMIC AND DISCIPLINARY CULTURE IN SETTING EXPECTATIONS

Academic units are central to improving the quality of undergraduate education because they are the primary loci for cultural change. When students decide to major in a particular discipline, or to complete a program, they are signing on to more than a single course: they are committing to be part of the unit for multiple years. Therefore, no matter how strongly one might express the sentiment that "STEM disciplines are independent of culture," faculty or students experience its culture, created—in part—by these units being social organizations. An important component of this culture is "sense of belonging." If students feel like they belong and feel supported in developing their own identity within the discipline, they are more likely to be motivated to continue in their degree and to be successful in their courses. Research has shown that sense of belonging is correlated with performance (Master & Meltzoff, 2020) and is an important component of persistence through to degree completion. And yet, STEM programs can be perceived as "chilly" and "hostile," and students can sometimes find it hard to identify a supportive and helpful advisor or mentor. This type of culture can create barriers to access (Jorstad et al., 2017; Marín-Spiotta et al., 2020), and an increasing number of students report switching out of a STEM major because of a competitive and/or unsupportive culture (Hunter, 2019).

While STEM environments can be chilly and hostile for instructors as well, disciplinary culture is powerful and many faculty members identify with and are more deeply connected to their unit or discipline than their institution (Austin et al., 2009). Some faculty members can primarily exist in separate unit-based worlds and may perceive themselves as having the greatest influence within their unit and see their unit as the space in which they could best create change if desired (Kezar et al., 2015; Tagg, 2012).

Another way to think of "culture" is as part of a unit's "identity." Although identity is often seen as the collection of characteristics of an individual, academic units have identities, too. By considering their unit's identity, faculty can work together to develop a place where they and their students can belong (e.g., The AIP National Task Force to Elevate African American Representation in Undergraduate Physics & Astronomy, 2020). Academic units include faculty and instructors at all levels, staff, and students (in some cases, graduate and undergraduate). They include adjunct instructors whose primary place of "belonging" may be elsewhere. Developing a welcoming identity means working together to identify collective goals, where faculty talk about teaching and work together to improve their courses and create a place that makes students say, "Hey, I want to be part of that!"

Culture also extends to the curriculum. STEM instructors may have little experience discussing their ideas about teaching or creating courses with others. As scholars protected by academic freedom, they may feel that this right means that they can teach what they want without being challenged or facing repercussions. This is, however, a misinterpretation of the meaning of academic freedom. Academic freedom is intended to protect unexpected or unconventional research findings, not to justify poor teaching. The collective faculty (sometimes in collaboration with a disciplinary society or a professional association) holds responsibility for defining the general parameters that govern teaching expectations and approaches. As a body, they place constraints on the actions of instructors in their teaching to ensure that it fits within the professional norms of their disciplines. This means that academic units have the responsibility to define the appropriate general parameters of content and pedagogical approach within the courses for which they are responsible, providing faculty with the general parameters within which they exercise their freedom.

The role of professional standards and competence within academic freedom points to the important connection between academic units and professional societies and between disciplinary and departmental/unit culture. The culture within a unit may arise from the experience of the discipline's culture that is sometimes nurtured at professional meetings and within the practices of the larger profession (Austin, 1994, 1996; Finnegan & Gamson, 1996; Lee, 2007; Martin et al., 2015; Murzi et al., 2016, 2021; Tierney & Lanford, 2018). Therefore, sustained change at the unit level will be influenced by efforts to change or sustain the status quo in the larger discipline and profession.

Academic disciplines reflect conditions within the broader system of higher education. Chapter 2 briefly explores the history of how the higher education system in the United States has, from the beginning, involved systemic inequities based in part on a conception of science that is Western and Eurocentric (Mensah & Jackson, 2018; Morton et al., 2023). Throughout its development, the undergraduate curriculum has been both a reflection and perpetuation of its context. In the early history of the United States, most colonial college teachers were White men, who implemented a highly religious and Eurocentric curriculum consisting of languages (e.g., Greek, Latin) and the liberal arts (e.g., grammar, logic, arithmetic, geometry, music, etc.; Rudolph, 2021). In the late 1700s, some became interested in Europe's Enlightenment movement, which introduced the basic tenets of Western science and other secular philosophies (Chalmers, 2013). Enlightenment ideas of specialized inquiry and the unrestricted pursuit of knowledge spread to university instructors in the Americas, and colonial faculty who had typically taught according to the interests of their college leadership and the church now used the concept of intellectual freedom to set up space and structures for more clearly defined disciplinary study (Cetina, 1999). They accomplished this by drawing boundaries around themselves and those that were interested in similar subject matter, initiating "academic territories," which grew into what are now called academic disciplines (Becher & Trowler, 2001).

Within these boundaries, scholars developed preferences for ways of framing, knowing, and studying the subject matter drawn from European ideas (Abbott, 1988; Cetina, 1999; Gonzales, 2018; Traweek, 1993). Since not all people were invited into the creation of these disciplines, only some ideas and ways of knowing set the foundation. For example, the first international meeting of sociologists and organizers explicitly excluded Black and Indigenous thinkers, who had much to offer on social matters (Go, 2020). The exclusion of People of Color and their ideas meant that the disciplines were being formed with partial views of the world, all of which served as the basis for research that led to racial harm (e.g., forced sterilization, discriminatory immigration policies; Graves et al., 2022). This example is emblematic of the ways that many academic disciplines and their disciplinary societies perpetuated both racial and epistemic exclusion in ways that continue to haunt some of the disciplines today (Cech et al., 2017; Go, 2020; Gonzales et al., 2024c; Kerr, 2014; Settles et al., 2021; Wilder, 2013).

In tandem with the growth of the disciplines, faculty members believed themselves experts and made calls for freedom of intellectual inquiry (now known as academic freedom) to break away from the heavily guided, or directed, curricular and intellectual work imposed by college leaders (Tiede, 2015). Rather than teaching what college and religious leaders defined, faculty wanted to develop and oversee the curriculum, have more control over their work, and have a larger role in any decision making that would shape the conditions of their work (e.g., shared governance; Tiede, 2015). This became a feature of American post-secondary education—the emphasis on elective and general education and the central role of faculty in planning curricular sequences.

This role of the faculty results in a curriculum that is constantly in flux (e.g., the enacted curriculum combines foundational knowledge with contemporary advances and debates in the field, which reflects its increasing complexity; Lattuca & Brown, 2023; Lattuca & Stark, 2011). Curricular decisions by academic units may therefore reflect the dominant views in the discipline or compromises based on disagreements from faculty in different subdisciplines instead of thoughtful analysis of the desired learning outcomes for undergraduates. In addition, when making curriculum decisions, designing courses, and teaching (e.g., developing the intended curriculum and then realizing the enacted curriculum), instructors commonly rely on Western histories and narratives around how knowledge has been and should be created (Álvarez & Coolsaet, 2020; McGinty & Bang, 2016; Medin & Bang, 2014), privilege Western scientific methods (Page-Reeves et al., 2019; Smith, 2021), prioritize disciplinary methods and norms over interdisciplinary approaches (Gonzales et al., 2024c, Holley, 2009; O'Meara et al., 2023; Settles et al., 2021), and conceptualize student success in highly individualized ways (Brayboy, 2005; Lopez, 2021). These practices may be so deeply entrenched that they are unrecognized as conscious choices that faculty make in designing a curriculum, and changing these approaches requires deep, transformative change (Kania et al., 2018; Liera, 2023; Liera & Desir, 2023).

At the same time, faculty face external pressure as institutional leaders, legislators, and students increasingly call for curricular efficiencies that allow students to graduate quicker and reduce their debt burden (Lattuca & Brown, 2023). The desire for efficiencies often focuses on students who experience delays or challenges in making progress toward their degree. Misalignment occurs between the intended and experienced curricula due to inadequate coordination by the academic unit, irregular offerings of critical required courses, course combinations that produce high failure rates, "weed-out" introductory courses, and overall curricular complexity. Fixing this misalignment can better serve students in an equitable and affective manner and help avoid exacerbating inequities caused by students' social position, sense of belonging in a major or discipline, and a lack of awareness of the hidden curriculum (Andarvazh et al., 2017; Jackson, 1968; Snyder, 1971), all of which reduce persistence and increase time to degree. That is, course structures and graduation requirements can both convey academic content and knowledge of the discipline and be aligned with common pathways taken by students to providing students with realistic routes toward degrees that work for their personal circumstances.

FOCUS ON COURSE AND PROGRAM LEARNING OUTCOMES

As mentioned above, academic units have many factors and influences that go into the determination of the curriculum. One key influence should be the learning outcomes discussed extensively at the course level in Chapter 5 and that emerged out of *Principle 1: Active engagement*; one effective way to do this is to outline the scope of the disciplinary learning that students will actively engage in during their time in a course or program. In addition, articulation of program-level learning outcomes (PLOs) lays the foundation for *Principle 7: Intentionality and transparency* at the program level. Articulating PLOs ensures that success is clearly defined in terms of measurable outcomes, providing the endpoint that students will reach.

When considering program learning outcomes, *Principle 5: Multiple forms of data* is useful both for defining program outcomes and for measuring whether or not they are being met. In terms of defining program outcomes, academic units may consider qualitative data ranging from student goals to the needs/expectations of future employers, graduate schools, and professional schools. Program learning outcomes can be measured by taking key assessments in relevant courses to demonstrate different levels of achievement of specific PLOs disaggregated by different student groups. While this requires considerable commitment, regular data collection and measurement, sometimes achieved through a learning management system, can lead to substantial insights and improve overall program effectiveness.

Developing high-quality, well-articulated program-level outcomes is the work not of a single faculty member or department chair, but of all of the faculty and instructors who are engaged in a program. Engaging all instructors in the development of learning outcomes ensures that PLOs represent consensus, and that individual instructors will be more likely to make connections in their own courses to the program outcomes (Clark & Hsu, 2023). There are both challenges and opportunities to including a full range of instructor perspectives in these conversations. The example described in Box 6-1 shows how all members of a department can work together to audit their existing curriculum and determine what they as a group wish to prioritize for improvement across the courses offered. Though faculty often treat their courses as stand-alone entities, students experience courses collectively and benefit when they see coherence across the courses and also how each course is connected to the program outcomes.

Designing Curricula That Prepare Students for Life and Work

PLOs are the foundation of the intended curriculum and critical to transparency (*Principle 7: Intentionality and transparency*): they articulate the knowledge, skills, and dispositions expected of students who complete a given program. PLOs communicate to students, faculty, administrators, and external groups like accreditors and employers what constitutes mastery at that level in that discipline (Aloi et al., 2003).

When groups of instructors are working together to design (or redesign) the curriculum for a degree, major or minor program, or certificate, starting with program-level learning outcomes gives them the ability to use a backward design approach as discussed in Chapter 5 (Wiggins & McTighe, 2005) to align the intended and enacted curriculums. PLOs provide guidance for developing course-level learning outcomes that support students in achieving the program-level outcomes. In addition, program-level learning outcomes are the basis for the development of programmatic assessments and application of the outcomes in a curriculum matrix (see example in Figure 6-1 and associated material in Box 6-1) to determine where the outcomes are introduced, practiced, and needed throughout the curriculum (Clark & Hsu, 2023; Towns, 2010).

Program Learning Outcomes	Take 1 of 2				Take All																					
	GEOL 101: Physical Geology (4)		**GEOS 101:** Global Environmental Sci (4)		**GEOS 200:** Evolution of W. N. Am. (4)		**GEOS 212:** Water in the West (4)		**GEOS 220:** Seeing the Unseen: An Intro to Geophysics (4)		**GEOS 300:** Earth Materials (4)		**GEOS 313:** Geomorphology (4)		**GEOS 314:** Structural Geology (4)		**GEOS 315:** Sedimentation & Stratigraphy (4)		**GEOS 357:** Computation in Geosciences (3)		**GEOG 360:** Introduction to GIS (3)		**GEOS 482:** Experiences in Geoscience Field Studies (6)		**FF: GEOS 487** Capstone & Technical Communication (3)	
PLO 1: Integrate geoscientific principles to infer and demonstrate knowledge of Earth system processes	PF	B	PF	B	PF	D	PF	D	PF	P	PF	P	PF	P			PF	P	SF	B			PF	P	PF	P
PLO 2: Formulate geoscientific research questions and hypotheses and design ways to test them					PF	D	SF	B	SF	B	SF	D	SF	D	SF	B	SF	D	PF	P			PF	P		
PLO 3: Collect, process, analyze, and interpret various types of geoscientific data (e.g. field, lab, synthetic)	PF	B	SF	B	PF	P	SF	B	SF	B	PF	D	PF	P	PF	D	PF	P	PF	P	PF	D	PF	P		
PLO 4: Communicate scientific ideas & their societal relevance in a variety of formats (verbal, written, graphical) to diverse audiences	PF	B	SF	B	PF	D	SF	B	SF	D	PF	D	PF	D	SF	D	SF	B	SF	D	SF	D	PF	P	PF	P
PLO 5: Apply physics, chemistry, math, and computational methods to solve problems in the geosciences	SF	B			PF	D	PF	D	PF	P	PF	D	SF	D	PF	P	SF	B	PF	P	SF	D	PF	P		
PLO 6: Evaluate professional preparation in the field of geosciences and how it relates to their career goals					SF	B	SF	B	SF	B			SF	P	SF	B	SF	D			SF	D	PF	P	PF	P

FIGURE 6-1 Curriculum matrix sample for an undergraduate program in the geosciences.
NOTE: An example of a portion of a curriculum matrix for an undergraduate program in the geosciences showing program-level learning outcomes and courses in which they are addressed. NOTE: Each column has two designations. The first indicates the degree of emphasis placed on the outcome in the associated course: Primary Focus (PF); Secondary Focus (SF). The second indicates the level of competency the student will achieve in each course: Beginning (B); Developing (D); Proficient (P). For additional information on the use of matrices see https://serc.carleton.edu/departments/degree_programs/matrix.html
SOURCE: Committee generated based on information related to the National Association of Geoscience Teachers example in Box 6-1.

BOX 6-1
Using a Curriculum Matrix in the Geosciences

Since 2014, the National Association of Geoscience Teachers has been running a Traveling Workshops Program (TWP) to help geoscience departments in building stronger and more inclusive cultures, curricula, and courses (Egger & Robinson, 2024). A pair of experienced TWP facilitators works with department leaders to develop a workshop that meets the needs of the department, typically run over two days. One of the most common components of these workshops is developing and using a matrix to conduct a curriculum audit.

Prior to the workshop, facilitators ask participants (all faculty and instructors in a department or program) to do some homework. The homework includes a reflection prompt to envision a student who has successfully completed the program: what knowledge, skills, and dispositions does this student possess, and how has the program helped them develop these characteristics? The facilitators collect these reflections and share themes and commonalities with all participants. These commonalities are then used to develop or refine program learning outcomes. The characteristics of a successful student that are agreed upon by all participants are typically *skills*, whereas existing program outcomes may be focused on *content knowledge*, which participants tend to disagree on in that they differ about the relative importance of different topics.

The new and/or revised learning outcomes are then incorporated into a curriculum matrix. In general, the curriculum matrix is a way to visualize the extent to which a department is supporting its students in meeting their program learning outcomes: program learning outcomes are listed on one axis and individual courses on the other, and in each box, faculty can indicate whether a skill is introduced, developed, or expected in that course (the exact schema can vary).[a]

The initial completion of the matrix generates highly productive discussions. In some cases, groups realize that a learning outcome is over- or underemphasized in the existing curriculum, leading to changes in courses. In other cases, they realize that the program learning outcomes do not truly reflect what they emphasize in their courses, and they revise the outcomes. The matrix thus becomes a living document that instructors can continually refer and add to.

Importantly, these exercises are engaged in as a team—full participation of everyone in the department facilitates shared knowledge about what is going on in others' courses and is a critical component of successful implementation. In post-workshop evaluations, participants commonly mention the team approach with broad participation and the curriculum matrix as the most valuable things they learned. From 2014 to 2024, facilitators have led departments through the matrix approach activity at more than 80 institutions, including two-year colleges, small, private liberal arts schools, and large research universities.

[a]Figure 6-1 provides an example, and additional information on the use of matrices can be found at https://serc.carleton.edu/departments/degree_programs/matrix.html
SOURCE: Egger and Robinson (2024).

Well-articulated program outcomes allow for flexibility in the curriculum (related to *Principle 6: Flexibility and responsiveness*). Clear articulation between program outcomes and course outcomes allows courses to be designed, chosen, and incorporated into the curriculum on the basis of how they help students make progress toward the program outcomes rather than individual instructor preferences. This clear articulation can be particularly useful for transfer students, whose receiving institution may recognize that they have already met certain outcomes articulated by the intended curriculum through a different collection of courses taken at their previous institution, allowing them to make faster progress toward their degree. Creating a framework where students understand their course choices in terms of outcomes instead of required courses may potentially provide increased clarity, flexibility, and leveraging of prior knowledge and may help attract more students to enter and continue in the program (for more information see the discussion of specifications grading in Chapter 8). Students can also gain a level of ownership that builds directly on affective aspects of learning, social belonging, and identify as a STEM practitioner.

PLOs also describe the specific knowledge, skills, and dispositions for which the instructors in different STEM disciplines and at different institutions are responsible for writing and implementing, leading to variations (e.g., Clark & Hsu, 2023). In most STEM disciplines and at most institutions, instructors involved in a degree program are responsible for writing and implementing program learning outcomes, and thus the specific knowledge, skills, and dispositions described vary across institutions (e.g., Clark & Hsu, 2023). To ensure that program learning outcomes are meaningfully designed and incorporated throughout a degree program in an intentional and transparent way, lessons can be learned from STEM disciplines for which accrediting bodies provide expected learning outcomes and use those as one basis for program accreditation, including chemistry (e.g., Towns, 2010) and engineering (e.g., Spurlin et al., 2008).

Career and Technical Education Curricula Integrate Workforce Needs

What is now commonly referred to as "career and technical education" (CTE) is an important part of the higher educational STEM landscape and includes education that typically occurs at community colleges and prepares students for careers in health care, advanced manufacturing, biotechnology, and more. In many cases, graduates of CTE programs enter the workforce in jobs that are poised for advancement within that industry sector, providing that the student obtains, or already has, appropriate educational credentials. The incorporation of job-readiness programming in higher education has gone through significant historical shifts with the decline in vocational training programs and a more recent rise in CTE programs (Benavot, 1983; Kim, 2021). The current structure of CTE programs sometimes provides credentials that do not contribute to the requirements for four-year degrees; this can hamper students who wish to pursue further education after taking CTE courses (Hong et al., 2021; Soliz, 2023). Current CTE programs do often provide education on technical skills, employability skills (sometimes described as "soft skills"), and academic knowledge, and these could be recognized in transferable credentials that are parallel to those other students acquire through liberal arts or general educational courses (Lindsay et al., 2024; Matthews, 2022).

The Perkins Act and its subsequent reauthorization[3] (discussed in Chapter 2), together with other legislation and proposed government initiatives, has played a major role in supporting an "education-to-work pipeline," with particular impacts on CTE in community and technical colleges (Cushing et al., 2019). The 2006 Carl D. Perkins Career and Technical Education Improvement Act (Perkins IV)[4] was reauthorized and updated in 2018 as the Strengthening Career and Technical Education for the 21st Century Act.[5] The 2018 update included expansion of targeted funding (Edgerton, 2022). One important aspect of these acts is that, in contrast to the way that traditional disciplinary academic units make decisions about course content and major requirements, local educational agencies (LEAs) are required to assess the implementation of the curriculum. This puts the LEAs in the position of overseeing aspects of pedagogy, professional learning, and curriculum development (Cushing et al., 2019).

When educators work with local industry to identify the components of student education in those industries, students' ability to join the workforce with appropriate competencies can be significantly enhanced. Technical skills, professional "employability skills," and academic preparation are all needed for work. This results in a situation in which faculty at the instructional, department, and institutional levels benefit from gaining knowledge of the local industry and aligning their teaching methods, course and program content, and physical resources such as instrumentation and classroom spaces to align with the workforce needs of the community. This can be done in a variety of ways, including work with local advisory boards, the U.S. Department of Labor, state agencies, and directly with employers.

It is worth noting that in the context of this culture of alignment with community workforce needs, CTE at large is generally adaptive and nimble. This means that programs are able to adapt to evolving employer

[3] Carl D. Perkins Vocational and Technical Education Act, 20 U.S.C. § 2301 (1984).

[4] Carl D. Perkins Career and Technical Education Improvement Act, 20 U.S.C. § 2301 (2006).

[5] Strengthening Career and Technical Education for the 21st Century Act, 2018.

needs—for example, ensuring students acquire a variety of skills when technology or priorities change the hiring needs. CTE programs frequently recognize that employers value employees with more than just focused technical skills and include learning outcomes related to work skills as well. What used to be called "terminal" or "vocational" education is being transformed into what Kisker et al. likened to "a LEGO brick construction where degrees, certificates, and other non-degree credentials can be put together in various formations to enable educational and career advancement" (Kisker et al., 2023, p. 385). These curricular pathways, in recent years, have taken on the form of "stacked credentials" in which a student can, for example, work toward a certificate, and enter the workforce with entry-level skills while continuing toward a B.S. degree or higher. Likewise, a student with a non-CTE degree may return to school to obtain a certificate or an applied associate degree in order to gain job skills for career advancement or career transition.

CONSIDER CURRICULAR COMPLEXITY AND COHERENCE

There are several key factors beyond the desired learning outcomes to keep in mind when making decisions about curriculum. As alluded to above, these include the ways instructors will enact the curriculum and the ways that students will experience the curriculum. Specifically, it is very useful for academic units to consider their existing curriculum and what is and is not working well with it. Below we present one approach that can help with that process: curriculum audits. We then discuss the key role of foundational courses and the need to consider the academic and personal goals of the students taking the foundational courses in the units' purview. For example, chemistry departments frequently have many students in their foundational courses who intend to study life sciences, health, sciences, or engineering, among other fields, in addition to those who may be interested in specializing in chemistry. It is therefore valuable to consider the ways existing formats and structures for foundational courses do or do not serve the students who are likely to enroll. The role that foundational courses often play as "weed-out" courses that discourage students from pursuing further study is also an important consideration for curriculum design as is the potential for the toxic course combinations (such as students who take calculus and chemistry in their first term as undergraduate) discussed in the previous chapter.

Auditing Curricula

One tool that can be used to help achieve this is Curricular Analytics,[6] a freely available software program that allows users to create visualizations of curricula and model student pathways to identify bottlenecks and other friction points. The Curricular Analytics Project,[7] led by the Association for Undergraduate Education at Research Universities (UERU) uses this software in its study of the connection between curricular structure and complexity and student outcomes such as time to degree, retention, and graduation rates across multiple research universities and STEM disciplines. It is increasingly recognized that assessment professionals can play a critical role in designing, developing, and evaluating Curricular Analytics to improve student learning and reducing student dropouts (De Silva et al., 2024).

Attending to Foundational Courses

Foundational courses and course sequences are critical to student motivation, persistence, and sense of belonging (see Chapter 3 for more detail). The structure and offerings of these courses is often determined not by a single instructor, but by a group of instructors or an academic unit; therefore, coordination and collaboration are needed to make change (e.g., Herman et al., 2018; Matz et al., 2018). A collaborative environment is crucial to this type of transformation effort to improve STEM education and the formation of communities of practice can help instructors to work together to make instruction more student centered (Gehrke & Kezar, 2017; Kezar et al., 2017). Studies have examined how developing communities of practice for a particular course or course sequence can bring together the group of people involved to then work together toward implementing more equitable and effective practices (Benabentos et al., 2021; Tomkin et al., 2019). In cases where courses or course sequences are articulated between institutions (e.g., two-year and four-year transfer agreements) or taught at multiple campuses of a single institution, engaging instructors in a community of practice can enhance communication and coordination (Martinez et al., 2022). Some of the complexities that result from students taking courses across institutions and academic units is discussed further in the section on how to align policies and approaches later in this chapter. Communities of practice and their role in professional learning and development are discussed further in Chapter 8.

---

[6] More information on Curricular Analytics is available at https://curricularanalytics.org/home

[7] More information on the Curricular Analytics Project is available at https://www.ueru.org/ueru-communities/curricular-analytics-project

Foundational courses are often taught in multiple sections even on one campus in order to decrease class size, and some institutions use course coordinators to manage the overall effort (Bazett & Clough, 2021; Dettori & Settle, 2005; Sathianathan, 1997; Villalobos et al., 2021). An appropriately prepared course coordinator can help ensure that equitable and effective teaching practices are employed by all instructors, including teaching/learning assistants (Bressoud & Rasmussen, 2015). Coordinators can help instructors to work collectively and collaboratively, reflect on their pedagogical approaches, and share resources and approaches with each other. The instructional team can reflect upon the effectiveness of their approach. One retrospective study of course coordinators for introductory mathematics found three drivers for change that coordinators are equipped to offer when they understand the local context and culture: (a) provide materials and tools, (b) encourage collaboration and communication, and (c) encourage (and provide) professional development (Williams et al., 2022).

The strategies for course design described in Chapter 5 can be implemented in multi-section courses and course sequences as well. Implementation in these settings benefits from a systemic approach that includes all members of the instructional team. Strategies that show promise for reforming introductory STEM courses include

- Developing learning outcomes that span multiple cognitive levels and include higher-order thinking skills (Clark & Hsu, 2023).
- Engaging students in work that makes explicit connections between content and their lives (Canning et al., 2018; Gosselin et al., 2019; James & LaDue, 2021).
- Increasing course structure and the use of active learning strategies (Casey et al., 2023; Freeman et al., 2011; Haak et al., 2011).
- Incorporating mixed assessment methods and de-emphasizing high-stakes exams (Cotner & Ballen, 2017; Ralph et al., 2022).
- Engaging a faculty community with disaggregated student data in an equity mentoring format.

Making these changes in courses typically described as "weed-out" courses (Weston et al., 2019) may require a more substantial shift in culture. In many STEM fields, there are expectations that students will develop a common set of competencies by taking certain required courses that use predetermined assessment strategies in a specific sequence (e.g., Yother et al., 2022). Faculty members may worry that if their department adopts curricula or teaching methods that do not align with disciplinary norms and expectations, their program's reputation and prestige may suffer (e.g., O'Meara et al., 2023). Professional socialization may lead to the perpetuation of weed-out courses more so than explicit decisions by an academic unit or curriculum committee (Weston et al., 2019). As such, examining the assumptions about introductory courses and their roles, coupled with exploration of the data of who succeeds in these courses, can open the door to broader change in approach (Weston et al., 2019).

The role of mathematics requirements, course sequencing, and availability has received significant attention as a potential barrier to participation in STEM degrees. Within the past decade, a substantial portion of open-access institutions have implemented accelerated courses in developmental math, recognizing that early math coursework potentially serves as a roadblock not just to STEM degree attainment but to degree attainment broadly (e.g., Rutschow et al., 2019). Again, while much of this work focuses on the community college context, a series of longitudinal randomized controlled trials conducted among The City University of New York students observed that co-requisite math remediation has significantly greater benefits than just remediation (Logue et al., 2019). Rather than having students taking developmental courses first, co-requisite remediation involves placing underprepared students directly into college-level courses with co-requisite supports, such as in-class tutoring, online learning laboratories, or a supplemental class (Cerna et al., 2023). Some corequisite courses integrated culturally relevant instruction and the implementation of such courses increased students' understanding of the course content and their coursework engagement (Cerna et al., 2023). It is worth noting that co-requisite remediation requires a restructuring of the curriculum that creates new interdependencies and reconfigures students' trajectories. Understanding the impact of approaches such as co-requisite remediation and supporting students in navigating these new pathways ultimately requires coordination across disciplines and academic as well as an institutional commitment to support the necessary changes to processes, policies, and institutional structures.

ALIGN POLICIES AND APPROACHES

Academic units and programs typically include members at different ranks with a range of emphases in their roles. Unit leaders may not always feel they have the power or authority to advance change, yet they generally do have the ability to get issues onto the agenda of the unit. This ability could be used to elevate attention to instruction and to engage instructors in discussions about how existing policies do or do not contribute to equitable and effective teaching practices. As articulated in Chapter 4 under *Principle 6: Flexibility and responsiveness* and *Principle 7: Intentionality and transparency*, both formal policies and unspoken and implicit assumptions can influence many aspects of teaching and learning.

For example, many STEM units and disciplines have expectations about grading practices, academic integrity, and assignment deadlines that may have been established to support outdated views of standards and rigor. When norm-based grading (i.e., grading on a curve) is used to evaluate students relative to one another as opposed to evaluating whether or not each student has met the course learning goals, artificial factors determine the distribution of final grades in courses and systemic inequities are exacerbated (Bowen & Cooper, 2021). These policies and practices stand in the way of equitable and effective teaching for all students.

There is a growing body of literature on the design of assessments that are more equitable, are less prone to academic integrity violations, and maintain the standards expected by faculty (Denaro et al., 2022; Eslami et al., 2024; Webb & Paul, 2023). This includes alternative approaches to determining grades for students as described in Chapter 5, such as specifications grading, contract grading, mastery-based grading, and ungrading (Blum & Kohn, 2020; Nilson & Stanny, 2023; Tsoi et al., 2019).

Without buy-in and support of the unit leader and members, alignment between policies and teaching approaches at this structural level is not truly sustainable, and this can lead to significantly different teaching approaches across courses, which can cause confusion among students and sometimes outright conflict between instructors. It is not the case that everyone and every course needs to be the same, but it is desirable that approaches used are acceptable to the unit as a whole and that they collectively support defined unit goals. Ideally, the learning goals for the courses and programs would be communicated clearly and transparently to students, with an explanation as to how the variety of approaches is used achieve these goals. The Departmental Action Team approach described in Box 6-2 is one example of how members of an academic unit can work together to advance change and build consensus among unit members.

Another critical issue for academic units in the alignment of policies and approaches is the criteria for review, tenure, and promotion, which codifies what is valued within a faculty members' work (discussed further later in this chapter). For VITAL educators (visiting faculty, instructors, teaching assistants, adjunct faculty, and lecturers), these criteria are important for fair and equitable review of performance that could lead to contract renewal. For tenure-track faculty at research universities, criteria for promotion place a greater value on research productivity over teaching effectiveness. In many teaching-focused universities, substantial evidence of teaching is important, but may emphasize numerical scores on student evaluations or number of students served over the use of equitable and effective practices. In both cases, there is an external disincentive to modify or overhaul courses or change current teaching practices. While criteria for review are the purview of the unit, they can be modified to strengthen the role of effective and equitable teaching in review, tenure, and promotion.

BOX 6-2
How Departmental Action Teams Advance Equity

Departmental Action Teams (DATs) consist of fewer than ten faculty, students, and staff representing various groups within a single department that meet regularly for multiple semesters. Following an action research paradigm, DAT projects support the implementation and institutionalization of change and promote better use of research on learning and systemic change. They are driven by six core principles (Quan, 2019, as cited in DAT, n.d.; Reinholz et al., 2021, p. 130):

1. Students are partners in the educational process.
2. Work focuses on achieving collective positive outcomes.
3. Data collection, analysis, and interpretation inform decision making.
4. Collaboration between group members is enjoyable, productive, and rewarding.
5. Continuous improvement is an upheld practice.
6. Work is grounded in a commitment to equity, inclusion, and social justice.

DAT participants decide on the focus for their own group. External and internal facilitators with different expertise in research, institutional change, and supporting collaborative groups help the participants create a shared vision and goals. DAT participation can be incentivized in many ways, such as through service credit or performance reviews.

DATs have focused on various initiatives in the past (Ngai et al., 2020):

- Developing a new undergraduate major
- Developing assessment plans
- Monthly seminars on diversity, equity, and inclusion
- A multi-year undergraduate skills assessment
- Program-level student learning outcomes
- Ongoing study of student experiences for the purposes of improving the undergraduate program
- Implementation of a peer mentoring program

While most institutions have unit- and institution-based metrics and/or dashboards to look at student retention and completion, fewer have disaggregated those outcomes via student demographics and intersections of identities, and even fewer have shared disaggregated D, F, and withdraw rates and GPA outcomes or linked measures of incoming student opportunity with outcomes or social mobility measures (Shapiro & Tang, 2019). Tools to do this kind of data analysis are growing (see Chapter 9). In general, many of the approaches taken at the unit level can work at the institution level. Aggregating values but allowing the disaggregation by unit and student intersecting identities can point out inequities across the various parts of an institution. While a dashboard that is able to show the data and allow for multiple disaggregation is technically achievable, there is often no particular individual or group that is responsible for interrogating and making sense of such data. At some research universities, an individual in the office of undergraduate education, an educational effectiveness leader, and/or a leader of a teaching center may take on such an activity. Without adequate support from institutional leadership, unit leaders, and faculty, the potential impact of their work tends to be limited. Some institutions may choose to outsource such work to consultants and/or private companies, but often the level of inquiry will be shallow, focused primarily on retention and graduation, often with limited disaggregation and/or buy-in by academic units and their faculty. Others house these efforts in central offices (e.g., California State University System Office and the California Community Colleges Chancellor's Office), where such tools have been created and made widely accessible, but it has been less clear who is responsible for reviewing and acting on the data within academic units.

In considering the use of data to understand if change is successful, one example is the assessment of the impact of the Vision and Change in Undergraduate Biology initiative and the development of the Vision and Change document in the biological sciences. This document was written to provide guidance for pedagogy and curricula in U.S. undergraduate biology (American Association for the Advancement of Science, 2009). In addition, a validated tool for assessing the implementation of the Vision and Change document, the BioSkills Guide (Clemmons et al., 2020), has been developed and validated base on the input from biology faculty from various institutions. Vision and Change makes use of some approaches highlighted in this chapter such as the articulation of learning outcomes; it provides general outcomes from professionals in the field that can be used by departments to establish specific learning outcomes for their programs.

A study of Vision and Change efforts provided the ability to compare three levels of the curriculum: (a) intended curriculum, learning outcomes recommended at the program level or planned at the course level; (b) enacted curriculum, learning outcomes taught and/or assessed in a course; and (c) experienced curriculum, learning outcomes reported by students as being taught (Clemmons et al., 2022). This three-part curricular model is important to evaluate as it can help assess how effective the departmental level of reform (intended curriculum) can be at creating effective and equitable outcomes at the student level (experienced curriculum). A key step is for individual faculty to embrace the program outcomes that are expected to be in their course and commit to teaching them (enacted curriculum). Clemmons et al. used the BioSkills curriculum survey to evaluate the effectiveness of adoption of Vision and Change learning outcomes; their work provides evidence of how to measure this process, and a snapshot of the status of the initiative across a number of biology departments. As one might expect, there remains important work to be done to align the three levels of curriculum, but the power of this assessment illustrates important next steps. For example, Clemmons et al. were able to identify learning outcomes that are less likely to appear in assessments, pointing to the need for more work in this space. This is especially important given that they also found that the assessment of learning outcomes increased the likelihood of students recognizing that the particular learning outcomes were part of the course.

Consider Student Experiences Taking Courses Across Multiple Academic Units

The *enacted* curriculum sets a path for students to achieve an end goal—a credential, or degree. But students' variability in reaching the common end goal (e.g., the range of *experienced* curricula) is shaped by their individual momentum and trajectory. Students' academic momentum is influenced by their background, previous coursework, access to advising, sense of belonging, willingness to accrue debt, relationships with instructors, quality of teaching, and many other factors (Wang, 2017; Zhang, 2022). That is, academic momentum may be slowed when the experienced curriculum does not align with the intended curriculum. Many of the challenges lie in building the pathway across academic units and institutions; therefore, institutional leaders may need to coordinate cross-unit conversations to ensure alignment and consistency within their institution or to revisit articulation agreements with feeder colleges, which determine which courses transfer between institutions. The enacted and experienced curriculum spans academic units: essentially all STEM disciplines require some courses that are "outside" the discipline and department in which the major is housed. They also span institutions, as when students transfer or take a course at another institution. This is especially true for foundational course sequences that rely on each other in terms of content covered as well as courses in related fields that rely on specific cross-disciplinary content. For instance, the second general chemistry course builds on the first content and may also rely on math courses while introductory biology may build upon elements of the general chemistry courses. Data can be used to understand outcome consistency and coordination within and across courses enabling the majority of students taking the courses to engage in the relevant content in a fairly consistent manner. This consistency can be coupled with increased coordination between departments to improve the utility of introductory courses rather than acting as screens, or barriers, to student retention.

In biology, an introductory course may rely on both chemistry and mathematics knowledge for successful completion. Often these co- or prerequisite relationships have not been reviewed for years, and courses in other departments may have been used intentionally or unintentionally as "filters" to limit the students that get through instead of ensuring that students gain the knowledge and skills needed to be successful in the course (Weston et al., 2019). For example, some biology programs may require calculus and introductory chemistry courses before enrollment, even though the necessary chemistry is taught in the biology courses and calculus is not used at all. Analysis of the curriculum audits discussed above can sometimes make clear that the prerequisite courses were used as barriers to limit who enters. Data tools to measure, clarify, and support these types of situations and help identify ways to improve them are nascent. Some campuses have minimized these issues by adopting a "common goods" approach to the introductory STEM courses whereby the instructors teaching these courses come together as a community to uncover and minimize toxic course combinations and unnecessary co- and prerequisites. For example, to increase student retention and success in engineering, Wright State University developed a freshman-level engineering math course which did not require traditional math prerequisites and instead moved core engineering courses earlier in the program, redefining the way in which engineering math was taught (Klingbeil, 2004).

Potentially more challenging, but equally important, is the need to coordinate across not just academic units but entire institutions, especially between two-year and four-year institutions, in order to ensure support for transfer student success. Preparation for transfer and post-transfer success in STEM present several additional structural barriers that students must navigate. Unstructured curricular and programmatic choices have been a longstanding challenge (Bailey et al., 2015a; Van Noy et al., 2016). As alluded to above, this can lead students to take courses outside of what is required for their programs, which can delay them in receiving the credentials they are pursuing (Packard et al., 2012; Wang, 2020).

Measure Curricular Complexity to Understand Student Experiences

There are a number of emerging data approaches that can help address issues of curricular complexity. Student flows through the curriculum can be studied via Sankey diagrams, such as those enabled by the free UC Davis Ribbon tool[8] (Bradforth et al., 2015) or available in many popular visual-

[8] More information on the UC Davis Ribbon Tool is available at https://cee.ucdavis.edu/tools

ization programs (Tableau,[9] Power BI,[10] SAS® Visual Analytics[11]). These tools make it easy to understand how students flow in and out of majors, if there are discrepancies between different groups of students, and identify areas for further investigation. See examples in Chapter 9.

Program leaders can also examine the impact of pre- and co-requisite structures on time to degree. The UERU Curricular Analytics Project mentioned earlier has developed a tool to help identify potential curricular bottlenecks and also logistical ones where students who may not succeed in a course the first time can be delayed up to a year in their degree progression if that course is only offered during one term each academic year. Groups that manage curricular programs can also discuss in detail which skills and knowledge are needed for particular courses (e.g., which specific quantitative skills are expected for an upper-level course) and bring that information to other departments to determine which courses should be prerequisites and which are not necessary for students to be successful. This process can help streamline the curriculum and increase the intentionality and transparency of the curriculum to students (related to *Principle 7: Intentionality and transparency*). In addition, identifying the specific skills and knowledge can support alternative means for students to demonstrate mastery of skills to succeed in a course, which provides flexibility (related to *Principle 6: Flexibility and responsiveness*) for students who transfer or return to degree programs after time in the workforce.

Local as well as larger-scale sources of information (e.g., University of California Undergraduate Experience Survey,[12] National Survey of Student Engagement[13]) can be critical in determining if there are inequities that are manifesting in differences in retention, completion, and opportunity for students from different groups. Policies related to who is allowed to enter a major and how the criteria may change depending on route in (direct or transfer), course repeat policies, minimum grade for progress, registration and billing, accommodation approach, timing for course withdrawal, and more can affect different student groups differently, and may create challenges to equitable instruction and outcomes. All of these sources of information, along with more traditional measures (i.e., grades and completion rates) of who is succeeding in introductory courses and who is struggling, can paint a fuller picture and help identify areas for improvement.

---

[9] More information on Tableau is available at https://www.tableau.com/

[10] More information on Power BI is available at https://powerbi.microsoft.com/

[11] More information on SAS Visual Analytics is available at https://www.sas.com/en_us/software/visual-analytics.html

[12] More information about the University of California Undergraduate Experience Survey is available at https://www.ucop.edu/institutional-research-academic-planning/services/survey-services/UCUES.html

[13] https://nsse.indiana.edu/nsse/index.html

Another challenge in STEM education is ensuring that lower-division courses appropriately prepare students for their upper-division courses (e.g., Hsu et al., 2008). This design challenge involves taking a developmental approach, considering the knowledge and skills that students can develop in lower-division courses that they can build on in upper-division courses and subsequent careers. Successfully considering these challenges can help to make the learning goals for individual courses and for majors or programs more transparent as well as more intentional (*Principle 7: Intentionality and transparency*). This developmental approach can help identify the key concepts it is important for students to learn and facilitate a move away from a focus on content coverage (Petersen et al., 2020). When the volume of material students encounter is appropriate for the length of the course, students may be more able to develop deeper understanding of the content. In some academic units longstanding traditions about course ownership and the sense that coverage of certain topics must be preserved can make these types of changes challenging and significant changes to course content and teaching approaches are likely to require a collective department effort to have the potential for success.

The considerations around course content and sequencing are even more numerous at community colleges where students intend to transfer to multiple four-year institutions. While articulation agreements can facilitate this process by providing documentation of what courses will transfer for credit at the new institution, many are based on outdated learning outcomes that may not have been revisited for many years. Community college faculty may feel constrained in making changes to courses because they are articulated to a four-year college. Yet, instructors at the four-year college may be unaware of these agreements and never have the chance to look at syllabi and grant credit to students for having taken other equivalent courses solely because a previous agreement was already in place.

Evaluation of Teaching

The changes in teaching strategies and classroom culture needed to achieve equitable and effective teaching will originate with and be led by the instructor. This requires significant and sustained effort. Instructors have many competing demands on their time and in some contexts are incentivized and rewarded for their research. In most higher education contexts instructors are now playing an expanded role in supporting the increasingly nuanced aspects of the student experience. Instructors have long needed to support students by providing accommodations for learning or physical disabilities. They must also attend to providing appropriate support to students with diverse gender identities and students who are underserved due to race/ethnicity, transfer status, country of origin, and other factors.

These aspects are critically important in creating an inclusive and equitable learning environment in which all students can succeed. But they are also skills that an instructor must learn and must be able to attend to: in other words, these skills require more time and effort from an instructor than was assumed decades ago. Therefore, a message that these efforts are valued and supported by academic units and institutions can be a powerful motivator.

Equitable and effective teaching is unlikely to happen in a widespread manner if the work is not valued by academic units, considered in teaching evaluations, and rewarded equitably and reliably. The reliability and depth of information provided by student surveys is not robust enough to allow an academic unit to properly evaluate any given members teaching and newer approaches that give better insights into teaching behaviors have been proposed (discussed later in this section).

Institutions are beginning to explore "holistic" approaches to evaluate the increased complexities of teaching (Follmer Greenhoot et al., 2020; National Academies, 2020; Weaver et al., 2020). Holistic evaluation systems involve the collection of multiple forms of evidence which represent the perspective and voices of students, the instructor, and some third parties (Krishnan et al., 2022; Transforming Higher Education Multidimensional Evaluation of Teaching, n.d.). For example, the traditional method of collecting end-of-course student surveys can be one form of evidence representing the student voice and perspective. For instructors, evidence could include the course materials (e.g., the syllabus, course assessments, assignments) and samples of student work. Instructors can also solicit external letters describing the impact of their work, provide a citation for research articles or conference presentations on education research, or prepare a reflection on their teaching and how they plan to adjust in the future.

Third-party evidence can supplement both the instructor and student evidence. One common form of evidence is a peer observation carried out by another instructor or member of a teaching and learning center. The observation is facilitated by a validated observation tool or rubric (e.g., COPUS,[14] TDOP,[15] TQF,[16] CUE,[17] etc.) accompanied by a pre-observation discussion with the instructor to understand the structure and goals of the course. The observations themselves should span a substantial portion of the term in order to gain a complete understanding of the dynamics of the

[14] More information about the Classroom Observation Protocol for the Undergraduate STEM (COPUS) is available at https://cwsei.ubc.ca/resources/tools/copus.html

[15] More information about the Teaching Dimensions Observational Protocol (TDOP) is available at https://tdop.wceruw.org/

[16] More information about the Teaching Quality Framework (TQF) is available at https://www.colorado.edu/teaching-quality-framework/about-tqf

[17] More information about the tools developed by the Center for Urban Education (CUE) is available https://www.cue-tools.usc.edu/all-tools

course and the student-student and student-instructor interactions. Thus, in a holistic evaluation system, all of this evidence is placed in context and helps ensure a more complete and accurate evaluation.

Holistic evaluation systems can also include multiple categories (or dimensions) of work. These dimensions will depend on the alignment of the cultures and values of the unit or institution with its educational mission. The Benchmarks for Teaching Effectiveness approach at the University of Kansas (Follmer Greenhoot et al., 2020) has seven dimensions: goals, content, and alignment; teaching practices; class climate; achievement of learning outcomes; reflection and iterative growth; mentoring and advising; and involvement in teaching service, scholarship, or community. Each of these can be examined through more than one lens using varying forms of evidence. Another example is the Holistic Evaluation of Teaching (HET) project at UCLA[18] which uses four dimensions to define excellent teaching and carry out their evaluations: it engages students, is equitable, is learning centered and responsive, and strives to improve. As these examples show, there are different ways to define these dimensions in support of equitable and effective teaching.

To best support these efforts, the evaluation of teaching must support instructors with both the formative and summative feedback they need about student learning and about their teaching approaches (see discussions in Chapter 5 and National Academies, 2020). Students unfamiliar with the methods are sometimes resistant to active learning approaches (Andrews et al., 2020; Finelli et al., 2018; Tharayil et al., 2018). It has been reported that instructors making a transition to the teaching practices advocated in this report fear a decrease in students survey scores, and this could be a deterrent to faculty choosing to reform their teaching practices; however, there is little evidence to support such declines (Henderson et al., 2018).

SUMMARY

Academic units (e.g., departments, interdisciplinary programs, etc.) are located at a key level of institutional change where they may be able to influence the larger institutional policies and certainly can influence instructor behavior by providing opportunities, support, and incentives for attention to teaching and equity. When members of the academic unit agree to act collectively and come to agreement about course, major, or program learning outcomes, the unit provides a structure for developing a clearly articulated curricular structure that supports those learning outcomes. This in turn provides a solid foundation for creating equitable and effective teaching at

[18] More information about UCLA's Holistic Evaluation of Teaching HET project is available at https://teaching.ucla.edu/programs/holistic-evaluation-of-teaching/

the course level. It is the culture of the academic unit that acts as the starting point for increasing inclusion and fostering a welcoming environment at all levels. These units can then work to improve curriculum so that it is based on learning goals and provides equitable and effective pathways for students to achieve these goals.

Conclusion 6.1: Academic units hold collective responsibility for ensuring that (a) educators working under their auspices have the resources and supports they need to provide equitable and effective undergraduate science, technology, engineering, and mathematics (STEM) learning experiences, and (b) all learning experiences they oversee, including courses, laboratories, field experiences, research experiences, and prerequisite and other requirements for programs and majors, provide equitable and effective STEM learning experiences for students.

Conclusion 6.2: Making science, technology, engineering, and mathematics (STEM) instruction equitable and effective requires support and guidance from academic units and institutions in ways that balance instructors' autonomy with the goal of providing high-quality learning experiences in STEM for all students.

Conclusion 6.3: Academic units play a major role in decisions and policies about teaching, including how teaching is valued, recognized, evaluated, and rewarded. Academic unit decisions and policies related to teaching can impede or promote the implementation of equitable and effective teaching strategies.

Conclusion 6.4: Barriers to students' success can arise from the structure of course offerings and requirements. Students are often expected to take a sequence of science, technology, engineering, and mathematics courses, but the connections between the courses are often not well coordinated, and the overall goals for what students will learn across the sequence are not always well articulated.

Conclusion 6.5: Focused attention on examining and improving the coherence of learning goals across course sequences, programs, and majors can (a) help educators clarify the overall goals for students and facilitate improvements in individual courses, (b) facilitate alignment to the Principles for Equitable and Effective Instruction, (c) increase transparency and improve student outcomes, and (d) provide a means to collect data to assess the impact of curricular changes.

7

Student Pathways Through Undergraduate STEM Curricula

The committee recognizes that their charge could be narrowly interpreted as a series of issues related to individual science, technology, engineering, and mathematics (STEM) courses, but that this focus would miss many important aspects that influence whether students experience equitable and effective STEM learning experiences. Students experience undergraduate STEM education as a series of courses and also as an array of interconnected interactions with peers, advisors, academic units, and various offices in one or, often, more than one college or university. These student experiences vary due to institution type, discipline, program structure, and course format in addition to more student-specific academic and non-academic factors (e.g., race, gender, etc.; see Chapters 2 and 3 for a more detailed discussion). In the big picture the key issue to keep in mind is that less than half of undergraduates are first-time full-time college students coming straight from high school graduation (National Center for Education Statistics, 2024b).

This chapter explores some aspects of the varied, complex pathways students take through STEM education and into the workforce. It acknowledges that students do not simply follow the designed or enacted curriculum described in Chapter 6; instead, there is an experienced curriculum: the way students actually navigate undergraduate STEM curricula. The chapter begins with a discussion of the complex and nuanced concept of motivation to pursue STEM, recognizing that in this space student agency and employment goals interact with instructor and societal expectations. It links the concept of motivation to the Principles for Equitable and Effective Teaching, as described in Chapters 4 and 5. We then go on to discuss the development of a STEM identity. Along with this, we investigate some of the specific decision and transition points where students sometimes switch away from studying STEM, or from post-secondary education altogether. This includes a closer look at the transition from high school to college, transfer between institutions, and other aspects of student experiences in higher education institutions.

STUDENT MOTIVATION TO PURSUE STEM AND DEVELOPMENT OF STEM IDENTITY

Students choose to study STEM for a variety of reasons including in- and out-of-school experiences with STEM topics and issues before enrolling in college (*Principle 3: Affective and social dimensions*). Students may be motivated to study STEM because of their curiosity about the natural or designed world, a desire to use STEM to improve the world, and/or a perception about the value or importance of STEM in society. Recent empirical work has highlighted the roles of aspirations, motivation, and attitudes in STEM education and learning (e.g., Kujawa, 2013; Wang, 2013b; Wang et al., 2017a,b, 2020). One study found that students describe affective reasons for choosing to study STEM more frequently than they indicated a choice of STEM because it would lead to a future career or financial rewards (Thiry & Weston, 2019). Another key aspect of students' decisions to study STEM related to their perceptions of themselves and their abilities. Many students report having chosen a STEM major because they are interested in or passionate about the subject area, that they enjoy it, and are skilled in it. Research has shown that students' math and science self-efficacy beliefs positively predict intent to transfer into STEM fields (Wang et al., 2017a).

Development of a STEM identity can also influence students' choice of field of study and how they navigate that pathway, a topic captured in *Principle 4: Identity and a sense of belonging* (Rodriguez et al., 2019a; Teshera-Levye et al., 2023). One study explored how focusing on identity development can improve success in STEM for Women of Color (Rodriguez et al., 2017). This may be particularly important for community college students who often have less extensive ties to disciplinary research communities and sometimes have lower levels of STEM identity (Teshera-Levye et al., 2023). Additionally, studies have shown the importance of STEM instructors' mindset beliefs (Canning et al., 2022; Muenks et al., 2020; White et al., 2024). Emphasizing the potential for growth, rather than emphasizing fixed abilities, can indicate to students that STEM fields offer opportunities to fulfill their goals. Students can perceive when faculty endorse growth- versus fixed-mindset beliefs and designed STEM courses to advance communal and individual goals; these perceptions can increase students' interest in pursuing STEM education and careers (Fuesting et al., 2019).

TRANSITIONS FROM HIGH SCHOOL TO COLLEGE

The transition from high school to college is a critical period when students who feel underprepared may choose to switch out of intended STEM majors (Thiry, 2019). While many students take STEM courses in high school, the opportunity to access these courses and the preparation that they provide for success in undergraduate STEM education is not equitable. Studies have shown that exposure to STEM preparatory college coursework varies significantly by race, geography, and community income. *Call to Action for Science Education: Building Opportunity for the Future*, published by the National Academies in 2021, reported that

> high-poverty schools are at least 1.5 times as likely as low-poverty schools to lack advanced coursework in mathematics and science (NASEM, 2019a) [...] 14 percent of schools that enroll the fewest numbers of Black, Latino/a and Indigenous students offer no biology courses, 18 percent offer no chemistry courses and 31 percent offer no physics courses. In contrast, in schools that enroll large percentages of Black, Latino/a and Indigenous students, 29 percent offer no biology courses, 42 percent offer no chemistry courses, and 59 percent offer no physics courses. Similar trends in lack of access to science courses can be seen in schools enrolling significant numbers of students living at or below the poverty line (ExcelinEd, 2018). (pp. 30–31)

There are many strategies that programs and institutions use to try to mitigate the challenges of this transition and support students. Some programs target specific student populations (by geography, discipline, or student identity). while others are open to the wider student population. Out-of-school learning at museums and in clubs as well as internships provide students access to STEM while they are still in high school. Dual enrollment programs or options engage students in academic learning at the college level while they are in high school. Advising and mentoring approaches can help students learn about potential career options and postsecondary educational opportunities. State initiatives sometimes provide vocational learning opportunities. In this section we go into more detail on dual enrollment, bridge programs, and supports for students in foundational courses.

Dual Enrollment Courses and Programs

Dual enrollment courses and programs (also known as concurrent enrollment or dual credit) have emerged as a means of providing a way for students to enroll in college courses while still in high school. These courses and programs enable students to access advanced courses and to accrue college credits early and sometimes at a lower cost than for high school graduates. These opportunities expand student exposure to college STEM courses (Zinth, 2014, 2019), and in several states, they have an intentional focus on students who would otherwise not have access to them (e.g., Martinez et al., 2017). Dual enrollment courses and programs enable students interested in STEM to study topics that are not available to them in their regular course offerings and may help increase engagement, motivation, or STEM identity—all from choosing to participate in a special course. These courses can be offered at a high school, on a college campus, or online. Secondary school teachers may be required to have certain credentials (e.g., a master's degree in the discipline) to teach these courses. One type of dual enrollment program involves Early College High Schools, some of which have a specialized curriculum in STEM, health care, K–12 teacher preparation, or another more targeted field than the typical high school curriculum. These schools can get students on track to an undergraduate degree earlier by providing additional information about what college is like or more information about STEM pathways and careers. Exposure to college STEM courses via dual credit enrollment has been shown to have a significant positive impact on STEM career intention (Corin et al., 2020). Dual enrollment can also reduce total college tuition costs (which can be especially helpful for students and families in low-income brackets) and accelerate college degree attainment (Ison, 2022; Lee et al., 2022; Partridge et al., 2021; Schaller et al., 2023). However, dual enrollment can be challenging for students to navigate in multiple ways. There are equity issues to consider (Hooper & Harrington, 2022; Williams & Perry, 2020). Furthermore, students can encounter different expectations on college campuses than they would in their high schools (Hu & Chan, 2021). Dual enrollment experiences also may alter their previous college plans in unanticipated ways. For example, students may feel constrained to continue their education at in-state schools where they are more likely to be granted credit for courses already taken, since not all colleges or universities will accept the credits they have already earned or may restrict which of those credits can count toward their intended major. One study found that dual enrollment students were less likely to receive bachelor's degrees if they did not enter a four-year institution immediately after high school (Jagesic et al., 2022). Additional research would be beneficial to better understand the positive experiences some dual enrollment students have in career and technical education (CTE) pathways (Edmunds et al., 2024).

Bridge and First-Year Support Programs

Many institutions have found ways to support students by investing in STEM readiness, such as mathematics and introductory science courses. These programs provide supports ranging from pre-college engagement to wrap-around services in critical foundational courses (Hallet et al., 2020; Kezar & Kitchen, 2020).

Bridge programs are often designed to start in the summer to prepare students for fall courses and can include social events as well as academic initiatives. These programs are designed to build community and provide early intervention to support the performance of students who may benefit from additional resources to increase their ability to succeed in foundational courses (Bradford et al., 2021; Cabrera et al., 2013; Ghazzawi et al., 2021; Grace-Odeleye & Santiago, 2019; Hallett et al., 2020; Kallison & Stader, 2012; Palmer et al., 2010). Such initiatives may also be called a variation on Summer Success Academy, Summer Start, or Jump Start (e.g., Albany State University,[1] Coppin State University,[2] Durham Technical College,[3] George Washington University,[4] and Clemson University[5]).

There are also examples of strategies and models that can disrupt the culture of "weeding out" students in the collegiate space and provide the support and resources needed for all students to thrive equitably (Aizenman et al., 2022). California State University–Fresno, for example, proactively developed a learning community approach called the Building Opportunities through Networks of Discovery (BOND) program that has been proven to effectively support first-year student retention in STEM pathways (Cowan et al., 2022). This program counters the traditional "weed-out" method of education by fostering an environment where first-year students are supported, nurtured, and ultimately prepared for higher-level STEM courses. It provides students with dedicated courses on scientific method

---

[1] More information about the Summer Success Academy at Albany State University is available at https://www.asurams.edu/enrollment-management/summersuccess.php

[2] More information about the Summer Academic Success Academy at Coppin State University is available at https://www.coppin.edu/sasa

[3] More information about the Summer Success Academy at Durham Technical College is available at https://www.durhamtech.edu/summer-camps/summer-success-academy

[4] More information about the GW Jump Start Summer Success Program at George Washington University is available at https://studentsuccess.gwu.edu/gw-jump-start-summer-success-program

[5] More infomration about the Summer Start Program at Clemson University is available at https://www.clemson.edu/admissions/summer-start/index.html

and evidence use, a community, peer mentors, guaranteed enrollment in other courses, and technology support.[6]

NAVIGATING PATHWAYS WITHIN COLLEGE

Once students enroll at a college or university, there are several factors that define their experienced curriculum or the actual STEM pathway they end up taking (see Chapter 6 for more discussion of intended, enacted, and experiences curricula). These include the choices students make about how, when, and where to take courses, and their experiences within those courses. Poor teaching, poorly designed courses, and harsh grading practices influence their decisions to persist in STEM (Holland, 2019). Other factors include personal circumstances, finances, age, family status, and the availability of accessible learning opportunities (e.g., Holland et al., 2019b). As a result of these complex, interrelated factors, students do not always journey linearly through higher education. As discussed in Chapter 3, students take courses within an institution, vertically between institutions (e.g., transfer from a community college to a four-year institution), and laterally between institutions (e.g., transfer from one four-year institution to another). In this section, we explore the factors that influence student choice in the experienced curriculum—that is, how they navigate pathways of study in their undergraduate education.

STEM fields are known for their highly structured curriculum with specific prerequisites and a relatively rigid order in which courses need to be taken. This can require students to understand complexities of the *intended* curriculum (e.g., the program-level outcomes for a degree, certificate, or program developed by academic units or a group of instructors, as described in Chapter 6). Instructors may easily see why certain prerequisites are needed or understand why a major requires courses offered by another department or program (such as why engineering students need to take calculus, or why biology students need to take chemistry). However, it can be hard for students to understand when an entire course is required when only a fraction of the material is relevant for future study in their major. These requirements are not only confusing to students; they can at times develop a life of their own as tools that decrease enrollment in higher-level courses (when students fail or become discouraged by the course requirements they are sometimes not able to progress on in the curriculum). This complexity of the curriculum can have a number of unintended consequences, including added time to degree and decreased motivation to persist. A few studies have sought to analyze how students experience STEM education in terms

---

[6] More about the CSM BOND program at Fresno State University is available at https://csm.fresnostate.edu/fye/index.html

of the curricular structures they must navigate (e.g., Lattuca & Stark, 2009; Smart et al., 2000). Students make course choices with limited insight into why courses are ordered the way that they are. The research that is available suggests a murky relationship between the enacted and experienced curricula (Lattuca & Brown, 2023). Some institutions have developed support structures to help students identify and navigate pathways through the first couple years of college (see Box 7-1 for an example).

BOX 7-1
Pathway Reform at Fond du Lac Tribal and Community College

Fond du Lac Tribal and Community College (FDLTCC) in Cloquet, Minnesota, serves many Indigenous students. Its main tribal affiliation is with the Fond du Lac Band of Lake Superior Chippewa, although it also serves the Mille Lacs Band of Ojibwe of northeastern Minnesota (Goose, 2024). It offers biology and general sciences transfer pathway courses as well as nursing, health, and environmental sciences programs in addition to a few other programs.[a]

FDLTCC is one of the colleges in the 2017 Tribal College and University cohort of the Achieving the Dream (ATD) network. ATD works with institutions, mainly community colleges, to improve student success by supporting college instructors and administrators in making change.

The institution recently received a spotlight award from Achieving the Dream in recognition of the success they have had in several metrics that measure student progress through their educational journeys. Through multiple coordinated initiatives, they have achieved at-scale reform in an institution that serves students of many cultures, but with needs that are unique to the institution, location, and identities of staff and students.

Momentum metrics track student progress in the early years that are associated with their outcomes in the later years. Metrics are conceptually grouped into (a) credit momentum measuring the number of college-level credits student completed in their first year, (b) gateway course momentum measuring the take-and-pass rate of math and English courses in their first year, and (c) persistence momentum measuring the retention rate from the first to the second term (Belfield et al., 2019).

The college's targeted approach included the implementation of a co-requisite math model that resulted in increases in learning and outcomes and an elevated math enrollment. The model was designed to serve low enrollment in math class and low completion rates. Students receive maximum exposure to ideas and concepts through taking developmental math and college-level statistics in the same semester. The percentage of students placed in developmental education that completed college-level math satisfactorily increased from 18% in the 2019–2020 academic year to 61% in 2022–2023 (Achieving the Dream, 2024).

[a] https://fdltcc.edu/degrees-certificates/degree-programs/

When students must declare a major upon application to a college or university, they often do not yet understand what the course or career path would be like in that discipline. This may lead to a desire to change majors or may complicate their effort to navigate the curriculum. When students do not need to declare a major until later, they sometimes make choices that lead to a longer time to degree by not entering a course sequence at the start of their undergraduate studies. When more students would like to choose a major than the academic unit can support, the navigation gets even more complex. Some majors are designated as limited enrollment, sometimes with higher admissions standards, and students are restricted from choosing that program or encounter restrictions on joining after enrollment. Programs sometimes also choose to create other tools for managing the size of their programs, such as setting GPA requirements, rules about credit accrual, or academic performance in a specific course as a prerequisite for admission; these allow popular majors to manage their cohort and course sizes (Nespor, 2012). Student decisions to repeat content or to enroll (or avoid) remediation courses are potentially informed by their intended major and their goals. For example, students intending to go into medicine are often quite focused on GPA, and their grades in foundational STEM courses can influence whether they are able to continue in their chosen field (Barr et al., 2008; Lovecchio & Dundes, 2002; Stratton & Elam, 2014; Zhang et al., 2020). These gatekeeping mechanisms often rely on courses that cross departments, which can further complicate individual students' pathways (e.g., their experienced curriculum).

Because pathways do not necessarily follow a simple or linear progression, instructors and academic leaders would benefit from studying course sequences to identify the coursework structure of STEM majors. As an example, research on students' pathways into and through chemical engineering courses is shown in Figure 7-1. In their first year, students take introductory and advanced general chemistry before progressing into their chemical engineering coursework. At the start of their second year, students take an introductory chemical engineering course, an "assessment" course that includes the equivalency of a candidacy exam, and continue to progress through organic chemistry. The initial chemistry sequence is a prerequisite for introductory chemical engineering, the assessment, and the organic chemistry course. These courses then yield a set of complex interdependencies where organic chemistry is the gateway to chemical thermodynamics. To be off track in only one set of interdependencies threatens to forestall all of the momentum of a student in their coursework trajectory (Brown et al., 2023).

Another important element to consider is the impact of departmental, college, and university policies on student pathways through undergraduate STEM learning. Numerous policies can impact students' ability to begin or

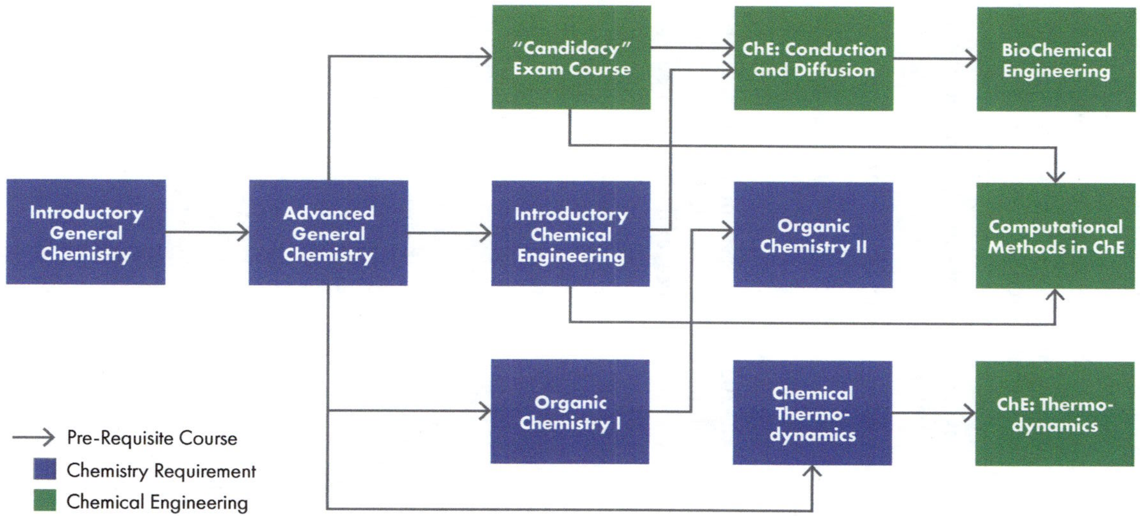

FIGURE 7-1 Chemistry prerequisite pathways for chemical engineering majors.
NOTE: The pathway illustrated only represents the chemistry requirements for chemical engineering majors and the requisite courses that they feed into. It does not include the equally complex general education and engineering gateway courses also required of students. Missing are required math course, other introductory STEM courses, and breadth courses that prepare students to participate as citizens in a pluralistic democracy.
SOURCE: Brown (2024).

continue studying STEM, such as those related to course withdrawal, who can repeat a course and what happens to the prior grade, cutoffs for course passing, number of times a course can be repeated, limited enrollment major policies, transfer articulations, and registration policies. Policies that mainly apply to instructors also influence the extent of equitable and effective effective teaching (e.g., policies around how teaching evaluation is considered in merit and promotion, approaches to evaluating teaching, expectations of teaching from various faculty types, teaching professional development expectations, resources for various levels of faculty that are teaching, representation of faculty in various teaching roles in teaching decisions).

The Role of Teaching and Learning Environments

Learning environments play a key role in student learning, with quantitative survey data and student interviews alike reinforcing that students frequently encounter gendered or chilly STEM learning environments (Jorstad et al., 2017; Marco-Bujosa et al., 2021; Wickersham & Wang, 2016). These issues extend across settings and modalities, including in-person and online courses, laboratory and field work experiences, and also as co-curricular activities (e.g., Cayubit, 2021; Kaufmann & Vallade, 2022). While most studies focus on classroom learning environments, undergraduates frequently engage in learning outside the classroom as well. Undergraduate research, internships, and co-ops are common (e.g., the University of Toronto's Professional Experience Year,[7] cooperative education at Drexel University,[8] the co-op program at Northeastern University,[9] etc.). These approaches provide opportunity for students to align experience in STEM alongside professionals in their disciplines and to clarify their career plans as they learn. They also provide an opportunity for students to build on their interests in alignment with *Principle 2: Leveraging diverse interests, goals, knowledge, and experiences.*

Another approach that builds on student interests, goals, knowledge, and experiences is competency-based education (CBE) or outcome-based education (Chappell et al., 2020; Morcke et al., 2013). CBE allows students to apply their prior knowledge and experience to attain a degree at a more customized pace depending on their existing skills and knowledge and level of support needs (Johnstone & Soares, 2014). CBE can sometimes

[7] More information about the Professional Experience Year is available at https://undergrad.engineering.utoronto.ca/experiential-learning/professional-experience-year-pey/

[8] More information about Drexel cooperative education is available at https://drexel.edu/academics/co-op

[9] More information about the co-op programs at Northeastern University is available at https://www.northeastern.edu/experiential-learning/co-op/

be a better fit for students who do not enjoy traditional classroom experiences and would prefer to have a more self-directed learning experience (Boyer et al., 2022). Some CBE programs are designed to help bridge the college-to-career gap by giving learners the real-world skills needed for their chosen profession. For example, South Texas College offered an Affordable Baccalaureate Program[10] beginning in 2014 that offered credit for prior learning and experiences, such as training taken in the military as well as a one-price model where students could take seven-week online courses toward a bachelor's degree in fields such as computer and information technologies, medical and health services, technology management, or nursing (Ashford, 2019). Western Governors University (WGU)[11] works entirely on a CBE model, where students pay a flat rate per session and can earn as many credits as desired in six months.[12] All courses are online but offered via two different models. One study by WGU faculty found that the "enhanced" online instruction afforded students more control over the order and pace of the content, and practice and assessments were given in various interactive formats (Gyll & Hayes, 2024).

Existing research on students' learning and progress along STEM pathways concentrates on the classroom environment and the role of faculty. These environments can shape a student's experience and success, with supportive, warmer environments resulting in greater beliefs in STEM skills (e.g., Stack Hankey et al., 2019) and greater success overall (Starobin et al., 2016). For commuter students, and for community college students in particular, the classroom space tends to be the major (if not the sole) venue where they engage with professors and fellow students on campus (Deil-Amen, 2011). While community colleges are generally credited for their positive learning environments (Allen et al., 2022), evidence is mixed concerning the environments in CTE and STEM disciplines. Bahr et al. (2023b) tested the impact of STEM environments on students leaving STEM, even if they have demonstrated potential in their STEM courses. The results of their multilevel logistic regression model of student data from the community college system in California indicated complex experiences with what they termed marginalizing environments. On the other hand, in a small qualitative study, Berhane et al. (2023) showed that, at community colleges, Black engineering students' persistence and transfer pathways

---

[10] More information about the Texas Affordable Baccalaureate Program is available at https://er.educause.edu/articles/2015/4/the-texas-affordable-baccalaureate-program

[11] More information about Western Governors University is available at https://nces.ed.gov/ipeds/institution-profile/433387

[12] More information about the course structure at Western Governors University is available at https://www.wgu.edu/student-experience.html

were bolstered by positive engineering environments that featured engaging classrooms and strong advisor support.

Research using observations and student interviews suggested that there are gendered experiences in CTE environments and that, although such environments seemed supportive on the surface, women encountered discriminatory interactions with peers. This ethnographic case study of CTE students conducted at a mid-Atlantic community college identified consistent female isolation, pedagogy denoted by traditional lecture and a competitive classroom environment, and gendered language that invalidated women and their learning (Lester, 2010; Lester et al., 2016, 2017). Because such experiences can make these students feel isolated and like they do not belong or cannot succeed in STEM fields, they may lose confidence or become disengaged in learning. These experiences have an added layer of complexity for students with intersecting identities, such as women of color. Choi's (2024) narrative interviews of 12 current or former community college Women of Color in STEM highlighted feelings of isolation as both women and students of color, as well as pushing back on both gender and cultural norms. While Allen et al. (2022) found similar gendered and racialized experiences based on interviews with Black women in STEM starting at community colleges, the experiences were concentrated at four-year institutions after they transferred. Regardless of where these experiences occur, People of Color and/or women pursuing STEM disciplines often draw on their resilience or other coping mechanisms to persist despite hostile learning environments (e.g., Acevedo et al., 2021). These results collectively show that teaching and learning in STEM remains a critical area in need of revisiting to improve student pathways and success among these groups.

Empirical work on community college environments in STEM also focuses on faculty attitudes, behaviors, and interactions. For instance, Packard et al. (2011) interviewed 30 female students in STEM from five community colleges. Drawing on a phenomenological approach, findings revealed faculty to be inspiring with their knowledge, experience, patience, caring nature, and encouragement for these students, which helped them learn and persist. Allen et al.'s (2022) grounded theory study using 120 student interviews in North Carolina showed that some students in STEM had positive classroom experiences like rewarding hands-on work and faculty who encouraged their pursuit and success in STEM at the community college. In another study, Jackson and Laanan (2015) applied hierarchical sequential regression models on survey data from community college STEM transfer students in a Midwest state. They found that students' experiences with community college faculty tended to yield a positive adjustment when transferring to a university. These findings collectively show that community college faculty tend to play a supportive role as students navigate STEM learning and pathways.

Career and Technical Education Programs

In the community college context, CTE and STEM are distinct areas with significant overlap (Michaels & Liu, 2020). STEM encompasses science, technology, engineering, and mathematics disciplinary areas and their subdisciplines and often denotes the academic transfer courses that are aimed at building toward advanced STEM studies at a four-year institution (Van Noy & Zeidenberg, 2017). CTE, also referred to as technical, occupational, and vocational education (Kisker et al., 2023), spans from high school into post-secondary education (Association for Career & Technical Education, 2024). CTE fields represent a wide range of disciplines (e.g., health, business, manufacturing, etc.) focused on developing knowledge and skills for industry needs.[13] CTE courses often lead to intact sub-baccalaureate-level credentials for entry into the workforce and are traditionally not intended for transfer. That is, "CTE provides occupational preparation and training that often culminates in shorter-term credentials such as certificates; it may or may not provide credits that can be used for college degrees" (Dalporto & Tessler, 2020). However, in more recent years, there has been a growth in offerings that are transferrable at the baccalaureate level (Bragg & Soler, 2017; Bragg et al., 2022; Makela et al., 2012; Wright-Kim, 2022).

There are various pathways through CTE programs, including traditional certificates, diplomas, associate degrees, and even bachelor's degrees (Van Noy & Zeidenberg, 2017). Stackable credentials, also known as microcredentials, are sequential qualifications that students can build on toward higher-level credentials (Bohn & McConville, 2018; Perea, 2020); they have also emerged in recent years as additional routes students can take in CTE. Career pathway programs represent yet another route, this one involving partnering with local employers; these do not require students to leave their jobs for extended periods (Soliz, 2023). Instead, career pathways provide interconnected programs that lead to credentials but allow students several points of departure if they want or need to return to their jobs (Soliz, 2023).

[13] Based on the definitions by the National Center for Education Statistics and the Association for Career & Technical Education, CTE includes agriculture, arts and communication, natural resources, business, management, finance, communications, computer and information sciences, construction, education, engineering, architecture, health sciences, hospitality, manufacturing, marketing, protective services, and transportation, to name a few (Association for Career & Technical Education, 2024; National Center for Education Statistics, n.d.a).

Experiences of Diverse Student Populations

Students' prior knowledge influences how they learn (as reflected in *Principle 2: Leveraging diverse interests, goals, knowledge, and experiences).* Students from underrepresented backgrounds in STEM pathways encounter disparate experiences within and beyond the classroom. Research reveals that students of color, women, older students, and individuals with mental health and learning challenges have unique experiences in these disciplines that impact how they learn, progress, and succeed (Hurtado et al., 2008) Empirical work focused on students of color in STEM, particularly Black and Latina/o students, is limited but growing. This line of research illuminates both similarities with and departures from general community college student experiences in STEM. Qaqish et al.'s (2020) narrative examination of interviews with 13 Black engineering students revealed the role of community with other students and faculty in facilitating their learning success. Qualitative research on Black students in STEM more broadly points to cultural, science, and STEM identities as important elements that bolster their experiences and success (García et al., 2019; Jackson Smith, 2016). With regard to Latina/o students, existing evidence tends to underscore the invalidation that this group encounters, such as unsupportive faculty, limited guidance and mentoring, and a lack of sense of belonging (Acevedo et al., 2021). This requires that these students rely on their resilience, resistance, and aspirations to persist in STEM (e.g., Acevedo et al., 2021; Choi, 2024; Lawson & Fong, 2024; Rincón et al., 2020). Rincón et al.'s (2020) phenomenological study based on 16 student interviews suggests that that Latinx students in STEM resisted institutional values and expectations that focused on the individual and instead centered community to persist. Similarly, women and women of color in STEM navigate complicated community college environments. Starobin and Laanan (2008) analyzed interviews with women in STEM from two community colleges and discovered that women encountered stereotypes or a lack of support in pursuing STEM.

Based on their analysis of a national sample from the Community College Student Experience Questionnaire, Strayhorn et al. (2013) revealed that Black and White students in STEM were more satisfied with their community college experience than Latina/o students. At the same time, the researchers also found that Latina/o students experienced greater learning gains compared with their White counterparts. These findings suggest that learning and experiences are complicated, warranting additional research to unpack these variations across different student identities. Berhane et al. (2023) conducted interviews and focus groups with Black community college students in engineering and found that the students felt largely supported by their community colleges, particularly with regard to personal connections with faculty and advisor guidance in navigating and securing institutional resources.

There is limited but growing work on adults in STEM/CTE programs. Based on interviews with 18 adult students who transferred from a community college into engineering at a four-year institution, Allen and Zhang (2016) found that these students were highly motivated and strategic in navigating STEM pathways and learning. These students still encounter learning environments that impact their sense of belonging and confidence in their ability to succeed, as revealed in Wang's (2020) mixed methods longitudinal study, which showed that adult students studying STEM pointed out that their classrooms and course activities tended to be designed with traditional-aged students in mind. As a result, being in learning spaces that do not recognize and value the adult student experience can negatively shaped those students' self-perceptions as learners. This is an opportunity for institutions and faculty to push back on these narratives of adult students and instead provide evidence and encouragement that they can equally succeed. For community college students, for whom there is a greater prevalence of non-academic responsibilities such as employment and family care (Baugus, 2019; Bryant, 2016; Deil-Amen, 2011; Lovell, 2014), payoff, fit, transferability, place, flexibility, and mobility are important factors (Wickersham, 2020).

The prevalence of students with disabilities in the undergraduate population continues to grow, and colleges and universities are working to adapt and support these students (Center for Higher Education Policy and Practice, 2024a; Chini, 20243; Perez & Johnston, 2023). The programs and supports currently available vary widely; disability resource or service centers are now common, and there has been an increase in focused support programs, sometimes at an additional cost on top of tuition (Aquino & Scott, 2022; Kravetz & Wax, 2023; Li et al., 2023; Rush, 2023; West, 2019). Online courses and programs for students with disabilities are also receiving increased attention (Center for Higher Education Policy and Practice, 2024b). Looking at a nationally representative sample of students with autism spectrum disorder who majored in STEM, Wei et al. (2014) found that these students were more likely to persist and transfer as compared with their counterparts in non-STEM fields. Interviews with CTE instructors at two community colleges revealed that faculty were challenged by how to best support disabled students during college and transition them successfully into the workforce, but they also recognized the value of the innovative insights these students can bring CTE programs and fields (Nachman, 2024). A study drawing on qualitative interviews with students with high-incidence disabilities in STEM (Friedensen et al., 2021) showed that those who had attended a community college commented on the strong support they received there.

Holistically supporting the diverse needs of underserved students in an equitable way requires funding, with external funding a common source. Federal programs such as TRIO (U.S. Department of Education, 2024b) and the Building Infrastructure Leading to Diversity (BUILD) initiative (U.S. Department of Health and Human Services, 2024) are examples of externally funded programs that provide wrap-around support for students as they enter and proceed through higher education. TRIO includes eight federal programs for low-income individuals, first-generation college students, and individuals with disabilities. The TRIO programs include Upward Bound Math-Science (U.S. Department of Education, 2023) and Ronald E. McNair Postbaccalaureate Achievement (U.S. Department of Education, 2024a), among others. Programs such as these can provide the practices that have been shown to promote STEM identity, persistence, and intention to proceed in STEM education and careers (Linn et al., 2015; National Academies, 2019b; Ramos et al., 2024), and academic success (Aikens et al., 2017; Atkins et al., 2020). Examples of these practices include undergraduate research experiences, mentoring, cultural events, and financial literacy support (U.S. Department of Education, 2024b). Similarly, the National Institutes of Health funds the BUILD initiative to promote innovative strategies and programming to enhance representation in biomedical research careers. Mentoring and exposure to research are focal points for these programs as well (U.S. Department of Health and Human Services, 2024). Collectively, these programs can address the holistic needs of students, supporting them in their learning pathway through undergraduate STEM and as they journey toward careers in STEM or postgraduate education. Despite their demonstrated successes, only a fraction (approximately 10% for TRIO programs) of eligible students have opportunities to participate in these types of externally funded programs (Kisker et al., 2023).

Other funding opportunities focus on more specific populations or disciplines. For example, Opportunities for Enhancing Diversity in the Geosciences, a funding program at the National Science Foundation, ran from 2001 to 2013, granting over $50 million to approximately 200 projects that spanned a wide range of audiences, institution types, and strategies (Karsten, 2019). One of the commonly employed strategies that addressed barriers to participation is building pathways into and through the geosciences at two-year colleges and Minority Serving Institutions. These pathways were only effective and sustained beyond the grant period, however, through authentic institutional collaborations and partnerships in which each institution (and their representatives) are full, respected partners.

TRANSFER BETWEEN INSTITUTIONS

Community colleges and technical colleges provide educational opportunities for a large segment of the U.S. population: nearly half of first-time undergraduate students are enrolled in community colleges (Mountjoy, 2022). Community colleges typically offer associate (two-year) degrees and certifications, and many community college students plan to transfer to four-year colleges/universities to obtain additional degrees (bachelor's, master's, and others). However, the transfer process looks different depending on the institutions involved, state educational policies, and other critical factors. In many cases students who have completed courses with good grades at community colleges have trouble receiving credit for these learning experiences at the institutions where they wish to transfer. These receiving institutions are often not as supportive in helping students to navigate continued STEM study as they could be (Jabbar et al., 2021; Thiry et al., 2023).

Without intentional support and intervention, students pursuing STEM education through community and technical colleges tend to experience low completion and transfer rates. For all fields of study, national data reveal that 16% of students who start at community colleges attained a bachelor's degree within six years, despite 80% saying that was their goal (Van Noy & Zeidenberg, 2017). National enrollment data show that of all transfer-aspiring students aiming to major in STEM, only about 12% ended up transferring into a STEM major within six years (Wang, 2013a). This pattern has persisted through the years, with some state-level estimates demonstrating STEM transfer to hover around 7% within three years of starting at community college and STEM bachelor's degree completion to be even lower among all entering transfer-intending students, barely 4% (Fink et al., 2024). There are disparities in outcomes based on race and ethnicity. Fink et al. (2024) report that states with the largest share of community college students who are low-income, Black, or older fall below the national average in terms of bachelor's completion rates. Velasco et al. (2024) report that 10% of Hispanic students who begin and finish at a baccalaureate-granting institution earn a degree in science and mathematics; only 6% of Hispanic students who transfer from a community college and graduate with a bachelor's degree earn one in a science or mathematics discipline.

These outcomes suggest a continued misalignment between access and success and reflect the fact that students' goals continue to be (dis)served by a highly complex, convoluted STEM transfer system (Taylor & Jain, 2017; Wang, 2020; Wickersham, 2020). This system includes limited program and/or transfer structures (Bailey et al., 2015a) and a variety of momentum and friction points (Wang, 2015, 2017). Research on post-STEM transfer experiences suggests one issue may be a less supportive overall environment for students at receiving institutions. Many students reported their community college spaces to be more positive and supportive than the institutions they transferred to (Allen et al., 2022). These findings align with work by Flores et al. (2023), who conducted 12 focus groups with students and found that transfer students pointed to faculty attitudes and behaviors in STEM that created a hierarchical, competitive environment that ultimately marginalized transfer students. Elliott and Lakin's (2020) research further revealed that faculty assumptions of students' prior knowledge resulted in a challenging and marginalizing learning environment. Focusing on computing in particular, Blaney et al. (2024) combined surveys and interviews with women transfer students in southern California, bringing to light a lack of receptive environments experienced by students in this discipline post transfer. This evidence largely indicates that post-transfer STEM learning spaces continue to present significant challenges and friction points for community college students.

Over the past few decades, many states have improved formal partnerships and articulation agreements in an attempt to facilitate transfer pathways and make it easier for students to continue their studies after community college. These partnerships and articulation agreements often serve as major factors that support pathways into STEM departments and majors. For example, in Georgia, core courses that are taken and passed at community colleges within the University System of Georgia (USG) automatically transfer to any four-year institution in the state system provided that the major is the same (University System of Georgia, n.d.). Two-year transfers from outside USG must go through equivalency evaluation to see if credits are accepted and used to satisfy degree requirements. For transfers from community colleges to private institutions, the policies and procedures will be determined at an institutional level. In recent years, transfers from technical colleges (where the focus is on learning technical skills and practicing skills needed for the workforce) to four-year institutions have increased, suggesting that students who desire higher education have myriad options as to how they access, navigate, and curate their educational pathways.

There are several aspects of articulation agreements that can be targeted to better support equitable and effective outcomes for students across institution types. Partnerships in which instructors form relationships across institutions and develop an understanding of the student populations and their goals and experiences seem to lead to better supports and resources to help students navigate the transfer and ultimately earn a degree. An example of this type of multi-institutional program pathway is the (STEM) network, a five-institution consortium consisting of two community colleges and three private institutions located on Long Island, New York. This consortium leverages the proximity of the five institutions to increase pathway opportunities for students within the network (Santangelo et al., 2021b). Faculty from all five institutions play a critical and intentional role in defining and refining pathways for students, and strong collaboration and shared input are central to the success of this model. Another factor to consider is that not all colleges and universities offer all STEM fields of study. This is of particular interest for engineering. Multiple examples exist of "3-2" programs for engineering where students start at one institution and take general education as well as science and mathematics prerequisite courses during their first three years of undergraduate study and then move to another institution for two years to enroll in engineering-specific courses and ultimately earn a bachelor's or master's engineering degree; these programs feed from hundreds of mainly small colleges to universities such as Columbia University and Washington University in St. Louis.[14]

SUMMARY

Numerous small studies have been done that help increase understanding of pathways different student populations take in and through undergraduate STEM. These studies often focus on the supports provided by specialized programs designed to help defined student populations. While the experiences and results are often positive much work remains to determine how to adapt the useful insights from this type of work to larger systemic change efforts. Numerous analyses have examined student motivation and transitions from high school to post-secondary education and found variations in experiences between different subpopulations of students. Dual enrollment, CTE programs, and transfer pathways all illustrate the critical role that community colleges play in the overall undergraduate STEM education system. Increased attention by instructors and administrators to the preferences and circumstance of the large numbers of students who participate in these programs and pathways has the potential to help improve STEM learning experiences for many students.

Conclusion 7.1: Students in science, technology, engineering, and mathematics take many paths through the higher education landscape, including transitions within and across institutions and use of different modalities (e.g., online courses, hybrid/hyflex, in-person instruction, internships, and apprenticeships). Although the availability of diverse pathways provides choices and options for students, it also increases the complexity of their learning experiences. This diversity in learning experiences makes it even more important to employ equitable and effective instructional practices that are responsive to students' interests and previous experiences.

---

[14] For example, https://brownschool.washu.edu/academics/3-2-programs/ and https://gustavus.edu/engineering/dual_degree.php

Conclusion 7.2: Transitions from high school to post-secondary and from community colleges to baccalaureate-granting institutions are challenging for students to navigate and can exacerbate existing inequities. Mentorship, guidance, and support can facilitate the transitions, help students make informed decisions about their own learning, and potentially address inequities.

Conclusion 7.3: Students who transfer between institutions are often required to repeat courses because policies at the receiving institution (a) do not accept credits due to a perceived lack of quality, (b) are complex and hard to navigate, and (c) do not provide sufficient orientation and support for newly arrived students. Obstacles to smooth transfer pathways from community colleges to baccalaureate-granting institutions are likely to disproportionately impact first-generation, low-income, or minoritized students, further exacerbating their already disproportionate representation.

Conclusion 7.4: Career and technical education (CTE) is an important pathway to science, technology, engineering, and mathematics jobs. CTE programs often work collaboratively with industry advisory boards and employers to gain information that instructors and academic units can use for the backward design of competency-based curricula.

8

Supporting Equitable and Effective Teaching Through Ongoing Professional Learning and Development

This chapter builds in particular on the work of Chapter 4, which details the seven Principles for Equitable and Effective Teaching in undergraduate undergraduate science, technology, engineering, and mathematics (STEM) education, and Chapter 5, which provides examples of ways instructors can use the Principles. The present chapter focuses on the critical importance of professional learning and development (PLD) as part of a process of continuous improvement that seeks to achieve equitable and effective teaching in undergraduate STEM education. Continuous improvement is the long-term collective effort to make sustainable change based on data collection and analysis informing iterative cycles of change (Langley et al., 2009; Park et al., 2013; Shakman et al., 2020). PLD for equitable and effective teaching can provide instructors and leaders with critical lessons, guidance, and supports needed to confidently apply the Principles to their teaching practice as a component of their work and their institution's work toward continuous improvement.

The term PLD describes a range of formal experiences such as seminars and conferences, as well as less formal activities such as reading groups or peer mentorship that grow knowledge, skills, and abilities through community interactions or via self-directed learning activities (Nowell et al., 2018). Professional learning is focused on the active, social, and inquiry-based learning involved within professional success and includes the ways that instructors grow based on collaboration, reflection, combinations of experiences, and curiosity without a formal course or predesigned trajectory (Caffarella & Zinn, 1999; Webster-Wright, 2009). Continued engagement in PLD in general has many advantages over one-time workshops

(Bickerstaff & Cormier, 2015), and many effective programs are modeled after the idea that one workshop or intensive experience is not sufficient, and, rather, it is constant engagement in a community that supports changes in behavior. Instructors within STEM education have reported engaging in ongoing informal discussion with peers in the community to be beneficial in the long term (Chadha, 2022). We discuss PLD here as a key tool in the effort to improve undergraduate STEM teaching.

This chapter starts with a discussion of the critical need for ongoing PLD for equitable and effective education throughout an instructor's teaching career. It calls out the need for professional learning to encompass all instructor types, including VITAL instructors and even undergraduate learning assistants. It then presents approaches to developing common values and goals for teaching. Following this, we present short comments on some of the topics on which STEM instructors need expertise, including how students learn, course design, classroom practices, and equitable and effective teaching strategies. The chapter goes on to discuss methods for professional learning, including both formal and informal approaches. The important role of community in professional learning is explored, primarily through examples of ways instructors can connect with each other through professional societies and national networks, as well as locally within their academic unit or institution. The current and potential future role of digital tools and communities in professional learning is specifically called out as a promising method. The chapter concludes with some specific thoughts on how PLD for equitable and effective education can play a role in preparing future faculty, including some research on graduate students. Together, all of these approaches can help support instructors in developing and using equity-minded pedagogical practices and thereby support institutional efforts toward continuous change.

CURRENT NEED FOR PROFESSIONAL LEARNING

Many instructors have never received formal instruction in how to teach, in the science of learning, in how to assess learning, or in proven strategies to use in the classroom, laboratory, etc. Given the research showing that professional development for instructors in linked to student success, there is a clear need to engage instructors in PLD (Biswas et al., 2022; Wheeler & Bach, 2021). Ongoing educational development can increase awareness of equitable teaching practices, increase self-efficacy in implementation, and provide opportunities for the instructor to obtain feedback about, reflect on, and refine their teaching practices (Biswas et al., 2022; DeChenne et al., 2015; Duncan et al., 2023; O'Leary et al., 2020; Wheeler & Bach, 2021).

Lack of Preparation for Instruction

Learning how to teach has not been part of the core curriculum of STEM graduate education historically, even for those who act as graduate teaching assistants or are interested in future academic careers that involve teaching undergraduates. Instructors may have not been exposed to or had the opportunity to learn equitable and effective STEM teaching approaches, or to learn evidence-based teaching approaches or how the teaching experience might vary at different types of institutions (Gardner & Jones, 2011). For instance, a significant number of Ph.D. graduates teaching at community college feel less prepared than their counterparts working at research universities (Mitic et al., 2023). Additionally, because of variability in the value that institutions place on being an effective teacher, graduate teaching assistants and postdoctoral fellows might be dissuaded from pursuing opportunities to improve their teaching. This lack of opportunity to develop teaching skills can lead to situations where novice instructors lack the resources, guidance, and support needed to develop skills for equitable and effective teaching. Such a lack results in instructors teaching the ways they were taught, even if those approaches are not effective or equitable.

This cycle has its roots in a history of hyperfocus on content delivery approaches, which conflict with what is now known about how people best learn (National Academies of Sciences, Engineering, and Medicine [National Academies], 2018). This focus on content delivery is bolstered not only by these patterns of teaching how the instruction was taught—patterns that could be shifted with the help of PLD—but by the pressure felt by instructors to cover as much content as possible in the discipline (Oleson & Hora, 2014). This pressure can lead to overreliance on didactic approaches such as lecturing. For some disciplines, expectations about what is required for accreditation might lead to instructors teaching for content coverage rather focusing on equitable student learning outcomes, but it is a common pressure across all STEM disciplines (Tripp et al., 2024). This pressure to focus on content can be much stronger than any guidance instructors may receive through their limited PLD experiences. The history and culture of high-stakes testing in STEM as a conventional practice continues to exist even when it has been shown to lead to inequities, and many faculty may not be fully aware of the implications of their testing decisions on student experiences (Ballen et al., 2017; Cotner & Ballen, 2017; Odom et al., 2021). Even when PLD is available to help instructors change their teaching, instructors at some colleges and universities may face political forces that make it more challenging to apply these approaches to support all students. Instructors who do not engage in PLD do not have the motivation or support to reflect on their current teaching practices and interrogate their assumptions or develop new, more evidence-based ways to teach.

Improving Your Teaching

Engaging in ongoing PLD can benefit both new and experienced STEM instructors in different settings. Through further educational development, instructors at colleges and universities across ranks and appointment types can come to more equitable approaches to teaching than perhaps they experienced in their own time as students. As described in *Principle 7: Intentionality and transparency*, enacting equitable and effective teaching requires institutions, departments, and disciplinary societies to adopt a level of intentionality to ensure its presence in the classroom. They can do this by creating a culture that embraces ongoing PLD for all instructors by providing institutional structures and supports for educational development that are systematic (e.g., through centers for teaching and learning) and supporting initiatives in which instructors are expected to engage as part of their job responsibilities. Disciplinary professional societies can play key roles in providing educational development in equitable and effective teaching within disciplinary contexts, which can support those facing local political challenges. For example, it can be easier for an instructor to present ideas for change that others have published or shared and ask their colleagues to consider them than to share their own ideas directly. The Vision and Change approach (explained more fully in Chapter 6) is one model that uses this strategy to push change in life science departments (American Association for the Advancement of Science, 2009).

There are also challenges to address around PLD. Competing priorities within institutional rewards systems, such as lack of emphasis on quality instruction and lack of accountability to teach equitably, can hinder implementation. Even when PLD is available to help instructors change their teaching, instructors at some colleges and universities may face various forces that make it more challenging to apply these approaches to support all students. Recognized barriers include the need for time to engage in the professional development itself, a lack or reward for engaging in PLD, and a pressure to devote time to other responsibilities (Addy et al., 2021b). There are also disparities in professional development opportunities between different types of institutions or for instructors with different roles or appointment types. For example, VITAL educators are often left out of PLD opportunities (discussed in more detail below). Although many students from two-year institutions enter the STEM workforce, PLD opportunities are often lacking for instructors who enter such institutions directly from industry or from non-teaching positions in academic research (Frady, 2023; Twombly & Townsend, 2008).

Some institutional promotion, tenure, and review systems may discourage exploration in teaching, and this could discourage some instructors from taking the initiative necessary to transforming their practice to more equitable teaching approaches. Because of this lack of emphasis on improving instruction, graduate students, postdoctoral fellows, and faculty might need to seek out campus resources such as centers for teaching and learning or external support on their own accord or never engage in PLD.

Successful PLD involves instructors knowing the diverse attributes that their learners bring to their courses and having the flexibility to adapt to the needs of changing student populations. Also important is instructor awareness of the powerful influence that various socio-psychological phenomena—such as growth mindset, sense of belonging, microaggressions, stereotype threat, imposter phenomenon, and trauma—can have on the classroom experiences of diverse learners as well as instructors themselves (related to *Principle 3: Affective and social dimensions*). Awareness and responsiveness to the diverse assets that students bring to their courses can support equitable and effective learning (see *Principle 2: Leveraging diverse interests, goals, knowledge, and experiences* and *Principle 4: Identity and a sense of belonging*). As instructors engage in ongoing PLD and reflect on their own identity, power, and privilege, they are better able to understand how those have an impact on their teaching and make changes in their approach to create an equitable, student-centered teaching environment.

Including and Supporting VITAL Educators

One of the communities that is often excluded from intentional PLD are VITAL instructors, despite the fact that they make up over two-thirds of post-secondary instructors (American Association of University Professors, 2023). Because of the nature of their positions, VITAL educators may not be involved in the planning or decision making about when and how PLD is offered and thus may not be able to participate or fully engage. In many cases, these instructors have fewer institutional connections and less available time to connect with their academic units. They may also be new to teaching and sometimes hired immediately prior to the start of a term, resulting in less time to properly prepare. In addition, their academic units and institutions may not be providing them with any incentive to improve and may have low expectations for their participation or not provide compensation for time spent on PLD. And yet, their professional development is critical to advancing equitable and effective teaching in STEM (e.g., Lee et al., 2023) and academic units can play critical roles in the PLD for VITAL educators. Kezar (2013) describes various departmental cultures and their influences through 25 case studies. The study describes three departments that provided VITAL instructors with an orientation, mentoring, and course materials such as syllabi, and teaching expectations to support student learning as having a "learning culture." When VITAL instructors are teaching courses with multiple sections that have coordinators there may be structures and opportunities to engage them in professional learning and development (more information on course coordinators and PLD is in the section on community, below). Box 8-1 discusses concentrated efforts to increase support for this important group of educators in other ways.

KEY TOPICS FOR PROFESSIONAL LEARNING

Much work has been done to understand how instructors learn how to teach effectively (Shulman, 1986). The development of subject matter and pedagogical knowledge concurrently is critical since the two knowledge areas influence each other and together contribute to the development of the instructors' pedagogical content knowledge, e.g., the knowledge of how to teach specific subject matter (Andrews et al., 2022; Grossman, 1990). Fernández-Balboa and Stiehl (1995) found that college instructors develop their expertise in teaching through their expanding understanding of the

BOX 8-1
Supporting VITAL Educators

The Pullias Center for Higher Education was established in 2012 and has led a number of initiatives and created resources that support the work of VITAL educators, which include visiting faculty, instructors, teaching assistants, adjunct faculty, and lecturers, as defined in Chapter 1. The Pullias Center has recognized institutions for their support for non-tenure-track faculty through the Delphi Project, which focuses on better understanding trends in the instructional workforce. Several of these institutions have notable initiatives for VITAL educators within STEM disciplines and can serve as models for other institutions.

Embry-Riddle Aeronautical University's Rothwell Center for Teaching and Learning Excellence is a professional development series for adjunct faculty. The Rothwell Center for Teaching and Learning supports their VITAL faculty by requiring PLD and facilitating several other initiatives such as short workshops (synchronous and asynchronous), individual consultations, and faculty learning communities.

The University of Colorado Boulder's Center for STEM Learning Transforming Education, Supporting Teaching and Learning Excellence (TRESTLE) initiative is "a 7-institution NSF-funded project to support improvements in undergraduate STEM education through (1) supporting course design projects, (2) enhancing educational expertise in departments, and (3) building communities within and across campuses to enhance the impact of local experts."[a] The TRESTLE initiative consisted of several components to support VITAL educators in STEM disciplines: discussion groups, annual symposia, course development grants, and faculty learning communities.

---

[a] https://www.colorado.edu/csl/trestle-0

subject matter, their learners, instructional strategies, the contexts in which they teach, and their teaching beliefs and purposes. There is some evidence that STEM instructors develop teaching expertise largely through their experiences teaching and through reflection on whether student outcomes have been achieved (Lawrie et al., 2019). PLD is important in that it can help instructors develop an understanding of how people learn, how to use teaching practices with intentionality, and how to use equitable and effective approaches. The key topics for professional learning discussed in this section are important in part because they address some of the major barriers to implementing the Principles for Equitable and Effective Teaching. Instructors describe major personal and institutional barriers that can interfere with the adoption of equitable and effective teaching (Addy et al., 2021b). Personal barriers include not having an awareness of inclusive teaching approaches, not being aware of the diversity that exists within their student population, not noticing the classroom climate or its impact on students, not recognizing their own biases, a fear about making mistakes, not wanting to change teaching practices, not wanting to be responsible, and not knowing how to manage student-student interactions that were not inclusive (Addy et al., 2021b).

Institutional barriers include not being supported by administration, inadequate resources (including professional development), lack of incentives as tied to institutional rewards systems that place less emphasis on effective teaching, lack of diversity among instructors, racism, and sexism, as well as a lack of time to discuss inclusive teaching (Addy et al., 2021b). Notably, the findings of Addy et al. (2021b) highlight how some instructors express needs for more PLD and rewards systems that value equitable teaching.

All instructors need guidance and support to overcome barriers and develop expertise and a level of comfort with evidence-based instructional practices. As Chapter 5 discusses, the Principles can be used to design for learning and to create productive student-centered learning environments. While all of the topics mentioned in Chapter 5 are relevant, here we focus on some central topics of PLD as it promotes equitable and effective teaching that have been studied in the context of professional learning: course design, classroom practices, and awareness of beliefs, values, and positionalities related to teaching.

All of these important topics of PLD address a critical aspect of equitable and effective teaching practices, which is that the instructor does not simply know about them but also knows how to implement them. PLD that centers on the following topic areas, as well as others, can provide opportunities for instructors to learn to apply practices that have the potential to interrupt inequitable experiences.

Course Design

When designing for learning, a critical step is to develop clear learning goals for students and to use these in course design. Decisions about course content are naturally included in course design, but many other features and approaches also need to be considered when planning a course. Yee et al. (2023c) did a national survey and a large analysis of providers (for more information see the section below on Providers of Professional Learning and Development) of PLD to mathematics instructors to see what topics were critical for novice graduate students taking on an instructor role. These topics have broader relevance for all instructors, and some of the most critical topics were identified as learning how to (a) notice and manage challenges to equity, access, and success among undergraduates; (b) initiate and sustain a productive classroom culture; (c) use strategies to promote and facilitate collaborative learning; (d) foster student in-class engagement; (e) use methods for promoting whole-class discussion; (f) recognize teaching practices that create a sense of belonging among students; and (g) implement self-assessment in teaching (Yee et al., 2023c, p. 421). This list was used for an exercise by PLD providers in which they were asked to consider the needs of novice mathematics instructors and to sort and rank the goals accordingly. For graduate students learning about how to teach, these topics can be covered by PLD providers and can often be made more specific by laboratory and course coordinators.

Classroom Practices

Beyond course content topics, providers also strive to develop equitable and effective classroom practices by (a) using direct instruction, (b) using teacher questioning, and (c) actively engaging students in their own learning (see Chapter 3 for more on active learning). Reinholz's (2023) book on equitable and effective teaching discusses how teaching practices might be changed using what, how, and why questions, while McConnell et al. (2017) provide specific methods to incorporate active learning strategies. Rogers et al. (2022) identified three specific active learning strategies that were natural on-ramps for novice instructors (quick poll, think-pair-share, and conceptually based teacher questioning tasks). The College Mathematics Instructor Development Source (CoMInDS, 2020) resource suite provides full lessons in chemistry, physics, statistics, and mathematics that help PLD providers (who educate teaching assistants) to incorporate equitable and effective classroom practices. CoMInDS emphasizes *Principle 7: Intentionality and transparency* in the use of PLD so that graduate students understand the learning goals and objective of the practices. Additional classroom practices are described in the section of Chapter 5 on actively engaging students.

Awareness of Beliefs, Values, and Positionalities Related to Teaching

A STEM instructor who recognizes issues of power and privilege that are present in their classrooms and how their own identities and biases can impact their teaching and student learning (related to *Principle 4: Identity and a sense of belonging*) is better prepared to create equitable and effective learning experiences that allow students from diverse backgrounds to thrive. Awareness of beliefs, values, and positionality can be gained through opportunities that engage instructors in self-reflection on their role in the classroom, and on the significance of their own race, gender identity, or culture and how these intersect with the reasons they choose and implement certain teaching approaches. Additionally, instructors can informally observe peers teaching in classrooms that integrate evidence-based practices that promote equity and reflect on their own instructional efforts. PLD opportunities that support instructor self-reflection and self-awareness have the potential to enhance their future implementation of inclusive teaching approaches. One example of an opportunity along these lines is the conference called Opening the Pathway held as part of a National Science Foundation (NSF) Advanced Technological Education project. At this conference, participants learned about inclusive and Universal Design for Learning (UDL)-aligned course design (UDL is described in Chapter 5). They discussed and practiced effective pedagogical practices such as case-based learning that could be used in an introductory biology course and that would be particularly useful for deaf and hard of hearing students (Orndorf et al., 2022).

Multiple approaches can help instructors take steps toward changing their practice to be more equitable. One important step is for instructors to reflect on their instructional practices (*Principle 5: Multiple forms of data*). Obtaining feedback on course materials and sites can support reflection. Other possibilities include gathering feedback from courses by administering formative, anonymous mid-course surveys with items focused on the equity-minded approaches implemented, or having small group instructional feedback sessions conducted for a course. Instructors can maintain a teaching journal to document their own observations about their equitable teaching. Observing peers can also support instructors in reflecting on their own practices, as well as informing discussions and PLD experiences. Mentorship or peer partnerships can also provide opportunities to discuss teaching with colleagues.

It can sometimes be arranged for experts to observe class sessions and provide insight to instructors. An important aspect of the holistic review of teaching discussed in Chapter 6 is classroom observation in which instructors get feedback on their pedagogy from experts. Multiple classroom observation protocols have been developed to formalize observations such as the Classroom Observation Protocol for Undergraduate STEM (Smith et al., 2013), Equity Quantified In Participation (EQUIP; Reinholz et al., 2020), and the Protocol for Advancing Inclusive Teaching Efforts (Addy et al., 2022). While they can be used to provide formative feedback to instructors there are challenges in using them in a systematic and consistent way.[1] Challenges may include lack of buy-in from instructors and departments if there is no clear institutional strategy making this a priority, as well as lack of staffing and capacity to conduct these observations. At research institutions, heavy emphasis on research can create competing priorities with teaching; thus, usage is not typically widespread.

Observations and reflections can provide insights into pedagogical approaches and foster changes to improve equitable and effective teaching. Instructors can use tools in a diagnostic manner to identify which teaching approaches they currently favor and to consider opportunities for future instructional techniques. Instructors can also set equity goals and reflect over time on how their practices have changed and whether they are achieving their aims.

TECHNOLOGY AND PROFESSIONAL LEARNING

The work of teaching has become increasingly multifaceted, demanding much more from an instructor than simply "delivering" content. As active learning and other evidence-based practices have become more understood and accepted as strategies to support student learning, instructors have started learning ways to adapt their teaching. The increasing use of technology in education has also required instructors to learn and adopt new tools, from gradebooks that are now part of a learning management system to smart screens/boards, computerized testing, simulations for laboratory experiments, the integration of artificial intelligence (AI) into assignments and curriculum design, and communication tools that have propelled hybrid and flex formats for courses. Instructional technologies will continue to emerge and change, requiring all educators to be continuously learning and adapting their teaching.

Technology will continue to impact teaching and learning, and instructors will need to continue to develop and refine their expertise on how to integrate such tools within their disciplinary contexts as new technologies emerge (Chai et al., 2013; Dysart & Weckerle, 2015; Fernández-Batanero et al., 2022; Jaipal-Jamani et al., 2015; Keengwe et al., 2010; Kyei-Blankson et al., 2009; Manduca et al., 2017; Mercader & Gairín, 2020). Research suggests that the degree to which instructors use digital tools depends on factors such as their knowledge of how to incorporate them within their particular contexts, the discipline in which they teach, and policies at their

[1] Matthew Hora, presentation to the Committee, 2023.

institution (Marcelo & Yot-Domínguez, 2019). The Technological Pedagogical Content Knowledge framework, developed by Mishra and Koehler (2006), focuses on how technology, subject matter, and pedagogy interact to contribute to an instructor's technological pedagogical content knowledge. Therefore, it is important to consider different perspectives prior to the development and implementation of any educational technology.

A variety of digital tools can support equitable and effective teaching, and multiple criteria can be used to evaluate if these tools are suitable for PLD. These include whether instructors are aware of the tool and are able to feasibly and equitably use the tool (i.e., access and use of the tool should not be limited to only certain instructors, reflecting *Principle 7: Intentionality and transparency*). Like developing expertise in teaching, instructors can develop knowledge in how to use technology in ways that are equitable and effective. One of the main tools licensed by institutions is the learning management system (e.g., Canvas, Moodle, Brightspace, Blackboard), used to develop courses and share core and supplemental learning resources. Institutions may have instructional technologists who provide PLD for instructors to gain proficiency in using learning management systems and other licensed technologies such as polling software, assessment delivery and grading systems, discussion boards, social annotation tools, media production, and more. For purposes of equity, access to PLD for learning management systems would not be limited to only those who show an interest but rather available to all faculty (related to *Principle 7: Intentionality and transparency*).

PLD is also needed to navigate the affordances and pitfalls of emergent and changing technologies, and the myriad implications for equity introduced. Online courses (synchronous and asynchronous) can sometimes provide more equitable access to students if they would not otherwise be able to take the course, and open educational resources can provide students more equitable access to course material. Even disruptive technologies such as generative AI have the potential to advance equity by providing more personalized learning opportunities for students. In the case of AI in particular, PLD can provide essential guidance to instructors as they incorporate these new tools into their classrooms. AI poses complex challenges to academic integrity across disciplines as well as opportunities for learning, suggesting the need for PLD that supports instructors in finding and using new, equitable approaches to address these challenges (Mahmud, 2024). Without sufficient instructor preparation, instructors may find themselves at a disadvantage when working with those students who have access to and knowledge of how to use AI tools; these students may also have an unfair advantage over other students (Bowen & Watson, 2024).

Whether courses are fully online, fully onsite, or somewhere in between, digital tools can be leveraged to promote equitable and effective teaching in STEM disciplines. One prominent example in STEM is how polling tools can advance learning by promoting more equitable participation and deeper engagement in course material. For example, polling tools can be useful in peer instruction approaches where students actively problem-solve independently, share their own ideas via the poll, and then discuss the question in small groups to deepen their learning through their interactions with peers (Crouch & Mazur, 2001; Mazur, 1997). Multiple digital learning tool initiatives have been designed to support equity. The Gates Foundation has funded multiple grants[2] in an effort to create better online learning environments. That work has explored questions such as should the online curriculum be modular or structured? Standardized or custom? Designed for the instructor or the student? On one level these may seem like graphic-user-interface questions, but they are central to both learning and equity, especially when considering the demographics of students using courseware in online environments.

Another initiative around courseware is Carnegie Mellon University's Open Learning Initiative,[3] which strives to democratize learning through collaborative online communities with asynchronous courses that are not based on college credit, starting or ending date, or certification/completion. These courses are expansive uses of online education that include virtual experiments and community collaboration. Using these and other digital technologies and resources—not just in themselves, but in equitable and inclusive ways—requires PLD that supports instructors in such pursuits.

Additionally, there are digital PLD resources that explicitly promote equity. For example, an online observation tool called EQUIP[4] can be used together with an external observer to improve equitable teaching in the classroom.

COMMUNITY IS A KEY COMPONENT OF SUPPORTING STEM INSTRUCTORS

We now turn to communities, which can play an important role in PLD experiences. They can allow instructors to engage with other STEM instructors within or across similar communities (such as discipline or institution type) and share teaching approaches (a form of the transparency called for in *Principle 7: Intentionality and transparency*). Furthermore, communities

---

[2] More information about one of the undergraduate-level courseware initiatives is available at https://www.coursewarechallenge.org/

[3] More information about the Open Learning Initiative is available at https://oli.cmu.edu/courses/

[4] More information about EQUIP is available at https://www.equip.ninja/about https://www.equip.ninja/

can serve as valuable structures that support understanding of the role of equity in teaching and learning (Goldstein et al., 2017).

A community can be defined as a group where a shared identity around a topic promotes the intent to steward a domain of knowledge and to sustain learning about it (Wenger et al., 2002). Communities can be formal or informal, large or small, and connect locally or virtually. They can exist for a short period of time or persist indefinitely. There are multiple ways in which communities facilitate communication and work to sustain change. Below we discuss communities in education research, communities around academic units, institutional communities including centers for teaching and learning, and larger communities of the sort that connect people working in the same discipline or focusing on similar pedagogical goals.

Community in the Education Literature

Multiple types of communities have been discussed in the literature on system change in higher education, these include Communities of Practice (CoP), Professional Learning Communities (PLCs), and Networked Improvement Communities (NICs). Box 8-3, below, on the Inclusive STEM Teaching Project, mentions another type of community, the Faculty Learning Communities (Cox, 2004, 2005; Russel et al., 2017; Vescio et al., 2008) or Learning Communities, which also come up in the literature. Some people also refer to communities of transformation in STEM reform, which are a variation of Communities of Practice designed to focus on the change aspect of the community (Gehrke & Kezar, 2016). While there is not a definitive line between each type of community, we present information below on three types to illustrate the range of options and perspectives (Lenning et al., 2013). Each of these types of communities can help instructors learn about pedagogy and how to flexibly and responsively support equitable and effective teaching and learning.

Communities of Practice

Communities of Practice are defined by three main pillars: domain (shared knowledge), practice (uses of shared knowledge), and community (identity and collaboration around the practice; Wenger, 1999). Together, these three pillars define a community of members who use the domain and practices to connect as a group (Wegner & Nückles, 2015). Reinholz et al.'s (2021b) study of change theory in undergraduate STEM education used a large meta-analysis to illustrate that CoPs are the most commonly used community structure. CoPs often develop naturally from the participants, rather than from external or administrative influence. As such, they can include members from multiple levels (e.g., both instructors and administrators), depending on the domain and practice. By virtue of including members from multiple levels, CoPs are capable of adapting and being flexible (reflecting aspects of *Principle 6: Flexibility and responsiveness*). For example, a community may coalesce around a common goal (here, equitable and effective teaching) and work together on developing strategies and trying out practices in the courses they teach. More specifically, multiple instructors may want to create similar lesson plans on a digital cloud so that they can draw upon each other's experiences, try new teaching methods to help their students, and have equitable access to each other's effective ideas. However, what one instructor values about a lessons' equitable or effective features may not be clear in the shared lesson plan. Thus, an instructor may not use the shared lesson plan or think it is not valuable. If enough CoP members do not value a certain instructor's resources, that instructor's contributions may be written off, which can damage the member's sense of belonging to the CoP. If communication is used appropriately, this tension could be resolved by having all shared lesson plans begin by providing clear learning objectives, relative to equitable and effective teaching. This example demonstrates how tensions in the potential stage can grow or diminish a CoP.

CoPs typically involve groups of 5 to 15 instructors who are part of a cohort or who are focusing on a particular topic (Cox, 2004). By coming together and focusing on the implementation of effective and equitable teaching practices, CoPs can provide instructors with an additional support system, which can bring in additional resources including reading and discussing books focused on effective and equitable practices. Such CoPs could be developed to accommodate whatever instructional, departmental, or institutional needs exist. For example, a smaller group of STEM instructors within a department who are teaching similar courses or similar students can gather to discuss their equitable teaching practices and might engage in formative peer observations of teaching to learn from one another. A broader STEM or community-wide Community of Practice could be facilitated in part through centers for teaching and learning that focus on equitable teaching practices across disciplines. These cross-disciplinary communities can enable both interdisciplinary learning and collaboration. A great asset of the CoPs is that if the participating instructors are given autonomy in the way they design their courses, they can be flexible and responsive to varying changes impacting students and institutional structures (related to *Principle 6: Flexibility and responsiveness*).

Professional Learning Communities

PLCs are teams of educators that share ideas to enhance teaching (Blankenship & Ruona, 2007; Dufour, 2004). They are common in K–12 schools and also found at colleges and universities (Stoll et al., 2006; Vescio et al., 2008). Some describe them as more formally organized than CoPs in that they can be implemented by administrators (Brummer et al., 2024). Facilitators of PLCs can provide resources, organize group work, and cultivate community while building opportunities for learning via reflection (Margalef & Roblin, 2018). One small study found that those who participated in PLCs reported increased energy, enjoyment, and engagement in work, as well as an opportunity to reflect on teaching and expand skills and knowledge. These participants also reported developing more self-confidence and achieving a sense of accomplishment (McAnuff-Gumbs & Verbeck, 2013). PLCs could be helpful in promoting the use of equitable and effective teaching, when instructors work together to meet a common teaching goal. One case study found that Communities of Practice could support the adaptation of material from another institution for use in teaching inquiry-based mathematics courses (Brummer et al., 2024).

Networked Improvement Communities

NICs emphasize evidence-based research, known as improvement science, as a means to change (Bryk et al., 2015). This approach grew out of the recognition that translating good ideas from one educational setting to another generally has a low probability of success (Bryk et al., 2015, p.6). Improvement science has evolved by focusing on specific problems and implementing clear goals and drivers to methodically improve at scalable speed (Feygin et al., 2020; LeMahieu et al., 2017). A NIC can grow participants' understanding, using evidence in the Plan-Do-Study-Act (PDSA) cycle (Bryk et al., 2011; Poole & Germain, 2022). In this model, administrators and instructors work together to address a problem using change regulated by manageable and achievable goals using PDSA cycles. If one instructor finds great success in a STEM course using a specific active learning method for equitable and effective teaching, rather than the coordinator requiring all instructors of the same course to implement that method, the instructor could work with three other instructors through a lesson study design (Fernandez & Chokshi, 2002) to identify what characteristics and what results seem transferable. Thus, a NIC can have participants from many levels, but the pace at which the community grows is regulated by evidence collected (*Principle 5: Multiple forms of data*) through tools such as the PDSA cycle.

Institution-Level Communities

At an institutional level, multiple approaches can support improvements to community around teaching including STEM education centers, science education specialists, and Centers for Teaching and Learning

(CTLs). Science education specialists work directly with instructors in the academic unit to understand and apply better teaching methods (Wieman, 2017). Many centers focused on STEM teaching and learning were formed in the early 2000s although some have since merged with CTLs[5] (Carlisle & Weaver, 2015; Horii et al., 2015). Centers for teaching and learning can foster community across academic units and act as change agents on campuses through their goals, programs, and services (Wright, 2023). CTLs can help colleges and universities embed PLD within the institutions' culture through their programs. This of course requires adequate staffing and funding, and some level of alignment with institutional values and strategic goals around equitable and effective education (Coryell, 2016; Hines, 2017; Sorcinelli, 2002). Increasing the numbers of instructors engaged with PLD efforts builds up expertise at the institution and may allow for the creation of self-sustaining and robust structures that support equitable and effective teaching.

The work of CTLs has been conceptualized across four dimensions: hub, incubator, temple, and sieve (POD Network, n.d.). This framework, derived from the work of Stevens et al. (2008), can be used to describe how a CTL can support equitable and effective STEM teaching within an institution. As a hub, a CTL can bring together STEM instructors to share equitable teaching approaches and learn from one another, as well as highlight evidence-based teaching across STEM disciplines. As an incubator, the various instructor-level initiatives that the CTL offers can cultivate instructors as change agents who share their practices more widely within and beyond their academic units. As a temple, the CTL can be a place where STEM instructors talk about teaching and become inspired about equitable and effective instructional practices. Lastly, as a sieve, CTLs can share evidence-based practices for equitable teaching in STEM to increase awareness and dissemination of such practices across their campuses. In performing one or any number of these functions, CTLs can be critical partners to instructors, departments, and institutions.

Below is a list of potential ways that CTLs and STEM centers can directly support STEM instructors in their implementation of equitable and effective practices for instructors as well as academic units. The list is inspired by the work of Wright (2023), Hines (2017), Coryell (2016), and Sorcinelli (2002):

- Local communities of practice for and among STEM instructors
- Workshop series
- Department-specific workshops

[5] More information about the Network of STEM Education Centers can be found at https://www.aplu.org/our-work/2-fostering-research-innovation/stem-education-centers-network/

- Panel discussions
- Community book reads
- Sharing of teaching strategies
- Open classrooms to formatively observe courses on campus
- Course design institutes
- Course transformation grants
- Intensive multi-day initiatives
- Teaching symposia and conferences
- Climate studies for STEM departments
- Student perspectives sessions
- Consultations with individual instructors or departments
- Formative reviews of teaching focused on equitable teaching practices
- Teaching fellowships

Community and Academic Units

Academic units play critical roles in establishing cultures that support equitable and effective teaching. They can take actions and create structures for PLD that support their instructors in engaging in equitable and effective teaching. Young, minoritized, or part-time instructors may face pushback from learners when teaching equitably and effectively; this can be compounded by student bias and job security concerns. It is important for academic leaders to recognize these possibilities and provide intentional support to instructors. As articulated in *Principle 4: Identity and a sense of belonging*, identity can influence the experiences of instructors as well as their learners.

The role of academic units in teaching is discussed extensively in Chapter 6; here the Committee presents a few examples of potential academic unit-level actions that in their experience have the potential to elevate and address equitable and effective teaching via attention to multiple Principles:

- Conducting climate studies and obtaining data on existing inequities to identify opportunities for improvement
- Creating and implementing departmental or program-level strategic and assessment plans
- Facilitating discussions at team meetings on equitable teaching practices across courses
- Holding department or program retreats focused on equity
- Engaging in curricular revision to advance equity
- Hiring science education or STEM education experts to work with instructors

- Facilitating speaker series on approaches to equitable and effective teaching
- Creating teaching circles consisting of instructors teaching similar courses
- Identifying instructors with knowledge of pedagogy and equity issues who can serve as mentors or peer advisors
- Supporting instructors by facilitating review of teaching in a low-stakes formative manner in which the instructor receives feedback designed to inform improvement from a peer or expert serving as a critical friend (more on the "critical friend" approach can be found in Chapter 9)
- Advertising notable teaching examples and helping other faculty to learn from them
- Identifying instructors with knowledge of pedagogy and equity issues who can serve as mentors or peer advisors **and rewarding them for that work**
- Adjusting faculty schedules to ensure collaboration time is possible
- Paying VITAL faculty to participate in PLD and/or communities of transformation
- General support from departmental and program leadership and tenured colleagues when instructors integrate equitable teaching approaches
- Fostering a culture of inquiry and continuous improvement

Achieving a culture where equitable and effective STEM teaching and learning is valued will be difficult if there is not buy-in at all levels of the institution and PLD is an expectation. The list above includes a variety of intentional steps that instructors, units, and institutions can take to support sustained engagement with PLD around equitable and effective teaching practices. For example, when academic units discuss what types of PLD they want to undergo as a unit, they could choose to include lessons on assessment practices and how to best collect data to support the work of their faculty. Instructors could set yearly goals to identify one thing they could do to support their learning as an equitable instructor and what they might want to accomplish in the next two or three years, given that some approaches can take more time to fully implement. Institutional leaders who publicly support these efforts can encourage instructors to work toward equitable and effective teaching approaches. They can also play a key role in decision making by encouraging the unit to develop goals around learning.

A more specific example builds on the discussion in Chapter 6 on coordinators for multi-section courses; units can consider how these coordinators can function as change agents within communities of practice. A study of 19 coordinators and 53 instructors across introductory mathematics courses at seven institutions described a framework that illuminates how coordinators approach their work, categorizing them into a humanistic-growth orientation or a resource-managerial orientation (Martinez et al., 2022). They propose embedding professional development into the course coordinator role, pointing out that coordinators are well positioned to facilitate changes to teaching approaches.

When unit and institutional leaders recognize the varying ways that instructors might react to reform methods, they can develop strategies to support those who are ready and eager to modify their practices as well as those who might benefit from more time and support as they start their change journey. Instructors may also vary in the type of activities and modalities they find useful and variations offered could include on-campus to online to hybrid experiences. Institutions and departments may choose to invest in their own resources in PLD or encourage instructors to participate in external initiatives and compensate and schedule accordingly. An internal analysis on existing and desired PLD support for implementing effective and equitable teaching can inform development of strategic plans and identify the appropriate resources.

National Networks

Multiple national initiatives have worked to improve teaching by college STEM instructors (see Boxes 8-2, 8-3, and 8-4) through the formation of networks based on the idea that participation in PLD can lead to more equitable student learning outcomes. National networks can provide community when an instructor is isolated in their discipline, institution, and/or approach to pedagogy. These connections can be powerful sources of motivation and moral support as well as professional learning. CoPs discussed in an earlier section of this chapter are sometimes integrated into the design of networks to allow instructors to share their approaches and learn from each other. These kinds of networks can link engaged STEM faculty in learning communities that allow them to learn from instructors who are also actively teaching. Communities around teaching can form in all sorts of organizations.

Organizations focused on one institution type include the Association of American Universities (AAU), and the Association of Public and Land-Grant Universities (APLU). Achieving the Dream and the American Association of Community Colleges are two of the groups focused on community college stakeholders. The AAU Undergraduate STEM Education Initiative has elevated attention to evidence-based teaching and system change at the department level[6] (Coleman et al., 2019). APLU has coordinated a network of STEM education centers focused on undergraduate learning, among many other relevant projects. The American Association of Colleges and Universities links across institution types and serves as a network for education in higher education. Their Project Kaleidoscope initiative, including its regional networks, is of particular relevance for undergraduate learning.[7]

Places where instructors connect and build community in their discipline include numerous associations large and small, some focused on teaching and some more general in nature. Examples include the American Chemical Society, American Geophysical Union, American Society for Engineering Education, National Association of Biology Teachers, American Association of Physics Teachers, and the National Association of Geoscience Teachers, among many others. The activities of these groups vary but they sometimes provide workshops for new or experienced instructors and often serve as venues for instructors to meet others with similar goals and share resources.

Funders of STEM education and STEM education research have also supported communities. For example, the Inclusive Excellence (IE) Initiatives of the Howard Hughes Medical Institute (HHMI), especially the IE3 cohort, linked educators across institutions in work groups in an effort to foster community as they worked together to increase institutional capacity for inclusion of all students in science.[8] The annual principal investigator (PI) meetings of the Improving Undergraduate STEM Education (IUSE) initiative of the National Science Foundation are also a source of community for education researchers and change agents.[9] The PI meetings[10] and central hub[11] of NSF's Advanced Technological Education (ATE) program are a source of community for community college instructors engaged with career and technical education and partnership with employers in their communities.

Another group of organizations and associations are those focused on a particular underrepresented group, such as the American Indian Science and Engineering Society and the Society for Advancing Chicanos and Native

---

[6] More information about the AAU Undergraduate STEM Education Initiative is available at https://www.aau.edu/education-community-impact/undergraduate-education/undergraduate-stem-education-initiative

[7] More information about the Kaleidoscope Project is available at https://www.aacu.org/initiatives/project-kaleidoscope

[8] More information about the IE3 initiative of the HHMI is available at https://www.hhmi.org/programs/inclusive-excellence-3

[9] More information about IUSE is available at https://aaas-iuse.org/

[10] More information about the National ATE Principal Investigators Conference is available at https://www.aacc.nche.edu/programs/advanced-technological-education/ate-conference/

[11] More information about ATE is available at https://atecentral.net/

Americans in Science, and the Society for Black Engineers. Another category of group includes particular initiatives such as the Community College Presidents' Initiative in STEM, Sloan Equity & Inclusion in STEM Introductory Courses, and many others. In this next section we present three selected examples of some initiatives that focus on professional learning about teaching. The Student Experience Project (SEP) described in Box 8-2 focuses on instructors, mostly within STEM disciplines, who participate in professional development focused on growth mindset, belonging, revised

BOX 8-2
The Student Experience Project

SEP, led by the APLU, the Coalition of Urban Serving Universities; the College Transition Collaborative (now part of Equity Accelerator), Education Counsel, the Project for Education Research That Scales, and Shift, involves the facilitation of PLD experiences for six institutions. Instructors engaged in this project have access to several tools and modules. The Classroom Practices Library[a] consists of evidence-based approaches organized by six social-psychological constructs: belonging, growth-mindset culture, trust and fairness, identity safety, self-efficacy, and social connectedness. The identification and presentation of practices enable instructors to learn and focus on specific equity-minded practices in their classrooms that can advance equity.

The module *Your Syllabus as a Tool to Promote Student Equity, Belonging, and Growth* supports instructors in developing equity-focused course syllabi. They explore the following module topical areas: Why Growth Mindset Matters, Why Students' Sense of Belonging Matters, Communicating Growth Mindset, Normalizing Challenges, Communicating Care for Students, Valuing Diversity in the Classroom, and Communicating about Resources and Success. Two other modules, the *Academic Standing Toolkit, Social-Belonging for College Students* and the *Supporting Students in Times of Uncertainty* module, provide additional resources for instructors engaged in equity work.

The SEP provided teaching materials and related resources and PLD to support instructors in their approaches. The SEP also includes a handbook[b] with guidance on how to run CoPs, among other resources, to help instructors connect and share their practices. The institutions involved in the project used a variety of implementation strategies for their CoPs. This work can support instructors in applying *Principle 1: Active engagement* from the Principles for Equitable and Effective Teaching: students need opportunities to actively engage in disciplinary learning. The outcomes of the SEP have been positive with regards to students' sense of belonging and academic achievement in the course of instructors participating in the project. Instructors found the PLD to be meaningful in that it supported their efforts to teach and enabled them to connect better with students.

[a]https://accelerateequity.org/resource/practices-library/
[b]https://studentexperienceproject.org/handbook/

course syllabi, and using evidence-based equitable and effective practices in their classrooms (Student Experience Project, 2022a). As discussed later in this chapter, the Center for the Integration of Research, Teaching and Learning (CIRTL)[12] is another key group that has created a learning community to engage in systematic use of research methods to develop and implement teaching practices that advance learning. Their work focuses on graduate students as future educators of undergraduate students.

This project embodies several of the Principles for Equitable and Effective Teaching by providing PLD that focuses on *Principle 3: Affective and social dimensions*, *Principle 4: Identity and a sense of belonging*, *Principle 5: Multiple forms of data*, and *Principle 6: Flexibility and responsiveness.* Students reported increases in positive perceptions of their learning environments (*Principle 3: Affective and social dimensions*). D, F, and withdraw rates for students decreased. By engaging in this PLD opportunity and supporting students, many instructors reported that even their sense of belonging and job satisfaction increased (*Principle 4: Identity and a sense of belonging*).

The Inclusive STEM Teaching Project (ISTP; Box 8-3) is a large mainly online initiative that provides significant professional learning and development opportunities that instructors can join as individuals, as opposed to the focus of the SEP on specific institutions.[13]

The ISTP modules center identity of both students and instructors (*Principle 4: Identity and a sense of belonging*) and provide a systematic curriculum around pedagogy and inclusive teaching that all participants engage in in a carefully planned sequence. Another example of professional learning is the National Institute on Scientific Teaching (NIST). NIST has a more varied collection of opportunities that instructors can engage with on an ad hoc basis (see Box 8-4). Some choose to attend individual virtual learning sessions on defined topics while others have been able to participate in longer experiences.

As embodied within the case examples presented in Boxes 8-2, 8-3, and 8-4, the substance of promising approaches to STEM PLD in equitable and effective teaching involves building community, providing resources and tools, engaging with disciplinary content, practice applying approaches, and reflection on teaching.

Initiatives Through Disciplinary Professional Societies and Networks

Another critical source for creating PLD programs are disciplinary professional organizations and networks within STEM disciplines. These

[12] More information about CIRTL is available at https://cirtl.net/

[13] See https://www.inclusivestemteaching.org/

BOX 8-3
Inclusive STEM Teaching Project

Sponsored by the National Science Foundation (NSF), the Inclusive STEM Teaching Project (ISTP) is a massive open online course that engages instructors, graduate students, and postdoctoral fellows in virtual and local communities of practice to apply and share their learning. The modules center identity of both students and instructors and have four key features:

1. embodied case studies,
2. affinity spaces,
3. local and virtual learning communities, and
4. an inclusivity framework portfolio.

The course engages instructors in self-reflection as they complete the various activities, which ultimately leads to the development of an individual portfolio that synthesizes their inclusivity framework. The design features of the project empower institutions to locally engage by providing leadership opportunities for instructors to become facilitator and lead Inclusive STEM Project communities on their own campuses.

The program is designed to provide professional learning and development, a community, increased awareness, confidence, self-efficacy, reflection, and changes in behavior. Qualitative results show significant shifts in attitudes and planned practices, student benefits, and greater confidence. Mixed-methods studies are in progress.

SOURCE: Presented by Bennett Golderg and Sarah Chobot Hokanson on May 22, 2023, with information from www.inclusivestemteaching.org

groups can gather in ways that make space for *Principle 1: Active engagement* while also supporting the development of instructors' pedagogical content knowledge.

Sample networks in this category include BioQUEST Curriculum Consortium, the Process Oriented Guided Inquiry Learning Project, Project Kaleidoscope, and the Science Education for New Civic Engagements and Responsibilities. These groups have distinct philosophies that drive their work. They host "annual events, community-specific newsletters and journals, curricular materials, and sub-groups on more focused topics or made up of faculty who are geographically close to one another" (Gehrke & Kezar, 2016, p. 31). They provide spaces and a community for instructors to reflect on and modify their practices, bringing them into alignment with equitable and effective teaching approaches, and have led to a number of positive instructor and organizational outcomes, including for women and faculty of color in STEM fields.

BOX 8-4
National Institute on Scientific Teaching

The National Institute on Scientific Teaching (NIST) is a nonprofit organization that provides PLD opportunities for undergraduate STEM instructors (NIST, n.d.). Instructors have the opportunity to participate in institutes and learning communities focused on implementing evidence-based teaching practices in STEM, including equitable instructional approaches.

NIST was founded as the Summer Institutes in 2004 at the University of Wisconsin, Madison, as an effort to help implement the ideas in the 2003 National Academies report *BIO2010: Transforming Undergraduate Education for Future Research Biologists* (NRC, 2003).

It has evolved over time as the priorities and leadership have changed. Initial efforts were primarily multi-day workshops held at one institution, evolving to a number of summer institutes across the country. All of these workshops included teams of attendees so that participants came with others from their own institution.

NIST was formally established as a nonprofit organization in 2020. Current NIST programs include

- Addressing Challenges in Teaching
- Learning Sanctuary Institute
- Friday Afternoon Learning Community
- Mobile Summer Institutes.

In a study of alumni who attended one of the early scientific teaching institutes, a high percentage (87%, n = 135) self-reported more confidence using the evidence-based teaching strategies learned (Pfund et al., 2009). Two years after their participation, 98% were still making changes in their teaching practices, and 68% reported using evidence-based teaching practices in at least half of their courses.

NIST reports that its work demonstrates the power of STEM instructors coming together for an intentionally designed, intensive experience with supplemental supports to advance their teaching practices.

Additionally, the members of a variety of disciplinary societies actively conduct discipline-based education research (DBER) and present their work at conferences and other scholarly gatherings run by these communities of transformation. This work is often focused on equity and access issues and can provide an evidence base for STEM PLD efforts focused on equitable and effective teaching. Professional learning and development is often based on lessons learned from DBER, although that connection is not always transparent to PLD participants (Saitta & Donnelly, 2022).

PREPARING FUTURE INSTRUCTORS

A critical group in making undergraduate STEM education equitable and effective is graduate students and postdoctoral scholars, many of whom are future faculty and current VITAL educators. Experiences with evidence-based practices as both students and instructors can increase confidence in those individuals implementing them in their classrooms (Kraft et al., 2024a). As mentioned above, without having experienced active learning themselves, new faculty are likely to teach through lecture (Apkarian et al., 2021). In addition, the underrepresented graduate student and postdoctoral population in STEM is more representative of the U.S. population than faculty, with 19% minority doctoral students and 25% minority master's students (National Center for Science and Engineering Statistic, 2023b) compared to 10% minority faculty at four-year institutions (National Science Foundation & National Center for Science and Engineering Statistics, 2019). Providing timely professional learning focused on equitable and effective teaching for graduate students and postdocs thus has the potential to transform the system, producing a new generation of experienced instructors who can have an impact long into the future.

A focus on preparing doctoral students to transition into teaching careers is not new. In the 1990s, universities launched programs to prepare future faculty across a wide range of disciplines (von Hoene, 2020; Winter et al., 2018), and as of 2020, as many as 150 universities had programs that support professional learning for future faculty. With funding from the National Science Foundation, CIRTL was founded in 2003, with an explicit focus on graduate education and the STEM disciplines and a mission "to develop future faculty committed to implementing and advancing evidence-based teaching practices to enrich undergraduate education that is accessible to all learners" (Center for the Integration of Research, Teaching and Learning, n.d.). The CIRTL network has also received funding from other sources and now includes 45 universities. Relying on three core ideas, learning through diversity, teaching as research, and learning communities, CIRTL develops and implements programming for graduate students and postdoctoral fellows that fosters community within and across institutions (Hill, 2023). As a result of these long-term efforts, there is substantial evidence for the benefits; evaluations show that participants focus on learning goals for students and understand the nature of learning in order to apply effective teaching strategies to support specific learning goals (Hill et al., 2019a,b). CIRTL functions as a network and a community with shared leadership that has changed over time (Austin, 2021; Mathieu et al., 2020)

Key findings from longitudinal studies show that sustained participation in teaching-focused PLD as a doctoral student or postdoctoral fellow has both short- and long-term impacts. In the short term, participants gain self-efficacy (Connolly et al., 2018) and increase their sense of community with peers (Connolly et al., 2016). Notably, efforts to improve teaching skills have actually been reported to also enhance and improve their research skills (Feldon et al., 2016) and research confidence (Shortlidge & Eddy, 2018), suggesting that time spent on teaching may not detract from graduate students' disciplinary research but in fact may benefit it. In the long term, participants use more learner-centered approaches than their peers nearly ten years later (Emery et al., 2020), and are more likely to be in a tenure-track teaching position (Connolly et al., 2016), all without increasing their time to degree (Connolly et al., 2016).

However, these same findings highlight two persistent challenges that inhibit more widespread, deeper, and sustained engagement in teaching-focused PLD: (a) a lack of time, or lack of appropriately scheduled time to participate (Connolly et al., 2016), and (b) the perceived low priority given to development of teaching skills (Connolly et al., 2016) and perception that participation in teaching reduces effort and commitment to research (Shortlidge & Eddy, 2018). In other words, although effective opportunities are available for graduate students and postdocs to become better prepared for both their current and future teaching responsibilities, many do not make use of these opportunities to the extent that they could because such opportunities are not integrated into their programs (thus requiring extra time) or may not be supported by their community (thus being perceived as low value).

Overcoming these challenges requires attention not just to the availability of PLD for graduate students and postdocs, but to the value placed on teaching and professional development in teaching, and to the power dynamics that play a significant role in their choices (and perceived ability) to participate (National Academies, 2024c).

The dual role of graduate students as both instructors and students requires them to navigate complex policies, cultures, and power dynamics, particularly because they may be reliant on their funding as an instructor to support their role as a student. As a result, though graduate students and postdocs may desire to build their skills as an equitable and effective educator, they may not perceive those skills as valued or supported by their advisor, department, or program (or may be explicitly told that they are not valued), and thus choose not to participate.

Though there are a substantial and growing number of institutions that offer and often require training for their graduate teaching assistants (TAs), some institutions, departments, and colleges still lack such support, which has far-reaching consequences. In many cases, graduate students may teach the majority of laboratory sections, and in these settings may have the most direct contact with undergraduate students; thus, they have the potential to make connections that faculty does not necessarily have. Many graduate students have not had the opportunity to develop their skills as a teacher and are provided with minimal support structures when they begin teaching (Speer et al., 2005; Teasdale et al., 2019). As instructors, they may deliver pre-scripted laboratory procedures, create and facilitate laboratory exercises, as either recitation section facilitator or the instructor of record. When they play a supportive role for a course, they report to a faculty member who is the instructor of record for the course. This power dynamic between the instructor of record and the TA is critical: depending on how that power is wielded, TAs may have limited agency in their teaching experience, particularly in building their own skills and making decisions about how to transform a course to be more equitable and effective. They may also be looking to the instructor of record as a mentor in teaching, but if that instructor does not make use of equitable and effective strategies, they may be perpetuating and internalizing inequitable practices in response to power dynamics. Thus *Principle 7: Intentionality and transparency* is needed to articulate if not diffuse tension from these power dynamics.

As students, they must pass necessary departmental content-based exams and work closely with an academic mentor/advisor (Johnson & Nelson, 1999). If research is part of their work, they must also navigate the expectations of their primary investigator who may send messages like "focus less on teaching," "complete your teaching requirements as fast as possible," or "put less time into your teaching." As an instructor, these are difficult messages to hear and may be even more difficult to overcome if they strive to be effective educators. This can critically impact their identity and sense of belonging within the academy (*Principle 4: Identity and a sense of belonging*). Therefore, it is important for mentors and advisors to recognize their position in the relationship and make decisions that support the students in all their roles within the department.

Lessons Learned from the Preparation of Future K–12 Teachers

Teacher preparation programs are ubiquitous, though they are concentrated at the institutions formerly known as "normal schools" across the United States (Morey et al., 1997). Many of these teacher education programs have evolved to use an approach that involves pairing the apprentice teacher with an experienced master teacher and a university supervisor (e.g., Goodell & Koç, 2020). In the UTeach Replication Model, the apprentice teacher has sustained teaching experiences with a master teacher, who provides them with advice and guidance on how to put their educational theories into practice (Goodell & Koç, 2020). The university supervisor assures that the apprentice teacher is receiving the appropriate support and is not exploited. The supervisor can also mediate any challenges that arise between the master teacher and the apprentice teacher.

A similar model could support graduate students in their roles as teaching assistants, though the instructor of record may or may not be the person best situated to support them in implementing equitable and effective practices. The preparation of graduate students as instructors is highly variable across institutions and uneven within institutions. If a pedagogy course or seminar exists, the graduate student may be able to lean on the instructor for support, like the university supervisor in the model discussed above, but they may not be paired with a master teacher who can introduce them to equitable and effective practices.

Methods for Delivering Professional Learning and Development

Professional learning and development can occur either before or while the graduate students are teaching. Yee et al. (2023a) found the following structures to be the most dominant around the country:

- An orientation that often occurs before a graduate student teaches to set departmental expectations and give some information about teaching approaches.
- Seminars and pedagogy course(s) where a PLD provider facilitates situations and experiences to help graduate students become equitable and effective instructors.
- PLD through course coordination or co-requisite courses that may offer credentials for teaching.
- PLD that has expanded from K–12 in the use of mentoring with graduate students.

Johnson and Nelson (1999) argue that mentoring is central to "quality graduate education" (p. 205). Moreover, studies have shown that marginalized groups benefit greatly from mentored PLD (Crisp & Cruz, 2009). It is important to note that Johnson and Nelson (1999) did find that if the mentor is a faculty member, relationships are complicated and multifaceted because of the roles faculty must play, such as doctoral advisors and qualifying exam evaluators, and the power dynamics involved. Peer-mentoring is another option with less complexity as well as significant flexibility and responsiveness to any potential struggles that graduate students would have with teaching (Yee et al., 2023b). Similar to K–12 mentoring structures for new in-service teachers, a peer mentor (a fellow graduate student with experience teaching) can provide more options and flexibility for delivering PLD.

Mentoring and induction has been shown to be successful in teacher education (Portner, 2005). Moreover, it has been shown to be successful with novice DBER instructors, especially peer-mentoring (Yee et al., 2022, 2023b). Although teaching experience is necessary, it is not sufficient for mentoring because mentors need to understand their role and purpose in facilitating meaningful pedagogical decision-making conversations with protégés (Rogers & Steele, 2016). Consequently, the design of a mentor-based professional development curriculum should focus on preparing mentors to guide and support protégés' understanding of their pedagogical decisions (Boyle & Boice, 1998; Crisp & Cruz, 2009) One study compared spontaneous mentoring (talk to the mentor if there are problems) and systematic mentoring (meeting regularly every week), and found that the systematic mentoring was more effective in supporting graduate students and new faculty because the mentor could not prepare appropriately when it was spontaneous (Boyle & Boice, 1998). The same study also observed that the topics that dominated mentor meetings in decreasing order of frequency were (a) discussions of undergraduates, (b) teaching styles, (c) teaching-related goals, (d) grading issues, and (e) course preparation. Box 8-5 presents a specific example of mentoring of graduate students.

Providers of Professional Learning and Development

Structures for providers of graduate student PLD fall into two general categories. In one the provider's job is to support graduate student PLD by regularly designing, organizing, and modifying PLD opportunities

BOX 8-5
Peer-Mentoring for Graduate Students

Mentoring can have enormous effects with respect to change toward equitable and effective education. Yee et al. (2021, 2022, 2023b) have demonstrated how three universities' mathematics departments were able to implement a peer-mentor program to promote change toward using active learning strategies with graduate student instructors. These programs, while initially funded externally by the National Science Foundation, are now sustained by departments after showing (a) a significant drop (>5%) in DFW rates, (b) a drop in student complaint severity, and (c) a drop in student complaint frequency. Moreover, the peer-mentor program promoted a strong community of practice among all levels of graduate students because of the use of peer-mentoring rather than faculty mentoring. This successful change included multiple observations with post-observation feedback using the graduate student observation protocol (Yee et al., 2021) as well as small group biweekly meetings between the mentor and novices, to discuss teaching strategies. Fundamentally, departments supported this change because they saw improvement in teaching and allowed the implicit discussion of teaching among novices to become explicit as the peer-mentor program provided an open space for communication around teaching.

throughout their unit or the institution (e.g., COMInDS, 2020). In the second, the providers come into the unit or institution to offer PLD in addition to teaching other courses. In this second model, the structure and system has been established with a desired PLD curriculum. In both cases, the providers of PLD can be teaching, research, or adjunct faculty or staff (e.g., CMI Prep; see Yee et al., 2023c). Regardless of their title and role, the provider's success is dependent upon many other unit and institutional logistics and expectations. One specific group that has grown over the years are DBER scholars who have significant expertise in a content discipline and focus their scholarly activities on investigating learning and teaching in that discipline using a range of methods with deep grounding in the discipline's priorities, worldview, knowledge, and practices. Science faculty with education specialties have also been considered a critical group of DBER associates who have taken on their own role as change agents within units often associated as PLD providers (Bush et al., 2019). When academic units have access to such scholars as faculty and instructors, the other members of the unit can leverage their knowledge to improve their own understanding of pedagogy.

Developing Instructor Identity

Many graduate students have experience-based beliefs about teaching established from their role and identity as a learner. From a constructivist lens, to help graduate students grow, change, and identify what is possible and what decisions are necessary in order to prepare and teach, certain experiences with teaching can provide a safe way for these graduate students to validate their beliefs and decisions as instructors. This can take time and repeated teaching experiences. Some activities/experiences that providers have found to support graduate students in finding their teaching identity include

- Reflections on teaching
- Peer observations
- Self-observations via video
- Micro-teaching
- Mock teaching

Through these activities, graduate students (ideally) work within in a safe environment where they can wrestle with what they believe, what they observe, and how they want to approach their own teaching, possibly even writing a teaching philosophy. Such work, supported by mentors, can help graduate students synthesize pedagogical theory and practice.

Organizations such as the CIRTL described above offer initiatives for STEM instructors to address gaps in graduate student PLD by facilitating online courses, workshops, learning communities, and institutes. These programs can help graduate students develop instructor identity as they work with peers to learn about equity and inclusivity within the classroom. CIRTL also provides resources on topics such as teaching-as-research, instructor materials, and program evaluation that focus on ways that graduate students and novice teaching faculty can approach integration of their disciplinary and educational research in holistic ways.

Considerations for Postdoctoral Scholars

While the section above largely addressed graduate student instructional development in equitable and effective teaching, postdoctoral scholars may currently teach or plan to do so in their future academic careers, making PLD in equitable and effective teaching critical for them as well. If they plan to enter academia and teach, postdoctoral scholars can seek out opportunities to teach as guest lecturers or instructors or as instructors of record. Such investments in teaching can also lead to tensions with their research, depending on the culture of their unit and mentor expectations. They might also seek out PLD through centers for teaching and learning or external initiatives. A variety of special funded initiatives, such as Institutional Research and Academic Career Development Awards (IRACDA)[14] and The Harvard Medical School Curriculum Fellows Program (HMS CFP),[15] have provided opportunities for postdoctoral scholars to teach and/or pursue discipline-based education research in STEM. Other initiatives that support teaching postdoctoral scholars include the Carl Weiman Science Education Initiative[16] and the TRESTLE initiative.[17] Both programs focused on teaching and teaching innovation and were designed to support postdoctoral scholars in developing their effective and equitable teaching skills and practices. Postdoctoral scholars served as change agents by partnering with faculty to transform courses with better practices (Chasteen & Code, 2018; White et al., 2020).

[14] More information about the IRACDA program is available at https://www.nigms.nih.gov/training/careerdev/Pages/TWDInstRes.aspx

[15] More information about the HMS CFP is available at https://curriculumfellows.hms.harvard.edu/

[16] More information about the Carl Weiman Science Education Initiative is available at https://cwsei.ubc.ca/

[17] More Information about the TRESTLE initiative is available at https://trestlenetwork.ku.edu/

In a systematic review of literature, one major theme that arose with regards to PLD of postdoctoral scholars was an appreciation for developing their teaching and learning skills, including equitable teaching approaches such as active learning (Nowell et al., 2018). One of the studies cited in the review found that between the postdoctoral scholars who engaged in such programming and taught, and those who did not, there were no differences in their publications or the duration of their fellowship (Rybarczyk et al., 2011). While more research is needed, this finding counters the perception that postdoctoral scholars who engage in such development and teach are unable to be productive in their research.

Considerations for Undergraduate Learning Assistants

Undergraduate learning assistants (ULAs) provide peer support for other undergraduate students' education in many diverse learning environments. A ULA provides direct support to fellow undergraduates and would benefit from PLD on equitable and effective teaching. ULAs work in tutoring labs, run review sessions online or on campus for specific courses, or work in emporiums where undergraduates navigate an online curriculum and receive assistance on campus. They have typically successfully completed the course they are assisting; with this experience they can relate to the challenges fellow undergraduates (*Principle 3: Affective and social dimensions*) are facing better than faculty or graduate students, who have an influential power or privilege.

ULAs have been shown to have significant benefits for students and units. Data have shown that students in courses with ULAs have an increased sense of belonging and identity and the presence of ULAs lowers undergraduate STEM attrition (Barrasso & Spilios, 2021; Clements et al., 2022; Dawson et al., 2014). The differences between ULAs and graduate students are important and should affect the PLD opportunities they might most benefit from. First, unlike graduate teaching assistants, ULAs are not beholden to the unit, especially if their major is not in the unit for which they are assisting (e.g., a computer science major may be a ULA for a calculus course for non-mathematics majors). Additionally, ULAs may be getting paid from a CTL and may not be accountable to the instructor or course in the same way as a graduate student who is paid by the department. ULAs also often work with one class and one instructor, so they can help students in that class more directly and personally. Finally, as with graduate students, when disagreements or challenges arise between the instructor and ULA, PLD for ULAs can be provided so they understand their role and their purpose relative to the instructor of the course.

SUMMARY

Continuous improvement strategies are necessary to work toward equitable and effective teaching. When instructors engage together in communities, they can foster equitable and effective teaching by collaborating to improve pedagogical approaches and also contribute to changes to institutional and departmental cultures toward undergraduate instruction. Ongoing PLD in community is one means for improvement and has been shown to be more effective than single session or workshop style. PLD instructors may engage in PLD opportunities on their own campus or with others from their own academic unit or institution or may join national networks as an individual or as a member of a group. Sometimes community found outside of campus can be more closely aligned to an instructor's needs, such as when they connect instructors with others in their own discipline. All types of instructors, including tenured, tenure-track faculty, and VITAL educators, benefit from PLD. This includes graduate students and postdoctoral fellows engaged in teaching. Successful culture change toward equitable and effective teaching requires that people in all roles be included in PLD, communities, and initiatives. Because VITAL educators are often excluded from professional development opportunities and communities, we have called them out specifically for attention. However, increasing attention to VITAL educators will not help achieve equitable and effective learning experiences if there is not systemic change to increase the value of instruction itself.

Conclusion 8.1: Implementation of equitable and effective teaching is an ongoing process that necessitates all instructors (full-time faculty, VITAL educators, and postdocs with teaching roles) regularly engage in professional learning and development (PLD) throughout their careers. An important aspect of PLD is to cultivate the practice of reflection in which instructors review teaching experiences and how they can learn from those experiences in ways that will improve future teaching and learning. PLD can occur on campus or via technology and in both formal and informal ways.

Conclusion 8.2: Institutional support is needed to ensure that ongoing high-quality professional learning and development is available and accessible for all types of instructors.

Conclusion 8.3: Digital technologies present opportunities to enhance equitable and effective teaching in science, technology, engineering, and mathematics when they are introduced along with professional learning and development opportunities that provide guidance and support on appropriate use that does not magnify existing inequities.

9

Role of the Institution in Creating Equitable and Effective Learning Environments

Prior chapters have described the Principles for Equitable and Effective Teaching and their application in specific teaching and learning settings. Here, we turn to the implementation of the seven Principles at an institutional level. This discussion is grounded in a concept of implementation and change as processes that shape and are shaped by a number of interrelated dimensions within the institution. A goal of continuous improvement throughout the system is needed to work toward equitable and effective teaching and to achieve a student-ready college that values and focuses on student-centered approaches to learning. Institutional leadership at an institution is essential for articulating and prioritizing goals and providing the financial and human resources needed for significant change. That is, achieving equity-minded change in our current system is a challenging endeavor that will likely only succeed through gradual changes to mindset and actors on multiple levels being open to multiple possible interpretations of data (Culver et al., 2021; Equity-Based Teaching Collective, 2024; Kezar & Dizon, 2019; Kezar & Posselt, 2020; Kezar et al., 2008).

Figure 9-1, below, illustrates the various institutional dimensions that we consider in relation to the seven Principles in this report. At their core, the Principles are built around both the socio-cultural and cognitive dimensions that research shows interact in a dynamic way during learning, shown in Figure 9-1 at the center of the diagram. Implementing the Principles at an institution involves the interconnected participation of all levels of the campus: the instructors (e.g., those who are teaching), the academic units (e.g., those who manage the academic mission), and the institutional leaders (e.g., those who make policy and resource decisions that impact how teaching and learning can take place at the institution); this dimension is illustrated by the middle ring of Figure 9-1. And finally, as shown in the outer ring of Figure 9-1, all of this takes place within the institutional context—including its infrastructure, policies, and practices—which may support or be a barrier to enacting equitable and effective teaching. Moreover, aspects of the institutional context may be deeply entrenched, whether or not they are aligned with the current goals and vision of the institution. Examining these policies, practices, and infrastructure limitations is critical to supporting

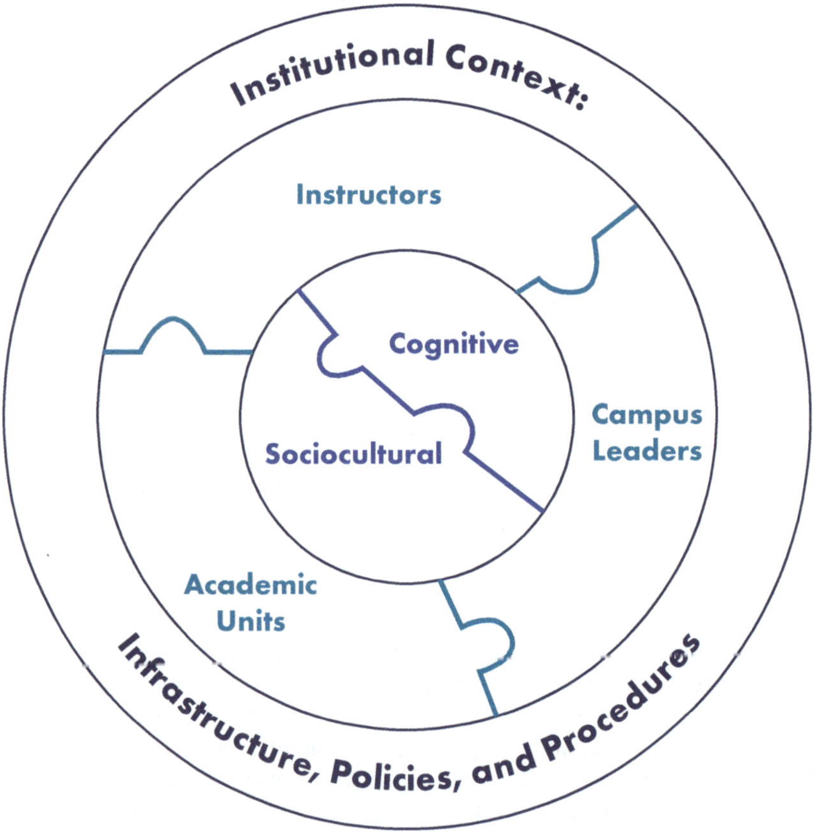

FIGURE 9-1 Institutional context impacts interactions and student learning.
NOTE: Inner circle: All learning involves a dynamic interaction between cognitive and socio-cultural processes and the Principles address both. Middle ring: Implementation of the Principles requires the integrated effort of individuals at multiple levels of the institution. Outer ring: Implementation of the Principles also depends on acknowledging the needs and challenges of the particular institutional context. The institutional context also impacts interactions of students, instructors, academic units, and campus leaders (middle ring) in ways that influence student learning (both cognitive and socio-cultural; inner circle).

continuous improvement and requires institutional leaders to be actively involved in changing them.

Higher education scholars often examine institutions from a "systems" perspective to understand and describe their change processes (Austin, 2011; Baecker, 2010; Henderson et al., 2011; Lemke & Sabelli, 2008; Scileppi, 1988). It has been posited that culture change requires multi-level aligned action and leadership from across an institution, including academic unit members and student affairs professionals, as well as deans, provosts, and presidents (Kezar, 2013; Kezar & Holcombe, 2015). It is highly unlikely that sustained and broad implementation of equitable and effective teaching will occur if an institution presumes that the responsibility for change lies only with individual instructors and what they do in their classes. While some particularly motivated and informed individuals may be able to implement change effectively and well, such efforts are unlikely to become the norm at the institution unless there is vertical support and horizontal integration for the Principles for Equitable and Effective Teaching. As implied by the outer ring of Figure 9-1, "Equity-minded teaching must be fostered not only by individuals but supported by the systems and conditions that surround individuals and their efforts" (Bensimon & Harris, 2023; Gonzales & Culpepper, 2024, p. 30; Liera & Desir, 2023).

CULTIVATE A CULTURE OF CONTINUOUS IMPROVEMENT

Improving science, technology, engineering, and mathematics (STEM) teaching at the undergraduate level so that it is more equitable and effective is an iterative process that requires sustained effort over time to ensure the best practices and policies are in place. That is, work to achieve equitable and effective learning environments is a journey and not a destination that can be defined today and reached tomorrow. The concept of continuous improvement, originally developed in manufacturing, can usefully be applied to this type of STEM education reform (Singh & Singh, 2015; Temponi, 2005). Continuous improvement does not focus on continual change but, rather, on evaluating the outcomes of a change and then using the information to guide actions to improve the process (Jha et al., 1996). Continuous improvement approaches can help to address the complexity of culture change and may be more likely to lead to sustainable transformation (Glover et al., 2015; Michela et al., 1996; Mitchell & Sickney, 2019; Reinholz et al., 2019. This process requires iterative cycles of evaluation, reflection, and action. By fostering a culture of continuous improvement, institutions can ensure that efforts to enhance equity and effectiveness in teaching are sustained and refined over time, creating lasting and impactful change in higher education.

Multiple national initiatives have approached teaching and learning through systemic approaches, including the National Academies of Sciences, Engineering, and Medicine's (National Academies') Roundtable on Systemic Change in Undergraduate STEM Education.[1] Studies have explored the concept of organizational change networks as a lever for systemic change by focusing on the examples of the Advanced Technology Education program of the National Science Foundation (NSF), the Bayview Alliance, the Center for the Integration of Research, Teaching and Learning (see Chapter 8), the network of STEM education centers, the Partnership for Undergraduate Life Sciences Education, and the Association for Undergraduate Education at Research Universities, all of which have been players in the effort to improve undergraduate STEM education (Austin et al., 2024). Recognizing all students, faculty, staff, administrators, and members of the public as valuable and capable, Effective Practices for Physics Programs (EP3)[2] provides structured resources informed by practices across the physics community to address challenges and make changes and improvements. Recognizing the challenges of teaching in complex ecosystems, the Equity-Based Teaching Collective, composed of faculty from American University, Florida International University, and the University of Connecticut, has created an ecosystem-based report for understanding the complex roles of different stakeholders and levers in the improvement of college teaching and how they (i.e., institutional leaders, centers for teaching and learning, deans and department chairs, faculty, and students) can interact to improve college teaching and promote equity-based teaching and equitable outcomes for Black, Indigenous, and low-income students. Their work included a large landscape analysis, interviews, and synthesis efforts that informed their recommendations and provided resources for the examples they cite (Equity-Based Teaching Collective, 2024).

Understanding Theories of Organizational Change

Structures, policies, practices, and operating principles of modern higher education replicated those first established by the colonial colleges before the nation's founding (see Chapter 2). These institutional underpinnings are difficult to change because they form part of the infrastructure of the institution's operation—they are entrenched and undergird the institutional culture. The changes that are needed now must be carried out intentionally and systemically rather than allowed to evolve slowly, in part because equitable experiences are morally urgent and in part because our interconnected society is changing more rapidly than ever before. The challenges faced

[1] More information is available at https://www.nationalacademies.org/our-work/roundtable-on-systemic-change-in-undergraduate-stem-education

[2] More information about EP3 is available at https://ep3guide.org/

by our society today are global and cross-disciplinary challenges. In order to prepare students to be contributors in today's world, there is a need to prepare a diversity of individuals who can bring their particular forms of creativity and problem solving to the challenges of this century.

Creating an equity-minded institution requires organizational change. Organizational change can be described, broadly, as being one of three types: first order, second order, or third order (Gonazales & Culpepper, 2024). These types are distinguished from one another by the extent to which existing structures are affected. Equity-minded change, generally and more specifically in support of teaching, is most likely to take hold when institutions invest simultaneously in first-, second-, and third-order change. Table 9-1 gives a brief description and example for each type of organizational change.

TABLE 9-1 Types of Organizational Change by Scope

Type of Change	Scope (e.g., depth, magnitude)	Example
First-Order Change	Targets, or is meant to be **compatible with, existing structures**, and thus does not seek to change those structures or their foundations. Does not affect the foundations or core of the organization.	Implementing a recruitment effort to diversify the STEM faculty and student body on a campus (see Hrabowski, 2012; Palmer et al., 2013)
Second-Order Change	**Targets relationships, practices, and norms** in phases or in ways that are otherwise limited/contained. These changes are often more significant than first order change but also do not address the core or foundations of an organization.	Implementing affinity groups wherein minoritized and marginalized students can build community and share strategies for navigating their disciplines and departments (see Villa et al., 2013)
Third-Order Change	Often described as deep, transformative, and implicit. **It targets the deepest foundations of the organization, or its core, including mental models.** Third-order change involves or assumes first- and second-order change and requires adjustments at the individual, sub-organization, and whole organization level.	Ongoing work to design educational and policy initiatives that enhance faculty, staff, and student understanding of the dominant culture-focused foundations of institutions, disciplines, etc. (see Liera, 2023)

SOURCES: Adapted from Gonzales and Culpepper (2024, p. 17), informed by ideas from Bartunek and Moch (1987) and Kania et al. (2018).

Most diversity efforts are what organizational theorists would deem first-order changes (Bartunek & Moch, 1987; Kania et al., 2018), which focus on change that can be quickly adopted—e.g., by doing "more" of what an organization does rather than fundamentally altering conditions within the organization. Some of these efforts are performative, such as public statements about the value that an institution places on inclusion. Some are actions, such as an invited speaker or an optional one-time workshop, which are unlikely to lead to any change and may not reach people who are least informed about issues of exclusion, privilege, and implicit bias. David Asai, former Senior Director for Science Education in the Howard Hughes Medical Institute, where his team developed initiatives advancing inclusive STEM learning, recently stated that "when confronted with the truth that STEM lacks diversity, our first impulse is to recruit more persons from the underrepresented groups" (personal correspondence from David Asai to Gabriela Weaver, October 2024). But starting with representation is a mistake, as shown by the failure to make progress in closing the racialized STEM completion gap even after three decades of diversity-centered interventions (Asai, 2020; Bernard & Cooperdock, 2018). A focus on equity and an equitable, inclusive environment can create a space that will be inviting to a diverse group of people—students, staff, and faculty (Griffin, 2020).

Many inclusion efforts tend to fall under second-order changes, as they focus on small and contained alterations to pre-existing practices and relationships (Bartunek & Moch, 1987; Kania et al., 2018). These are important and necessary because they begin to normalize the conversation about equity and provide some ways to act on it. An example of a second-order change that can be helpful is creating a forum where first-generation faculty members can meet with first-generation students and share experiences or provide encouragement about college life. Another example is to provide ongoing PLD for educators and administrators to learn about and recognize their own unconscious biases, and how these may affect their interactions with others and their decision making.

Any effort to make STEM more diverse, inclusive, and equitable demands the deepest and most difficult kind of change: third-order change. This approach requires new or revised policies and practices, long-term reallocation of resources, and ongoing learning and reflection to shift mental models about how academic units, colleges, universities, and/or the profession should work. These underlying models, structures, and culture are what maintain inequity and need to be addressed through transformational change (Kezar, 2018; McNair et al., 2020). As discussed earlier, contributions from all levels of the institution will be needed to achieve this depth of change. By their nature, institutions have nuanced and distributed systems of power and autonomy, and different stakeholders may have competing priorities (e.g., Vican et al., 2020). For this reason, transformation requires institutional leaders to take an active role in creating change by facilitating and supporting widespread efforts. Researchers have observed that norms that exist within professions tend to change when individuals observe others in their social group exhibiting different behaviors (e.g., individual-level change); when they view these behavior changes being adopted collectively (e.g., departmental and disciplinary change); and when they receive institutional rewards that validate and legitimize the change (e.g., college, university change; Tankard & Paluck, 2016).

Disruptive, third-order change requires institutional equity-mindedness. The presence of diversity (e.g., achieving a designation based on student demographics) is not sufficient to achieve this: institutional culture matters more. Equity-mindedness is necessary because the exclusion of certain classes of individuals from higher education is a systemic problem (Liera & Desir, 2023). Analysis and understanding of the problem are needed before implementing solutions—otherwise the result will be superficial change. Equity-mindedness also requires an awareness of the challenges faced by different populations of students, the practices that affect these students, and the importance of using data (specifically data disaggregated by the population of the students at the institution) to identify and address inequities (Bensimon, 2018; McNair et al., 2020). Success in implementing equity-mindedness requires a sense of shared responsibility and accountability for advancing equity in policies, practices, and norms, meaning equity is everyone's responsibility (Gonzales & Culpepper, 2024).

CREATE STUDENT-READY INSTITUTIONS

The experience of teaching and mentoring undergraduate students in STEM varies by institutional context, mission, and perhaps, most importantly, across levels of student preparedness to learn the course material. Concerns about underprepared college students are a perennial complaint across post-secondary education, and the COVID-19 pandemic magnified opportunity and preparedness gaps for many students (Bailey et al., 2021; National Academies, 2021). Rather than blaming students and other stakeholders (e.g., parents, high school teachers, the Pre-K–12 education system) or focusing on students' college readiness, McNair et al. (2016) argue for rejecting the concept of "college readiness," replacing it with "student-ready"—institutions that meet their admitted students where they are. Institutions ranging from community colleges to highly selective research universities have differing approaches to student admission (see Chapter 2 for more). No matter the process, the students who show up at these institutions have been admitted, and educators and administrators have an obligation to provide a learning environment that supports their education and learning. To create student-ready institutions requires attention to who has control or influence on which elements in the system. There is variation in the extent that instructors can influence the design of the course or curriculum design, but they usually have control over pedagogical approach and their classroom policies.

Assess Resources and Infrastructure

The creation of an effective and equitable institution that values, promotes, and rewards equitable and effective teaching and learning can be guided by the data and physical infrastructure made available at the instructor, classroom, course, department, college, and university leadership levels. While some instructors may be familiar with institutional graduation and retention data, sometimes disaggregated by demographic and additional variables, many have not had access to data at finer levels of detail. Even fewer have been able to connect instructional revenue and costs with student outcomes.

Physical infrastructure, including items such as classrooms and the pedagogical opportunities they afford, technology capabilities, student study spaces, experimentation spaces, learning laboratories, testing centers and more, and how these spaces are used and allocated for the purposes of teaching and learning, can affect both the costs and outcomes of the educational experiences. These issues are complicated by increasing demand for courses in certain disciplines (e.g., computer science), which has led to difficult choices at some institutions where course sizes have grown, responsibilities of instructors have increased, or student access to courses has been restricted (Alonso, 2023; Nguyen & Lewis, 2020). However, many institutions have worked to make courses more equitable and effective with minimal changes in instructional costs. An equitable and effective teaching approach emphasizes student access and success as metrics that are considered as part of the resource allocation process. A 2024 convening at the Howard Hughes Medical Institute (HHMI), the Financial Alignment with Inclusive Teaching Effectiveness (FAITE),[3] brought together institutional financial officers from the National Association of College and University Business Officers with institutional change agents, data analytics experts, and academic leaders. The primary purpose of the workshop was to determine approaches to align financial decisions with inclusive instructional practices and student success metrics. Discussion focused on how data can be used to drive informed decision making that supports institutional improvement, including balancing instructional costs with financial realities, supporting systemic change for increased access and equity, and developing

[3] More information about FAITE is available at https://ascnhighered.org/ASCN/cost_benefit.html

new organizational structures to sustain inclusive teaching innovations. While this type of work is just emerging, it has the ability to have a major impact on equitable and effective teaching since it is difficult to remove financial constraints from what is deemed possible, or desirable, in instructional activities.

The impact of institutional finances on STEM instruction can be seen, for example, when looking at the various roles of introductory STEM courses, both financial and educational. Introductory STEM courses are frequently taught to large numbers of students (and at research institutions are responsible for supporting many graduate students teaching assistants); they are therefore important for institutional revenue (Hatfield et al., 2022; Hopp et al., 2019). There are significant expenses with offering these courses as well, and this sometimes leads to the use of extra "differential" tuition costs for students as institutions try to recoup some of their expenses (Harwell, 2013; Wolniak et al., 2018). Foundational STEM courses have the highest breadth of incoming student backgrounds and expertise. and typically require a larger proportional investment in terms of instructional spaces, resources, learning materials, and preparation of instructors and teaching assistants, all of which are reflected in the financial data and are a key factor in student-centered financial planning.[4] These are just a sampling of the issues where combining various forms of data, including financial, can help inform institutional decision making about instruction and the extent to which equitable and effective teaching is prioritized. Institutional leaders often have to make difficult decisions about competing priorities and finite resources. Various forms of data, including financial data, can help administrators, leaders, and instructors to build a culture and infrastructure that supports equitable and effective teaching with an eye toward sustainable, long-term programmatic and instructional changes.

Infrastructure, policies, and practices also relate directly to data in terms of what data are available to whom and for what purposes. Data are often siloed within institutions, which inhibits evidence-informed decisions related to instruction, students, and instructional staff (Swing et al., 2016). Instructors and administrators are often unaware of the challenges that students face and the complexity of the classroom situations that can arise in STEM courses, as well as the bottlenecks created in STEM curriculum (as discussed in Chapters 6 and 7). Data, made usable in transparent and multi-dimensional representations, coupled with professional development around its interpretation and use, can provide substantial support for the creation of equitable and effective instructional environments. When

---

[4] More information about the benefits of student-centered financial planning is available at https://www.nacubo.org/Press-Releases/2024/NACUBO-Student-Success-Hub-Highlights-Financial-Links-to-Equitable-Student-Outcomes

financial data are also included, there is an opportunity for leadership, instructors, and business officers to work together to develop approaches that are feasible and prioritize equitable and effective teaching in a sustainable manner that benefits the institution as a whole.

Student-Focused Policies

One important function of institutional leaders in supporting equitable and effective teaching is an examination of policies that impact teaching and learning. One example of a policy that directly affects student success is transfer articulation (see Chapter 7). Credit hour limits, procedures for transfer requests, and agreements among local or state institutions must be decided by institutional administrators; academic advisors and program directors are responsible for developing course-to-course equivalencies; faculty are most likely to be the ones to look at course learning objectives and syllabi to ensure that the content meets the needs of the students within a given program (see Chapter 6). Institutional alignment across these efforts will ensure that decisions at each level are guided by the same values, promoting equitable and effective teaching for all students, as articulated in the seven Principles of this report. Lacking such alignment can lead to the exclusion of some groups of students. For example, when students transferring from a two-year college are not given equivalent credit, such as for a first-year biology course, only because a research institution does not believe the two-year college version of the course has sufficient "rigor," then populations of students who are likely to begin their higher education career through a two-year college route (a larger percentage of underrepresented, low-income, and/or first-generation students) will be systematically and unfairly penalized by the receiving institution requiring them to take a course a second time in their college career.

Other policies that affect students' equitable access to an excellent education are those related to the timing of course withdrawals and the impact of withdrawals on prior grades, policies connecting a student's permission to register for courses based on their account balance, practices around grades in a student's first term in college, academic integrity policies and how they are reported, monitored, and enforced, practices around admission to limited-enrollment degree programs, and rules and procedures related to changing a major. Students who must work in order to pay for school may be at a significant disadvantage when their ability to register for the following term's courses is held up. Each of these policies, when examined with an equity lens, can derail the educational plans of some students more than others based on their race, income level, or other identity characteristics. An equity lens, or "equity-mindedness," has been described by scholars (Bensimon, 2007, 2018) as a way of thinking that centers—brings attention to—and seeks to resolve persistent patterns of inequity. The underlying message is that the reasons behind any given policy or practice should be consistent with the educational mission of the institutions and not inadvertently put barriers in front of some groups of students.

Instructor-Focused Policies

Creating a student-ready institution that provides and supports equitable and effective teaching involves not only policies that directly affect students, but also those that have a direct impact on instructors and an indirect impact on students. Among these are the extent to which they have access to data about their students, support to utilize those data, expectations for teaching, such as numbers of courses/sections/students, modality of teaching, and time to prepare and support for improving teaching such as that provided by centers for teaching and learning or other related structures (Molinaro et al., 2020). It also matters how teaching assignments are allocated (to different categories of instructors) and resourced: support staff, types of teaching spaces, availability of needed equipment or materials, course scheduling, and so on. Some of these decisions rest solely within the purview of the academic unit (Chapter 6) but all of it can be influenced by policies and cultural expectations created by the institutional leadership. These policies and actions are embedded in the system depicted in Figure 9-1. In addition, realistic access to professional learning requires that institutional leaders provide realistic compensation for the time required for everyone who teaches to do that learning and subsequently apply it to their courses.

A practice that spans an entire institution—both across disciplines and vertically through levels of leadership—is creating true access to professional learning and development (PLD) and an expectation that faculty will participate (Chapter 8 discusses various approaches to PLD). While faculty have expertise in their academic discipline, formal preparation in methods of educating others varies. Furthermore, there is plentiful research demonstrating that some approaches to teaching are more effective and equitable than others in higher education (Freeman et al., 2014; Sathy & Moore, 2020; Theobald et al., 2020) It follows that professional learning is needed if institutions expect their instructors to educate in equitable and effective ways, and for all students to learn and graduate successfully. Access to professional learning means that all categories of faculty, instructors, and teaching assistants can develop the necessary skills with evidence-based pedagogies and inclusive teaching practices through ongoing programming and resources available to them through their institution or professional societies. As mentioned in Chapter 8's discussion of professional learning, a single workshop or isolated experience is not likely to be effective unless it instigates further engagement by instructors. In most situations, research has shown that long-term professional learning experiences are needed in order to increase the likelihood of success (Bifulco & Drue, 2023; Castillo-Montoya et al., 2023; Hakkola et al., 2021; Miller et al., 2022).

Compensation and hiring policies may also have an impact on student success at the institution. Hiring practices and how they influence the diversity of faculty across departments and faculty categories are important for developing an inclusive community for all students. Simply hiring diverse faculty is not enough. Work at all levels is needed to ensure that effective faculty are retained and promoted. Valuing teaching from all types of instructors is one step to cultivating an equitable environment.

These faculty-focused policies are an example of actions that require an alignment of efforts between unit practices and institutional policies. For example, one important component of faculty retention specifically related to teaching is how teaching evaluation, recognition, and reward practices are carried out. This is clearly a complex subject that interacts with many other components of the larger system, and one that does not always get prioritized by the academic unit or the institution.

Reflect on the Role of Grades

Letter grades are considered a staple of the educational system, but the history of the system is more complex than usually recognized today (Durm, 1993; Schneider & Hutt, 2013). In higher education, there have been numerous approaches to grading over the past several hundred years; a 100-point scale, common in the 19th century, was phased out in the 1900s such that by the 1940s an A–F approach was fairly ubiquitous, potentially still tied to a 100-point scale but considered more reliable due to potential inconsistencies with how points were assigned (Schinske & Tanner, 2014). A detailed description of both the history of grading and what grading is meant to achieve for students and the institution can be found in the paper by Schinske and Tanner (2014), including a discussion of the emergence of grading which is commonly associated with foundational STEM courses:

> As research on intellectual ability appeared to show that, like other continuous biological traits, levels of aptitude in a population conformed to a normal curve, some experts felt grades should similarly be distributed according to a curve in a classroom (Finkelstein, 1913). Distributing grades according to a normal curve was therefore considered as a solution to the subjective nature of grading and a way to minimize interrater differences in grading (Guskey,1994). Others worried that measuring aptitude was different from measuring levels of classroom performance, which might not be normally distributed (Schneider & Hutt, 2013). (Schinske & Tanner, 2014, p. 158).

More and more, the use of a normal distribution within the sample of an individual course has led to concerns about the validity of grades representing learning (Bowen & Cooper, 2021; Eyler, 2024). Some schools have experimented with the removal of grades in favor of assessment models like student portfolios or narrative grading, while others have looked at using "badges" or "microcredentials" to signify mastery of specific skills rather than approaches that assign letters or numbers without context and therefore do not connect grades to specific skills or abilities (Ferguson & Whitelock, 2024; Reed, 2023). Some institutions have chosen to not calculate grade point averages (GPAs) and/or not record failing grades (e.g., Burke, 2022), as repeating a course is considered penalty enough and recording failing grades creates a GPA burden that is very difficult to overcome. More recently, there have been suggestions of alternative grading approaches usable in classrooms (Townsley & Schmid, 2020) that attempt to make grading more relevant and equitable, including approaches such as specifications grading. Specifications grading is a term for a combination of multiple types of grading approaches. It includes mastery grading in which students demonstrate proficiency before continuing to the next topic as well as competency-based grading where students can show mastery through a choice of assessments. A variation is contract grading in which the instructor offers multiple options in advance and the students have choices about which components to complete, and the anticipated grade or requirement for credit is known in advance based on the choices selected by the student. The instructor selects the options for assignments in a way designed to ensure students meet the learning objectives for the course (Bonner, 2016; Howitz et al., 2021; Larson, 2023; Nilson, 2015; Townsley & Schmid, 2020).

Some research suggests that the most commonly used grading systems have the most negative impact on students with the lowest number of systemic advantages and that small differences in points awarded that lead to different letter grades can impact a student's choice of major (Castle et al., 2024; Dika & D'Amico, 2016; Koester et al., 2016; Li & Xia, 2024; Malespina & Singh, 2023; Matz et al., 2017; Seymour & Hunter, 2019; Whitcomb et al., 2021; Wright et al., 2016; Xie et al., 2015). Therefore, these approaches to grading create barriers to inclusive STEM outcomes at the course and program levels for students belonging to one or more of the commonly underrepresented groups: low socio-economic status; first-generation college attendance; female; lesbian, gay, bisexual, transgender, queer/questioning, intersex, asexual/aromantic/agender, plus other related identities (LGBTQIA+); and/or racial/ethnic minoritized status. Furthermore, even with all the variations in grading approaches—which arise for a range of factors, from different instructors teaching the same course to inconsistencies between courses in an academic unit, and from differences between academic units to the even more varied approaches that are possible between different institutions—it can be easy to make high-stakes decisions about who is qualified to continue in STEM, receive a STEM degree, and how worthy they are as graduates—all based on the imprecise measure of grades.

Campus leadership also has a role in shaping the use of grades; one face of this is to organize an analysis of the courses where inequities across groups are more prevalent, with particular emphasis on large, introductory courses. Such an audit of grading practices and outcomes requires follow-up with support for implementing improvements in grading practices that are supported by the literature to avoid introducing additional bias into the grading approaches (Bowen & Cooper, 2021; Ekstrom et al., 1994; Felder & Brent, 2024; Feldman, 2023; van Dusen et al., 2021).

In the end, administrators need to consider that historically, grades have been assigned a tremendous amount of value, but they are actually an approach that takes limited input and assigns those generalizations an outsized impact. Additional research on more holistic approaches to evaluating the capabilities of STEM students is needed, with special attention to emphasis on approaches that value the ability to learn and overcome struggle.

ANALYZE INSTITUTIONAL DATA

This section focuses on how data can be leveraged to define goals, measure progress, and guide movement toward equitable and effective STEM teaching at the institutional level. We purposefully choose to consider data as they pertain to the range of interrelated dimensions that together make up the institution, from the individual instructor in the classroom to the college or university administrator who makes and implements institution-wide policies. Data are crucial at every level as stakeholders think about goals, measure progress, and guide improvement. The committee acknowledges that structures and resources may vary widely among institutions, so we discuss issues from a general perspectives and guidance that can be applied in a variety of ways.

As reflected in *Principle 5: Multiple forms of data,* data and self-reflection are important tools that provide evidence to inform continuous improvement. Data alone, however, do not make change happen. Data are an input to decision making and one component of raising awareness of potential challenges in achieving equitable and effective teaching—an awareness that can be used to increase buy-in and participation across the institution. Without data, understanding what is and is not working in undergraduate education, and why, becomes extremely difficult, leaving stakeholders to make decisions based on anecdotal experiences and individual perspectives. It is crucial, then, to use data to determine what the potential challenges are and to discern what further data points might be needed to craft a solution.

Data are part of a complex system that can help reveal insights into intent, support, and culture and can reveal information about these various factors and their interrelationships. Thus, it is important to remain aware of the power dynamics at play when data are gathered, interpreted, and used to inform action. As Taylor (2020) described, leaders of student success initiatives are increasingly pressured to use the language of data-driven decision making to justify programs and their corresponding results. There may also be significant challenges for everyone involved in student success initiatives to access the data used to drive decision-making processes, and data-driven decision making can pit student success initiatives against each other by setting up competition for resources, and silence institutional personnel who push back against data-driven reform efforts (Taylor, 2020). Taylor's analysis shows that quantitative data are often inappropriately treated as superior to qualitative data points when both are valuable. The perspectives and life experiences of the people designing studies and those collecting and analyzing qualitative and quantitative data influence the categories that are chosen and many other aspects of data use (Castillo & Gillborn, 2022; Delamont, 2012; Gillborn et al., 2023; Hatch, 2023).

Ways of Using Data

There are multiple types of data and multiple ways to use data. Both quantitative and qualitative data can be used for strategic planning, program evaluation, and instructors' annual reviews. Quantitative data may comprise the student outcomes that programs often use to gauge students' progress, including course pass/fail/withdrawal rates, Fall-to-Fall retention, enrollment numbers, and student responses to class evaluations, among others. Qualitative data may be in-class assessments given by the instructor asking students how they feel about their learning (e.g., exit tickets students submit before leaving class, Plus/Delta charts where students submit quick answers to what added value (plus) and what should be changed (delta), exit interviews when students leave or graduate from programs; focus groups and individual interviews with students; and content analyses of artifacts (e.g., syllabi, student assignments). Different data points can be used to guide planning and action at the course, program, department, college, and institutional levels. McNair et al.'s (2020) book *From Equity Talk to Equity Walk: Expanding Practitioner Knowledge for Racial Justice in Higher Education* provides a thorough discussion of how equity-informed data can guide reform at multiple levels. The book is centered around themes of great relevance to equitable and effective education and how to promote equity through alignment of mission and priorities, and strategies. Institutions can invest in or fine-tune their data structure to support such missions and priorities and to inform strategies. For example, Meraz (2022) described an effort in the California community college system wherein faculty were given access to an equity dashboard that allowed faculty to view the academic performance of their students based on gender, race, and ethnicity. These data, along with targeted professional development resources and communities of practice, allowed faculty to diagnose issues in their teaching and make improvements (Carlson, 2022; Gonzales & Culpepper, 2024; Meraz, 2022).

Thoughtful data collection and usage involves three important areas: intent, guidance, and cultural context. Each of these areas can be considered at the class, academic unit, or institutional level. Here we provide examples at various levels as all are relevant to the thinking of institutional leaders using data to drive change.

The intent behind collecting and using data can span from supportive to supportive and critical (called here as "critical friend") to purely judgmental. Take, for instance, the range of responses to the instructor of a course with a large gap in D, F, and withdraw (DFW) rates by gender or race. A purely supportive approach may ask questions to better understand the situation and why inequities exist and what is within the instructor's control to alter; a slightly more critical friend might highlight teaching practices that have been shown to reduce DFW rates with the hope that the instructor sees the value in engaging in professional development in these areas. A critical friend approach could employ the supportive approach, acknowledging that a change is needed to improve the situation, but also work with the instructor to identify and strongly suggest potential interventions while supporting ongoing data exploration. A judgmental approach would label the instructor as not able to work with different groups of students and take some punitive action based on the judgment.

At the department level, a department chair may see data that one or more of their introductory courses have an unacceptable DFW rate of 30% to 60%. A supportive approach in this case might consist of acknowledging the poor outcomes with colleagues and blaming the admissions unit, the preparation of the students, and/or their willingness to work hard. If adopting a critical friend perspective, the chair could acknowledge the challenge of working with students from varied backgrounds, acknowledge the rates are unacceptable, and create a plan supporting instructor development and course structure and pedagogical experimentation to work toward improvement. A judgmental perspective may have the chair decide that the current instructors are incapable and replace them with a new group to try again and hope for a better result. An important point is that the intent can be aimed toward the students, the instructors, and/or the administrators. What appears to be supportive, critical, or judgmental can dramatically change based on who the actions are aimed at. Box 9-1 gives a brief example of

BOX 9-1
Moving Toward Equity via Course Redesign

Using the disaggregated data for formative and summative course redesigns has led to marked improvements in student success. For instance, the data on DFW rates for students in math gateway courses at the Department of Mathematics at The University of Texas at San Antonio helped to drive initiatives for change.

The institution made decisions that decreased class sizes, increased the salaries of the faculty teaching these courses, and brought in more teaching assistants to provide students with personalized support.

Increased performance in mathematics was seen, with the D, F, and withdraw rate on these courses dropping from 35% in Fall 2019 to 25% in Fall 2021. Furthermore, these gains were sustained over time and through the challenges of the pandemic.

Academic innovation is fundamentally rooted in data-informed strategies, underscoring the importance of consistent data analysis to shape effective educational practices (*Principle 5: Multiple forms of data*). This precise approach enables specific interventions tailored to the diverse needs of student groups (*Principle 2: Leveraging diverse interests, goals, knowledge, and experiences*).

SOURCES: Vito et al. (2024); Gutiérrez (n.d.).

how data have been used by an institution to inform redesign of courses in ways that promote higher student success.

In connection with intent comes the approach toward guidance. Some instructors will receive significant guidance on how to use data and others will be left to figure it out on their own. When considering the main ways that instructional data are shared with instructors and administrators, it is often via a report or dashboard. Those modalities by themselves do not dictate the level of guidance that accompanies them, but often they end up as stand-alone tools that are intended to inspire the "necessary" actions in their users but do not clearly identify or enumerate those actions.

Some reports and dashboards come with informational material to provide guidance both for interpretation and potential actions. This guidance can be written into the report and/or part of a compilation of interlinked dashboards, each with its own individual guidance, or can come in the form of formalized instruction. The lessons can be short term, allowing full access upon completion, and/or can take the form of a more extended learning community where faculty and administrators are exposed to the assumptions, limitations, and capabilities of the data along with ideas for structuring student-centered asset-based conversations and actions at the level of instructors and department administrators.

A few examples of this work include (a) the Foundational Course Initiative (FCI)[5] at the University of Michigan where large introductory courses are revised with departmental teams working with the Center for Research on Learning & Teaching and supported by extensive disaggregated data, (b) the Indiana University faculty Learning Analytics Learning Community,[6] (c) the California State University Equity Dashboards and Community College dashboards,[7] and (d) the Sloan Equity & Inclusion in STEM Introductory Courses Stem Equity Learning Community project[8] and resulting course equity reports and communication approach (Carlson, 2022; Meraz, 2022, Rehrey et al., 2019).

Often, these more elaborate approaches are facilitated by teaching and learning center staff, an institutional researcher/learning analytics expert, and/or an administrator focused on educational effectiveness. Since guidance in data interpretation always comes with a point of view, the perspective of the author/deliverer of the guidance needs to be explicit to avoid concerns of hidden messages. In the learning community situation, the group facilitator helps to guide, but not completely dictate, the direction of conversation allowing this approach to often be more palatable and accessible to multiple viewpoints and interpretations of the data (Margalef & Roblin, 2018; Ortquist-Ahrens & Torosyan, 2009).

Lastly, we turn to the importance of cultural context. Culture includes behaviors, norms, and expectations defined at the disciplinary, institutional, and departmental levels with disciplinary and departmental norms often playing the key role in STEM fields. The setting in which data are interpreted can influence how they are perceived and interpreted, and potentially which actions are taken based on them. Potential questions to ask to help reflect on the setting, culture, and context that might be influencing data use include the following: Does the discipline pride itself on the complexity of their area? Is interdisciplinarity valued? Is there a belief that few are able to succeed in the area due to exceptional intellect needed to succeed? Is there greater value placed on abstract/theoretical components than applied? Does the department believe they are one of the few upholding rigor? Does the institution espouse and reward an equity-minded student-centered perspective toward undergraduate education? The answers to these questions and more could affect what data will be collected, who they will be shared with,

[5] More information about the FCI is available at https://crlt.umich.edu/fci

[6] More information about the Learning Community is available at https://ctl.indianapolis.iu.edu/Programs/teaching-with-learning-analytics

[7] More information about the Course Equity Portal is available at https://cep-info.dashboards.calstate.edu/

[8] More information about the SEISMIC Collaboration is available at https://www.seismicproject.org/about/overview/

how they will be perceived and, ultimately, what impact they may have on STEM education.

Even after the data and approach to their use are clear in the form of intent, guidance, and cultural context, it is still important to consider the individual, or individuals, using the data and their own individual experiences with data and with teaching. Often STEM faculty and administrators have dealt primarily with quantitative data. While they will often have some experience with survey data, data from sources such as observations, focus groups, and interviews can be less familiar. In addition, some STEM focused researchers may be uncomfortable incorporating qualitative data that apply to feelings, perceptions, and opinions, and may benefit from guidance on how this type of data can be interpreted.

Measuring Progress in Multiple Ways

The measurement of progress implies the use of one or more forms of data to make informed decisions about the current state as well as suggest metrics for a desired state. Two forms of data, and an intermediate form, are important to consider: quantitative, qualitative, and categorical (a mixed form containing features/elements of both). Quantitative data are numerical (e.g., age, test outcomes, number of credits attempted, percent of total points, course enrollment, etc.), tend to answer questions such as how many, how much, and how often, and are usually collected as part of the institution's standard processes (admissions, Registrar) and through various assessments. Qualitative data describe perceptions, characteristics, behaviors, and experiences (e.g., course experience/evaluation of teaching, sense of belonging, perceptions of classroom and campus climate, etc.), tend to answer questions such as what, why, and how, and are collected through surveys, focus groups, interviews, and/or observation.

The intermediate form of categorical data (e.g., gender, Pell eligibility,[9] race/ethnicity, major, letter grade, enrollment type, prior schooling, veteran, etc.) is based on generally constructed definitions and is usually collected through questionnaires or derived based on quantitative data (Pell status). Categorical data are generally considered qualitative, but they are separated here as they are based less on experience or opinion and more on shared definitions which tend to be mostly stable over time but are subject to the understanding of those that define it. For example, the dominant racial/ethnic group defines who is in the underrepresented group, but the

[9] Pell-eligible students are those from families with low household income. The precise income levels vary with family size and several other factors. Students access Pell grants via the Free Application for Federal Student Aid. Pell grants are frequently used as a proxy for social and economic status in discussion of higher education.

definition is subject to interpretation and can change over time. This can be seen in how Asian/Asian-American workers are not considered underrepresented in science and engineering fields by the National Center for Science and Engineering, National Science Foundation (NCSES, 2023a), while the Department of Education classifies Asian American and Native American Pacific Islander Serving Institutions as Minority Serving Institutions based on their percentage of Asian/Asian-American students. Neither of the definitions used make the actual people involved immune to experiences similar to other minoritized groups. Categorical data also tend to raise a small number of questions of objectivity, though maybe it should raise more. Classification is complex but useful for data analysis. First-generation attendance, Pell eligibility, gender, and other categorical variables can and often do change definition over time so some students may fit one or more of these categories in any given academic year but not in the next.

In general, quantitative data hold a privileged position in STEM conversations likely due to the similarity in numerical analysis approaches applied in STEM research. Qualitative data often are the least appreciated in STEM as they are often relegated to the realm of "opinion" because they relates to perception and experience, realms most often associated with social sciences (which many research funding agencies in the United States recognize as part of STEM but many natural and physical scientists may not). Even with these challenges in what type of data may be favored, to cultivate equitable and effective teaching, data can be used to depict the lived experience of the students. This need will most often require all three forms of data to be available for analysis and interpretation.

Data Dashboards and Decision Making

Understanding what types of data are useful to measure progress does not mean they are readily available to those who can use them to support and enhance equitable and effective teaching. In most higher education settings, whether community college, four-year liberal arts, or comprehensive research institutions, the data are often siloed in a combination of settings that can include numerous categories:

- Admissions: past student records and demographics
- Registrar: course and program registrations and outcomes
- Financial aid: Pell grants and scholarships
- Personnel: instructor information
- Individual classrooms: course elements, student participation, and assessments
- Departments: evaluations and teaching assignments
- Special programs: participation

- Advising: participation and reasons
- Supports: tutoring and other support participation
- Budget and finance: income and expenses
- Facilities: classroom space affordances
- Health: physical and mental
- Extracurricular participation: clubs, sports
- Alumni: post-graduation outcomes

Depending on the size and resources of an institution, some of the data-collecting and interpreting functions may be combined. An institutional research entity (from one individual to many individuals) may have the express duty of combining data from multiple data silos and reporting this synthesis to leadership, with a subset of data used in reporting to a broader campus community. Externally administered undergraduate experience surveys (e.g., University of California Undergraduate Experience Survey,[10] National Survey of Student Engagement,[11] Community College Survey of Student Engagement,[12] and student surveys by the Higher Education Research Institute[13]) can also inform improvement efforts. Data from surveys can provide a window into student experiences at the department, college, and institution levels over time, highlighting positive and negative trends. These tools can be expensive for institutions, however, and it may be difficult to get students to spend the time needed to provide the necessary information, which can result in low response rates and less helpful data.

Data governance and security, from completely absent to highly evolved, also determines the process and availability of data for informing equitable and effective teaching. Some institutions have handed over the process of data ingestion, clean-up, analysis, and visualization to private entities, often at substantial cost. This can lead to limited access for individual instructors. Local efforts focused on equity in introductory STEM courses have developed in a variety of institutions including those associated with the Association of American Universities (AAU) STEM initiative,[14] NSF Improving Undergraduate STEM Education grants, HHMI Inclusive Excellence

---

[10] More information about the University of California Undergraduate Experience Survey is available at https://www.ucop.edu/institutional-research-academic-planning/services/survey-services/UCUES.html

[11] More information about the National Survey of Student Engagement is available at https://nsse.indiana.edu/

[12] More information about the Community College Survey of Student Engagement is available at https://www.ccsse.org/

[13] More information about the surveys conducted by the Higher Education Research Institute is available at https://heri.ucla.edu/overview-of-surveys/

[14] More information about AAU's STEM initiative is available at https://www.aau.edu/education-community-impact/undergraduate-education/undergraduate-stem-education-initiative

projects,[15] and the Sloan Foundation-funded Sloan Equity & Inclusion in STEM Introductory Courses (SEISMIC) Collaboration.[16] Some institutional efforts turn into national-level consulting approaches such as Georgia State University's National Institute for Student Success.[17] In general, external funding has enabled a variety of tools and approaches to be developed and disseminated to a broader number of schools. While attempts at understanding how equity-focused visualizations can impact faculty thinking (Reinholz et al., 2023), more complex collections of visualizations and suggestions are available in the form of course equity reports.[18]

Here we present several examples of data dashboards or other tools for collecting, collating, analyzing, and visualizing data. These examples were chosen to illustrate a variety of approaches and a variety of data types. Most of the tools have other features we do not explore here as well as new features that may have been recently added or are currently under development. Because tools of this complexity are relatively new, the impact that such approaches could have on efforts to achieve equitable and effective teaching has not been methodically studied. We share them here for their potential promise and for the kinds of questions they can raise for decision makers. An approach for making your own dashboard[19] to visualize inequities has also been described (Tatapudy et al., 2024).

Box 9-2 shows an example of an equity dashboard that provides data on academic units that provide courses for students who are majoring in another field. This example was chosen to illustrate how thinking of donor and acceptor departments can inform the pathways students take through their undergraduate education. The student flows as they leave one major and declare another can be considered in the context of the number of effectors students hold. An effector is term that signifies a student as belonging to an underserved group and serves as a mechanism for better understanding inequities. The University of California, Santa Barbara, has used this tool along with a suite of complimentary tools to improve understanding of student experiences and has coupled the tools with professional development on their use.

Box 9-3 shows a different type of equity dashboard that is designed for use by an instructor and is easily accessible from course software they are

[15] More information about the HHMI Inclusive Excellence projects is available at https://www.hhmi.org/programs/inclusive-excellence-3

[16] More information about the SEISMIC Collaboration is available at https://www.seismicproject.org/

[17] More information about NISS is available at https://niss.gsu.edu/

[18] More information about course equity reports is available at https://www.seismicproject.org/seismic-central/the_selc_grant/

[19] https://theobaldlab.shinyapps.io/visualizinginequities/

BOX 9-2
Equity Dashboards at the University of California, Santa Barbara

The University of California, Santa Barbara (UCSB) has created a guided pathway system for instructors and administrators to engage with data. For these visualizations, the campus developed the terminology "effectors of opportunity"—e.g., systemic factors shown to have a relationship to educational access—to disaggregate the data. Students might hold 0, 1, 2, or 3 effectors: low-income, first-generation attendee, and/or member of a minoritized group (1, 2, 3), or none of these (0).

Via questions surrounding specific "pages" of extensive data dashboards, the pathway provides disaggregated visualizations for users to begin by examining quarter-by-quarter program-level patterns, such as a flow diagram showing graduation rates in the major for students who "start in" (see Figure 9-2-1) or "switch into" (see Figure 9-2-2) majors (for entering first-year or transfer students; note that UCSB is on the quarter system).

Then, depending on what users of the system observe, they can move to other visualizations to look at more specific points in the selected group's trajectories to learn more, e.g., at what point in the program different effector groups switch in/out via change of major; pre-major to major trajectories; etc. Next, users can look at disaggregated data focused on course performance at multiple levels (e.g., division, major, lower or upper division). Finally, instructors can receive course-specific reports and equity-focused questions relevant to teaching: Data-Enhanced Teaching and Learning (DETAiL), and the institution's Course Equity Reports (originally developed as part of the SEISMIC collaborative).

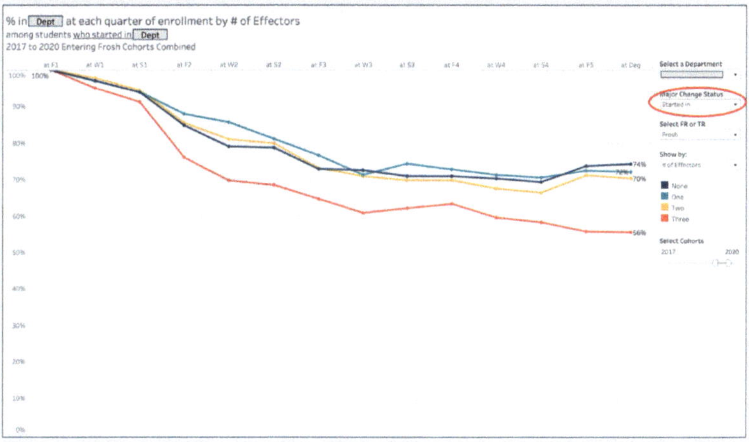

FIGURE 9-2-1 Percentage of students enrolled each quarter who started in that department.

continued

BOX 9-2 Continued

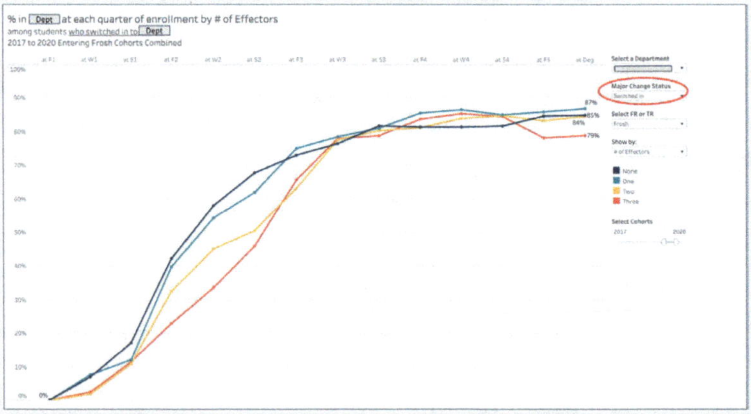

FIGURE 9-2-2 Percentage of students enrolled each quarter who switched into that department.
SOURCE: Data Dashboards, https://otl.ucsb.edu/data-dashboards (University of California, Santa Barbara, n.d.).

BOX 9-3
Equity Dashboards at University of Nebraska-Lincoln

At the University of Nebraska-Lincoln, every instructor can access course-specific dashboards through a customized link embedded in the course software. Instructors can view average assignment grades disaggregated by a wide variety of demographics, including first generation or rural/urban background. The assignments can be summed into assignment groups (see Figure 9-3-1).

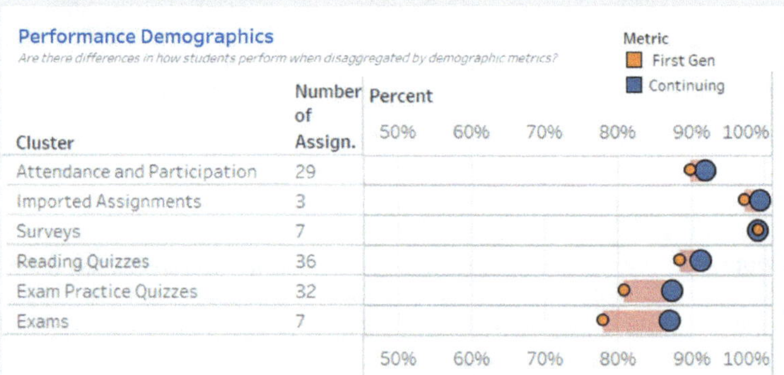

FIGURE 9-3-1 Performance on individual assignments.

BOX 9-3 Continued

Instructors can link out to another view that shows them their course DFW rates across semesters disaggregated by the same set of demographics (see Figure 9-3-2). For small enrollment courses, instructors can sum across semesters in order to reduce noise. These views are complemented by campus-wide initiatives to engage and support instructors in self-reflection as they trial pedagogical interventions.

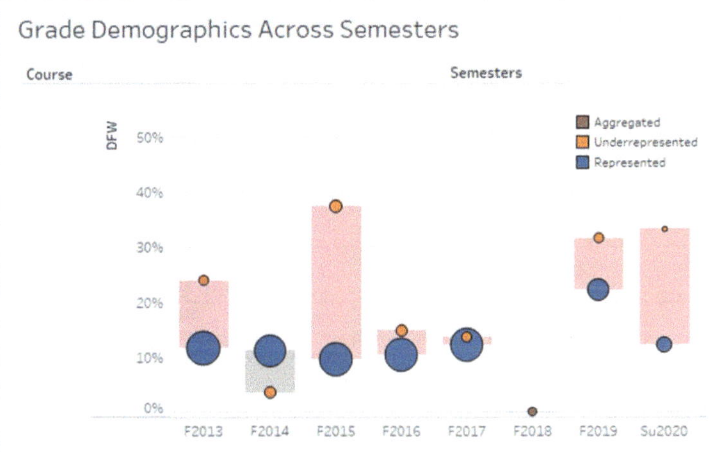

FIGURE 9-3-2 Data on DFW course grades across semesters.
SOURCE: Course Insights, https://analytics.unl.edu/ (University of Nebraska-Lincoln, n.d.).

already using. It illustrates how a set of tools can be created to visualize disaggregated data for course and department outcomes as well as disaggregated outcomes from the learning management system that is in use by the entire university. It is notable that this tool was made broadly available with minimal oversight at the University of Nebraska-Lincoln, and that the institution is slowly growing its community of users.

Box 9-4 shows a third example of equity dashboards that demonstrates how a tool can provide customized results for each instructor within a 24-institution system, the California State University system. It shows instructors disaggregated course outcomes along with any equity indicators observed in their data. Notably the data are coupled with guidance and self-reflection opportunities to help instructors consider the implications of what they see and determine how they can use it to decide where to focus their efforts at improving teaching.

BOX 9-4
Equity Dashboards at California State University

The California State University Course Equity Portal provides each faculty member across the whole system of 24 institutions with historical course grade records and identifies students with notable equity gaps in the rates at which they received low or non-passing grades. Criteria for selecting which courses to show faculty include effect size, overall size of the difference (e.g., must be greater than 10 percentage points difference), and recency. The portal intentionally biases presentation toward more recent terms rather than showing gaps in a course that may have occurred many years ago (see Figure 9-4-1).

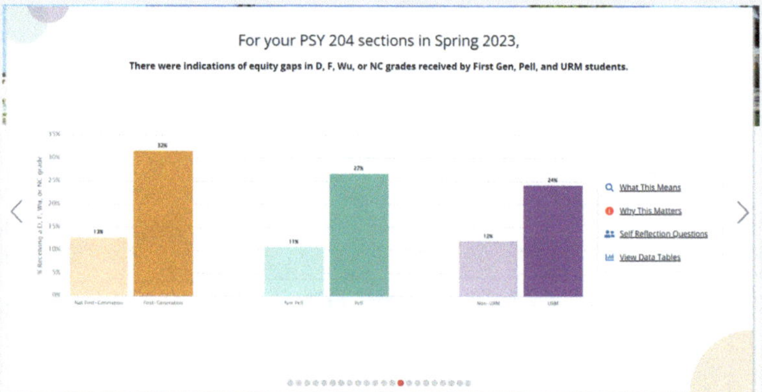

FIGURE 9-4-1 Disaggregated data on DFW course grades.

They include several pop-up FAQs explaining (a) what is shown and why it was selected/criteria used; (b) why it matters—some faculty may not see a clear connection between their in-class teaching and student contact and the long-term outcomes of their students (e.g., retention and graduation rates) so these connections are discussed; and (c) self-reflection questions (see Figure 9-4-2). This last is critical in part because it could be natural for instructors viewing data like these to slip into a defensive and/or deficit mindset; the self-reflection questions can help faculty move themselves toward more constructive/productive questions.

BOX 9-4 Continued

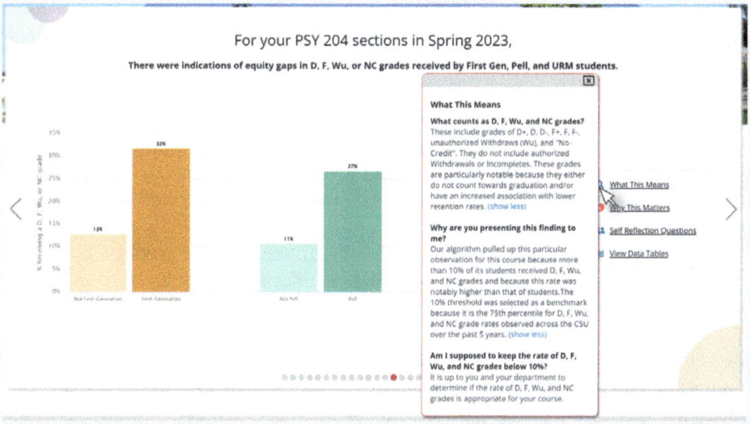

FIGURE 9-4-2 Explanatory text in dashboards designed to guide instructors in interpreting data.
SOURCE: Course Equity Portal, https://www.studentsuccessanalytics.com/courseEquityPortal.html (California State University, n.d.).

Box 9-5 presents one of the earliest tools (2016) that provided detailed aggregated student information to each instructor about the classes they have taught in the past as well as upcoming classes. Additionally, it provided instructors information on how different student characteristics, as well as intersectional identities, performed in the courses they taught, giving them a first-even view of inequities in outcomes. This tool provided a form of inspiration for the other three tools mentioned. Even though this is an old tool, it provides a clear way to see disparities in access by instructor and is notable in part because many across higher education still do not have access to such information on their own students.

Critically, users of data, whether instructors, department heads, or institutional administrators, need support and guidance to disaggregate, interpret, and use the data in ways that minimize bias (see, e.g., McNair et al., 2020). Simply providing data without context and appropriate discussion can lead to unintended consequences or encourage a deficit mindset. For example, predictive analytics could be used to identify students needing additional support or to label or exclude students. Equity gaps in student performance could be used to identify instructors needing additional support or professional learning opportunities, or to judge and punish.

BOX 9-5
Know Your Students at the University of California, Davis

Know Your Students (KYS) at the University of California, Davis (UC Davis) is a web application developed to help instructors plan and execute their courses. It provides information on learning and grades for small and large classes. KYS presents aggregate student demographics and academic data at the course level as well as student testimonials about their background and experience at UC Davis (see Figure 9-5-1). It also serves as a tool that instructors can use to survey students in a course, examine inequities at the assignment level, and reflect on the language used in recorded lectures.

The tool was designed with the intention of providing information that might inspire empathy and motivate course change efforts that could improve overall student learning and equity.

All users only have access to the courses they have taught. Any instructor who would like access to the full set of charts and visualizations showing demographic information about the students they teach as well as historical grade gaps must go through training and/or consultation with the teaching center. In the example, the full dashboard is shown as a strip at left with two highlighted sections showing general class demographic variables for current class (top) and specific equity gaps selectable by group over the time the course is taught (below).

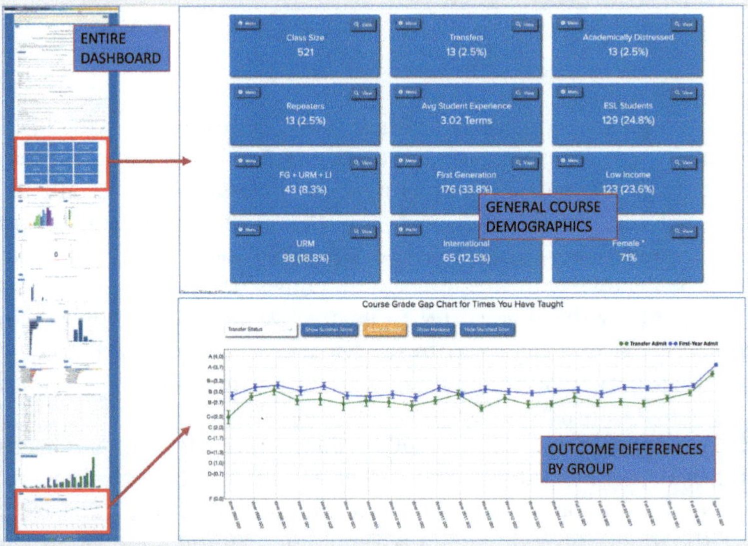

FIGURE 9-5-1 Aggregate student demographics and academic data at the course level.
SOURCE: Know Your Students, https://cee.ucdavis.edu/know-your-students (University of California, Davis, n.d.).

Tools and Approaches Across the Instructional System

While equitable and effective teaching might at first appear to be solely the domain of an individual instructor impacting their classroom, the reality is that moving toward teaching that is equitable can have a much broader impact when such change is approached systemically. Many introductory STEM courses are taught by groups of instructors that, when coordinated, can impact a much larger group of students than any individual instructor. In addition, courses connect with each other within and between departments, and none of them exist independently of academic unit and institutional policies (see Figure 9-2). Therefore, institutional leaders might have to consider these interconnections and the data about the courses in their decision-making process. Institution-level change can benefit from tools and approaches that measure and support progress across various levels of users from the individual to the instructor group to the academic unit, collection of academic units, and the whole campus. Specific ideas and approaches to data at the various levels have been illustrated in Chapters 6 on academic units, courses, and curriculum and Chapter 7 on pathways. Here we illustrate some of the interconnections across academic units that help explain why course-level data might be of interest to institutional leaders (Figure 9-2).

Similarly to how the data suggested by Figure 9-2 can be of use at multiple levels of the system, other course-level data can inform systemic change efforts. Buy-in to those systemic change efforts can be enhanced by sharing of data to STEM instructors when it is done in a thoughtful way and via useful informative tools. The majority of STEM instructors have been trained to look for and appreciate data. Unfortunately, in most higher education classrooms they are limited to the data that they generate by their students' level of learning through homework, quizzes, and tests. While these forms of data provide insights into students' performance, they tend to reflect the outcomes of students' prior opportunities rather than offering insights into potential inequities. As a result, these assessments offer limited guidance on how instructors or instructional teams can address and mitigate these inequities. Implementing alternative grading methods that assess specific learning outcomes can provide instructors with additional and more detailed data (see Chapter 5) and help them see the inequities that they might be able to address.

Administrative leaders can encourage and support instructors' access to valuable information such as who is enrolled, which can be shared via readily accessible dashboards or course reports. Real-time information about student engagement with course materials via the learning management system can help gauge who may need additional attention and system-level early warning systems can guide instructor-student interventions where they

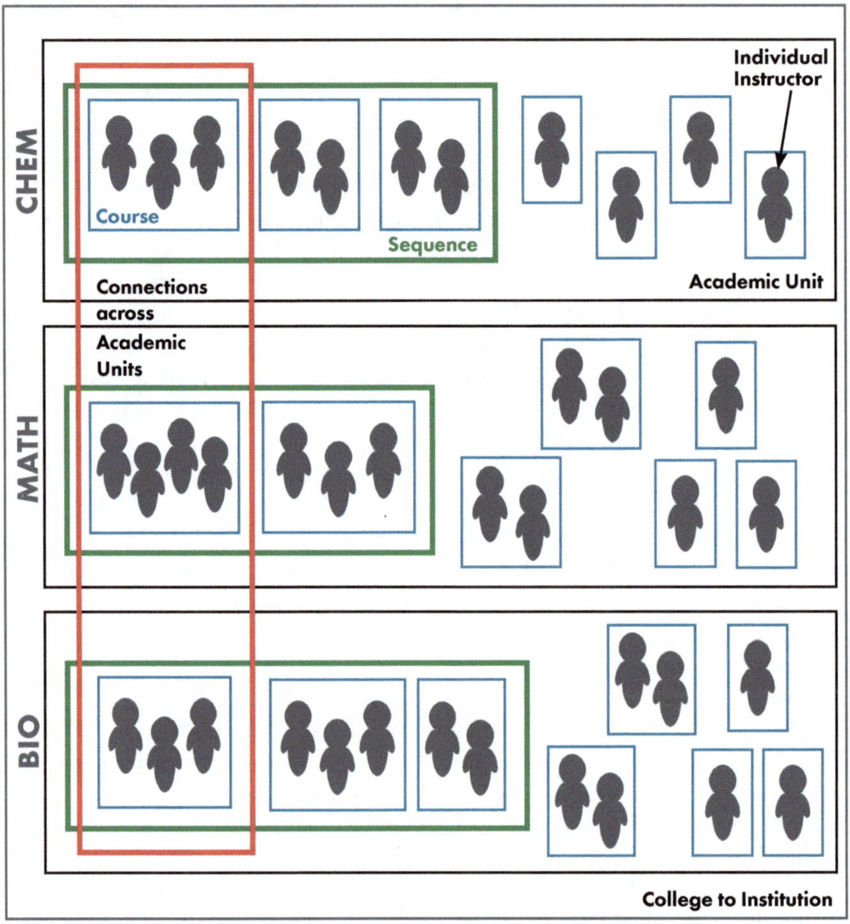

FIGURE 9-2 Course taking across multiple STEM departments.
NOTE: Data can be collected and analyzed at the level of individual instructors, at a course level, as connected between courses in a sequence, within an academic program, how courses connect between programs, as well as aggregated at the level of related academic units and/or the institution.

are most needed. Additionally, affective measures (qualitative or quantitative) such as sense of belonging and departmental climate can be part of a campus-wide data collection effort that is distributed back to departments and instructors and teaching and learning centers can help gather and interpret qualitative data that can help an instructor make instructional corrections when they still have the chance to impact student outcomes. In all these instances, departmental and institutional leaders can create the expectations and infrastructure for these forms of data to be normalized throughout academic units and the institution.

When considering course-level innovations to foster effective and equitable teaching, there are multiple approaches to data for instructors and instructional communities that are being employed. Course teams and learning communities rely heavily on administrative support both for data access as well as for resources to make a well-informed coordinated community possible. Groups of instructors could work together, informed by detailed disaggregated data of prior student outcomes, in order to create courses that prioritize equitable and effective teaching. Additionally, providing structure at the introductory levels via course coordinators, whose primary job is to create a team teaching a highly structured course that is meeting in multiple sections with multiple instructors throughout one term, can provide a consistent student experience that has continuous improvement at its core. Lastly, supporting departmental action teams (see Chapter 6) and interdepartmental learning communities can ensure that valuable instructional expertise gained in one discipline has the opportunity to impact other disciplines within related academic units. None of these activities can be optimized without data resources, compensation for time spent on this, and a clear message of the value of equitable and effective teaching communicated throughout the academic unit and institution.

When considering data at the level of the academic unit there are multiple opportunities that allow STEM units to gauge their progress toward equitable and effective teaching—teaching communicated throughout the academic unit and institution.

When considering data at the level of the academic unit there are multiple opportunities that allow STEM units to gauge their progress toward equitable and effective teaching, including

- Student flow
- Elements of program structure
- Course taking patterns
- Course outcomes
- Bottlenecks in the curriculum
- Climate
- Sense of belonging

Analysis can consider the data in relation to policies and potential for differential impact on different student groups. Student flow can be studied with tools that make clear the paths that students are taking into and out of programs. Such tools can help leaders of academic units determine where a deeper look is warranted. Program structure can help a program look at how their pre- and co-requisite structures enable or block the potential for timely graduation and whether current requirements reflect actual student needs. Bottlenecks in the curriculum can then be identified, and potential course and/or structural changes encouraged to smooth student progress in a program (see Chapter 6). Aside from logistical and course outcome improvements, one also needs to be aware of the climate, student perceptions, and their sense of belonging. Examining policies within a course, academic unit, and beyond can help instructors and administrators to understand the impact the accreted structures created have on equitable and effective student outcomes. For all this work, academic unit leadership and above need to ensure that data are available for all forms of improvement work and encourage data collection that is both qualitative and quantitative and that gives information of various types (e.g., student learning, student engagement, instructor engagement, teaching practices, instructor participation in PLD, etc.) as well as providing time, resources, and guidance on how to use these forms of data.

While some of the examples mentioned in this section focus at the academic unit level (e.g., the department), many of the same approaches mentioned will also work when reviewing these elements at the institutional level—whether that is within a college or school within a university, a collection of academic units, student services units, or the whole institution. In addition, as mentioned earlier, this level of data can be of value to institutional leaders working to make systemic change and to drive continuous improvement toward equitable and effective teaching.

VALUE AND REWARD TEACHING

Recognizing and rewarding faculty for implementing equitable teaching practices is essential to achieving equitable and effective undergraduate STEM education. The institutional reward system can support and encourage such teaching practices at the classroom and departmental levels by valuing teaching activities and rewarding equitable and effective teaching. This may be done through revised promotion and tenure criteria that value innovative and inclusive teaching, professional development opportunities, and appropriate compensation for the additional efforts required to transform teaching practices. Revised teaching evaluation processes are necessary to support these revised criteria. Aligning rewards with the goals of equitable and effective teaching can motivate educators to adopt and maintain these practices.

Different Approaches to Teaching Evaluation

Many higher education institutions nationwide have been using student end-of-term surveys as a form of teaching evaluation. In many cases, these surveys serve as the sole basis for judging the quality of teaching. While many of the surveys used include options for students to contribute written comments, the quantitative portion of the survey data tends to be the focus of annual faculty evaluations, such as considerations for merit raises or promotion. This is largely due to the ease with which the quantitative data are collected, processed, reported, and compared.

Such heavy reliance on this approach to evaluating teaching is a concern, particularly within the context of our larger conversation about inclusion and equity. Numerous studies have documented biases that exist in these student teaching surveys. While most studies on this subject have examined the effects of faculty gender on survey scores (Boring, 2017; Flaherty, 2022; MacNell et al., 2015; Mitchell & Martin, 2018), bias has also been seen to result from the instructor's race/ethnicity, accent, attractiveness, age, and LGBTQIA+ identity (Basow & Martin, 2012; Heffernan, 2021; Kreitzer & Sweet-Cushman, 2021). Furthermore, there is little evidence that the scores on these surveys correlate with measures of student learning or teaching quality, and some evidence to suggest that, in fact, they do not (Esarey & Valdes, 2020; Spooren et al., 2013). This is not to say that the student voice is not important in understanding what takes place in a course. Instead, the information provided by student end-of-term surveys must be understood as feedback and a reflection of the students' own experience, not as a measure of teaching quality, and used appropriately within that interpretation (D'Agostino & Kosegarten, 2015). One important way to do this is to include multiple sources of evidence about an instructor's teaching, as described in Chapter 8.

Holistic approaches to teaching evaluation (see Chapter 6) have the advantage that they can take into account the aspects of teaching that take place outside of a classroom setting—whether that be the laboratory, the field, or an online classroom—and would thus be invisible to students. For example, there is a significant amount of work that takes place before a course begins, such as planning a syllabus to include selected source materials, creating assessments and learning progressions, preparing course materials, and engaging in professional development. While students will see the finished products of these efforts, the reasoning behind them may not be evident to a student; yet the approach to these planning steps may indeed distinguish higher and lower quality teaching. Other components of teaching include advising students on such topics as their educational journeys, majors, career aspirations, specific courses, undergraduate research opportunities, or internships as well as engaging in community outreach, or carrying out scholarly studies on teaching. These and other aspects of teaching can be represented and properly valued in a holistic approach to teaching evaluation, balancing the limited information from the in-class feedback that has long been provided through student end-of-term surveys.

Reform of the Reward and Recognition System

Because the current approach of evaluating faculty teaching using primarily (or solely) student surveys is so deeply flawed, it is difficult to properly recognize and reward teaching with this approach to measurement. Therefore, we consider a discussion of the methods used for the evaluation of teaching a core component of a larger call to reform teaching and the educational experience for all students. Similar arguments have been made by others, such as the Boyer 2030 Commission report, which states, "Aligning the faculty rewards structure with the stated educational mission of the university is the most important reform we can make to ensure sustained, authentic institutional change in the quality of undergraduate education" (2022, p. 33). Similarly, others have said that when an institution uses a well-rounded process to measure and reward teaching it is both fairer to faculty members and better for students (McMurtrie & Supiano, 2021).

If considering the example of a college or university in which faculty have both a teaching and research requirement in their contract, every faculty member knows that they can achieve recognition for their innovations, productivity, and creativity in the arena of research. They are able to demonstrate their contributions through publications, grants, presentations, and other metrics of research productivity, which are occurring on a regular basis and hold legitimacy for others in the department or institution. This varied list of metrics underscores the reasons that a multi-dimensional approach to examining teaching quality is also needed. In fact, for faculty in disciplines where the connections between their discipline-based work and equity issues are less clear, attention to equity-minded teaching can be viewed as at best a distraction and, at worst, a waste of time (McGee, 2020; Perez et al., 2023). Creating a system of evaluating teaching that everyone at the institution can trust to be meaningful is a first step in raising the value of teaching in the reward and recognition system and ensuring that all teaching can be both equitable and excellent.

While the actions related to implementing a holistic teaching evaluation approach will take place at the department level of an institution, the work that will be required to formulate and use these practices will need support from institutional leaders. In fact, reform of faculty evaluation in ways that will support equity-minded teaching is a third-order organizational change (Marbach-Ad et al., 2016; Miller & Fairweather, 2016). However, without changes to campus-level faculty evaluation policies, including workload, annual and merit review, and promotion policies, it will be difficult to move equity-minded teaching into the core of an institution.

SUMMARY

The higher education space has many types of institutions that vary in their specifics. However, all institutions are responsible for implementing equitable and effective teaching, and all face challenges in this work as well. The committee acknowledges that the resources, structures, and titles of the actors may be very different in different types of institutions, but the need to provide courses for students resonates across disciplinary and institutional types. Data can be useful at all institution types and at all levels within institutions. Multiple types of data can be used to provide various perspectives on the components of the system and their interconnections and that can in turn inform decision making to improve equitable and effective teaching.

Conclusion 9.1: Policies and procedures at the institutional level can either impede or promote implementation of the Principles for Equitable and Effective Teaching. Change toward equitable and effective teaching will require coordinated effort from multiple levels of institutional leadership and a culture of growth that is responsive to the needs of students and instructors. Upper-level administrators (e.g., deans and provosts) can analyze and reform policies and practices so that the institutional reward system for faculty, instructors, and academic unit leaders is aligned with the goal of equitable and effective teaching and all stakeholders are supported in change efforts.

Conclusion 9.2: Institutional change is an ongoing process of continuous improvement that can include (a) opportunities to become familiar with goals and principles of change, (b) recognition of an academic unit's culture, (c) attention to power dynamics in the institution, and (d) communication among key stakeholders.

Conclusion 9.3: Data, both aggregated and disaggregated, are a key tool to understand, enact, and monitor change. Both quantitative and qualitative data are needed to fully understand what is happening in a system and to provide information to guide change efforts. Reflective analysis of data best guides policy and practice decisions and informs ongoing efforts at improvement. Grades, and the approaches to assigning them, do not convey the full complexity of information about student learning.

10

Recommendations for Current Action and Future Research

Addressing inequities within the system of higher education involves making changes at every level of the institution that enable instructors to improve instruction in ways that benefit all students. Designing, implementing, and improving equitable and effective teaching and learning requires coordinated and intentional action by a variety of stakeholders across and beyond the system of higher education, including not just instructors but also academic unit leaders, institutional leaders, researchers, governing boards, professional societies, funders of science, technology, engineering, and mathematics (STEM) education, and students themselves.

Working toward equitable and effective instruction involves continuous improvement with repeated cycles of reflection and innovation by instructors, both individually and collectively. This work demands the support of academic units and institutional leadership. Focused attention on examining and improving the coherence of learning goals across course sequences, programs, and majors can (a) help instructors clarify the overall goals for students and facilitate improvements in individual courses, (b) facilitate alignment of practices and policies at all levels with the Principles for Equitable and Effective Instruction, and (c) increase transparency and improve student outcomes.

Structural changes and collective responsibility within and across institutions will be necessary for sustained and successful implementation of equitable and effective teaching. These changes include ensuring that all instructors are empowered to provide equitable and effective STEM education and that they have the knowledge, skills, incentives, and supports needed to create welcoming STEM courses, built on knowledge about how students learn, in which all students have equal opportunity to succeed. Attention to the social dynamics and culture of the learning environment is a crucial component of understanding the systems and structures needed to support learning and the teaching in the classroom.

The Committee has analyzed evidence and examples throughout this report and presented conclusions as they arose in each chapter. This chapter does not recount the evidence presented throughout the document but does provide an overview of the implications we drew from that evidence. As can be seen from the conclusions shared in the earlier chapters, there is strong evidence to show that teaching practices can be improved to be more equitable and effective. The evidence is not as robust that changes to policies and priorities can support those necessary changes to teaching practices. However, together these changes have a high likelihood to help achieve a system in which all undergraduate STEM students experience equitable and effective learning experiences, feel belonging, and have the opportunity to succeed in their STEM courses and programs regardless of their identity or background.

The committee therefore authored recommendations for action that span the range of levels and actors in higher education. Making student-centered learning a central and explicit goal of course design is a necessary, but not sufficient, component of achieving equitable and effective learning experiences. The challenge of defining equitable and effective teaching is also partly a journey in helping the higher education community redefine what teaching means, and in so doing identifying the equity-based behaviors currently missing from our current notion of effective teaching. This redefinition requires individuals to reflect upon their own practices as well as work toward changes to the overall system. The recommendations therefore call for communication, questions, reflection, and discussion, not simply action. The committee recognizes that current political, social, and financial conditions make taking action on these recommendations challenging for actors in higher education and that achieving these ends should be a long-term goal, not one that contributes to burnout of instructors and administrators.

These recommendations apply across the wide range of types of institutions in which undergraduate STEM education occurs. Despite the varying sizes, priorities, and budgets, all institutions do share a responsibility for providing high-quality STEM learning experiences for all students. They are individually and collectively responsible for questioning longstanding policies and practices in undergraduate STEM education that have produced, perpetuated, and exacerbated differences in opportunities, experiences, and outcomes among post-secondary STEM students. This questioning, reflection, and evidence-based action is needed to ensure that all students—including those from lower socio-economic backgrounds, students of color, rural students, first-generation college goers, women, LGBTQIA+ students, veterans, parents and other caregivers, and students with disabilities—have equitable opportunities to learn about and engage in STEM.

TOWARD EQUITABLE AND EFFECTIVE LEARNING EXPERIENCES

STEM learning is shaped by the characteristics and experiences of learners, myriad social interactions, the broader cultural context, and policies at all levels. The identities and backgrounds of students and instructors alike influence these processes and outcomes. This is evident in the research, which finds that students from lower socio-economic backgrounds, students of color, first-generation college attendees, women, and students with disabilities are among the groups who have consistently fared worse in post-secondary STEM education.

Widespread use of teaching strategies that are not supported by research have contributed to the disparities in opportunity and outcomes for undergraduate STEM students. Recent changes in the demographics of the student population and pressures on higher education to meet the demands of the 21st century STEM workplace underscore the need to re-evaluate instructional practices in STEM and improve the learning experiences of undergraduate students in STEM courses. Instructional practices that take students' interests and experiences into account and provide them with authentic opportunities to engage with disciplinary content, practices, and analysis have been shown to be more effective than instructional practices that rely solely on lecture, reading, and memorization of content, procedures, and algorithms. In particular, students' experiences in foundational courses are especially important for their persistence in STEM, because often, these courses filter out students rather than deepen their engagement, interest, and understanding of STEM topics. Improving instruction in these courses specifically is an important lever for producing more equitable opportunities and outcomes for undergraduate STEM students.

Students in STEM take many paths through higher education, including transitions within and across institutions and use of different modalities (e.g., online courses, on-campus instruction, internships, and apprenticeships). There are barriers to students' success that arise from the current quality of instruction and the structure of course offerings and requirements. Students are usually expected to take a sequence of STEM courses that are often not well coordinated, and the overall goals for what students learn in individual courses and across course sequences are often not well articulated. While the availability of diverse pathways provides choices and options for students, it also increases the complexity of their learning experiences. This diversity in learning experiences makes it even more important to employ equitable and effective instructional practices that are responsive to students' interests and previous experiences.

Equitable and effective approaches make student learning and a student-centered approach the primary driver. This is in contrast to an instructor-centered course that schedules, policies, and assessments are intended to allow the instructor to cover a certain volume of content. Courses rooted in equitable and effective teaching (a) are designed around clear learning goals, (b) recognize the students' role in their own learning, and (c) cultivate environments that give students agency to engage in the course material in ways that welcome and respect their identities

The seven Principles for Equitable and Effective Teaching developed for this report by the Committee are derived from the evidence on learning and teaching. As discussed in detail in Chapter 4, these Principles are intended to inform the design and enactment of more equitable and effective pedagogical approaches. Using these Principles to improve undergraduate teaching and learning in STEM will require a commitment from leaders of STEM academic units and higher education institutions as well as from individual instructors. The Principles are as follows:

- Principle 1: Students need opportunities to actively engage in disciplinary learning
- Principle 2: Students' diverse interests, goals, knowledge, and experiences can be leveraged to enhance learning
- Principle 3: STEM learning involves affective and social dimensions
- Principle 4: Identity and sense of belonging shape STEM teaching and learning
- Principle 5: Multiple forms of data can provide evidence to inform improvement
- Principle 6: Flexibility and responsiveness to situational and contextual factors support student learning
- Principle 7: Intentionality and transparency create more equitable opportunities

Realizing equitable and effective teaching through the adoption of these Principles is a multi-level endeavor that involves individuals, academic units, and institutions. Individual or groups of instructors undertake continuous improvement through repeated cycles of innovation, implementation, and reflection/learning. Decisions and policies related to teaching can impede or promote the implementation of the seven Principles. Academic units hold collective responsibility for ensuring that instructors working under their auspices have the resources and supports they need to provide equitable and effective undergraduate STEM learning experiences, and that all learning experiences overseen by the academic unit, including courses, assessments, laboratories, field experiences, research experiences, and prerequisite and other requirements for programs and majors, provide equitable and effective STEM learning experiences for all students. Academic units (e.g., departments or programs) play a major role in decisions and policies about teaching assignments, career advancement, rewards, promotion, and tenure; these decisions explicitly or tacitly establish how teaching is valued, recognized, evaluated, and rewarded. In some academic units those teaching courses that are foundational or have large enrollments or that are designed for non-major learners are not treated with the same respect as those who teach upper-level courses focused on students majoring in the discipline. Academic unit decisions and policies related to teaching can impede or promote the implementation of equitable and effective teaching strategies. Institutional leadership can articulate and prioritize goals that align with the seven Principles and provide the financial and human resources that are needed for significant change at the system level.

RECOMMENDATIONS FOR IMPROVING INSTRUCTION AND COURSES

Achieving equitable and effective teaching and learning requires improving instruction and courses, and specific recommendations are provided here for steps toward those improvements. However, these changes will be difficult to achieve and will not have optimal impact if the subsequent recommendations on how to alter the existing systemic incentives are not also addressed.

Recommendation 1: Instructors, working independently and collaboratively, should use the Principles for Equitable and Effective Teaching to reflect on and revise their instructional practices, approaches to assessment, course syllabi and grading policies, and the selection and use of instructional resources. They should articulate clear learning goals for courses and use these learning goals to design instruction and assessment for courses in all modalities and settings, including online, in the classroom, in the laboratory, and in the field and continually reflect on and improve instructional practices over time based on student learning data.

Recommendation 2: Members of academic units collectively should take responsibility for reviewing the portfolio of courses offered and the sequencing of courses using the Principles for equitable and effective teaching. They should work collectively to define clear course and program learning outcomes and use them to refine and revise the content and pedagogy of course sequences and individual courses. As part of the

review, academic units should use both aggregated and disaggregated data of multiple forms to identify courses or course sequences that appear to be producing systematic, inequitable outcomes and undertake revisions to address them.

Recommendation 3: Developers of instructional materials and resources at institutions of higher education, non-profits, and companies should work collaboratively with experts in teaching and learning (and experienced instructors) to develop resources and materials, including educational and instructional technology, using the Principles for Equitable and Effective Teaching. as a guide for informing design from the initial stages of conceptualization. If developers attempt to use the Principles to modify a product in a later stage of development it is less likely that the resulting product will be equitable and effective. Developers should also work collaboratively with experts in teaching and learning (and experienced instructors) to create the professional learning, support, and guidance that instructors will need to equitably and effectively use their products.

RECOMMENDATIONS FOR VALUING AND SUPPORTING INSTRUCTORS

Changes to courses and instruction as recommended in the previous section require that academic units and institutions value teaching itself and the efforts instructors make to learn about and provide equitable learning experiences for students. The recommendations below convey multiple ways that academic units and institutions can engage in the continuous improvement process that is central to achieving equitable and effective teaching. **Recommendations 4–7** focus on how academic units and institutions can demonstrate that they value teaching and instructors and **Recommendations 8–10** on how they can support professional learning about teaching.

Continuous improvement requires support for all instructors to engage in professional learning and development (PLD) throughout their careers. The specific nature of the professional learning will likely vary over time as instructors develop expertise, but the goal of equitable and effective teaching necessitates an ongoing process of learning and reflection. This process of learning and reflection is important for everyone who engages with undergraduates in their courses and classrooms: full-time tenure-track faculty, teaching-track faculty, VITAL educators (visiting faculty, instructors, teaching assistants, adjunct faculty, lecturers), graduate student teaching assistants, postdoctoral fellows, undergraduate learning assistants, and others.

An important aspect of PLD is to cultivate a practice of reflection in which instructors review teaching experiences and how they can learn from those experiences in ways that will improve future teaching and learning. PLD can occur on campus or via technology and in both formal and informal ways. Digital technologies present opportunities to enhance equitable and effective teaching in STEM when they are introduced along with professional learning and development opportunities that provide guidance and support.

Institutional support is needed to ensure that ongoing high-quality PLD is available and accessible for all types of instructors. VITAL educators are often excluded from professional development opportunities and communities. The reasons for this vary but include lack of funding for time spent on PLD, exclusion from faculty or academic unit meetings and functions, and lack of appropriate venues for connecting with other instructors. Graduate students and postdoctoral scholars need professional learning and development to prepare for potential roles as future faculty in addition to professional learning and development related to any existing roles as instructors or teaching assistants.

Recommendation 4: Academic unit and institutional leaders should support participation of all instructors in professional learning and development grounded in the Principles for Equitable and Effective Teaching by providing resources, encouragement, and financial compensation. Specifically, they should foster a culture of improvement and change policies to provide incentives and compensation for instructors to engage in professional learning and development as part of their workload so that all instructors receive a base level of preparation before they begin teaching and are provided with, compensated for, and encouraged to participate in ongoing opportunities to continue improving their teaching. Implementation will involve coordinating with academic units to also compensate instructor time (such as course release, salary increase, or funding bonus) for developing or revising courses to align with equitable and effective teaching practices, potentially including changing lesson goals, changing instructional practices, and/or changing instructional tools.

Recommendation 5: Academic unit and institutional leaders should foster a support structure for instructors (e.g., centers for teaching and learning, science, technology, engineering, and mathematics education centers) that can (a) organize and offer accessible professional learning opportunities (including on campus, virtual, and asynchronous) that are grounded in the Principles for Equitable and Effective Teaching, and (b) support academic unit-level professional learning and development opportunities.

Recommendation 6: Graduate and postdoctoral program leaders should revise programs and expectations to make preparation for teaching an integral learning goal of programs. They should work to change cultures so that all participants are encouraged and supported in meaningful professional learning and development activities focused on teaching, learning, course design, and creating an equitable learning environment that embraces and promotes equitable and effective teaching. When teaching, graduate students and postdoctoral scholars should be supported by a mentor who has expertise in the use of the Principles to support equitable and effective teaching.

Recommendation 7: Academic unit leaders should develop policies and practices that value, recognize, and reward equitable and effective teaching. Steps they can take include

- Providing time in unit meetings to discuss teaching-related topics such as reviewing students' outcomes in courses, discussing the unit's strategy for continuous improvement of teaching, and sharing information about successes and challenges in teaching.
- Supporting individual and groups of instructors as they improve and revise their courses, including providing dedicated time to work on course revision or additional financial compensation.
- Encouraging and providing time and resources for collaboration among instructors to work on course and curriculum revision and redesign.
- Designing policies and practices for making teaching assignments that value the teaching of all courses and the contributions of all instructors regardless of their appointment type.
- Identifying and supporting cohorts of instructors who are dedicated to and interested in implementing equitable and effective teaching and providing them with leadership opportunities.
- Facilitating the access and use of relevant data that can help instructors identify and monitor differences and changes in student outcomes.

Recommendation 8: Academic unit leaders should revise practices around hiring and onboarding of new instructors so that teaching is an essential and valued component of the role. In hiring, job candidates should be evaluated by their ability to engage in equitable and effective teaching. Once hired, instructors should receive mentoring related to equitable and effective teaching and be provided with opportunities to engage in ongoing professional learning and development.

Recommendation 9: Academic unit leaders should use the Principles for Equitable and Effective Teaching as professional standards that form the basis of teaching evaluation processes. To achieve this goal, they should use evidence-based approaches to evaluate the entire portfolio of teaching-related activities. This holistic evaluation should go beyond student surveys to include other forms of evidence (e.g., structured teaching observations, analysis of teaching artifacts, course design, instructor reflections) in formative and holistic evaluation of teaching.

Recommendation 10: Academic unit and institutional leaders should include and value teaching during review processes for advancement and retention such that all instructors are expected and required to provide equitable and effective teaching.

- **Determine reappointment, raises, merit, promotion, and tenure in a clear and transparent way that rewards instructor work toward achieving equitable and effective teaching.**
- **Develop approaches for determining promotion and tenure that include holistic evidence-based evaluation of the faculty member's teaching.**
- **Develop processes for changes to salaries and titles that consider all different categories of employees who have teaching responsibilities, including visiting faculty, instructors, teaching assistants, adjunct faculty, and lecturers (VITAL instructors).**

RECOMMENDATIONS FOR MEASURING AND ADVANCING SYSTEM CHANGE

Change toward equitable and effective teaching requires coordinated effort at both institutional and national levels to achieve changes to policy and practice, and a culture of growth that is responsive to the needs of students and instructors. Institutional efforts to support continuous improvement are complex and require action on multiple levels within the institution as well as support and guidance from national actors such as funders and researchers with specialized expertise or resources. The following recommendations provide actions for leaders of institutions and academic units (**Recommendations 11 and 12**) and for national actors (**Recommendations 13–15**).

Equitable and effective teaching requires attention not only to what happens in courses, but also to the entire experience of students at the institution from their first encounters with post-secondary education, early transitions such as determining their next steps after foundational courses and choosing a major, all the way through searching for post-degree or post-credential employment or applying to graduate programs. Therefore, this multi-level coordination includes connections to student affairs, student success, disability resources centers, academic advisors, tutoring centers, and other professionals. Many of the specifics for how institutional leaders engage with these resources on their campuses are outside the scope of this study, yet essential to the success of change efforts toward equitable and effective STEM education and should be kept in mind as leaders work to follow our recommendations.

Institutional leaders can analyze and reform policies and practices so that incentives for faculty, instructors, and academic unit leaders are aligned with the goal of equitable and effective teaching and all stakeholders are supported in change efforts. Policies and procedures at the institutional level can either impede or promote implementation of the principles for equitable and effective teaching. Data, both aggregated and disaggregated, are a key tool to understand, enact, and monitor change. Both quantitative and qualitative data are needed to fully understand what is happening in a system and to provide information to guide change efforts. Institutional change at the deepest levels is an ongoing process. Reflective analysis of data best guides policy and practice decisions and informs ongoing efforts to improve.

Administrators can also analyze and reform policies and practices so that the institutional reward system for faculty, instructors, and academic unit leaders is aligned with the goal of equitable and effective teaching and all stakeholders are supported in change efforts. For example, grades and the approaches to assigning them do not fully convey the complexity and extent of student learning; policies that support student learning and that promote more equitable and effective grading approaches might be explored.

Institutional change toward equitable and effective education is an ongoing process of continuous improvement that can include (a) opportunities for institutional stakeholders at all levels to become familiar with the Principles for Equitable and Effective Teaching and why they are important; (b) attention to an academic unit's culture and the challenges of implementing change; (c) both top-down and bottom-up changes with attention to power dynamics in the institution and who holds positional power as well as who holds more informal power and influence; and (d) vigilant and transparent communication among key stakeholders.

Setting up processes for continuous improvement can have a larger long-term impact than seeking quick, dramatic change. Many actors outside institutions of higher education can contribute to the continuous improvement process through providing financial or informational resources as well as prioritizing and publicizing approaches aligned to the Principles for Equitable and Effective Teaching.

Recommendation 11: Institutional leaders should develop and support the infrastructure and approaches needed to collect, use, and monitor data about courses and programs, as well as student outcomes, experiences, belonging, and other affective measures. They should provide access to the system and to the data in a transparent way so that instructors and academic units can use it to improve teaching and learning. This will entail offering guidance to academic units about which metrics to review on a regular basis and multi-level strategies to investigate and decrease any gaps discovered. The systems should include qualitative and quantitative data from both internal and external (from studies or federal agencies) sources and allow for disaggregation of data by students' demographic characteristics so that revised policies and practices can be implemented to decrease disparities.

Recommendation 12: Members of academic units should take into account the complexity of the student undergraduate population and their varied goals and pathways to ensure that all students can equitably and effectively experience and benefit from the unit's courses, programs, and credentials. They should examine data for obstacles and barriers to undergraduate science, technology, engineering, and mathematics learning and apply the Principles for Equitable and Effective Teaching to smooth the educational journeys of their students. Academic units should analyze transition points, course offerings, student experiences, and student outcomes and use the information to remediate obstacles that limit student learning or student progress toward a credential, especially obstacles that disproportionately impact students who are members of underserved groups.

Recommendation 13: Professional, academic, and disciplinary societies and organizations should publicly endorse and elevate the Principles for Equitable and Effective Teaching and adopt them to guide their work related to undergraduate education. Specifically, they should

- Share clear position statements on and advocate for the importance of equitable and effective teaching with their members, constituents, and the public.
- Coordinate with teaching experts in their discipline to design, offer, or coordinate professional learning and development opportunities to support instructors in their discipline to implement equitable and effective teaching practices.
- Coordinate with teaching experts to develop, curate, and promote resources for addressing discipline-specific teaching needs.

- Offer events that showcase and disseminate practices, tools, data, and research related to implementing equitable and effective teaching.
- Cultivate professional learning and development communities for current and future instructors and encourage academic units to do the same.
- Include experts in equitable and effective teaching in society leadership.
- Review the guidelines for any accreditations that they administer and support academic units to implement these guidelines in ways that maximize equitable and effective teaching and learning.
- Promote comparative studies that help identify approaches that lead to more equitable outcomes, especially for foundational courses.

Recommendation 14: Oversight bodies should endorse and adopt the Principles for Equitable and Effective Teaching to guide their work. Through their oversight, they should require institutional leaders to demonstrate that work at their institution is being done in alignment with the Principles and that policies and procedures have been updated accordingly.

Recommendation 15: Funders should endorse and adopt the use of the Principles for Equitable and Effective Teaching to prioritize evidence-based projects that support both implementation of and research about equitable and effective teaching. Implementation funding should include support for ongoing professional learning and development activities at different types of institutions of higher education, especially those that have fewer resources. Research funding should include some long-term projects that study student experiences and outcomes over time. Implementation projects should include evaluation plans.

GUIDANCE FOR IMPLEMENTATION

The above recommendations provide specific guidance for key actors in the system of undergraduate STEM education. Because changes are needed by multiple actors and at multiple levels across the system the list of recommended actions is long.

While many have already begun work to improve teaching and learning, we provide here some starting points for a few selected key actors who are beginning or ramping up this work: institutional leaders, academic units, and instructors.

Actions for Institutional Leaders

Institutional leaders create the environment in which academic units and instructors of STEM courses adapt current policies, practices, and instructional methods to improve educational outcomes for all students. While some instructors and academic units will create equitable and effective environments on their own, getting to all instructors and academic units will require support and guidance to act. **Recommendations 5, 10, and 11** are critical in providing the support needed to make changes across the institutions. As a starting point, institutional leaders can ensure that their policies and practices reward teaching that leads to equitable outcomes. This can be done through merit and promotion processes (**Recommendation 10, bullet #1**). Critical to this could be revising the teaching evaluation process (**Recommendation 9**) or providing the data needed by academic units and instructors to improve courses, programs, student outcomes, experience, belonging, and other affective measures (**Recommendation 11**). Institutional leaders can provide the necessary support by ensuring that professional learning opportunities are available for all instructors (**Recommendation 5**).

Actions for Academic Unit Leaders

As discussed in Chapter 6, academic units have oversight and responsibility for the courses that students take and for STEM degrees and programs. They are also an organizing unit for the instructors who teach these courses. Leaders of academic units can start advancing this work by leading an effort to review curriculum and program learning goals and the structure of STEM programs (**Recommendation 2**) as well as how their programs align with the needs of the student population (**Recommendation 12**). This exploration is best informed by the use of quantitative and qualitative disaggregated data. Through this review and discussions with the faculty of the unit, leaders can help determine how to best support instructors, either individually or collectively, to learn about and adopt the instructional and curricular changes needed to create equitable and effective learning environments (**Recommendations 4, 5, and 7**) and how to include teaching in hiring, evaluations, and reward structures for instructors (**Recommendation 2, 9, and 10**).

Actions for Instructors

The principles presented in Chapter 4 provide a framework for instructors to apply **Recommendation 1** to decide what changes are needed to create equitable and effective learning environments for their students.

For many, starting with applying *Principle 1: Active engagement* to their course(s) will help them identify a place to begin (e.g., changes to assessments as discussed in Chapter 5) with **Recommendation 2** (use of data to identify inequitable outcomes in courses or course sequences) providing the information needed to determine whether the change(s) desired are happening and if the impacts are improving experiences and outcomes.

As discussed above, instructors need academic unit and institutional leaders to support them in this work by providing the reward structures (**Recommendation 10**) and professional development opportunities (**Recommendations 4 and 5**) needed. Taken together, the Principles and the report's recommendation will help instructors develop the continuous improvement mindset needed to support all students who take STEM courses and pursue STEM degrees.

RESEARCH AGENDA

While the Committee found extensive evidence to support their conclusions and inform their recommendations, they also found areas where their questions could not be answered due to lack of data or a need for future research. Informed by their analysis of the existing context and current research, the following areas of future research are proposed. This section lays out some categories of research that would help inform continued improvement in efforts to achieve equitable and effective learning experiences. For each category, a few themes are proposed to guide future studies of equitable and effective teaching and learning. A few specific examples are included for each theme to illustrate some of the types of research questions that fall under that theme. Across these categories, this research should be done in ways that illuminate and provide information about student learning in a wide range of modalities and across institution types.

Toward Equitable and Effective Learning Experiences

As the classroom becomes more diverse with students from a full range of identity groups, conducting more research and disaggregating data will help instructors better understand how to serve student needs. Discipline-based education research can provide information on specific courses of study. Meta-analyses, landscape analyses, causal research, and longitudinal studies would allow for greater understanding.

Student Pathways

To better understand undergraduate student experiences researchers can examine pathways for various categories of students, such as those who do not major in STEM fields, those who commute to school or learn primarily online, those who transfer institutions during their studies, as well as differences by gender, race, first-generation status, or other demographic categories. Potential research questions in this theme include

- What data are most effective in helping institutions track and modify the barriers and opportunities transfer students encounter at receiving institutions? To what extent do outcomes (e.g., rate of completion, total time to graduation, total cost of degree, retention in a STEM major or in STEM overall) differ for students who complete their bachelor's degree at one institution versus at multiple institutions?
- To what extent do students use the practices and concepts they learn as undergraduates in their future jobs? How frequently do students entering career and technical education (CTE) programs finish and obtain employment in their intended field? How does this differ across different types of CTE programs and how does it compare to the job and career pathways of non-CTE students?

Learning and Grading

Higher education has traditionally attempted to use grades to measure learning, but alternative grading approaches may better measure what students learn and their preparation to enter the workforce than traditional methods of assigning grades. Further research could help determine to what extent grades correlate with increased student understanding due to their experiences in courses or reflect differences in knowledge or privilege that students possess when they enter courses. Potential research questions in this theme include

- What methods for more holistic approaches to evaluating the capabilities of STEM students work best to demonstrate learning?
- What methods of measuring student engagement with their program content, relevant research experiences, and skills gained might inform decisions about how to make learning more student centered? To what extent do programmatic scale interventions alter student learning, sense of belonging, and sense of identity?
- What aspects of interdisciplinary or cross-disciplinary courses contribute to increases in student engagement, persistence, learning, or future employment prospects?

Valuing and Supporting Instructors

Significant changes have occurred in the composition of the instructional workforce over the past decades. Today's instructors are under significant pressures and stresses. Additional studies could provide information that would allow institutions to better support these instructors and their ability to provide equitable and effective learning experiences. The following themes and research questions are examples that could improve understanding of the instructional workforce and its role in equitable and effective teaching and learning.

Instructional Workforce

The percentage of the instructional workforce that is full-time tenured/tenure track has been declining. Research could explore the impact this may have had on the culture of academic units and institutions, including its potential impact on attitudes about teaching. Potential research questions in this theme include

- Are there differences in the approaches taken to teaching by those who more strongly identify as scientists versus educators? Are there differences in instructor identity? What aspects of identity are most important for instructors who teach CTE courses?
- Who are the VITAL STEM educators? Do demographics differ when comparing those who work at community colleges versus other types of institutions? What percentage of these educators would prefer a different type of employment? How do differences in compensation and benefits dictate the background and composition of the instructional workforce at different types of institutions?

Evaluating and Rewarding Teaching

Research could help to identify the features of a teaching evaluation and reward system that would support faculty adoption of equitable and effective teaching approaches and explore any ways that student outcomes change at institutions that have altered their teaching evaluation systems to reward equitable teaching practices. Potential research questions in this theme include

- How are instructional practices, particularly practices that contribute to an equitable and effective education, transferred between instructors? Does knowledge learned by one instructor pass to another? In what ways and to what extent?

- What rewards and incentives, given to faculty either individually or as a group/cohort, contribute to their use of instructional practices that create equitable and effective learning environments for all students?
- In which way can instruments for students' evaluation of teaching be co-created by faculty, administrators, and students? In turn, how could the data from student evaluations be combined with data from other sources to reimagine teaching evaluations that promote the Principles for Equitable and Effective Teaching?

Professional Learning and Development

Research on PLD could help to identify features that would best support instructors of various roles and appointment types (e.g., VITAL instructors, CTE instructors) and whether there are differences in PLD approaches that work better for different populations or those who teach in different course types, levels, or modalities.

- What are the impacts of pedagogical self-efficacy and pedagogical content knowledge on current and future faculty? How does instructor mindset about the usefulness of PLD influence their PLD engagement or behavior changes post PLD?
- How do CTE faculty seek out assistance with strengthening their teaching practice, and how do CTE faculty perceive themselves and their field in relation to the other STEM fields?
- What are the best rewards and recognitions to incentivize PLD?
- How do teaching awards given to individual faculty impact their career progression and/or the instructional practices used by their colleagues?
- What rewards and incentives, given to faculty either individually or as a group/cohort, contribute to their use of instructional practices that create equitable and effective learning environments for all students?

Advancing and Measuring Systemic Change

Achieving equitable and effective learning experiences for students requires setting goals and measuring progress toward those goals. The data needed to measure progress differ by institution type and for non-institutional actors such as funders, accreditors, and disciplinary societies. Additional studies that address questions like those listed below could provide information on approaches to data collection and sharing as well as deeper understanding of the overall system of higher education and the experiences of STEM students and instructors.

Using Institutional Data

Research could help to improve understanding of effective approaches for sharing data throughout an instructional system in ways that support equitable student outcomes and explore the kinds of data and ways of visualizing those data that instructors and administrators find most helpful in supporting their goals.

- What are some of the effective ways to share data with instructors and department administrators regarding equitable outcomes in courses and programs while taking an asset-based approach and focusing on systemically improving educational outcomes?
- How does the allocation of institutional resources (e.g., state appropriations and tuition dollars) incentivize the use of data to support and improve educational outcomes for all students?
- How can an institution quantify the cost and value of providing equitable and effective courses?

Trends in Student Enrollment and Outcomes

Research could increase understanding of trends in (a) overall completion rates, (b) STEM completion rates, (c) GPA gaps between different student populations, and (d) completion rate gaps between different student populations, including the extent to which state funding levels and tuition levels might correlate with these rates.

- How many students enroll in STEM courses each year? How many declare a major in STEM fields? How many complete a major in a STEM field? Who does not complete STEM degrees and why? To what extent have there been increases in non-completion rates due to mental health challenges?

Artificial Intelligence and the System of Undergraduate STEM Education

Research on generative and other forms of artificial intelligence (AI) could help determine issues that should be addressed if AI is used to analyze system data, support student learning, and/or support instructors in creating or implementing courses and learning experiences.

- What potential benefits and potential drawbacks might arise from the use of AI to assist in the interpretation of qualitative data from students about their learning experiences?

- How could AI assist instructors, academic units, and institutions in understanding student pathways though STEM programs?
- What role can AI tools play in supporting equitable and effective practices by instructors? What role can it play in course design and development? Can it assist with course and program learning outcome alignment?
- What role can AI tools serve in enhancing tutoring, navigating course content, and program pathways?

A FINAL WORD

STEM education is a wonderful opportunity for people to learn about the world around them—to become knowledgeable about natural processes, technological innovations, and the built environment in ways that enhance our quality of life. Looking ahead to the future needs of society, including economic growth and innovation, it is critical to improve understanding of how people learn, to continuously move toward more equitable and effective pedagogies, and to envision and enact ways to achieve changes in the system of higher education to facilitate design of educational experiences that provide more learners access to an equitable and effective undergraduate STEM education. Society will not fully benefit from the development and use of future discoveries and innovations if access continues to be restricted and not all people have opportunities to experience equitable and effective STEM education. These changes are necessary to provide the information, tools, and resources needed to address future challenges facing our society and our planet.

References

Abbott, A. (1988). *The system of professions: An essay on the division of expert labor*. The University of Chicago Press.

Acevedo, N., Nunez-Rivera, S., Casas, Y., Cruz, E., & Rivera, P. (2021). Enacting spiritual activism to develop a sense of belonging: Latina community college students choosing and persisting in STEM. *Journal of Women and Gender in Higher Education*, *14*(1), 59–78. https://doi.org/10.1080/26379112.2021.1891928

Acevedo-Gil, N., Santos, R. E., Alonso, L., & Solorzano, D. G. (2015). Latinas/os in community college developmental education: Increasing moments of academic and interpersonal validation. *Journal of Hispanic Higher Education*, *14*(2), 101–127. https://doi.org/10.1177/1538192715572893

Achieving the Dream. (2024). *Fond du Lac Tribal and Community College*. https://achievingthedream.org/wp-content/uploads/2024/02/2024-LMA-Spotlight-accessible.pdf

Addy, T. M., Dube, D., & Mitchell, K. A. (2024). *Enhancing inclusive instruction: Student perspectives and practical approaches for advancing equity in higher education*. Taylor & Francis.

Addy, T. M., Dube, D., Mitchell, K. A., & SoRelle, M. (2021a). *What inclusive instructors do: Principles and practices for excellence in college teaching*. Routledge.

Addy, T. M., Reeves, P. M., Dube, D., & Mitchell, K. A. (2021b). What really matters for instructors implementing equitable and inclusive teaching approaches. *To Improve the Academy: A Journal of Educational Development*, *40*(1). https://doi.org/10.3998/tia.182

Addy, T. M., Younas, H., Cetin, P., Rizk, M., Cham, F., Nwankpa, C., & Borzone, M. (2022). The development of the protocol for advancing inclusive teaching efforts (PAITE). *Journal of Educational Research and Practice*, *12*(0), 65–93. https://doi.org/10.5590/JERAP.2022.12.0.05

Ahmad, Z., & Al-Thani, N. J. (2022). Undergraduate research experience models: A systematic review of the literature from 2011 to 2021. *International Journal of Educational Research*, *114*, 101996.

Aikens, M. L., Robertson, M. M., Sadselia, S., Watkins, K., Evans, M., Runyon, C. R. Eby, L. T., & Dolan, E. L. (2017). Race and gender differences in undergraduate research mentoring structures and research outcomes. *CBE Life Sciences Education*, *16*(2), Article 34. https://doi.org/10.1187/cbe.16-07-0211

The AIP National Task Force to Elevate African American Representation in Undergraduate Physics & Astronomy. (2020). *The time is now: Systemic changes to increase African Americans with bachelor's degrees in physics and astronomy*. American Institute of Physics. https://www.aip.org/sites/default/files/aipcorp/files/teamup-full-report.pdf

Aizenman, J., King, C., Kling, T., Ramsey, L., Solomon, J., Waratuke, S., & Womack, C. (2022). Interdisciplinary research and STEM-focused social science curriculum support retention and impact perception of science in cohort of S-STEM scholarship students. *Journal of STEM Education: Innovations and Research*, *23*(1).

Al-Hussami, M., Saleh, M. Y., Hayajneh, F., Abdalkader, R. H., & Mahadeen, A. I. (2011). The effects of undergraduate nursing student-faculty interaction outside the classroom on college grade point average. *Nurse Education in Practice*, *11*(5), 320–326. https://doi.org/10.1016/j.nepr.2011.02.004

Albaili, M. (1998). Goal orientations, cognitive strategies, and academic achievement among United Arab Emirates college students. *Educational Psychology*, *18*(2), 195–203, https://www.tandfonline.com/doi/abs/10.1080/0144341980180205

Alex, P. (2022). Time to pull the plug on traditional grading? Supporters of mastery-based grading say it could promote equity. *Educational Next*, *22*(4).

Allen, D., Dancy, M., Stearns, E., Mickelson, R., & Bottia, M. (2022). Racism, sexism, and disconnection: Contrasting experiences of Black women in STEM before and after transfer from community college. *International Journal of STEM Education*, *9*, 20. https://doi.org/10.1186/s40594-022-00334-2

Allen, T. O., & Zhang, Y. (2016). Dedicated to their degrees: Adult transfer students in engineering baccalaureate programs. *Community College Review*, *44*(1), 70–86. https://doi.org/10.1177/0091552115617018

Almeqdad, Q. I., Alodat, A. M., Alquraan, M. F., Mohaidat, M. A., & Al-Makhzoomy, A. K. (2023). The effectiveness of universal design for learning: A systematic review of the literature and meta-analysis. *Cogent Education*, *10*(1), https://doi.org/10.1080/2331186X.2023.22118191

Aloi, S. L., Gardner, W. S., & Lusher, A. L. (2003). A framework for assessing general education outcomes within the majors. *The Journal of General Education*, *52*(4), 237–252.

Alonso, J. (2023, November 2). Universities can't accommodate all the computer science majors. *Inside Higher Ed*. https://www.insidehighered.com/news/students/academics/2023/11/02/high-demand-comp-sci-degrees-leads-enrollment-caps

Álvarez, L., & Coolsaet, B. (2020). Decolonizing environmental justice studies: A Latin American perspective. *Capitalism, Nature, Socialism*, *31*(2), 50–69. https://doi.org/10.1080/10455752.2018.1558272

American Academy of Arts and Sciences. (2017). *The future of undergraduate education, the future of America*. Commission on the Future of Undergraduate Education. https://www.amacad.org/publication/future-undergraduate-education

American Association for the Advancement of Science. (2009). *Vision and change in undergraduate biology education: A call to action*. https://www.aaas.org/sites/default/files/content_files/VC_report.pdf

American Association of University Professors. (2023, March). *Tenure and contingency in US higher education*. https://www.aaup.org/sites/default/files/AAUP%20Data%20Snapshot.pdf

American Mathematical Association of Two-Year Colleges. (2018). *IMPACT: Improving mathematical prowess and college teaching.* https://amatyc.org/resource/resmgr/impact/chapters/impact-full.pdf

Ames, C., & Archer, J. (1988). Achievement goals in the classroom: Students' learning strategies and motivation processes. *Journal of Educational Psychology, 80*(3), 260.

Andarvazh, M. R., Afshar, L., & Yazdani, S. (2017). Hidden curriculum: An analytical definition. *Academic Medicine, 16.* https://doi.org/10.22037/JME.V16I4.18061

Andrews, M. E., Graham, M., Prince, M., Borrego, M., Finelli, C. J., & Husman, J. (2020). Student resistance to active learning: Do instructors (mostly) get it wrong? *Australasian Journal of Engineering Education, 25*(2), 142–154.

Andrews, T. C., Speer, N. M., & Shultz, G. V. (2022). Building bridges: A review and synthesis of research on teaching knowledge for undergraduate instruction in science, engineering, and mathematics. *International Journal of STEM Education, 9*, Article 66. https://doi.org/10.1186/s40594-022-00380-w

Anthony-Stevens, V., & Matsaw, S. L., Jr. (2020). The productive uncertainty of Indigenous and decolonizing methodologies in the preparation of interdisciplinary STEM researchers. *Cultural Studies of Science Education, 15*(2), 595–613.

Apkarian, N., Henderson, C., Stains, M., Raker, J., Johnson, E., & Dancy, M. (2021). What really impacts the use of active learning in undergraduate STEM education? Results from a national survey of chemistry, mathematics, and physics instructors. *PLoS One, 16*(2), e0247544. https://doi.org/10.1371/journal.pone.0247544

Aquino, K. C., & Scott, S. (2022). The disability resource office and COVID-19: Disability and accessibility support during the pandemic within the two-year postsecondary environment. *Community College Journal of Research and Practice, 46*(12), 907–911. https://doi.org/10.1080/10668926.2021.2006825

Araghi, T., Busch, C. A., & Cooper, K. M. (2023). The aspects of active-learning science courses that exacerbate and alleviate depression in undergraduates. *CBE—Life Sciences Education, 22*(2), Article 26. https://doi.org/10.1187/cbe.22-10-0199

Archer-Kuhn, B., & MacKinnon, S. (2020). Inquiry-based learning in higher education: A pedagogy of trust. *Journal of Education and Training Studies, 8*(9), 1.

Armbruster, P., Patel, M., Johnson, E., & Weiss, M. (2009). Active learning and student-centered pedagogy improve student attitudes and performance in introductory biology. *CBE—Life Sciences Education, 8*(3), 203–213. https://doi.org/10.1187/cbe.09-03-0025

Arnold, K. E., & Pistilli, M. D. (2012). Course signals at Purdue: Using learning analytics to increase student success. In *Proceedings of the 2nd International Conference on Learning Analytics and Knowledge* (pp. 267–270). https://doi.org/10.1145/2330601.2330666

Aronson, B., & Laughter, J. (2016). The theory and practice of culturally relevant education: A synthesis of research across content areas. *Review of Educational Research, 86*(1), 163–206. https://doi.org/10.3102/0034654315582066

Artze-Vega, I., Darby, F., Dewsbury, B., & Imad, M. (2023). *The Norton guide to equity-minded teaching.* WW Norton.

Asai, D. J. (2020). Race matters. *Cell, 181*(4), 754–757. https://doi.org/10.1016/j.cell.2020.03.044

Ashcroft, J., Jaramillo, V., Blatti, J., Guan, S. S. A., Bui, A., Villasenor, V., Adamian, A., Chavira, G., Saetermoe, C., Le, E., Horowitz, B., Palacios, B., Williams, P. B., Brockman, E., & Moses, J. (2021). BUILDing equity in STEM: A collaborative undergraduate research program to increase achievement of underserved community college students. *Scholarship and Practice of Undergraduate Research, 4*(3), 47–58. https://doi.org/10.18833/spur/4/3/11

Ashford, E. (2019, August 20). CBE takes hold in Texas. *Community College Daily.* https://www.ccdaily.com/2019/08/cbe-takes-hold-texas/

Association for Career & Technical Education. (2024, February). *What is career and technical education?* [Infographic]. https://www.acteonline.org/wp-content/uploads/2024/06/ACTE_WhatIsCTE_Infographic_Feb2024.pdf

Association of American Universities. (n.d.). Undergraduate STEM education initiative. https://www.aau.edu/education-community-impact/undergraduate-education/undergraduate-stem-education-initiative?id=14357

Atchison, C. L., Marshall, A. M., & Collins, T. D., (2019). A multiple case study of inclusive learning communities enabling active participation in geoscience field courses for students with physical disabilities. *Journal of Geoscience Education*, *67*(4), 472–486.

Atkins, K., Dougan, B. M., Dromgold-Sermen, M. S., Potter, H., Sathy, V., & Panter, A. T. (2020). "Looking at Myself in the Future": How mentoring shapes scientific identity for STEM students from underrepresented groups. *International Journal of STEM Education*, 7, 1–15.

Auerbach, A. J., Higgins, M., Brickman, P., & Andrews, T. C. (2018). Teacher knowledge for active-learning instruction: Expert—novice comparison reveals differences. *CBE—Life Sciences Education*, *17*(1), Article 12. https://doi.org/10.1187/cbe.17-07-0149

Austin, A. E. (1994). Understanding and assessing faculty cultures and climates. *New Directions for Institutional Research*, *1994*(84), 47–63.

___. (1996). Institutional and departmental cultures: The relationship between teaching and research. *New Directions for Institutional Research*, *1996*(90), 57–66.

___. (2011). [Promoting evidence-based change in undergraduate science education]. Paper commissioned by the Board on Science Education of the National Academies, National Research Council. https://sites.nationalacademies.org/cs/groups/dbassesite/documents/webpage/dbasse_072578.pdf

Austin, A. E., Campa, H., III, Pfund, C., Gillian-Daniel, D. L., Mathieu, R., & Stoddart, J. (2009). Preparing STEM doctoral students for future faculty careers. *New Directions for Teaching & Learning*, *117*, 83–95. https://doi.org/10.1002/tl.346

Austin, A. E., Singer, S. R., Grimm, A., Baker, V. L., & Shanks, L. B. (2024). Organization Change Networks (OCNs): An emerging framework for understanding their development and functioning. *Innovative Higher Education*. https://doi.org/10.1007/s10755-024-09750-4

Avargil, S., Lavi, R., & Dori, Y. J. (2018). Students' metacognition and metacognitive strategies in science education. In *Cognition, metacognition, and culture in STEM education: Learning, teaching and assessment* (pp. 33–64).

Azevedo, R., Mudrick, N., Taub, M., & Wortha, F. (2017). Coupling between metacognition and emotions during STEM learning with advanced learning technologies: A critical analysis, implications for future research, and design of learning systems. *Teachers College Record*, *119*(13).

Bahr, P. R., Jackson, G., McNaughtan, J., Oster, M., & Gross, J. (2017). Unrealized potential: Community college pathways to STEM baccalaureate degrees. *The Journal of Higher Education, 88*(3), 430–478. https://doi.org/10.1080/00221546.2016.1257313

Bahr, P. R., Jones, E. S., & Skiles, J. (2023a). Investigating the viability of transfer pathways to STEM degrees: Do community colleges prepare students for success in university STEM courses? *Community College Review*, *51*(4), 567–592.

Bahr, P. R., McNaughtan, J., & Jackson, G. R. (2023b). Reducing the loss of community college students who demonstrate potential in STEM. *Research in Higher Education*, *64*(5), 675–704. https://doi.org/10.1007/s11162-022-09713-8

Bailey, D. H., Duncan, G. J., Murnane, R. J., & Au Yeung, N. (2021). Achievement gaps in the wake of COVID-19. *Educational Researcher*, *50*(5), 266–275.

Bailey, T., Jaggers, S., & Jenkins, D. (2015a). *Redesigning America's community colleges: A clearer path to student success*. Harvard University Press.

Bailey, T. R., Jaggars, S., & Jenkins, P. D. (2015b, March). *What we know about guided pathways*. Community College Research Center, Teachers College, Columbia University. https://ccrc.tc.columbia.edu/wp-content/uploads/2015/04/What-We-Know-Guided-Pathways.pdf

Baldwin, R. G., & Wawrzynski, M. R. (2011). Contingent faculty as teachers: What we know; what we need to know. *American Behavioral Scientist*, *55*(11), 1485–1509. https://doi.org/10.1177/0002764211409194

Ballen, C. J., Salehi, S., & Cotner, S. (2017). Exams disadvantage women in introductory biology. *PLoS One*, *12*(10), e0186419. https://doi.org/10.1371/journal.pone.0186419

Balta, N., Michinov, N., Balyimez, S., & Ayaz, M. F. (2017). A meta-analysis of the effect of peer instruction on learning gain: Identification of informational and cultural moderators. *International Journal of Educational Research, 86*, 66–77.

Bang, M., & Medin, D. (2010). Cultural processes in science education: Supporting the navigation of multiple epistemologies. *Science Education*, *94*(6), 1008–1026.

Bang, M., Medin, D., Washinawatok, K., & Chapman, S. (2010). Innovations in culturally based science education through partnerships and community. In M. S. Kwine & I. M. Saleh (Eds.), *New science of learning: Cognition, computers and collaboration in education* (pp. 569–592).

Bang, M., Warren, B., Rosebery, A. S., & Medin, D. (2012). Desettling expectations in science education. *Human Development*, *55*(5–6), 302–318. https://doi.org/10.1159/000345322

Bangera, G., & Brownell, S. E. (2014). Course-based undergraduate research experiences can make scientific research more inclusive. *CBE–Life Sciences Education*, *13*(4), 573–738. https://doi.org/10.1187/cbe.14-06-0099

Barbera, S. A., Berkshire, S. D., Boronat, C. B., & Kennedy, M. H. (2020). Review of undergraduate student retention and graduation since 2010: Patterns, predictions, and recommendations for 2020. *Journal of College Student Retention: Research, Theory & Practice*, *22*(2), 227–250.

Barker, L., Hovey, C. L., & Thompson, L. D. (2014). Results of a large-scale, multi-institutional study of undergraduate retention in computing. *IEEE Frontiers in Education Conference*, 1–8. https://doi.org/10.1109/FIE.2014.7044267

Barlow, A. E., & Villarejo, M. (2004). Making a difference for minorities: Evaluation of an educational enrichment program. *Journal of Research in Science Teaching*, *41*(9), 861–881. https://doi.org/10.1002/tea.20029

Barnes, M. E., & Brownell, S. E. (2017). A call to use cultural competence when teaching evolution to religious college students: Introducing religious cultural competence in evolution education (ReCCEE). *CBE—Life Sciences Education*, *16*(4), es4. https://doi.org/10.1187/cbe.17-04-0062

Barr, D. A., Gonzalez, M. E., & Wanat, S. F. (2008). The leaky pipeline: Factors associated with early decline in interest in premedical studies among underrepresented minority undergraduate students. *Academic Medicine*, *83*(5), 503–511.

Barrasso, A. P., & Spilios, K. E. (2021). A scoping review of literature assessing the impact of the learning assistant model. *International Journal of STEM Education*, *8*, Article 12, 1–18. https://doi.org/10.1186/s40594-020-00267-8

Barron, H. A., Brown, J. C., Cotner, S. (2021). The culturally responsive science teaching practices of undergraduate biology teaching assistants. *Journal of Research in Science Teaching, 58*(9), 1320–1358. https://doi.org/10.1002/tea.21711

Bartunek, J. M., & Moch, M. K. (1987). First-order, second-order, and third-order change and organization development interventions: A cognitive approach. *The Journal of Applied Behavioral Science*, *23*(4), 483–500. https://doi.org/10.1177/002188638702300404

Basow, S. A., & Martin, L. J. (2012). Bias in student evaluations. In M. E. Kite (Ed.), *Effective evaluation of teaching: A guide for faculty and administrators* (pp. 40–49). Society for the Teaching of Psychology. http://teachpsych.org/ebooks/evals2012/index.php

Baugus, K. E. (2019). Food insecurity, inadequate childcare, & transportation disadvantage: Student retention and persistence of community college students. *Community College Journal of Research and Practice*, *44*(8), 608–622. https://doi.org/10.1080/10668926.2019.1627956

Bawa, P. (2016). Retention in online courses: Exploring issues and solutions—A literature review. *Sage Open*, *6*(1), 2158244015621777. https://doi.org/10.1177/2158244015621777

Bayles, T., & Morrell, C. (2018). Creating an equitable learning environment. *Chemical Engineering Education*, *52*(2), 143–151.

Bazett, T., & Clough, C. L. (2021). Course coordination as an avenue to departmental culture change. *Primus*, 31(3-5), 467–482.

Beardall, T. R. (2022). Settler simultaneity and anti-indigenous racism at land-grant universities. *Sociology of Race and Ethnicity*, *8*(1), 197–212.

Becher, T., & Trowler, P. (2001). *Academic tribes and territories: Intellectual enquiry and the culture of disciplines*. McGraw-Hill Education.

Behbahanian, A., Davis, E. L., & Roberts, N. A. (2018, June). Open educational resources in the undergraduate engineering curriculum: A materials science case study. In *2018 ASEE Annual Conference & Exposition.*

Behling, K. T., & Tobin, T. J. (2018). *Reach everyone, teach everyone: Universal design for learning in higher education.* West Virginia University Press.

Beilock, S. L., Gunderson, E. A., Ramirez, G., & Levine, S. C. (2010). Female teachers' math anxiety affect girls' math achievement. *Proceedings of the National Academy of Sciences*, *107*(5), 1860–1863. https://doi.org/10.1073/pnas.0910967107

Belanger, A. L., Joshi, M. P., Fuesting, M. A., Weisgram, E. S., Claypool, H. M., & Diekman, A. B. (2020). Putting belonging in context: Communal affordances signal belonging in STEM. *Personality and Social Psychology Bulletin*, *46*(8), 1186–1204. https://doi.org/10.1177/0146167219897181

Belfield, C. R., Jenkins, D., & Fink, J. (2019, July). *Early momentum metrics: Leading indicators for community college improvement* (CCRC Research Brief). Community College Research Center, Teachers College, Columbia University. https://ccrc.tc.columbia.edu/publications/early-momentum-metrics-leading-indicators.html

Bell, A. E., Spencer, S. J., Iserman, E., & Logel, C. E. (2003). Stereotype threat and women's performance in engineering. *Journal of Engineering Education*, *92*(4), 307–312.

Bell, P., Van Horne, K., & Cheng, B. H. (2017). Designing learning environments for equitable disciplinary identification. *Journal of the Learning Sciences*, *26*(3), 367–375. https://doi.org/10.1080/10508406.2017.1336021

Benabentos, R., Hazari, Z., Stanford, J. S., Potvin, G., Marsteller, P., Thompson, K. V., Cassone, V. M., Murasko, D., & Kramer, L. (2021). Measuring the implementation of student-centered teaching strategies in lower- and upper-division STEM courses. *Journal of Geoscience Education*, *69*(4), 342–356. https://doi.org/10.1080/10899995.2020.1768005

Benaduce, A. P., & Brinn, L. (2024). Reenvisioning office hours to increase participation and engagement. *Journal of College Science Teaching*, *53*(4), 364–366. https://doi.org/10.1080/0047231X.2024.2363127

Benavot, A. (1983). The rise and decline of vocational education. *Sociology of Education*, 63–76.

Bennett, J. C., Lattuca, L, Redd, K., & York, T. (2020). *Strengthening pathways to faculty careers in STEM: Recommendations for systemic change to support underrepresented groups*. Association of Public and Land-Grant Universities.

Bennett, R. E. (2011). Formative assessment: A critical review. *Assessment in Education: Principles, Policy, and Practice*, *18*(1), 5–25. https://doi.org/10.1080/0969594X.2010.513678

Bensimon, E. M. (2007). The underestimated significance of practitioner knowledge in the scholarship of student success. *The Review of Higher Education*, *30*(4), 441–469. https://doi.org/10.1353/rhe.2007.0032

___. (2018). Reclaiming racial justice in equity. *Change: The Magazine of Higher Learning*, *50*(3–4), 95–98. https://doi.org/10.1080/00091383.2018.1509623

Bensimon, E. M., & Harris, F. (2023). The mediational means of enacting equity-mindedness among community college practitioners. In E. M. Bensimon & L. Malcom (Eds.), *Confronting equity issues on campus* (pp. 216–246). Routledge.

Bensimon, E. M., Ward, K., & Sanders, K. (2000). *The department chair's role in developing new faculty into teachers and scholars*. Anker Publishing Company, Inc.

Berhane, B., Onuma, F., Buenaflor, S., Fries-Britt, S., & Ogwo, A. (2023). "They helped me to get through": Investigating institutional sources of support at two-year colleges that facilitate the transfer and persistence of Black engineering students. *Community College Review*, *51*(1), 103–127. https://doi.org/10.1177/00915521221125901

Berhane, B. T., Secules, S., & Onuma, F. J. (2020). Learning while Black: Identity formation and experience for five Black men who transferred into engineering undergraduate programs. *Journal of Women and Minorities in Science and Engineering*, *26*(2), 93–124. https://doi.org/10.1615/JWomenMinorScienEng.2020024994

Bernard, S. (2010). To enable learning, put (emotional) safety first. *Edutopia*. George Lucas Educational Foundation. https://www.edutopia.org/neuroscience-brain-based-learning-emotional-safety

Bernard, R. E., & Cooperdock, E. H. G. (2018). No progress on diversity in 40 years. *Nature Geoscience*, *11*(5), 292–295. https://doi.org/10.1038/s41561-018-0116-6

Bernardi, F., Brown, C., Davis, L., Ephraim, M., Moody, R., & Trubko, R. (2024). Cultivating inclusivity in introductory undergraduate STEM course syllabi. *Humanities and Social Sciences Communications*, *11*, Article 784. https://doi.org/10.1057/s41599-024-03276-y

Bernstein, D. J., & Huber, M. T. (2006). *What is good teaching. Raising the bar through scholarship assessed* [Presentation]. International Society for the Scholarship of Teaching and Learning.

Bernstein, J. L., & Ginsberg, S. M. (2009). Toward an integrated model of the scholarship of teaching and learning and faculty development. *Journal on Centers for Teaching and Learning*, *1*, 57–72.

Betz, A. R., King, B., Grauer, B., Montelone, B., Wiley, Z., & Thurston, L. (2021). Improving academic self-concept and STEM identity through a research immersion: Pathways to STEM summer program. *Frontiers in Education, 6*, 674817.

Bickerstaff, S., & Cormier, M. S. (2015). Examining faculty questions to facilitate instructional improvement in higher education. *Studies in Educational Evaluation*, *46*, 74–80. https://doi.org/10.1016/j.stueduc.2014.11.004

Bier, N., Moore, S., & Van Velsen, M. (2019). Instrumenting courseware and leveraging data with the Open Learning Initiative (OLI). In *Companion Proceedings 9th International Learning Analytics & Knowledge Conference.*

Bier, N., Stamper, J., Moore, S., Siegel, D., & Anbar, A. (2023). OLI Torus: A next-generation, open platform for adaptive courseware development, delivery, and research. In *Companion Proceedings of the 13th International Learning Analytics & Knowledge Conference.*

Bifulco, C., & Drue, C. (2023). A collaborative model for faculty development: Helping faculty develop inclusive teaching practices. *To Improve the Academy: A Journal of Educational Development*, *42*(2), Article 5. https://doi.org/10.3998/tia.3168

Binning, K. R., Doucette, D., Conrique, B. G., & Singh, C. (2024). Unlocking the benefits of gender diversity: How an ecological-belonging intervention enhances performance in science classrooms. *Psychological Sciences*, *35*(3), 226–238. https://doi.org/10.1177/09567976231222534

Binning, K. R., Kaufmann, N., McGreevy, E. M., Fotuhi, O., Chen, S., Marshman, E., Kalender, Z. Y., Limeri, L., Betancur, L., & Singh, C. (2020). Changing social contexts to foster equity in college science courses: An ecological-belonging intervention. *Psychological Science*, *31*(9), 1059–1070. https://doi.org/10.1177/0956797620929984

Biswas, S., Benabentos, R., Brewe, E., Potvin, G., Edward, J., Kravec, M., & Kramer, L. (2022). Institutionalizing evidence-based STEM reform through faculty professional development and support structures. *International Journal of STEM Education*, *9*(1), 36.

Bitting, K. S., McCartney, M. J., Denning, K. R., & Roberts, J. A. (2018). Conceptual learning outcomes of virtual experiential learning: Results of Google Earth exploration in introductory geoscience courses. *Research in Science Education*, *48*(3), 533–548. https://doi.org/10.1007/s11165-016-9577-z

Black, P., & Wiliam, D. (2009). Developing the theory of formative assessment. *Educational Assessment, Evaluation, and Accountability*, *21*, 5–31. https://doi.org/10.1007/s11092-008-9068-5

Black, S., Byars-Winston, A., Cabrera, I., & Pfund, C. (2022). Enhancing research mentors' cultural awareness in STEM: A mentor training intervention. *UI Journal*, *13*(1), 36522.

Blaney, J. M., Hernandez, T. E., Feldon, D. F., & Wofford, A. M. (2024). Transfer student receptivity in patriarchal STEM contexts: Evidence of gendered transfer student stigma in computer science from a mixed methods study. *Community College Review*, 1–33. https://doi.org/10.1177/00915521231218233

Blankenship, S. S., & Ruona, W. E. (2007, February 28–March 4). *Professional learning communities and communities of practice: A comparison of models, literature review* [Presentation]. Paper presented at the Academy of Human Resource Development International Research Conference in The Americas, Indianapolis, IN, USA.

Blatt, L., Schunn, C. D., Votruba-Drzal, E., & Rottman, B. M. (2020). Variation in which key motivational and academic resources relate to academic performance disparities across introductory college courses. *International Journal of STEM Education*, *7*, Article 58. https://doi.org/10.1186/s40594-020-00253-0

Bligh, D. A. (2000). *What's the use of lectures?: First U.S. edition of the classic work on lecturing*. Jossey-Bass.

Bliss, T. J., Hilton, J., III, Wiley, D., & Thanos, K. (2013). The cost and quality of open textbooks: Perceptions of community college faculty and students. *First Monday*, *18*, 1.

Blum, S. D. (2020). Just one change (just kidding): Ungrading and its necessary accompaniments. In S. D. Blum & A. Kohn, *Ungrading: Why rating students undermines learning (and what to do instead)* (pp. 53–73). West Virginia University Press.

Blum, S. D., & Kohn, A. (2020). *Ungrading: Why rating students undermines learning (and what to do instead)*. West Virginia University Press.

Boatman, A., & Long, B. T. (2018). Does remediation work for all students? How the effects of postsecondary remedial and developmental courses vary by level of academic preparation. *Educational Evaluation and Policy Analysis*, *40*(1), 29–58. https://doi.org/10.3102/0162373717715708

Bohn, S., & McConville, S. (2018). Stackable credentials in career education at California community colleges. *Public Policy Institute of California*. https://www.ppic.org/publication/stackable-credentials-in-career-education-at-california-community-colleges/

Bolkan, S., & Goodboy, A. K. (2009). Transformational leadership in the classroom: Fostering student learning, student participation, and teacher credibility. *Journal of Instructional Psychology*, *36*(4), 296–306.

Bond, C. E., Pugsley, J. H., Kedar, L., Ledingham, S. R., Skupinska, M. Z., Gluzinski, T. K., & Boath, M. L. (2022). Learning outcomes, learning support, and cohort cohesion on a virtual field trip: An analysis of student and staff perceptions. *Geoscience Communication*, *5*(4), 307–323. https://doi.org/10.5194/gc-5-307-2022

Bonner, M. W. (2016). Grading rigor in counselor education: A specifications grading framework. *Educational Research Quarterly, 39*(4), 21–42.

Booker, K. C., & Campbell-Whatley, G. D. (2018). How faculty create learning environments for diversity and inclusion. *InSight: A Journal of Scholarly Teaching, 13*, 14–27.

Borda, E., Shumacher, E., Hanley, D., Geary, E., Warren, S., Ispen, C., & Stredicke, L. (2020). Initial implementation of active learning strategies in large, lecture STEM courses: Lessons learned from a multi-institutional, interdisciplinary STEM faculty development program. *International Journal of STEM Education, 7*, Article 4. https://doi.org/10.1186/s40594-020-0203-2

Boring, A. (2017). Gender biases in student evaluations of teaching. *Journal of Public Economics, 145*, 27–41. http://dx.doi.org/10.1016/j.jpubeco.2016.11.006

Borrego, M., & Henderson, C. (2014). Increasing the use of evidence-based teaching in STEM higher education: A comparison of eight change strategies. *Journal of Engineering Education, 103*(2), 220–252. https://doi.org/10.1002/jee.20040

Boss, G. J., Davis, T. J., Porter, C. J., & Moore, C. M. (2019). Second to none: Contingent women of color faculty in the classroom. In R. B. Jeffries (Ed.), *Diversity, equity, and inclusivity in contemporary higher education* (pp. 211–225). IGI Global.

Bottia, M. C., Stearns, E., Mickelson, R. A., Moller, S., & Parler, A. D. (2015). The relationships among high school STEM learning experiences and students' intent to declare and declaration of a STEM major in college. *Teachers College Record, 117*(3), 1–46. https://doi.org/10.1177/016146811511700308

Boucher, K., Murphy, M., Bartell, D., Smail, J., Logel, C., & Danek, J. (2021). Centering the student experience: What faculty and institutions can do to advance equity. *Change: The Magazine of Higher Learning, 53*(6), 42–50. https://doi.org/10.1080/00091383.2021.1987804

Bowen, J. A., & Watson, C. E. (2024). *Teaching with AI: A practical guide to a new era of human learning.* Johns Hopkins University Press.

Bowen, R. S., & Cooper, M. M. (2021). Grading on a curve as a systemic issue of equity in chemistry education. *Journal of Chemical Education, 99*(1), 185–194.

Bowen, W. G., & Bok, D. (1998). *The shape of the river: Long-term consequences of considering race in college and university admissions.* Princeton University Press.

The Boyer 2030 Commission. (2022). *The equity/excellence imperative: A 2030 blueprint for undergraduate education at research universities.* The Association for Undergraduate Education at Research Universities. https://doi.org/10.37514/CUS-B.2022.1503

Boyer, N. R., Mason, J., Cleary, M. N., & Telkamp, J. A. (2022). An exploration of how competency-based education can support self-directed learners and learning. In P. Hughes & J. Yarbrough (Eds.), *Self-directed learning and the academic evolution from pedagogy to andragogy* (pp. 193–208). IGI Global.

Boyle, P., & Boice, B. (1998). Systematic mentoring for new faculty teachers and graduate teaching assistants. *Innovative Higher Education*, 22(3), 157–179. https://doi.org/10.1023/A:1025183225886

Bradford, B. C., Beier, M. E., & Oswald, F. L. (2021). A meta-analysis of university STEM summer bridge program effectiveness. *CBE—Life Sciences Education, 20*(2), Article 21.

Bradforth, S. E., Miller, E. R., Dichtel, W. R., Leibovich, A. K., Feig, A. L., Martin, J. D., Bjorkman, K. S., Schultz, Z. D., & Smith, T. L. (2015). University learning: Improve undergraduate science education. *Nature, 523*, 282–284. https://doi.org/10.1038/523282a

Bragg, D. D., & Soler, M. C. (2017). Policy narratives on applied baccalaureate degrees: Implications for student access to and progression through college in the United States. *Journal of Vocational Education & Training, 69*(1), 123–146. https://doi.org/10.1080/13636820.2017.1289550

Brame, C. J., & Biel, R. (2015). *Group work: Using cooperative learning groups effectively*. Center for Teaching. https://cft.vanderbilt.edu/guides-sub-pages/setting-up-and-facilitating-group-work-using-cooperative-learning-groups-effectively/

Branch, M. A. (2015, September/October). Renewed debate over renaming Calhoun. *Yale Alumni Magazine*. https://www.yalealumnimagazine.com/articles/4153-calhoun-college-renaming

Branchaw, J. L., Butz, A. R., & Smith, A. R. (2020). Evaluation of the second edition of entering research: A customizable curriculum for apprentice-style undergraduate and graduate research training programs and courses. *CBE—Life Sciences Education*, *19*(1), Article 11. https://doi.org/10.1187/cbe.19-04-0073

Bransford, J. D., & Johnson, M. K. (1972). Contextual prerequisites for understanding: Some investigations of comprehension and recall. *Journal of Verbal Learning & Verbal Behavior*, *11*(6), 717–726. https://doi.org/10.1016/S0022-5371(72)80006-9

Brathwaite, J. R., Fay, M. P., & Moussa, A. (2021). *Improving developmental and college-level mathematics: Prominent reforms and the need to address equity* (CCRC Working Papers No. 124). Community College Research Center, Teachers College, Columbia University. https://ccrc.tc.columbia.edu/publications/improving-developmental-college-level-mathematics.html

Braxton, J. M., Eimers, M. T., & Bayer, A. E. (1996). The implications of teaching norms for the improvement of undergraduate education. *The Journal of Higher Education*, *67*(6), 603–625.

Brayboy, B. M. J. (2005). Toward a tribal critical race theory in education. *The Urban Review*, *37*(5), 425–446. https://doi.org/10.1007/s11256-005-0018-y

Bressoud, D., & Rasmussen, C. (2015). Seven characteristics of successful calculus programs. *Notices of the AMS*, *62*(2), 144–146. http://dx.doi.org/10.1090/noti1209

Bressoud, D. M. (2014). [Attracting and retaining students to complete two-and four-year undergraduate degrees in STEM: The role of undergraduate mathematics education]. Commissioned paper prepared for the Committee on Barriers and Opportunities in Completing 2-Year and 4-Year STEM Degrees. The National Academies Press. https://doi.org/10.17226/21739

___. (2021). The strange role of calculus in the United States. *ZDM–Mathematics Education*, *53*(3), 521–533.

Brint, S. G., & Karabel, J. (1989). *The diverted dream: Community colleges and the promise of educational opportunity in America, 1900–1985*. Oxford University Press.

Brod, G. (2021). Toward an understanding of when prior knowledge helps or hinders learning. *NPJ Science of Learning*, *6*(1), 24.

Brown, A. L., & Campione, J. C. (1994). Guided discovery in a community of learners. In K. McGilly (Ed.), *Classroom lessons: Integrating cognitive theory and classroom practice* (pp. 229–270). MIT Press.

Brown, A. M., & Nurser, T. A. (2011). *Students as change agents-new ways of engaging with learning and teaching in higher education*. Higher Education Academy.

Brown, M., DeMonbrun, R. M., & Teasley, S. (2018). Taken together: Conceptualizing students' concurrent course enrollment across the post-secondary curriculum using temporal analytics. *Journal of Learning Analytics*, *5*(3), 60–72. https://doi.org/10.18608/jla.2018.53.5

Brown, M. (2024). [Toxic combinations, content repetition, and delayed momentum: Conceptualizing the emerging evidence on curricular complexity in 4-year institutions as an influence on equitable and effective teaching in undergraduate STEM education]. Commissioned paper prepared for the Committee on Equitable and Effective Teaching in Undergraduate STEM Education: A Framework for Institutions, Educators, and Disciplines. The National Academies Press.

Brown, M. G., Lamm, M. H., & Alam, M. I. (2023, June). Board 235: Chemical engineers in chemistry coursework: Longitudinal impacts on engineering identity. In *2023 ASEE Annual Conference & Exposition.*

Brownell, S. E., Freeman, S., Wenderoth, M. P., & Crowe, A. J. (2014). BioCore guide: A tool for interpreting the core concepts for vision and change for biology majors. *CBE—Life Sciences Education, 13*(2), 200–211. https://doi.org/10.1187/cbe.13-12-0233

Brownlie, N., Burke, K., & van der Laan, L. (2024). Quality indicators of effective teacher-created summative assessment. *Quality Assurance in Education*, *32*(1), 30–45.

Brummer, J., Yee, S., & Wakefield, N. (2024). Collaborating on inquiry-based mathematics education curricula with graduate student instructors to establish an equitable and sustainable community of practice. *PRIMUS*, *34*(7), 714–734. https://doi.org/10.1080/10511970.2023.2222278

Bryant, N. (2016). *The influence of the TRIO student support services program on first-generation students: An exploratory study* (Publication No. 10190954) [Doctoral dissertation, University of Massachusetts Boston]. ProQuest Dissertations Publishing.

Bryk, A. S., Gomez, L. M., & Grunow, A. (2011). Getting ideas into action: Building networked improvement communities in education. In *Frontiers in sociology of education* (pp. 127–162). Springer.

Bryk, A. S., Gomez, L. M., Grunow, A., & LeMahieu, P. G. (2015). *Learning to improve: How America's schools can get better at getting better*. Harvard Education Press.

Buchan, T. A., Kruse, S., Todd, J., & Tyson, L. (2020). A transformative approach to incorporating adaptive courseware: Strategic implementation, backward design and research-based teaching practices. *Current Issues in Emerging ELearning*, *7*(1), 3.

Bullock, C. D. (2003). Online collection of midterm student feedback. *New Directions for Teaching and Learning*, *96*, 95–102.

Bureau, J. S., Howard, J. L., Chong, J. X., & Guay, F. (2022). Pathways to student motivation: A meta-analysis of antecedents of autonomous and controlled motivations. *Review of Educational Research*, *92*(1), 46–72.

Bureau of Labor Statistics. (2022). *Occupational employment projections data, special tabulations of 2022-32 employment projections*. https://www.bls.gov/emp/data/occupational-data.htm

Burke, A., Okrent, A., & Hale, K. (2022). *Science and engineering indicators 2022: The state of U.S. science and engineering* (NSB-2022-1). National Science Board, National Science Foundation. https://ncses.nsf.gov/pubs/nsb20221/u-s-and-global-stem-education-and-labor-force

Burke, M. (2022, April 26). Letter grades on way out? Why some University of California departments may use alternatives. *EdSource*. https://edsource.org/2022/letter-grades-on-way-out-why-some-university-of-california-departments-may-use-alternatives/670994

Burmeister, K. C., Atchison, C. L., Egger, A. E., Rademacher, L. K., Ryker, K., & Tikoff, B. (2020). Meeting the challenge; how the geoscience community provided robust online capstone experiences in response to the COVID-19 pandemic [Virtual conference session]. Geological Society of America Annual Meeting. https://doi.org/10.1130/abs/2020AM-358012

Burmeister, K., Rademacher, L., & Ryker, K. (2020). Learning outcomes. *Teach the Earth, Teaching with Online Field Experiences*. https://serc.carleton.edu/NAGTWorkshops/online_field/learning_outcomes.html

Burt, B. A., Stone, B. D., Motshubi, R., & Baber, L. D. (2023). STEM validation among underrepresented students: Leveraging insights from a STEM diversity program to broaden participation. *Journal of Diversity in Higher Education*, *16*(1), 53–65. https://doi.org/10.1037/dhe0000300

Busch, C. A., Cooper, K. M., & Brownell, S. E. (2023). Women drive efforts to highlight concealable stigmatized identities in US academic science and engineering. *PLoS One*, *18*(7), e0287795. https://doi.org/10.1371/journal.pone.0287795

Bush, S. D., Stevens, M. T., Tanner, K. D., & Williams, K. S. (2019). Evolving roles of scientists as change agents in science education over a decade: SFES roles beyond disciple-based education research. *Science Advances*, *5*(6), eaav6403. https://doi.org/10.1126/sciadv.aav6403

Byrne, C. L., Shipman, A. S., & Mumford, M. D. (2010). The effects of forecasting on creative problem-solving: An experimental study. *Creativity Research Journal*, *22*(2), 119–138.

Byun, S. Y., Meece, J. L., & Irvin, M. J. (2012). Rural-nonrural disparities in postsecondary educational attainment revisited. *American Educational Research Journal*, *49*(3), 412–437.

Cabrera, N. L., Miner, D. D., & Milem, J. F. (2013). Can a summer bridge program impact first-year persistence and performance?: A case study of the new start summer program. *Research in Higher Education*, *54*, 481–498.

Caffarella, R. S., & Zinn, L. F. (1999). Professional development for faculty: A conceptual framework of barriers and supports. *Innovative Higher Education*, *23*(4), 241–254. https://doi.org/10.1023/A:1022978806131

Cafferty, P. (2021). Point of view: Taking the office hour out of the office. *Journal of College Science Teaching*, *50*(3), 3–7. https://doi.org/10.1080/0047231X.2021.12290501

Cain, J., Medina, M., Romanelli, F., & Persky, A. (2022). Deficiencies of traditional grading systems and recommendations for the future. *American Journal of Pharmaceutical Education*, *86*(7), 8850. https://doi.org/10.5688/ajpe8850

California State University. (n.d.). Course equity portal. https://www.studentsuccessanalytics.com/courseEquityPortal.html

Campbell, C. M. (2023). *Great college teaching: Where it happens and how to foster it everywhere*. Harvard Education Press.

Campbell, R., Clark, D., & OShaughnessy, J. (2020). Introduction to the special issue on implementing mastery grading in the undergraduate mathematics classroom. *PRIMUS*, *30*(8–10), 837–848.

Canning, E. A., & Harackiewicz, J. M. (2015). Teach it, don't preach it: The differential effects of directly-communicated and self-generated utility value information. *Motivation Science*, *1*(1), 47–71. https://doi.org/10.1037/mot0000015

Canning, E. A., Harackiewicz, J. M., Priniski, S. J., Hecht, C. A., Tibbetts, Y., & Hyde, J. S. (2018). Improving performance and retention in introductory biology with a utility-value intervention. *Journal of Educational Psychology*, *110*(6), 834–849. https://doi.org/10.1037/edu0000244

Canning, E. A., & Limeri, L. B. (2023). Theoretical and methodological directions in mindset intervention research. *Social and Personality Psychology Compass*, *17*(6), e12758. https://doi.org/10.1111/spc3.12758

Canning, E. A., Muenks, K., Green, D. J., & Murphy, M. C. (2019). STEM faculty who believe ability is fixed have larger racial achievement gaps and inspire less student motivation in their classes. *Science Advances*, *5*(2), eaau4734. https://doi.org/10.1126/sciadv.aau4734

Canning, E. A., Ozier, E., Williams, H. E., AlRasheed, R., & Murphy, M. C. (2022). Professors who signal a fixed mindset about ability undermine women's performance in STEM. *Social Psychological and Personality Science*, *13*(5), 927–937. https://doi.org/10.1177/19485506211030398

Canning, E. A., White, M., & Davis, W. B. (2024). Growth mindset messages from instructors improve academic performance among first-generation college students. *CBE—Life Sciences Education*, *23*(2), 1–9. https://doi.org/10.1187/cbe.23-07-0131

Capone, R. (2022). Blended learning and student-centered active learning environment: A case study with STEM undergraduate students. *Canadian Journal of Science, Mathematics and Technology Education*, *22*(1), 210–236. https://doi.org/10.1007/s42330-022-00195-5

Carabajal, I. G., & Atchison, C. L. (2020). An investigation of accessible and inclusive instructional field practices in US geoscience departments. *Advances in Geosciences, 53*, 53–63. https://doi.org/10.5194/adgeo-53-53-2020

Carabajal, I. G., Marshall, A. M., & Atchison, C. L. (2017). A synthesis of instructional strategies in geoscience education literature that address barriers to inclusion for students with disabilities. *Journal of Geoscience Education*, *65*(4), 531–541. https://doi.org/10.5408/16-211.1

Carlisle, D. L., & Weaver, G. C. (2018). STEM education centers: Catalyzing the improvement of undergraduate STEM education. *International Journal of STEM Education*, *5*, 1–21.

Carlone, H. B., & Johnson, A. (2007). Understanding the science experiences of successful women of color: Science identity as an analytic lens. *Journal of Research in Science Teaching: The Official Journal of the National Association for Research in Science Teaching*, *44*(8), 1187–1218. https://doi.org/10.1002/tea.20237

Carlson, E. R. (2022). *Personalized coaching model to address equity gaps in student learning outcomes: A program evaluation* [Doctoral dissertation, New Jersey City University].

Carnevale, A. P., Strohl, J., Campbell, K. P., Gulish, A., Cheah, B., Nyhof, E., & Fix, L. (2024). *Learning and earning by degrees: Gains in college degree attainment have enriched the nation and every state, but racial and gender inequality persists.* Georgetown University, Center on Education and the Workforce. https://cew.georgetown.edu/wp-content/uploads/CEW-attainment-gains-full_report.pdf

Carroll, J. B., & Wolverton, M. (2004). Who becomes a chair? *New Directions for Higher Education*, *2004*(126), 3–10. https://doi.org/10.1002/he.144

Carter, L. (2006). Postcolonial interventions within science education: Using postcolonial ideas to reconsider cultural diversity scholarship. *Educational Philosophy and Theory*, *38*(5), 677–691. https://doi.org/10.1111/j.1469-5812.2006.00219.x

Casey, J. R., Supriya, K., Shaked, S., Caram, J. R., Russell, A., & Courey, A. J. (2023). Participation in a high-structure general chemistry course increases student sense of belonging and persistence to organic chemistry. *Journal of Chemical Education*, *100*(8), 2860–2872. https://doi.org/10.1021/acs.jchemed.2c01253

Casper, A. M., Eddy, S. L., & Freeman, S. (2019). True grit: Passion and persistence make an innovative course design work. *PLoS Biology*, *17*(7), e3000359. https://doi.org/10.1371/journal.pbio.3000359

CAST. (n. d.). About Universal Design for Learning. https://www.cast.org/impact/universal-design-for-learning-udl

Castillo, W., & Gillborn, D. (2022). *How to "QuantCrit": Practices and questions for education data researchers and users.* (EdWorking Paper No. 22-546). Annenberg Institute at Brown University. https://doi.org/10.26300/v5kh-dd65

Castillo-Montoya, M. (2020). The challenges and tensions in equity-minded teaching. *Change: The Magazine of Higher Learning*, *52*(2), 74–78. https://doi.org/10.1080/00091383.2020.1732791

Castillo-Montoya, M., Bolitzer, L. A., & Santiago-Sotto, S. (2023). Reimagining faculty development: Activating instructional development for diversity, equity, and inclusion. In L. W. Perna (Ed.), *Higher education: Handbook of theory and research* (Vol. 38, pp. 415–481). Springer Cham.

Castillo-Montoya, M., & Ives, J. (2020). A liberating education: Integrating funds of knowledge and disciplinary knowledge to create tools for students' lives. *New Directions for Teaching and Learning*, *2020*(164), 39–48.

Castle, S. D., Byrd, W. C., Koester, B. P., Pearson, M. I., Bonem, E., Caporale, N., Cwik, S., Denaro, K., Fiorini, S., Li, Y., Mead, C., Rypkema, H., Sweeder, R. D., Valdivia Medinaceli, M. B., Whitcomb, K. M., Brownell, S. E., Levesque-Bristol, C., Molinaro, M., Singh, C., McKay, T. A., & Matz, R. L. (2024). Systemic advantage has a meaningful relationship with grade outcomes in students' early STEM courses at six research universities. *International Journal of STEM Education*, *11*, Article 14. https://doi.org/10.1186/s40594-024-00474-7

Cavanagh, A. J., Chen, X., Bathgate, M., Frederick, J., Hanauer, D. I., & Graham, M. J. (2018). Trust, growth mindset, and student commitment to active learning in a college science course. *CBE—Life Sciences Education*, *17*(1), Article 10.

Cayubit, R. F. O. (2021). Why learning environment matters? An analysis on how the learning environment influences the academic motivation, learning strategies and engagement of college students. *Learning Environments Research*, *25*(2), 581–599. https://doi.org/10.1007/s10984-021-09382-x

CBE—Life Sciences Education. (2024). *Special issue—Equity, inclusion, access, and justice in biology education.* The American Society for Cell Biology. https://www.lifescied.org/equity-special-issue/

Cech, E. A., Metz, A., Smith, J. L., & deVries, K. (2017). Epistemological dominance and social inequality: Experiences of Native American science, engineering, and health student. *Science, Technology, & Human Values*, *42*(5), 743–774. https://doi.org/10.1177/0162243916687037

Center for Excellence in Teaching and Learning. (n.d.). *Activating prior knowledge.* Virginia Polytechnic Institute and State University. https://teaching.vt.edu/teachingresources/adjustinginstruction/priorknowledge.html

Center for Higher Education Policy and Practice. (2024a). *How learner-centered higher education design and delivery accelerates equitable access and outcomes.* https://www.chepp.org/wp-content/uploads/2024/01/CHEPP_ONLINE-BY-DESIGN_WHITE-PAPER85.pdf

___. (2024b). *Online by design: How accessibility is fundamental to learner-centered design.* https://www.chepp.org/wp-content/uploads/2024/07/CHEPP_ACCESSIBILITY_WHITE-PAPER_v5.pdf

Center for the Integration of Research, Teaching and Learning. (n.d.) *About CIRTL.* https://cirtl.net/about/

Center for Urban Education, Rossier School of Education. (2015). *Five principles for creating equity by design.* University of Southern California. https://welcome.solano.edu/wp-content/uploads/2021/01/CUE_equity_design_principles.pdf

Cerna, O., Plancarte, V., Raufman, J., & Mahecha-Rodriguez, J. (2023). *Lessons from the Dana Center's Corequisite Research Design Collaborative Study. Research Brief.* Center for the Analysis of Postsecondary Readiness.

Cetina, K. K. (1999). *Epistemic cultures: How the sciences make knowledge.* Harvard University Press.

Chadha, D. (2022). How do we prepare to teach? Exploring science lecturers' authentic approaches to teaching in higher education. *Research in Science Education*, *52*(2), 635–653. https://doi.org/10.1007/s11165-020-09972-4

Chai, C. S., Koh, J. H. L., & Tsai, C. C. (2013). A review of technological pedagogical content knowledge. *Journal of Educational Technology & Society*, *16*(2), 31–51.

Chalmers, A. F. (2013). *What is this thing called science?* (4th ed.). Hackett Publishing Company, Inc.

Chandar, S., Crum, R., Pennino, E., Ishikawa, C., Ghosh Hajra, S., & McDonald, K. (2023). Ten tips for developing a more inviting syllabus. *Journal of Microbiology and Biology Education*, *24*(3), e00032–23.

Chang, M. J., Sharkness, J., Hurtado, S., & Newman, C. B. (2014). What matters in college for retaining aspiring scientists and engineers from underrepresented racial groups. *Journal of Research in Science Teaching, 51*(5), 555–580. https://doi.org/10.1002/tea.21146

Chappell, C., Gonczi, A., & Hager, P. (2020). Competency-based education. In G. Foley (Ed.), *Understanding adult education and training* (pp. 191–205). Routledge.

Chase, M. K. (2020). Student voice in STEM classroom assessment practice: A pilot intervention. *Research & Practice in Assessment, 15*(2), n2.

Chasteen, S. V., & Code, W. J. (2018). *The science education initiative handbook: A practical guide to fostering change in university courses and faculty by embedding discipline-based education specialists within departments.* University of Colorado Boulder.

Chi, M. T., & Wylie, R. (2014). The ICAP framework: Linking cognitive engagement to active learning outcomes. *Educational Psychologist, 49*(4), 219–243. https://doi.org/10.1080/00461520.2014.965823

Chiarella, D., & Vurro, G. (2020). Fieldwork and disability: An overview for an inclusive experience. *Geological Magazine, 157*(11), 1933–1938.

Chini, J. (2024). [Describing disability: Language and models]. Commissioned paper prepared for the National Academies of Sciences, Engineering, and Medicine. Committee on Beyond Compliance: Promoting the Success of People with Disabilities in the STEM Workforce.

Choi, Y. H. (2024). Master narratives and resistance narratives: How women of color on community college STEM education pathways push back. *Community College Review, 52*(3), 263–288. https://doi.org/10.1177/00915521241238746

Christe, B. (2013). The importance of faculty-student connections in STEM disciplines: A literature review. *Journal of STEM Education, 14*(3), 22–26.

Chu, D. (2006). *The department chair primer: Leading and managing academic departments* (Vol. 64). Jossey-Bass.

Chun, E., & Evans, A. (2023). *The challenges of minoritized contingent faculty in higher education.* Purdue University Press.

Clark, D., & Talbert, R. (2023). *Grading for growth: A guide to alternative grading practices that promote authentic learning and studied engagement in higher education.* Taylor & Francis.

Clark, I. (2012). Formative assessment: Assessment is for self-regulated learning. *Educational Psychology Review, 24*, 205–249.

Clark, N., & Hsu, J. L. (2023). Insight from biology program learning outcomes: Implications for teaching, learning, and assessment. *CBE—Life Sciences Education, 22*(1), Article 5. https://doi.org/10.1187/cbe.22-09-0177

Clements, T. P., Friedman, K. L., Johnson, H. J., Meier, C. J., Watkins, J., Brockman, A. J., & Brame, C. J. (2022). "It made me feel like a bigger part of the STEM community": Incorporation of learning assistants enhances students' sense of belonging in a large introductory biology course. *CBE—Life Sciences Education, 21*(2), Article 26. https://doi.org/10.1187/cbe.21-09-0287

Clemmons, A. W., Donovan, D. A., Theobald, E. J., & Crowe, A. J. (2022). Using the intended–enacted–experienced curriculum model to map the vision and change core competencies in undergraduate biology programs and courses. *CBE—Life Sciences Education, 21*(1), Article 6. https://doi.org/10.1187/cbe.21-02-0054

Clemmons, A. W., Timbrook, J., Herron, J. C., & Crowe, A. J. (2020). BioSkills Guide: Development and national validation of a tool for interpreting the *Vision and Change* core competencies. *CBE—Life Sciences Education, 19*(4). https://doi.org/10.1187/cbe.19-11-0259

Cohen, G. L., Garcia, J., Apfel, N., & Master, A. (2006). Reducing the racial achievement gap: A social-psychological intervention. *Science, 313*(5791), 1307–1310. https://doi.org/10.1126/science.1128317

Cohen, G. L., Garcia, J., Purdie-Vaughns, V., Apfel, N., & Brzustoski, P. (2009). Recursive processes in self-affirmation: Intervening to close the minority achievement gap. *Science, 324*(5925), 400–403. https://doi.org/10.1126/science.1170769

Cohen, G. L., & Sherman, D. K. (2014). The psychology of change: Self-affirmation and social psychological intervention. *Annual Review of Psychology*, *65*, 333–371. https://doi.org/10.1146/annurev-psych-010213-115137

Cohen, G. L., Steele, C. M., & Ross, L. D. (1999). The mentor's dilemma: Providing critical feedback across the racial divide. *Personality and Social Psychology Bulletin*, *25*(10), 1302–1318. https://doi.org/10.1177/0146167299258011

Cohen, R., & Kelly, A. M. (2020). Mathematics as a factor in community college STEM performance, persistence, and degree attainment. *Journal of Research in Science Teaching*, *57*(2), 279–307. https://doi.org/10.1002/tea.21594

Cole, D., & Griffin, K. A. (2013). Advancing the study of student-faculty interaction: A focus on diverse students and faculty. In M. B. Paulson (Ed.), *Higher education: Handbook of theory and research* (Vol. 28, pp. 561–611). Springer Netherlands.

Coleman, M. S., Smith, T. L., & Miller, E. R. (2019). Catalysts for achieving sustained improvement in the quality of undergraduate STEM education. *Dædalus*, *148*(4), 29–46.

Collins, T. (1997). For openers, an inclusive course syllabus. In W. E. Campbell & K. A. Smith (Eds.), *New paradigms for college teaching* (pp. 79–102). Interaction Book Company.

CoMInds. (2020). CoMInDs Hub. https://www.comindshub.org/

Community College Research Center. (2022). *Community college FAQs*. https://ccrc.tc.columbia.edu/community-college-faqs.html

Connell, G. L., Donovan, D. A., & Theobald, E. J. (2023). Forming groups in large-enrollment biology class: Group permanence matters more than group size. *CBE—Life Sciences Education, 22*(4), Article 37. https://doi.org/10.1187/cbe.22-08-0172

Connolly, M. R., Savoy, J. N., Lee, Y.-G., & Hill, L. B. (2016). *Building a better future STEM faculty: How doctoral teaching programs can improve undergraduate education.* Wisconsin Center for Education Research, University of Wisconsin-Madison.

___. (2018). The effects of doctoral teaching development on early-career STEM scholars' college teaching self-efficacy. *CBE—Life Sciences Education*, *17*(1), Article 14. https://doi.org/10.1187/cbe.17-02-0039

Considine, H., Nedic, Z., & Nafalski, A. (2017, June). Assisting students in online experimentation. In *2017 4th Experiment@ International Conference (exp. At'17)* (pp. 47–51). IEEE. https://ieeexplore.ieee.org/document/7984371

Cook, E., Kennedy, E., & McGuire, S. Y. (2013). Effect of teaching metacognitive learning strategies on performance in general chemistry courses. *Journal of Chemical Education*, *90*(8), 961–967.

Cooke, M., Breitbart, M., Cooperdock, E., Levin, N., Niemi, N., Bell, C., Stevens, L., & Viskupic, K. (2021). First-year graduate courses foster inclusion. *Nature Geoscience*, *14*(8), 539–540. https://doi.org/10.1038/s41561-021-00800-6

Cook-Sather, A., Bovill, C., & Felten, P. (2014). *Engaging students as partners in learning and teaching: A guide for faculty*. Jossey-Bass

Cook-Sather, A., Salmeron, D., & Smith, T. (2023, June). Humanizing STEM education through student-faculty pedagogical partnerships. *Frontiers in Education*, *8*, 1153087. https://doi.org/10.3389/feduc.2023.1153087

Cooper, K. M., & Brownell, S. E. (2016). Coming out in class: Challenges and benefits of active learning in a biology classroom for LGBTQIA students. *CBE—Life Sciences Education*, *15*(3), Article 37. https://doi.org/10.1187/cbe.16-01-0074

Cooper, K. M., Downing, V. R., & Brownell, S. E. (2018). The influence of active learning practices on student anxiety in large-enrollment college science classrooms. *International Journal of STEM Education*, *5*(1), 23. https://doi.org/10.1186/s40594-018-0123-6

Corin, E. N., Sonnert, G., & Sadler, P. M. (2020). The role of dual enrollment STEM coursework in increasing STEM career interest among American high school students. *Teachers College Record*, *122*(2), 1–26. https://doi.org/10.1177/016146812012200210

Coryell, J. E. (2016). Creating and sustaining teaching and learning centers: US models of resources and support, lessons learned, and building a culture of teaching and learning excellence. *Excellence and Innovation in Learning and Teaching.*

Costello, M. A., Nagel, A. G., Hunt, G. L., Rivens, A. J., Hazelwood, O. A., Pettit, C., & Allen, J. P. (2022). Facilitating connection to enhance college student well-being: Evaluation of an experiential group program. *American Journal of Community Psychology*, *70*(3–4), 314–326. https://doi.org/10.1002/ajcp.12601

Cotner, S., & Ballen, C. J. (2017). Can mixed assessment methods make biology classes more equitable? *PLoS One*, *12*(12), e0189610. https://doi.org/10.1371/journal.pone.0189610

Covarrubias, R., Valle, I., Laiduc, G., & Azmitia, M. (2019). "You never become fully independent": Family roles and independence in first-generation college students. *Journal of Adolescent Research*, *34*(4), 381–410.

Cowan, C. C., Brady, M., Arvizu, J., Reece, A., Weinman, B., & Zivot, M. (2022). Cultivating not weeding: STEM first year learning community fosters student persistence and engagement. *Journal of College Student Retention: Research, Theory & Practice*, *26*(2), 500–527. https://doi.org/10.1177/15210251221093749

Cox, A. (2005). What are communities of practice? A comparative review of four seminal works. *Journal of Information Science*, *31*(6), 527–540. https://journals.sagepub.com/doi/10.1177/0165551505057016

Cox, M. D. (2004). Introduction to faculty learning communities. *New Directions for Teaching and Learning*, *2004*(97), 5–23. https://doi.org/10.1002/tl.129

Cozart, D. L., Horan, E. M., & Frome, G. (2021). Rethinking the traditional textbook: A case for Open Educational Resources (OER) and no-cost learning materials. *Teaching & Learning Inquiry*, *9*(2), n2.

Crenshaw, K. (1989). Demarginalizing the intersection of race and sex: A Black feminist critique of antidiscrimination doctrine, feminist theory and antiracist politics. *University of Chicago Legal Forum*, *1989*(1), Article 8, 139–167. http://chicagounbound.uchicago.edu/uclf/vol1989/iss1/8

Crisp, G., & Cruz, I. (2009). Mentoring college students: A critical review of the literature between 1990 and 2007. *Research in Higher Education*, *50*, 525–545. https://doi.org/10.1007/s11162-009-9130-2

Croizet, J. C., & Claire, T. (1998). Extending the concept of stereotype threat to social class: The intellectual underperformance of students from low socioeconomic backgrounds. *Personality and Social Psychology Bulletin*, *24*(6), 588–594. https://doi.org/10.1177/0146167298246003

Croizet, J. C., & Millet, M. (2012). Social class and test performance: From stereotype threat to symbolic violence and vice versa. In M. Inzlicht & T. Schmader (Eds.), *Stereotype threat: Theory, process and application* (pp. 188–201). Oxford University Press.

Crouch, C. H., & Mazur, E. (2001). Peer instruction: Ten years of experience and results. *American Journal of Physics*, *69*(9), 970–977.

Cruz, C. L., Holmberg-Douglas, N., Onuska, N. P. R., McManus, J. B., MacKenzie, I. A., Hutson, B. L., Eskew, N. A., & Nicewicz, D. A. (2020). Development of a large-enrollment course-based research experience in an undergraduate organic chemistry laboratory: Structure–function relationships in pyrylium photoredox catalysts. *Journal of Chemical Education*, *97*(6), 1572–1578. https://doi.org/10.1021/acs.jchemed.9b00786

Culver, K. C., & Kezar, A. (2020). *The impacts of 2020 on advancement of non-tenure track and adjunct faculty*. Pullias Center for Higher Education, University of Southern California. https://nap.nationalacademies.org/resource/26405/6_The_Impacts_of_2020_on_Advancement_of_Contingent_Faculty-Culver_Kezar.pdf

Culver, K. C., Harper, J., & Kezar, A. (2021). *Design for equity in higher education.* Pullias Center for Higher Education.

Culver, K. C., Kezar, A., & Koren, E. R. (2023). Improving access and inclusion for VITAL faculty in the scholarship of teaching and learning through sustained professional development programs. *Innovative Higher Education, 48*(6), 1071–1094.

Curley, B., & Downey, J. (2024). Implementation of alternative grading methods in a mathematical statistics course. *Journal of Statistics and Data Science Education, 32*(3), 272–282.

Cushing, E., English, D., Therriault, S., & Lavinson, R. (2019). *Developing a college and career-ready workforce: An analysis of ESSA, Perkins V, IDEA, and WIOA.* College and Career Readiness and Success Center, American Institutes for Research.

D'Agostino, S., & Kosegarten, J. (2015). Reevaluating teaching evaluations. *Liberal Education, Summer*, 58–63.

Dalporto, H., & Tessler, B. (2020, April). *Voices from the field: How community colleges are advancing equity in career and technical education.* MDRC.

Dancy, M., & Hodari, A. K. (2023). How well-intentioned white male physicists maintain ignorance of inequity and justify inaction. *International Journal of STEM Education, 10*, Article 45. https://doi.org/10.1186/s40594-023-00433-8

Dancy, M., Rainey, K., Stearns, E., Mickelson, R., & Moller, S. (2020). Undergraduates' awareness of White and male privilege in STEM. *International Journal of STEM Education, 7*, Article 52. https://doi.org/10.1186/s40594-020-00250-3

Dasgupta, N. (2013). Implicit attitudes and beliefs adapt to situations: A decade of research on the malleability of implicit prejudice, stereotypes, and the self-concept. *Advances in Experimental Social Psychology, 47*, 233–279. https://doi.org/10.1016/B978-0-12-407236-7.00005-X

___. (2023). To make science and engineering more diverse, make research socially relevant: Science and engineering disciplines sometimes struggle to connect research with social benefits and to retain diverse students. Solving one problem can solve the other. *Issues in Science and Technology, 40*(1), 76–80. https://doi.org/10.58875/MAAC9457

Davies, P. L., Schelly, C. L., & Spooner, C. L. (2013). Measuring the effectiveness of Universal Design for Learning intervention for postsecondary education. *Journal of Postsecondary Education and Disability, 26*(3), 195–220.

Dawson, P., van der Meer, J., Skalicky, J., & Cowley, K. (2014). On the effectiveness of supplemental instruction: A systematic review of supplemental instruction and peer-assisted study sessions literature between 2001 and 2010. *Review of Educational Research, 84*(4), 609–639. https://doi.org/10.3102/0034654314540007

De Silva, L. M. H., Rodriguez-Triana, M. J., Chounta, I. A., & Pishtari, G. (2024). Curriculum analytics in higher education institutions: A systematic literature review. *Journal of Computing in Higher Education*, 1–47.

DeChenne, S. E., Koziol, N., Needham, M., & Enochs, L. (2015). Modeling sources of teaching self-efficacy for science, technology, engineering, and mathematics graduate teaching assistants. *CBE—Life Sciences Education, 14*(3), Article 32.

Deil-Amen, R. (2011). Socio-academic integrative moments: Rethinking academic and social integration among two-year college students in career-related programs. *The Journal of Higher Education, 82*(1), 54–91. https://doi.org/10.1080/00221546.2011.11779085

Deitz, S., & Freyman, C. (2024). *The state of U.S. science and engineering 2024* (NSB-2024-3). National Science Board, National Science Foundation. https://ncses.nsf.gov/pubs/nsb20243

Deitz, S., & Henke, R. (2023). *Higher education in science and engineering: Science and engineering indicators 2024* (NSB-2023-32). National Science Board, National Science Foundation. https://ncses.nsf.gov/pubs/nsb202332/

Delamont, S. (Ed.). (2012). *Handbook of qualitative research in education.* Edward Elgar Publishing.

Dempsey, P., & Huber, T. (2020, May 20). *Using standards-based grading to reduce mathematics anxiety: A review of literature* (ED605522). ERIC. https://files.eric.ed.gov/fulltext/ED605522.pdf

Denaro, K., Dennin, K., Dennin, M., & Sato, B. (2022). Identifying systemic inequity in higher education and opportunities for improvement. *PLoS One, 17*(4), e0264059. https://doi.org/10.1371/journal.pone.0264059

Dennehy, T. C., & Dasgupta, N. (2017). Female peer mentors early in college increase women's positive academic experiences and retention in engineering. *Proceedings of the National Academy of Sciences, 114*(23), 5964–5969. https://doi.org/10.1073/pnas.1613117114

Dennin, M., Schultz, Z. D., Feig, A., Finkelstein, N., Greenhoot, A. F., Hildreth, M., Leibovich, A. K., Martin, J. D., Moldwin, M. B., O'Dowd, D. K., Posey, L. A., Smith, T. L., & Miller, E. R. (2017). Aligning practice to policies: Changing the culture to recognize and reward teaching at research universities. *CBE—Life Sciences Education, 16*(4), es5. https://doi.org/10.1187/cbe.17-02-0032

Departmental Action Team. (n.d.). Departmental Action Team Project. https://dat-project.org

DeSilver, D. (2019). A majority of US colleges admit most students who apply. *Pew Research Center.* https://www.pewresearch.org/short-reads/2019/04/09/a-majority-of-u-s-colleges-admit-most-students-who-apply/

Dettori, L., & Settle, A. (2005). Course mentoring: Toward achieving consistency in the curriculum. *Information Systems Education Journal, 3.*

Devlin, M., & Samarawickrema, G. (2010). The criteria of effective teaching in a changing higher education context. *Higher Education Research & Development, 29*(2), 111–124. https://doi.org/10.1080/07294360903244398

Dewsbury, B. M. (2020). Deep teaching in a college STEM classroom. *Cultural Studies of Science Education, 15*(1), 169–191. https://doi.org/10.1007/s11422-018-9891-z

Dewsbury, B. M., Swanson, H. J., Moseman-Valtierra, S., & Caulkins, J. (2022). Inclusive and active pedagogies reduce academic outcome gaps and improve long-term performance. *PLoS One, 17*(6), e0268620. https://doi.org/10.1371/journal.pone.0268620

Diamond, M. R. (2004). The usefulness of structured mid-term feedback as a catalyst for change in higher education classes. *Active Learning in Higher Education, 5*(3), 217–231. https://doi.org/10.1177/1469787404046845

Diaz Eaton, C., Bonner, K., Cangialosi, K., Dewsbury, B., Diamond-Stanic, M., Douma, J., Smith, M., Taylor, R., Wojdak, J., & Wilfong, K. (2022). Sustainability and justice: Challenges and opportunities for an open STEM education. *CBE—Life Sciences Education, 21*(3), es4. https://doi/10.1187/cbe.20-08-0180

DiBenedetto, K., Peters, E. E., & Voight, M. (2021). *Ensuring a more equitable future: Colleges as models for equitable employment.* Postsecondary Value Commission.

Diegelman-Parente, A. (2011). The use of mastery learning with competency-based grading in an organic chemistry course. *Journal of College Science Teaching, 40*(5), 50.

Diekman, A. B., Brown, E. R., Johnston, A. M., & Clark, E. K. (2010). Seeking congruity between goals and roles: A new look at why women opt out of science, technology, engineering, and mathematics careers. *Psychological Science, 21*(8), 1051–1057. https://doi.org/10.1177/0956797610377342

Diekman, A. B., Clark, E. K., Johnston, A. M., Brown, E. R., & Steinberg, M. (2011). Malleability in communal goals and beliefs influences attraction to stem careers: Evidence for a goal congruity perspective. *Journal of Personality and Social Psychology, 101*(5), 902–918. https://doi.org/10/1037/a0025199

Dika, S. L., & D'Amico, M. M. (2016). Early experiences and integration in the persistence of first-generation college students in STEM and non-STEM majors. *Journal of Research in Science Teaching, 53*(3), 368–383. https://onlinelibrary.wiley.com/doi/10.1002/tea.21301

Donovan, D. A., Connell, G. A., & Grunspan, D. Z. (2018). Student learning outcomes and attitudes using three methods of group formation in a nonmajors biology class. *CBE—Life Sciences Education*, *17*(4), Article 60. https://doi.org/10.1187/cbe.17-12-0283

Dori, Y. J., Mevarech, Z. R., & Baker, D. R. (2018). Cognition, metacognition, and culture in STEM education. *Innovations in Science Education and Technology*, *24*, 386.

Dortch, D., & Patel, C. (2017). Black undergraduate women and their sense of belonging in STEM at predominantly White institutions. *NASPA Journal About Women in Higher Education*, *10*(2), 202–215. https://doi.org/10.1080/19407882.2017.1331854

Downing, V. R., Cooper, K. M., Cala, J. M., Gin, L. E., & Brownell, S. E. (2020). Fear of negative evaluation and student anxiety in community college active-learning science courses. *CBE—Life Sciences Education*, *19*(2), Article 20. https://doi.org/10.1187/cbe.19-09-0186

Driessen, E. P., Knight, J. K., Smith, M. K., & Ballen, C. J. (2020). Demystifying the meaning of active learning in postsecondary biology education. *CBE—Life Sciences Education*, *19*(4), Article 52.

DuFour, R. (2004). What is a "professional learning community"? *Educational Leadership*, *61*(8), 6–11.

Dunbar-Ortiz, R. (2021). *Not "a nation of immigrants": Settler colonialism, white supremacy, and a history of erasure and exclusion*. Beacon Press.

___. (2023). *An Indigenous peoples' history of the United States*. Beacon Press.

Duncan, V. L., Holt, E. A., & Keenan, S. M. (2023, September). Creating an equitable and inclusive STEM classroom: A qualitative meta-synthesis of approaches and practices in higher education. *Frontiers in Education*, *8*, 1154652.

Durm, M. W. (1993). An A is not an A is not an A: A history of grading. *The Educational Forum*, *57*(3), 294–297. https://doi.org/10.1080/00131729309335429

Durodoye, R., Gumpertz, M., Wilson, A., Griffith, E., & Ahmad, S. (2020). Tenure and promotion outcomes at four large land grant universities: Examining the roles of gender, race and academic discipline. *Research in Higher Education*, *61*, 628–651. https://doi.org/10.1007/s11162-019-09573-9

Dweck, C. S. (1986). Motivational processes affecting learning. *American Psychologist*, *41*(10), 1040.

___. (1999). *Self-theories: Their role in motivation, personality, and development*. Psychology Press.

___. (2006). *Mindset: The new psychology of success*. Random House.

Dweck, C. S., & Elliott, E. S. (1983). Achievement motivation. In P. Mussen & E. M. Hetherington (Eds.), *Handbook of child psychology* (Vol. 4, pp. 643–691). John Wiley & Sons.

Dweck, C. S., & Leggett, E. L. (1988). A social-cognitive approach to motivation and personality. *Psychological Review*, *95*(2), 256–273.

Dyer, W. G., Jr., Dyer, J. H., & Dyer, W. G. (2013). *Team building: Proven strategies for improving team performance*. John Wiley & Sons.

Dysart, S. A., & Weckerle, C. (2015). Professional development in higher education: A model for meaningful technology integration. *Journal of Information Technology Education. Innovations in Practice*, *14*, 255.

Eagan, K., Hurtado, H., Figueroa, T., & Hughes, B. (2014). [Examining STEM pathways among students who begin college at four-year institutions]. Commissioned paper prepared for the Committee on Barriers and Opportunities in Completing 2- and 4- Year STEM Degrees, National Academies of Sciences, Engineering, and Medicine.

Eberly, M. B., Newton, S. E., & Wiggins, R. A. (2001). The syllabus as a tool for student-centered learning. *The Journal of General Education*, 56–74.

Ebert-May, D., Brewer, C., & Allred, S. (1997). Innovation in large lectures: Teaching for active learning. *Bioscience, 47*(9), 601–607. https://doi.org/10.2307/1313166

Eccles, J. S., Wigfield, A., & Schiefele, U. (1998). Motivation to succeed. In N. Eisenberg (Ed.), *Handbook of child psychology, Vol. 3: Social, emotional, and personality development* (5th ed.). Wiley.

Eddy, S. L., Brownell, S. E., Thummaphan, P., Lan, M. C., & Wenderoth, M. P. (2015). Caution, student experience may vary: Social identities impact a student's experience in peer discussions. *CBE—Life Sciences Education, 14*(4), Article 45. https://doi.org/10.1187/cbe.15-05-0108

Eddy, S. L., & Hogan, K. A. (2014). Getting under the hood: How and for whom does increasing course structure work? *CBE—Life Sciences Education, 13*(3), 453–468. https://doi.org/10.1187/cbe.14-03-0050

Edgerton, A. K. (2022). *Strengthening career and technical education for the 21st Century Act (Perkins V): A primer.* Congressional Research Service.

Edmunds, J. A., Unlu, F., Phillips, B., Mulhern, C., & Hutchins, B. C. (2024). CTE-focused dual enrollment: Participation and outcomes. *Education Finance and Policy, 19*(4), 612–633.

Edwards, J. D., Barthelemy, R. S., & Frey, R. F. (2022). Relationship between course-level social belonging (sense of belonging and belonging uncertainty) and academic performance in general chemistry 1. *Journal of Chemical Education, 99*(1), 71–82. https://doi.org/10.1021/acs.jchemed.1c00405

Edwards, J. D., Torres, H. L., & Frey, R. F. (2023). The effect of social belonging on persistence to general chemistry 2. *Journal of Chemical Education, 100*(11), 4190–4199. https://doi.org/10.1021/acs.jchemed.2c01048

Edwards, R. (1999). The academic department: How does it fit into the university reform agenda? *Change: The Magazine of Higher Learning, 31*(5), 16–27. https://doi.org/10.1080/00091389909604219

Egger, A. E. (2019). The role of introductory geoscience courses in preparing teachers—And all students—For the future: Are we making the grade? *GSA Today, 29*(10), 4–10. https://doi.org/10.1130/GSATG393A.1

Egger, A. E., & Robinson, W. (2024). Geoscience departments can "phone a friend" for support. *Eos, 105*. https://doi.org/10.1029/2024EO240266.

Egger, A. E., Viskupic, K., & Iverson, E. R. (2019). *Results of the National Geoscience Faulty Survey (2004-2016).* National Association of Geoscience Teachers. https://cdn.serc.carleton.edu/files/NAGTWorkshops/CE_geo_survey/nationalsurveyreportforagu.v3.pdf

Ekstrom, R. B., Villegas, A. M., Bruschi, B. A., & Cline, F. A. (1994). College grades: An exploratory study of policies and practices. *ETS Research Report Series, 1994*(1), i–33.

El Baze, J. A., Stowe, S., Hood, S., Lawford, H., Jensen, M., & Hull, K. (2018). Academic anxiety in higher education: Causes, implications, and potential solutions. *HAPS Educator, 22*(3), 208–219.

Elliott, D. C., & Lakin, J. M. (2020). Running the STEM gauntlet: The complicity of four-year universities in the transfer penalty. *Research in Higher Education, 61*, 540–565. https://doi.org/10.1007/s11162-019-09586-4

Elliott, E. S., & Dweck, C. S. (1988). Goals: An approach to motivation and achievement. *Journal of Personality and Social Psychology, 54*(1), 5–12. https://psycnet.apa.org/doiLanding?doi=10.1037%2F0022-3514.54.1.5

Ellis, J., Fosdick, B. K., & Rasmussen, C. (2016). Women 1.5 times more likely to leave STEM pipeline after calculus compared to men: Lack of mathematical confidence a potential culprit. *PLoS One, 11*(7), e0157447. https://doi.org/10.1371/journal.pone.0157447

Emery, N. C., Maher, J. M., & Ebert-May, D. (2020). Early-career faculty practice learner-centered teaching up to 9 years after postdoctoral professional development. *Science Advances*, 6(25), eaba2091. https://doi.org/10.1126/sciadv.aba2091

England, B. J., Brigati, J. R., Schussler, E. E., & Chen, M. M. (2019). Student anxiety and perception of difficulty impact performance and persistence in introductory biology courses. *CBE—Life Sciences Education*, *18*(2), Article 21.

Equity-Based Teaching Collective. (2024). *Equity-based teaching in higher education: The levers that institutions can use for scaling improvement*. Equity-Based Teaching Collective. https://transformlearning.everylearnereverywhere.org/equity-teaching/equitybased-teaching-report/

Erickson, O. A., Cole, R. B., Isaacs, J. M., Alvarez-Clare, S., Arnold, J., Augustus-Wallace, A., Ayoob, J. C., Berkowitz, A., Branchaw, J., Burgio, K. R., Cannon, C. H., Ceballos, R. M., Cohen, C. S., Coller, H., Disney, J., Doze, V. A., Eggers, M. J., Farina, S., Ferguson, E. L., Gray, J. J., ... Dolan, E. L. (2022). "How do we do this at a distance?!" A descriptive study of remote undergraduate research programs during COVID-19. *CBE—Life Sciences Education*, *21*(1), Article 1. https://doi.org/10.1187/cbe.21-05-0125

Esarey, J., & Valdes, N. (2020). Unbiased, reliable, and valid student evaluations can still be unfair. *Assessment & Evaluation in Higher Education*, *45*(8), 1106–1120. https://doi.org/10.1080/02602938.2020.1724875.

Eslami, M., Denaro, K., Collins, P., Sumarsono, J. M., Dennin, M., & Sato, B. (2024). How syllabi relate to outcomes in higher education: A study of syllabi learner-centeredness and grade inequities in STEM. *PLoS One*, *19*(4), e0301331. https://doi.org/10.1371/journal.pone.0301331

Espinosa, L. (2011). Pipelines and pathways: Women of color in undergraduate STEM majors and the college experiences that contribute to persistence. *Harvard Educational Review*, *81*(2), 209–241. https://doi.org/10.17763/haer.81.2.92315ww157656k3u

Espinosa, L. L., Turk, J. M., & Taylor, M. (2017). *Pulling back the curtain: Enrollment and outcomes at Minority Serving Institutions*. American Council on Education & Center for Policy Research and Strategy. https://www.acenet.edu/Documents/Pulling-Back-the-Curtain-Enrollment-and-Outcomes-at-MSIs.pdf

Evans, C. A., Chen, R., & Hudes, R. P. (2020). Understanding determinants for STEM major choice among students beginning community college. *Community College Review*, *48*(3), 227–251. https://doi.org/10.1177/0091552120917214

Eyler, J. R. (2024). *Failing our future: How grades harm students, and what we can do about it*. JHU Press.

ExcelinEd. (2018). *College and career pathways: Equity and access*. https://www.excelined.org/wp-content/uploads/2018/10/ExcelinEd.Report.CollegeCareerPathways.CRDC-Analysis.2018.pdf

Fairweather, J. (2008). [Linking evidence and promising practices in science, technology, engineering, and mathematics (STEM) undergraduate education: A status report for the National Academies' National Research Council Board on Science Education]. Commissioned paper for the National Academies Workshop: Evidence on Promising Practices in Undergraduate Science, Technology, Engineering, and Mathematics (STEM) Education. https://www.nsf.gov/attachments/117803/public/Xc--Linking_Evidence--Fairweather.pdf

Fairweather, J. S. (2002). The mythologies of faculty productivity: Implications for institutional policy and decision making. *The Journal of Higher Education*, *71*(1), 26–48. https://doi.org/10.1080/00221546.2002.11777129

Farrar, V. S., Aguayo, B.-Y. C., & Caporale, N. (2023). Gendered performance gaps in an upper-division biology course: Academic, demographic, environmental, and affective factors. *CBE—Life Sciences Education*, *22*(4), 1–23. https://doi.org/10.1187/cbe.23-03-0041

Felder, R. M., & Brent, R. (2024). *Teaching and learning STEM: A practical guide*. John Wiley & Sons.

Feldman, J. (2023). *Grading for equity: What it is, why it matters, and how it can transform schools and classrooms*. Corwin Press.

Feldon, D. F., Shukla, K. D., & Anne Maher, M. (2016). Faculty–student coauthorship as a means to enhance STEM graduate students' research skills. *International Journal for Researcher Development*, 7(2), 178–191.

Feola, S., Lewis, J. E., McAlpin, J. D., Prevost, L. B., Skvoretz, J., Stains, M., Couch, B. A., Earl, B., Ziker, J. P., Lane, A. K., & Shadle, S. E. (2023). STEM education institutional change projects: Examining enacted approaches through the lens of the Four Categories of Change Strategies Model. *International Journal of STEM Education, 10*, Article 67. https://doi.org/10.1186/s40594-023-00458-z

Ferguson, R., & Whitelock, D. (2024). Assessing microcredentials. In R. Ferguson & D. Whitelock, *Microcredentials for excellence: A practical guide* (p. 173).

Fernandez, C., & Chokshi, S. (2002). A practical guide to translating lesson study for a US setting. *Phi Delta Kappan, 84*(2), 128–134. https://doi.org/10.1177/003172170208400208

Fernández-Balboa, J. M., & Stiehl, J. (1995). The generic nature of pedagogical content knowledge among college professors. *Teaching and Teacher Education, 11*(3), 293–306. https://doi.org/10.1016/0742-051X(94)00030-A

Fernández-Batanero, J. M., Montenegro-Rueda, M., Fernández-Cerero, J., & García-Martínez, I. (2022). Digital competences for teacher professional development. Systematic review. *European Journal of Teacher Education, 45*(4), 513–531.

Ferns, S., Hickey, R., & Williams, H. (2021). Ungrading, supporting our students through a pedagogy of care. *International Journal for Cross-Disciplinary Subjects in Education, 12*(2), 4500–4504. https://doi.org/10.20533/ijcdse.2042.6364.2021.0550

Ferrare, J. J. (2019). A multi-institutional analysis of instructional beliefs and practices in gateway courses to the sciences. *CBE—Life Sciences Education, 18*(2), Article 26. https://doi.org/10.1187/cbe.17-12-0257

Feygin, A., Nolan, L., Hickling, A., & Friedman, L. (2020, January). *Evidence for networked improvement communities: A systematic review of the literature.* American Institutes for Research. https://www.air.org/sites/default/files/NIC-Systematic-Review-Report-123019-Jan-2020.pdf

Fiegener, M. K., & Proudfoot, S. L. (2013). *Baccalaureate origins of US-trained S&E doctorate recipients* (NSF No. 13-323). National Science Foundation.

Finelli, C. J., Nguyen, K., DeMonbrun, M., Borrego, M., Prince, M., Husman, J., Henderson, C., Shekhar, P., & Waters, C. K. (2018). Reducing student resistance to active learning: Strategies for instructors. *Journal of College Science Teaching, 47*(5).

Fink, A., Frey, R. F., & Solomon, E. D. (2020). Belonging in general chemistry predicts first-year undergraduates' performance and attrition. *Chemistry Education Research and Practice, 21*(4), 1042–1062. https://doi.org/10.1039/D0RP00053A

Fink, J., Myers, T., Sparks, D., & Smith Jaggars, S. (2024). Toward a practical set of STEM transfer program momentum metrics. *Research in Higher Education, 65*(2), 259–282. https://doi.org/10.1007/s11162-023-09759-2

Finkelstein, I. E. (1913). *The marking system in theory and practice* (No. 10). Warwick & York.

Finkelstein, N., Greenhoot, A. F., Weaver, G., & Austin, A. E. (2020). A department-level cultural change project: Transforming evaluation of teaching. In K. White, A. Beach, N. Finkelstein, C. Henderson, S. Simkins, L. Slakey, M. Stains, G. Weaver, & L. Whitehead (Eds.), *Transforming institutions: Accelerating systemic change in higher education.* Pressbooks.

Finnegan, D. E., & Gamson, Z. F. (1996). Disciplinary adaptations to research culture in comprehensive institutions. *The Review of Higher Education, 19*(2), 141–177.

Fisher, K. M., (2004). The importance of prior knowledge in college science instruction. In D. W. Sunal, E. L. Wright, & J. B. Day (Eds.), *Reform in undergraduate science teaching for the 21st century* (pp. 69–94). Information Age Publishing.

Fitzsimmons, S. J., Carlson, K., Kerpelman, L.C., & Stoner, D. (1990). A *preliminary evaluation of the Research Experiences for Undergraduates (REU) Program of the National Science Foundation*. National Science Foundation.

Flaherty, C. (2022, October 30). Ratings and gender bias, over time. *Insider Higher Ed*. https://www.insidehighered.com/news/2022/10/31/ratings-and-bias-against-women-over-time

Fleischner, T. L., Espinoza, R. E., Gerrish, G. A., Greene, H. W., Kimmerer, R. W., Lacey, E. A., Pace, S., Parrish, J. K., Swain, H. M., Trombulak, S. C., Weisberg, S., Winkler, D. W., & Zander, L. (2017). Teaching biology in the field: Importance, challenges, and solutions. *BioScience*, *67*(6), 558–567. https://doi.org/10.1093/biosci/bix036

Fletcher, E. C., Lasonen, J. L., & Hernandez-Gantes, V. M. (2013). What is CTE?: Practitioners struggle to define their field in the United States. *International Journal of Adult Vocational Education and Technology (IJAVET)*, *4*(1), 16–30. http://doi.org/10.4018/javet.2013010102

Flores, G. M., Bañuelos, M., & Harris, P. R. (2023). "What are you doing here?": Examining minoritized undergraduate student experiences in STEM at a minority serving institution. *Journal for STEM Education Research*, 7, 181–204. https://doi.org/10.1007/s41979-023-00103-y

Follmer Greenhoot, A., Ward, D., Bernstein, D., Patterson, M. M., & Colyott, K. (2020). Benchmarks for teaching effectiveness. *Center for Teaching Excellence*. https://cte.ku.edu/evaluating-teaching

Fornauf, B. S., & Erickson, J. D. (2020). Toward an inclusive pedagogy through universal design for learning in higher education: A review of the literature. *Journal of Postsecondary Education and Disability*, *33*(2), 183–199.

Fox Tree, J. E., & Vaid, J. (2022). Why so few, still? Challenges to attracting, advancing, and keeping women faculty of color in academia. *Frontiers in Sociology*, *6*. https://doi.org/10.3389/fsoc.2021.792198

Frady, K. (2023). Challenges, barriers, and opportunities for two-year college STEM professional development. In S. M. Linder, C. M. Lee, S. K. Stefl, & K. High (Eds.), *Handbook of STEM faculty development* (pp. 27–38). Information Age Publishing.

Freeman, S., Eddy, S. L., McDonough, M., Smith, M. K., Okoroafor, N., Jordt, H., & Wenderoth, M. P. (2014). Active learning increases student performance in science, engineering, and mathematics. *Proceedings of the National Academy of Sciences*, *111*(23), 8410–8415. https://doi.org/10.1073/pnas.1319030111

Freeman, S., Haak, D., & Wenderoth, M. P. (2011). Increased course structure improves performance in introductory biology. *CBE—Life Sciences Education*, *10*(2), 175–186. https://doi.org/10.1187/cbe.10-08-0105

Freeman, S., O'Connor, E., Parks, J. W., Cunningham, M., Hurley, D., Dirks, C., & Wenderoth, M. P. (2007). Prescribed active learning increases performance in introductory biology. *CBE—Life Sciences Education*, *6*(2), 132–139. https://doi.org/10.1187/cbe.06-09-0194

Friedensen, R., Lauterbach, A., Kimball, A., & Mwangi, C. E. (2021). Students with high-incidence disabilities in STEM: Barriers encountered in postsecondary learning environments. *Journal of Postsecondary Education and Disability*, *34*(1), 77–90.

Fries-Britt, S., & White-Lewis, D. (2020). In pursuit of meaningful relationships: How black males perceive faculty interactions in STEM. *The Urban Review*, *52*(3), 521–540. https://doi.org/10.1007/s11256-020-00559-x

Fry, R., Kennedy, B., & Funk, C. (2021). *STEM jobs see uneven progress in increasing gender, racial, and ethnic diversity*. Pew Research Center. https://www.pewresearch.org/science/2021/04/01/stem-jobs-see-uneven-progress-in-increasing-gender-racial-and-ethnic-diversity/

Fryberg, S. A., & Markus, H. R. (2007). Cultural models of education in American Indian, Asian American and European American contexts. *Social Psychology of Education*, *10*, 213–246.

Fuesting, M. A., Diekman, A. B., Boucher, K. L., Murphy, M. C., Manson, D. L., & Safer, B. L. (2019). Growing STEM: Perceived faculty mindset as an indicator of communal affordances in STEM. *Journal of Personality and Social Psychology, 117*(2), 260–281. https://doi.org/10.1037/pspa0000154

Fuesting, M. A., Diekman, A. B., & Hudiburgh, L. (2017). From classroom to career: The unique role of communal processes in predicting interest in STEM careers. *Social Psychology of Education, 20*(4), 875–896. https://doi.org/10.1007/s11218-017-9398-6

Fujii, A. (2024). Exploring autonomy support and learning preference in higher education: introducing a flexible and personalized learning environment with technology. *Discover Education, 3*(1), 26.

Fuller, R., Brown, M. K., & Smith, K. (Eds.). (2023). *Adjunct faculty voices: Cultivating professional development and community at the front lines of higher education.* Taylor & Francis.

Funk, C., & Parker, K. (2018, January 9). *Diversity in the STEM workforce varies widely across jobs.* Pew Research Center. https://www.pewresearch.org/social-trends/2018/01/09/diversity-in-the-stem-workforce-varies-widely-across-jobs/#:~:text=Growth%20of%20employment%20in%20STEM,overall%20employment%20grew%20only%2034%25

Gao, Z., Heckman, S., & Lynch, C. (2022, February). Who uses office hours? A comparison of in-person and virtual office hours utilization. In *Proceedings of the 53rd ACM Technical Symposium on Computer Science Education* (Vol. 1, pp. 300–306). https://doi.org/10.1145/3478431.3499334

García, H. A., Bryan, K., & McNaughtan, J. (2019). "Why not?": How STEM identity development promotes black transfer and transition. *Journal of Negro Education, 88*(3), 343–357.

Garcia, H. A., McNaughtan, J., & Nehls, K. (2017). The current and future state of contingent faculty. *New Directions for Institutional Research, 2017*(176), 111–115.

Gardner, G. E., & Jones, M. G. (2011). Pedagogical preparation of the science graduate teaching assistant: Challenges and implications. *Science Educator, 20*(2), 31–41. https://eric.ed.gov/?id=EJ960634

Garvey, J. C., & Dolan, C. V. (2021). Queer and trans college student success: A comprehensive review and call to action. In *Higher education: Handbook of theory and research* (Vol. 36, pp. 161–215).

Gasiewski, J. A., Eagan, M. K., Garcia, G. A., Hurtado, S., & Chang, M. J. (2012, March 01). From gatekeeping to engagement: A multicontextual, mixed method study of student academic engagement in introductory STEM courses. *Research in Higher Education, 53*(2), 229–261. https://doi.org/10.1007/s11162-011-9247-y

Gay, G. (2002). Preparing for culturally responsive teaching. *Journal of Teacher Education, 53*(2), 106–116. https://doi.org/10.1177/0022487102053002003

___. (2018). *Culturally responsive teaching: Theory, research, and practice.* Teachers College Press.

Gebauer, R. (2019). The critical nature of intentionality when supporting academically underprepared students through learning communities. *Learning Communities: Research & Practice, 7*(1), 3.

Gehrke, S., & Kezar, A. (2016). STEM reform outcomes through communities of transformation. *Change: The Magazine of Higher Learning, 48*(1), 30–38. https://doi.org/10.1080/00091383.2016.1121084

___. (2017). The roles of STEM faculty communities of practice in institional and departmental reform in higher education. *American Educational Research Journal, 54*(5), 803–833.

Ghanat, S. T., Kaklamanos, J., Ziotopoulou, K., Immanuel, S., & Fallon, D. J. (2016, June). A multi-institutional study of pre-and post-course knowledge surveys in undergraduate geotechnical engineering courses. In *2016 ASEE Annual Conference & Exposition.*

Ghazzawi, D., Pattison, D., & Horn, C. (2021, July). Persistence of underrepresented minorities in STEM fields: Are summer bridge programs sufficient? *Frontiers in Education*, *6*, 630529.

Gildersleeve, R. E., Croom, N. N., & Vasquez, P. L. (2011). “Am I going crazy?!”: A critical race analysis of doctoral education. *Equity & Excellence in Education*, *44*(1), 93–114. https://doi.org/10.1080/10665684.2011.539472

Gillborn, D., Warmington, P., & Demack, S. (2017). QuantCrit: education, policy, ‘Big Data’ and principles for a critical race theory of statistics. *Race Ethnicity and Education*, *21*(2), 158–179. https://doi.org/10.1080/13613324.2017.1377417

Gilley, B., Atchison, C., Feig, A., & Stokes, A. (2015). Impact of inclusive field trips. *Nature Geoscience, 8*(8), 579–580.

Gilley, B. H., & Clarkston, B. (2014). Collaborative testing: Evidence of learning in a controlled in-class study of undergraduate students. *Journal of College Science Teaching*, *43*(3), 83–91.

Gin, L. E., Guerrero, F. A., Cooper, K. M., & Brownell, S. E. (2020). Is active learning accessible? Exploring the process of providing accommodations to students with disabilities. *CBE—Life Sciences Education*, *19*(4), es12. https://doi.org/10.1187/cbe.20-03-0049

Gin, L. E., Scott, R. A., Pfeiffer, L. D., Zheng, Y., Cooper, K. M., & Brownell, S. E. (2021). It’s in the syllabus...or is it? How biology syllabi can serve as communication tools for creating inclusive classrooms at a large-enrollment research institution. *Advances in Physiology Education*, *45*(2), 224–240. https://doi.org/10.1152/advan.00119.2020

Glassick C. E., Huber, M. T., & Maeroff, G. I. (1997). *Scholarship assessed: Evaluation of the professoriate.* Jossey-Bass.

Glisson, H. E. (2023). *The dynamics of belonging among undergraduate women in engineering* [Doctoral dissertation, Virginia Polytechnic Institute and State University]. http://hdl.handle.net/10919/116339

Glover, W. J., Farris, J. A., & Van Aken, E. M. (2015). The relationship between continuous improvement and rapid improvement sustainability. *International Journal of Production Research*, *53*(13), 4068–4086.

Go, J. (2020). Race, empire, and epistemic exclusion: Or the structures of sociological thought. *Sociological Theory*, *38*(2), 79–100. https://www.jstor.org/stable/26953572

Golde, C. M., & Dore, T. M. (2001). *At cross purposes: What the experiences of today’s doctoral students reveal about doctoral education.* Pew Charitable Trusts. https://users.ssc.wisc.edu/~oliver/sociology/PhDEducationreport.pdf

Goldstein, B. E., Chase, C., Frankel-Goldwater, L., Osborne-Gowey, J., Risien, J., & Schweizer, S. (2017). Transforming with a soft touch: Comparing four learning networks. *Systems Research and Behavioral Science*, *34*(5), 537–543.

Gong, H. J., Park, H., & Hagood, T. C. (2023). Peer learning in STEM: A qualitative study of a student oriented active learning intervention program. *Interactive Learning Environments*, *31*(4), 1922–1932.

Gonzales, L. D. (2018). Subverting and minding boundaries: The intellectual work of women. *The Journal of Higher Education*, *89*(5), 677–701. https://doi.org/10.1080/00221546.2018.1434278

Gonzales, L. D., Bhangal, N. K., Stokes, C., & Rosales, J. (2024a). Faculty hiring: Exercising professional jurisdiction over epistemic matters. *The Journal of Higher Education*, 1–26. https://doi.org/10.1080/00221546.2024.2301915

Gonzales, L. D., & Culpepper, D. K. (2024). [A framework for change agents: Fostering equity-minded change within and across STEM tea and learning contexts]. Commissioned paper prepared for the Committee on Equitable and Effective Teaching in Undergraduate STEM Education: A Framework for Institutions, Educators, and Disciplines. The National Academies Press.

Gonzales, L. D., Culpepper, D., & Anderson, J. (2024b). An analysis of academic hiring research and practice and a lens for the future: How labor justice can make a better academy. In L. W. Perna (Ed.), *Higher education: Handbook of theory and research* (Vol. 39, pp. 381–471). Springer Nature Switzerland.

Gonzales, L. D., Pasque, P. A., Farris, K. D., & Hansen, J. M. (2024c). Epistemic injustice and legitimacy in U.S. doctoral education: A systematic review of literature. *Review of Educational Research*, *94*(3), 423–464. https://doi.org/10.3102/00346543231187628

González, N., Moll, L. C., & Amanti, C. (Eds.). (2005). *Funds of knowledge: Theorizing practices in households, communities, and classrooms.* Routledge.

Gonzales, P. M., Blanton, H., & Williams, K. J. (2002). The effects of stereotype threat and double-minority status on the test performance of Latino women. *Personality and Social Psychology Bulletin*, *28*(5), 659–670. https://doi.org/10.1177/0146167202288010

González-Stokas, A. G. (2023). *Reparative universities: Why diversity alone won't solve racism in higher ed.* John Hopkins University Press.

Goodell, J. E., & Koç, S. (Eds.). (2020). *Preparing STEM teachers: The UTeach replication model.* Information Age Publishing.

Goose, M. (2024). "Aaniikoobidooyaang" — Tying things together: Ojibwe language revitalization at Fond du Lac Tribal and Community College. *Tribal College Journal of American Indian Higher Education*, *35*(3).

Gordon, C., Snare, J., & Rajasekhar, Y. (2024). Incorporating learning sciences' best practices into STEM courseware. In *INTED2024 Proceedings* (pp. 7076–7085). IATED.

Goss, H. (2022). Student learning outcomes assessment in higher education and in academic libraries: A review of the literature. *The Journal of Academic Librarianship*, *48*(2), 102485.

Gosselin, D. C., Manduca, C. A., Bralower, T. J., & Egger, A. E. (2019). Preparing students to address grand challenges and wicked problems: The InTeGrate Approach. In D. C. Gosselin, A. E. Egger, & J. J. Taber (Eds.), *Interdisciplinary teaching about earth and the environment for a sustainable future.* Springer. https://doi.org/10.1007/978-3-030-03273-9

Grace-Odeleye, B., & Santiago, J. (2019). A review of some diverse models of summer bridge programs for first-generation and at-risk college students. *Administrative Issues Journal: Connecting Education, Practice, and Research*, *9*(1), 35–47.

Graham, S., Hebert, M., & Harris, K. R. (2015). Formative assessment and writing: A meta-analysis. *The Elementary School Journal*, *115*(4), 523–547. https://doi.org/10.1086/681947

Grangeat, M., Harrison, C., & Dolin, J. (2021). Exploring assessment in STEM inquiry learning classrooms. *International Journal of Science Education*, *43*(3), 345–361. https://www.tandfonline.com/doi/full/10.1080/09500693.2021.1903617

Grant, J. (2021). No, I'm not crazy: A Black feminist perspective of gaslighting within doctoral socialization. *International Journal of Qualitative Studies in Education*, *34*(10), 939–947. https://doi.org/10.1080/09518398.2021.1930258

Graves, B. C. (2023). Specifications grading to promote student engagement, motivation, and learning: Possibilities and cautions. *Assessing Writing*, *57*, Article 100754. https://doi.org/10.1016/j.asw.2023.100754

Graves, J. L., Jr., Kearney, M., Barabino, G., & Malcom, S. (2022). Inequality in science and the case for a new agenda. *Proceedings of the National Academy of Sciences*, *119*(10), e2117831119. https://doi.org/10.1073/pnas.2117831119

Griffin, K. A. (2020). Institutional barriers, strategies, and benefits to increasing the representation of women and men of color in the professoriate. *Higher Education: Handbook of Theory and Research*, *35*, 1–73. https://doi.org/10.1007/978-3-030-11743-6_4-1

Griffin, K. A., Bennett, J. C., & Harris, J. (2013). Marginalizing merit?: Gender differences in Black faculty D/discourses on tenure, advancement, and professional success. *The Review of Higher Education*, *36*(4), 489–512.

Griffith, A. S., & Altinay, Z. (2020). A framework to assess higher education faculty workload in US universities. *Innovations in Education and Teaching International, 57*(6), 691–700.

Grossman, P. L. (1990). *The making of a teacher: Teacher knowledge & teacher education.* Teachers College Press.

Gube, M. (2019). *Higher ideation: Supporting creative thinking and adaptive expertise in undergraduate STEM students.* McGill University.

Gube, M., & Lajoie, S. (2020). Adaptive expertise and creative thinking: A synthetic review and implications for practice. *Thinking Skills and Creativity, 35*, 100630.

Guerrero, M., & Rod, A. B. (2013). Engaging in office hours: A study of student-faculty interaction and academic performance. *Journal of Political Science Education, 9*(4), 403–416. https://doi.org/10.1080/15512169.2013.835554

Guskey, T. R. (1994). Making the grade: What benefits students. *Educational Leadership, 52*(2), 14–20.

Gutiérrez, J. B. (n.d.). *A department, transformed.* UTSA College of Sciences. https://sciences.utsa.edu/mathematics/word-from-chair.html

Guzzardo, M. T., Khosla, N., Adams, A. L., Bussmann, J. D., Engleman, A., Ingraham, N., Gamba, R., Jones-Bey, A., Moore, M. D., Toosi, N. R., & Taylor, S. (2021). "The ones that care make all the difference": Perspectives on student-faculty relationships. *Innovative Higher Education, 46*(1), 41–58. https://doi.org/10.1007/s10755-020-09522-w

Gyll, S. P., & Hayes, H. (2024). Training for better transfer in an online competency-based higher education program: Using enhanced technology-based instruction to improve student learning and assessment outcomes. *Journal of Applied Testing Technology.* http://www.jattjournal.net/index.php/atp/article/view/173213

Haak, D. C., HilleRisLambers, J., Pitre, E., & Freeman, S. (2011). Increased structure and active learning reduce the achievement gap in introductory biology. *Science, 332*(6034), 1213–1216. https://doi.org/10.1126/science.1204820

Hackerson, E. L., Slominiski, T., Johnson, N., Buncher, J. B., Ismael, S., Singlemann, L., Leontyev, A., Knopps, A. G., McDarby, A., Nguyen, J. J., Condry, D. L. J., Nyachwaya, J. M., Wissman, K. T., Falkner, W., Grieger, K., Montplaisir, L., Hodgson, A., & Momsen, J. L. (2024). Alternative grading practices in undergraduate STEM education: A scoping review. *Disciplinary and Interdisciplinary Science Education Research, 6*(1), 15.

Hagenauer, G. & Volet, S. E. (2014). Teacher–student relationship at university: An important yet under-researched field. *Oxford Review of Education, 40*(3), 370–388. https://doi.org/10.1080/03054985.2014.921613

Hakkola, L., Ruben, M. A., McDonnell, C., Herakova, L. L., Buchanan, R., & Robbie, K. (2021). An equity-minded approach to faculty development in a community of practice. *Innovative Higher Education, 46*, 393–410. https://doi.org/10.1007/s10755-020-09540-8

Halamish, V., & Bjork, R. A. (2011). When does testing enhance retention? A distribution-based interpretation of retrieval as a memory modifier. *Journal of Experimental Psychology: Learning, Memory, and Cognition, 37*(4), 801–812. https://doi.org/10.1037/a0023219

Hallett, R. E., Kezar, A., Perez, R. J., & Kitchen, J. A. (2020). A typology of college transition and support programs: Situating a 2-year comprehensive college transition program within college access. *American Behavioral Scientist, 64*(3), 230–252. https://doi.org/10.1177/0002764219869410

Hammond, Z. (2014). *Culturally responsive teaching and the brain: Promoting authentic engagement and rigor among culturally and linguistically diverse students.* Corwin Press.

Hampel, R. (2021). Book review of *The amateur hour: A history of college teaching in America* by Jonathan Zimmerman. *Teaching History: A Journal of Methods, 46*(1), 27–28.

Han, S., Liu, D., & Lv, Y. (2022). The influence of psychological safety on students' creativity in project-based learning: The mediating role of psychological empowerment. *Frontiers in Psychology, 13.* https://www.frontiersin.org/articles/10.3389/fpsyg.2022.865123/full

Hanauer, D. I., Graham, M. J., & Hatfull, G. F. (2016). A measure of college student persistence in the sciences (PITS). *CBE—Life Sciences Education, 15*(4), Article 54. https://doi.org/10.1187/cbe.15-09-0185

Hansen, M. J., Palakal, M. J., & White, L. (2023). The importance of STEM sense of belonging and academic hope in enhancing persistence for low-income, underrepresented STEM students. *Journal for STEM Education Research, 7*, 155–180. https://doi.org/10.1007/s41979-023-00096-8

Hanson, M. (December 2024). College enrollment & student demographic statistics. *Education Data Initiative*. https://educationdata.org/college-enrollment-statistics

Harackiewicz, J. M., Canning, E. A., Tibbetts, Y., Giffen, C. J., Blair, S. S., Rouse, D. I., & Hyde, J. S. (2014). Closing the social class achievement gap for first-generation students in undergraduate biology. *Journal of Educational Psychology, 196*(2), 375–389. https://doi.org/10.1037/a0034679

Harackiewicz, J. M., Smith, J. L., & Priniski, S. J. (2016). Interest matters: The importance of promoting interest in education. *Policy Insights from the Behavioral and Brain Sciences, 3*(2), 220–227. https://doi.org/10.1177/2372732216655542

Harding, S. (2008). *Sciences from below: Feminisms, postcolonialities, and modernities*. Duke University Press.

Harlow, D. B., Otero, V. K., Leak, A. E., Robinson, S., Price, E., & Goldberg, F. (2020). Learning about teaching and learning while learning physics: An analysis of 15 years of responsive curriculum development. *Physical Review Physics Education Research, 16*(2), 020155. https://doi.org/10.1103/PhysRevPhysEducRes.16.020155

Harper, R. P., Weston, T. J., & Seymour, E. (2019). Students' perceptions of good STEM teaching. In E. Seymour & A.-B. Hunter (Eds.), *Talking about leaving revisited: Persistence, relocation, and loss in undergraduate STEM education* (pp. 245–276). Springer International Publishing. https://doi.org/10.1007/978-3-030-25304-2_8

Harris, L. M., Campbell, J. T., & Brophy, A. L. (Eds.). (2019). *Slavery and the university: History and legacies*. University of Georgia Press.

Harris, R. B., Mack, M. R., Bryant, J., Theobald, E. J., & Freeman, S. (2020). Reducing achievement gaps in undergraduate general chemistry could lift underrepresented students into a "hyperpersistent zone." *Science Advances, 6*(24), eaaz5687. https://doi.org/10.1126/sciadv.aaz5687

Harrison, C., & Tanner, K. D. (2018). Language matters: Considering microaggressions in science. *CBE—Life Sciences Education, 17*(1), fe4.

Harrison, J. M., & Williams, V. R. (2023). *A guide to curriculum mapping: Creating a collaborative, transformative, and learner-centered curriculum*. Taylor & Francis.

Harsh, J. A., Maltese, A. V., & Tai, R. H. (2012). A perspective of gender differences in chemistry and physics undergraduate research experiences. *Journal of Chemical Education, 89*, 1364–1370. https://doi.org/10.1021/ed200581m

Harsy, A., Carlson, C., & Klamerus, L. (2021). An analysis of the impact of mastery-based testing in mathematics courses. *PRIMUS, 31*(10), 1071–1088. https://doi.org/10.1080/10511970.2020.1809041

Hartikainen, S., Pylväs, L., & Nokelainen, P. (2022). Engineering students' perceptions of teaching: Teacher-created atmosphere and teaching procedures as triggers of student emotions. *European Journal of Engineering Education, 47*(5), 814–832.

Harwell, E. (2013). *Students' perceptions of differential tuition based on academic program and the impact on major choice* [Doctoral dissertation, University of Illinois at Urbana-Champaign].

Hastings, E. C., & West, R. L. (2011). Goal orientation and self-efficacy in relation to memory in adulthood. *Aging, Neuropsychology, and Cognition, 18*(4), 471–493. https://doi.org/10.1080/13825 585.2011.575926

Hatch, J. A. (2023). *Doing qualitative research in education settings.* State University of New York Press.

Hatfield, N., Brown, N., & Topaz, C. M. (2022). Do introductory courses disproportionately drive minoritized students out of STEM pathways? *PNAS Nexus, 1*(4), 1–10. https://doi.org/10.1093/pnasnexus/pgac167

Hatmaker, D. M. (2013). Engineering identity: Gender and professional identity negotiation among women engineer. *Gender, Work, and Organization, 20*(4), 382–396. https://doi.org/10.1111/j.1468-0432.2012.00589.x

Hattan, C., Alexander, P. A., & Lupo, S. M. (2024). Leveraging what students know to make sense of texts: What the research says about prior knowledge activation. *Review of Educational Research, 94*(1), 73–111.

Haynes, C., & Patton, L. D. (2019). From racial resistance to racial consciousness: Engaging White STEM faculty in pedagogical transformation. *Journal of Cases in Educational Leadership, 22*(2), 85–98. https://doi.org/10.1177/1555458919829845

Hazari, Z., Sadler, P. M., & Sonnert, G. (2013). The science identity of college students: Exploring the intersection of gender, race, and ethnicity. *Journal of College Science Teaching, 42*(5), 82–91.

Hecht, C. A., Bryan, C. J., & Yeager, D. S. (2023). A values-aligned intervention fosters growth mindset–supportive teaching and reduces inequality in educational outcomes. *Proceedings of the National Academy of Sciences, 120*(25), e2210704120.

Hecht, C. A., Latham, A, G., Buskrirk, R. E., Hansen, D. R., & Yeager, D. S. (2022). Peer-modeled mindsets: An approach to customizing life sciences studying interventions. *CBE—Life Sciences Education, 21*(4), Article 82. https://doi.org/10.1187/cbe.22-07-0143

Heffernan, T. (2021). Sexism, racism, prejudice, and bias: A literature review and synthesis of research surrounding student evaluations of courses and teaching. *Assessment and Evaluation in Higher Education, 27*(1), 144–154. https://www.tandfonline.com/doi/full/10.1080/02602938.2021.1888075

Henderson, B. C., Beach, A., & Finkelstein, N. (2011). Facilitating change in undergraduate STEM instructional practices: An analytic review of the literature. *Journal of Research in Science Teaching, 48*(8), 952–984. https://doi.org/10.1002/tea.20439

Henderson, C., Khan, R., & Dancy, M. (2018). Will my student evaluations decrease if I adopt an active learning instructional strategy? *American Journal of Physics, 86*(12), 934–942.

Henry, M. A., Shorter, S., Charkoudian, L., Heemstra, J. M., & Corwin, L. A. (2019). *FAIL* is not a four-letter word: A theoretical framework for exploring undergraduate students' approaches to academic challenge and responses to failure in STEM learning environments. *CBE—Life Sciences Education, 18*(1), Article 11. https://doi.org/10.1187/cbe.18-06-0108

Heringer, R. (2018). The pertinence of a culturally relevant pedagogy in internationalized higher education. *International Education Studies, 12*(1), 1–9. https://doi.org/10.5539/ies.v12n1p1

Herman, G. L., Greene, J. C., Hahn, L. D., Mestre, J. P., Tomkin, J. H., & West, M. (2018). Changing the teaching culture in introductory STEM courses at a large research university. *Journal of College Science Teaching, 47*(6), 32–38. https://doi.org/10.2505/4/jcst18_047_06_32

Hernandez, P. R., Schultz, P. W., Estrada, M., Woodcock, A., & Chance, R. C. (2013). Sustaining optimal motivation: A longitudinal analysis of interventions to broaden participation of underrepresented students in STEM. *Journal of Educational Psychology, 105*(1), 89–107. https://doi.org/10.1037/a0029691

Hess, R. A., Erickson, O. A., Cole, R. B., Isaacs, J. M., Alvarez-Clare, S., Arnold, J., Augustus-Wallace, A., Ayoob, J. C., Berkowitz, A., Branchaw, J., Burgio, K. R., Cannon, C. H., Ceballos, R. M., Cohen, C. S., Coller, H., Disney, J., Doze, V. A., Eggers, M. J., Ferguson, E. L., Gray, J. J., Greenberg, J. T., Hoffmann, Al., Jensen,-Ryan, D., ... Dolan, E. L. (2023). Virtually the same? Evaluating the effectiveness of remote undergraduate research experiences. *CBE—Life Sciences Education*, *22*(2), Article 25. https://doi.org/10.1187/cbe.22-01-0001

Higher Education Act of 1965, Pub. L. No. 89-329, 79 Stat. 1219 (1965), codified as amended at 20 U.S.C. § 1070 et seq.

Hill, L. B. (2023). Advancing SoTL through boundary-spanning leadership: A study of four CIRTL institutions. *Innovative Higher Education*, *48*(6), 1033–1054.

Hill, L. B., Austin, A. E., Bantawa, B., & Savoy, J. N. (2019a). Factors of success: Building and sustaining teaching professional development opportunities for doctoral students and postdocs. *Higher Education Research & Development*, *38*(6), 1168–1182.

Hill, L. B., Savoy, J. N., Austin, A. E., & Bantawa, B. (2019b). The impact of multi-institutional STEM reform networks on member institutions: A case study of CIRTL. *Innovative Higher Education*, *44*, 187–202.

Hilliard, J., Kear, K., Donelan, H., & Heaney, C. (2020). Students' experiences of anxiety in an assessed, online, collaborative project. *Computers & Education*, *143*, 103675.

Hilton, J. (2016). Open educational resources and college textbook choices: A review of research on efficacy and perceptions. *Educational Technology Research and Development*, *64*, 573–590.

Hines, S. R. (2017). Evaluating centers for teaching and learning: A field-tested model. *To Improve the Academy*, *36*(2), 89–100.

Hispanic Association of Colleges and Universities. (2024). About Hispanic-Serving Institutions (HSIs). https://www.hacu.net/hacu/About_HSIs.asp

Hogan, K. A., & Sathy, V. (2022). *Inclusive teaching: Strategies for promoting equity in the college classroom*. West Virginia University Press.

Holland, D. G. (2019). The struggle to belong and thrive. In E. Seymour & A.-B. Hunter (Eds.), *Talking about leaving revisited: Persistence, relocation, and loss in undergraduate STEM education* (pp. 277–327). Springer International Publishing. https://doi.org/10.1007/978-3-030-25304-2_9

Holland, D. G., Harper, R. P., Hunter, A.-B., Weston, T. J., & Seymour, E. (2019a). The processes and consequences of switching, including the loss of high-performing STEM majors. In E. Seymour & A.-B. Hunter (Eds.), *Talking about leaving revisited: Persistence, relocation, and loss in undergraduate STEM education* (pp. 329–369). Springer Cham. https://doi.org/10.1007/978-3-030-25304-2_10

Holland, D. G., Harper, R. P., & Seymour, E. (2019b). Influences beyond college that shape revised choices. In E. Seymour & A.-B. Hunter (Eds.), *Talking about leaving revisited: Persistence, relocation, and loss in undergraduate STEM education* (pp. 371–398). Springer. https://doi.org/10.1007/978-3-030-25304-2_11

Holland Zahner, D. G., & Harper, R. P. (2022). Validation of belonging among underrepresented undergraduates in STEM majors: Comparison of former transfer and non-transfer students. *Journal of College Student Retention: Research, Theory & Practice*, 15210251221146119.

Holley, K. (2009). The challenge of an interdisciplinary curriculum: A cultural analysis of a doctoral-degree program in neuroscience. *Higher Education*, *58*, 241–255. https://doi.org/10.1007/s10734-008-9193-6

Hong, A., Etemadi, A., & Hilliard, A. (2021). *Credential quality in career and technical education*. Project on Workforce at Harvard Summer Fellowship Series.

Hood, S., Barrickman, N., Djerdjian, N., Farr, M., Magner, S., Roychowdhury, H., Gerrits, R., Lawford, H., Ott, B., Ross, K., Paige, O., Stowe, S., Jensen, M., & Hull, K. (2021). "I like and prefer to work alone": Social anxiety, academic self-efficacy, and students' perceptions of active learning. *CBE—Life Sciences Education*, *20*(1), Article 12. https://doi.org/10.1187/cbe.19-12-0271

Hooper, K. M., & Harrington, C. (2022). Equity gaps in dual enrollment. *Impacting Education: Journal on Transforming Professional Practice*, *7*(3), 20–26.

Hopp, R., Britson, C., Mukhopadhyay, S., Goldina, A., Chapman, M., & Nielsen, M. (2019). Teaching assistants in human anatomy and physiology: Their prevalence, recruitment strategies, funding, retention, and training. *HAPS Educator*, *23*(2), 367–384.

Horii, C., Redd, K., Ouellett, M., Finkelstein, N., Beach, A., Carlisle, D., Shadle, S., & Weaver, G. (2015, November). *Collaborating at the centers: Report from a STEM education transformation workshop involving leaders of centers for teaching and learning and STEM education centers*. Collaborating at the Centers Workshop.

Howard, J. L., Bureau, J. S., Guay, F., Chong, J. X. Y., & Ryan, R. M. (2021). Student motivation and associated outcomes: A meta-analysis from self-determination theory. *Perspectives on Psychological Science*, *16*(6), 1300–1323. https://doi.org/10.1177/1745691620966789

Howitz, W. J., McKnelly, K. J., & Link, R. D. (2021). Developing and implementing a specifications grading system in an organic chemistry laboratory course. *Journal of Chemical Education*, *98*(2), 385–394. https://doi.org/10.1021/acs.jchemed.0c00450

Hrabowski, F. A., III. (2012). Broadening participation in the American STEM workforce. *BioScience*, *62*(4), 325–326. https://doi.org/10.1525/bio.2012.62.4.2

Hsu, E., Murphy, T. J., & Treisman, U. (2008). Supporting high achievement in introductory mathematics courses: What we have learned from 30 years of the emerging scholars program. In M. P. Carlson & C. Rasmussen (Eds.), *Making the connection: Research to practice in undergraduate mathematics education* (Vol. 73, pp. 203–218). Mathematical Association of America.

Hu, X., & Chan, H. Y. (2021). Does delivery location matter? A national study of the impact of dual enrollment on college readiness and early academic momentum. *Teachers College Record*, *123*(4), 1–32.

Huber, N. S. (2002). Approaching leadership education in the new millennium. *Journal of Leadership Education*, *1*(1), 25–34.

Hudesman, J., Crosby, S., Flugman, B., Issac, S., Everson, H., & Clay, D. B. (2013). Using formative assessment and metacognition to improve student achievement. *Journal of Developmental Education*, *37*(1), 2.

Hughes, B. E. (2018). Coming out in STEM: Factors affecting retention of sexual minority STEM students. *Science Advances*, *4*(3), eaao6373. https://doi.org/10.1126/sciadv.aao6373

Hulleman, C. S., Godes, O., Hendricks, B. L., & Harackiewicz, J. M. (2010). Enhancing interest and performance with a utility value intervention. *Journal of Educational Psychology*, *102*(4), 880–895. https://doi.org/10.1037/a0019506

Hunter, A.-B. (2019). Why undergraduates leave STEM majors: Changes over the last two decades. In E. Seymour & A.-B. Hunter (Eds.), *Talking about leaving revisited: Persistence, relocation, and loss in undergraduate STEM education* (pp. 87–114). Springer Cham. https://doi.org/10.1007/978-3-030-25304-2_3

Hurlburt, S., & McGarrah, M. (2016). *Cost savings or cost shifting? The relationship between part-time contingent faculty and institutional spending*. Delta Cost Project at American Institutes for Research. https://www.air.org/sites/default/files/downloads/report/Cost-Savings-or-Cost-Shifting-Contingent-Faculty-November-2016.pdf

Hurtado, S., Cabrera, N. L., Lin, M. H., Arellano, L., & Espinosa, L. L. (2008). Diversifying science: Underrepresented student experiences in structured research programs. *Research in Higher Education*, *50*, 189–214.

Hurtado, S., & Carter, D. F. (1997). Effects of college transition and perceptions of the campus racial climate on Latino college students' sense of belonging. *Sociology of Education*, *70*(4), 324–345.

Hutchings, P. (1996). Building a new culture of teaching & learning. *About Campus*, *1*(5), 4–8. https://doi.org/10.1002/abc.6190010502

Hutchings, P., Huber, M. T., & Ciccone, A. (2011). *The scholarship of teaching and learning reconsidered: Institutional integration and impact*. Jossey-Bass.

Hyson, A. R., Bonham, B., Hood, S., Deutschman, M. C., Seithers, L. C., Hull, K., & Jensen, M. (2021). Professional development, shifting perspectives, and instructional change among community college anatomy and physiology instructors. *CBE—Life Sciences Education*, *20*(3), Article 49. https://doi.org/10.1187/cbe.21-02-0037

Ing, M., Burnette, J. M., Azzam, T., & Wessler, S. R. (2021). Participation in a course-based undergraduate research experience results in higher grades in the companion lecture course. *Educational Researcher*, *50*(4), 205–214. https://doi.org/10.3102/0013189X20968097

The Institute for College Access and Success (2023). *National rural college completion trends, challenges, and solutions*. https://ticas.org/wp-content/uploads/2023/12/2023.-Rural-College-Completion-National-Primer_v2.pdf

Institute of International Education. (2024, November 18). *Report on International Educational Exchange*. https://opendoorsdata.org/annual-release/international-students/#key-findings

Irons, A., & Elkington, S. (2021). *Enhancing learning through formative assessment and feedback*. Routledge.

Ison, M. P. (2022). Dual enrollment, performance-based funding, and the completion agenda: An analysis of post-secondary credential outcomes of dual enrollment students by credential type. *Community College Review*, *50*(1), 51–70.

Ives, J., & Castillo-Montoya, M. (2020). First-generation college students as academic learners: A systematic review. *Review of Educational Research*, *90*(2), 139–178.

Izzo, M. V. & Bauer, W. M. (2015). Universal design for learning: Enhancing achievement and employment of STEM students with disabilities. *Universal Access in the Information Society*, *14*, 17–27. https://doi.org/10.1007/s10209-013-0332-1

Jabbar, H., Epstein, E., Sánchez, J., & Hartman, C. (2021). Thinking through transfer: Examining how community college students make transfer decisions. *Community College Review*, *49*(1), 3–29.

Jackson, D. L., & Laanan, F. S. (2015). Desiring to fit: Fostering the success of community college transfer students in STEM. *Community College Journal of Research and Practice*, *39*(2), 132–149. https://doi.org/10.1080/10668926.2012.762565

Jackson, M. A., Tran, A., Wenderoth, M. P., & Doherty, J. H. (2018). Peer vs. self-grading of practice exams: Which is better? *CBE—Life Sciences Education*, *17*(3), es44. https://doi.org/10.1187/cbe.18-04-0052

Jackson, P. (1968). *Life in classrooms*. Holt, Rinehart and Winston.

Jackson Smith, D. (2016). Operating in the middle: The experiences of African American female transfer students in STEM degree programs at HBCUs. *Community College Journal of Research and Practice*, *40*(12), 1025–1039. https://doi.org/10.1080/10668926.2016.1206841

Jagesic, S., Ewing, M., Wyatt, J. N., & Feng, J. (2022). Unintended consequences: Understanding the relationship between dual enrollment participation, college undermatch, and bachelor's degree attainment. *Research in Higher Education*, *63*(1), 119–139.

Jaimes, P. (2021). *Reimagining diversity in STEM: Using an assets-based capital framework model to explore the career trajectory of scientists from underrepresented groups*. Michigan State University.

Jaipal-Jamani, K., Figg, C., Gallagher, T., Scott, R. M., & Ciampa, K. (2015). Collaborative professional development in higher education: Developing knowledge of technology enhanced teaching. *Journal of Effective Teaching*, *15*(2), 30–44.

James, N. M., & LaDue, N. D. (2021). Pedagogical reform in an introductory chemistry course and the importance of curricular alignment. *Journal of Chemical Education*, *98*(11), 3421–3430. https://doi.org/10.1021/acs.jchemed.1c00688

Jenner, B. M. (2017). Student veterans and the transition to higher education: Integrating existing literatures. *Journal of Veterans Studies*, *2*(2), 26–44.

Jensen, G. M., Hack, L. M., Nordstrom, T., Gwyer, J., & Mostrom, E. (2017). National study of excellence and innovation in physical therapist education: Part 2—a call to reform. *Physical Therapy*, *97*(9), 875–888.

Jha, S., Noori, H., & Michela, J. L. (1996). The dynamics of continuous improvement: Aligning organizational attributes and activities for quality and productivity. *International Journal of Quality Science*, *1*(1), 19–47. https://doi.org/10.1108/13598539610117975

Johnson, A., & Elliott, S. (2020). Culturally relevant pedagogy: A model to guide cultural transformation in STEM departments. *Journal of Microbiology & Biology Education*, *21*(1). https://doi.org/10.1128/jmbe.v21i1.2097

Johnson, D. W., Johnson, R. T., & Smith, K. (2007). The state of cooperative learning in postsecondary and professional settings. *Educational Psychology Review*, *19*, 15–29. https://doi.org/10.1007/s10648-006-9038-8

Johnson, D. W., Johnson, R. T., & Smith, K. A. (1998). Cooperative learning returns to college what evidence is there that it works? *Change: The Magazine of Higher Learning*, *30*(4), 26–35. https://doi.org/10.1080/00091389809602629

Johnson, J., & Bozeman, B. (2012). Perspective: Adopting an asset bundles model to support and advance minority students' careers in academic medicine and the scientific pipeline. *Academic Medicine*, *87*(11), 1488–1495.

Johnson, W. B., & Nelson, N. (1999). Mentor-protégé relationships in graduate training: Some ethical concerns. *Ethics and Behavior*, *9*(3), 189–210. https://doi.org/10.1207/s15327019eb0903_1

Johnstone, S. M., & Soares, L. (2014). Principles for developing competency-based education programs. *Change: The Magazine of Higher Learning*, *46*(2), 12–19.

Jones, M. T., Barlow, A. E., & Villarejo, M. (2010). Importance of undergraduate research for minority persistence and achievement in biology. *The Journal of Higher Education*, *81*(1), 82–115. https://doi.org/10.1080/00221546.2010.11778971

Jonsson, A., & Svingby, G. (2007). The use of scoring rubrics: Reliability, validity, and educational consequences. *Educational Research Review*, *2*(2), 130–144. https://doi.org/10.1016/j.edurev.2007.05.002

Jorstad, J., Starobin, S. S., Chen, Y., & Kollasch, A. (2017). STEM aspiration: The influence of social capital and chilly climate on female community college students. *Community College Journal of Research and Practice*, *41*(4–5), 253–266. https://doi.org/10.1080/10668926.2016.1251358

Kallison, J. M., Jr., & Stader, D. L. (2012). Effectiveness of summer bridge programs in enhancing college readiness. *Community College Journal of Research and Practice*, *36*(5), 340–357.

Kania, J., Kramer, M., & Senge, P. (2018). *The water of systems change*. FSG. https://www.fsg.org/resource/water_of_systems_change/

Karandjeff, K., & Schiorring, E. (2011). Career and technical education (CTE) transfer research project: Improving transfer pathways for California community college students in CTE programs. *Journal of Applied Research in the Community College*, *18*(2), 39–48.

Kardash, C. A. M., & Wallace, M. L. (2001). The perceptions of science classes survey: What undergraduate science reform efforts really need to address. *Journal of Educational Psychology*, *93*(1), 199–210.

Karpicke, J. D., Butler, A. C., & Roediger, H. L., III. (2009). Metacognitive strategies in student learning: Do students practise retrieval when they study on their own? *Memory*, *17*(4), 471–479. https://doi.org/10.1080/09658210802647009

Karsten, J. L. (2019). Insights from the OEDG program on broadening participation in the geosciences. *Journal of Geoscience Education*, *67*(4), 287–299.

Katz, V. S., Jordan, A. B., & Ognyanova, K. (2021). Digital inequality, faculty communication, and remote learning experiences during the COVID-19 pandemic: A survey of U.S. undergraduates. *PLoS One*, *16*(2), e0246641. https://doi.org/10.1371/journal.pone.0246641

Katzman, S. D., Hurst-Kennedy, J., Barrera, A., Talley, J., Javazon, E., Diaz, M., & Anzovino, M. E. (2021). The effect of specifications grading on students' learning and attitudes in an undergraduate-level cell biology course. *Journal of Microbiology & Biology Education*, *22*(3), e00200–e00221. https://doi.org/10.1128/jmbe.00200-21

Kaufmann, R., & Vallade, J. I. (2022). Exploring connections in the online learning environment: Student perceptions or rapport, climate, and loneliness. *Interactive Learning Environments*, *30*(10), 1794–1808. https://doi.org/10.1080/10494820.2020.1749670

Kay, R. H., & LeSage, A. (2009). Examining the benefits and challenges of using audience response systems: A review of the literature. *Computers & Education*, *53*(3), 819–827. https://doi.org/10.1016/j.compedu.2009.05.001

Keengwe, J., Georgina, D., & Wachira, P. (2010). Faculty training strategies to enhance pedagogy-technology integration. *International Journal of Information and Communication Technology Education (IJICTE)*, *6*(3), 1–10.

Keith-Le, J. A., & Morgan, M. P. (Eds.). (2020). *Faculty experiences in active learning: A collection of strategies for implementing active learning across disciplines*. J. Murrey Atkins Library.

Kember, D., Leung, D. Y., & McNaught, C. (2008). A workshop activity to demonstrate that approaches to learning are influenced by the teaching and learning environment. *Active Learning in Higher Education*, *9*(1), 43–56. https://doi.org/10.1177/1469787407086745

Kerr, J. (2014). Western epistemic dominance and colonial structures: Considerations for thought and practice in programs of teacher education. *Decolonization: Indigeneity, Education & Society*, *3*(2).

Keutzer, C. S. (1993). Midterm evaluation of teaching provides helpful feedback to instructors. *Teaching of Psychology*, *20*(4), 238–240. https://doi.org/10.1207/s15328023top2004_12

Kezar, A. (2013). *How colleges change: Understanding, leading, and enacting change* (1st ed.). Routledge.

___. (2018). *How colleges change: Understanding, leading, and enacting change* (2nd ed.). Routledge.

Kezar, A., & Dizon, J. P. M. (2019). Renewing and revitalizing shared governance: A social justice and equity framework. In *Higher education administration for social justice and equity* (pp. 21–42). Routledge.

Kezar, A., Gehrke, S., & Bernstein-Sierra, S. (2017). Designing for success in STEM communities of practice: Philosophy and personal interactions. *The Review of Higher Education*, *40*(2), 217–244.

Kezar, A., Gehrke, S., & Elrod, S. (2015). Implicit theories of change as a barrier to change on college campuses: An examination of STEM reform. *The Review of Higher Education*, *38*(4), 479–506. https://dx.doi.org/10.1353/rhe.2015.0026

Kezar, A., Glenn, W. J., Lester, J., & Nakamoto, J. (2008). Examining organizational contextual features that affect implementation of equity initiatives. *The Journal of Higher Education*, *79*(2), 125–159.

Kezar, A., & Holcombe, E. (2015). Institutional transformation in STEM: Insights from change research and the Keck-PKAL Project. In G. C. Weaver, W. D. Burgess, A. L. Childress, & L. L. Slakey (Eds.), *Transforming institutions: 21st century undergraduate STEM education* (pp. 35–48). Purdue University Press.

Kezar, A., & Kitchen, J. A. (2020). Supporting first-generation, low-income, and underrepresented students' transitions to college through comprehensive and integrated programs. *American Behavioral Scientist*, *64*(3), 223–229. https://doi.org/10.1177/0002764219869397

Kezar, A., & Posselt, J. (2020). Higher education administration for social justice and equity. *Critical Perspectives for Leadership.*

Kezar, A. J. (2013). Departmental cultures and non-tenure-track faculty: Willingness, capacity, and opportunity to perform at four-year institutions. *The Journal of Higher Education*, *84*(2), 153–188. https://doi.org/10.1080/00221546.2013.11777284

Kezar, K., & Acuna, A. L. (2020). Gender inequality and the new faculty majority. In N. S. Niemi & N. B. Weaver-Hightower (Eds.), *The Wiley handbook of gender equity in higher education.* John Wiley & Sons.

Kim, A. (2021, August 11). History and background: Career prep. *Education Writers Association.* https://ewa.org/issues/career-technical-education/history-background-career-prep

Kim, Y. A., Cox, J., Southard, K. M., Elfring, L., Blowers, P., & Talanquer, V. (2019). Learning researchers: Promoting formative assessment in STEM courses. *Journal of College Science Teaching*, *48*(5), 36–41. https://doi.org/10.1080/0047231X.2019.12290474

King, A. (1993). From sage on the stage to guide on the side. *College Teaching*, *41*(1), 30–35. https://doi.org/10.1080/87567555.1993.9926781

King-Sears, M. E., Stefanidis, A., Evmenova, A. S., Rao, K., Mergen, R. L., Owen, L. S., & Strimel, M. M. (2023). Achievement of learners receiving UDL instruction: A meta-analysis. *Teaching and Teacher Education*, *122*, 103596.

Kingston, N., & Nash, B. (2011). Formative assessment: A meta-analysis and a call for research. *Educational Measurement: Issues and Practice*, *30*(4), 28–37. https://doi.org/10.1111/j.1745-3992.2011.00220.x

Kinnunen, P., Butler, M., Morgan, M., Nylen, A., Peters, A. K., Sinclair, J., Kalvala, S., & Pesonen, E. (2018). Understanding initial undergraduate expectations and identity in computing studies. *European Journal of Engineering Education*, *43*(2), 201–218. https://doi.org/10.1080/03043797.2016.1146233

Kisker, C. B., Cohen, A. M., & Brawer, F. B. (2023). *The American community college.* Jossey-Bass.

Kitchen, J. A., Cole, D., Rivera, G., & Hallett, R. (2020). The impact of a college transition program proactive advising intervention on self-efficacy. *Journal of Student Affairs Research and Practice*, *58*(1), 29–43. https://www.tandfonline.com/doi/full/10.1080/19496591.2020.1717963

Kiyama, J. M., & Rios-Aguilar, C. (2017). *Funds of knowledge in higher education honoring students' cultural experiences and resources as strengths.* Routledge.

Klingbeil, N. (2004, June). Rethinking engineering mathematics education: A model for increased retention, motivation, and success in engineering. In *2004 Annual Conference.*

Klyce, A., & Ryker, K. (2023). What does a degree in geology actually mean? A systematic evaluation of courses required to earn a bachelor of science in geology in the United States. *Journal of Geoscience Education*, *71*(1), 3–19. https://doi.org/10.1080/10899995.2022.2076201

Kober, N. (2015). *Reaching students: What research says about effective instruction in undergraduate science and engineering.* The National Academies Press. https://doi.org/10.17226/18687

Koch, A. K. (2017). It's about the gateway courses: Defining and contextualizing the issue. *New Directions for Higher Education*, *2017*(180), 11–17. https://doi.org/10.1002/he.20257

Koester, B. P., Grom, G., & McKay, T. A. (2016). Patterns of gendered performance difference in introductory STEM courses. *arXiv*. https://arxiv.org/abs/1608.07565

Koricich, A., Chen, X., & Hughes, R. P. (2018). Understanding the effects of rurality and socioeconomic status on college attendance and institutional choice in the United States. *The Review of Higher Education*, *41*(2), 281–305.

Koutsouris, G., Mountford-Zimdars, A., & Dingwall, K. (2021). The 'ideal' higher education student: Understanding the hidden curriculum to enable institutional change. *Research in Post-Compulsory Education*, 26(2), 131–147. https://doi.org/10.1080/13596748.2021.1909921

Kraft, A. R., Atieh, E. L., Shi, L. & Stains, M. (2024a). Prior experiences as students and instructors play a critical role in instructors' decision to adopt evidence-based instructional practices. *International Journal of STEM Education*, *11*, Article 18. https://doi.org/10.1186/s40594-024-00478-3

Kraft, T., & Hernández Rodríguez, O. (2024b). Lesson study in science teacher preparation programs: A literature review. *International Journal for Lesson & Learning Studies*, *13*(2), 116–129. https://doi.org/10.1108/IJLLS-12-2023-0181

Kravets, M., & Wax, I. (2023). *The K&W Guide to colleges for students with learning differences, 16th edition: 350+ schools with programs or services for students with ADHD, ASD, or Lea.* Princeton Review.

Kreitzer, R. J., & Sweet-Cushman, J. (2021). Evaluating student evaluations of teaching: A review of measurement and equity bias in sets and recommendations for ethical reform. *Journal of Academic Ethics*, *20*, 73–84. https://doi.org/10.1007/s10805-021-09400-w

Kressler, B., & Kressler, J. (2020). Diverse student perceptions of active learning in a large enrollment STEM course. *Journal of the Scholarship of Teaching and Learning*, *20*(1). https://doi.org/10.14434/josotl.v20i1.24688

Krim, J. S., Cote, L. E., Schwartz, R. S., Stone, E. M., Cleeves, J. J., Barry, K. J., Burgess, W., Buxner, S. R., Gerton, J. M., Horvath, L., Keller, J. M., Lee, S. C., Locke, S. M., & Rebar, B. M. (2019). Models and impacts of science research experiences: A review of the literature of CUREs, UREs, and TREs. *CBE—Life Sciences Education*, *18*(4), Article 65. https://doi.org/10/1187/cbe.19-03-0069

Krishnan, S., Gehrtz, J., Lemons, P. P., Dolan, E. L., Brickman, P., & Andrews, T. C. (2022). Guides to Advance Teaching Evaluation (GATEs): A resource for STEM departments planning robust and equitable evaluation practices. *CBE—Life Sciences*, *21*, Article 42. https://doi.org/10.1187/cbe.21-08-0198.

Kroeper, K. M., Fried, A. C., & Murphy, M. C. (2022a). Towards fostering growth mindset classrooms: Identifying teaching behaviors that signal instructors' fixed and growth mindsets beliefs to students. *Social Psychology of Education*, *25*(2), 371–398. https://doi.org/10.1007/s11218-022-09689-4

Kroeper, K. M., Muenks, K., Canning, E. A., & Murphy, M. C. (2022b). An exploratory study of the behaviors that communicate perceived instructor mindset beliefs in college STEM classrooms. *Teaching and Teacher Education*, *114*, 103717. https://doi.org/10.1016/j.tate.2022.103717

Kuh, G. D. (2016). Making learning meaningful: Engaging students in ways that matter to them. *New Directions for Teaching and Learning*, *2016*(145), 49–56. https://doi.org/10.1002/tl.20174

Kujawa, T. A. (2013). The AAS to BAS pathway: Heating up the educational aspiration of CTE students. *Community College Journal of Research and Practice*, *37*(5), 356–364. https://doi.org/10.1080/10668926.2012.755648

Kumar, K. L., & Wideman, M. (2014). Accessible by design: Applying UDL principles in a first year undergraduate course. *Canadian Journal of Higher Education*, *44*(1), 125–147.

Kyei-Blankson, L., Keengwe, J., & Blankson, J. (2009). Faculty use and integration of technology in higher education. *AACE Review*, *17*(3), 199–213. https://www.learntechlib.org/primary/p/28362/

LaCosse, J., Canning, E. A., Bowman, N. A., Murphy, M. C., & Logel, C. (2020). A social-belonging intervention improves STEM outcomes for students who speak English as a second language. *Science Advances*, *6*(40), eabb6543. https://doi.org/10.1126/sciadv.abb6543

Ladson-Billings, G. (1995). But that's just good teaching! The case for culturally relevant pedagogy. *Theory Into Practice*, *34*(3), 159–165.

___. (2006). 'Yes, but how do we do it?': Practicing culturally relevant pedagogy. In J. Landsman & C. W. Lewis (Eds.), *White teachers/diverse classrooms: Creating inclusive schools, building on students' diversity, and providing true educational equity* (pp. 29–41). Routledge. https://www.taylorfrancis.com/chapters/edit/10.4324/9781003448709-6/yes-gloria-ladson-billings

___. (2014). Culturally relevant pedagogy 2.0: Aka the remix. *Harvard Educational Review*, *84*(1), 74–84. https://doi.org/10.17763/haer.84.1.p2rj131485484751

Laist, R., Sheehan, D., & Brewer, N. (Eds.). (2022). *UDL university: Designing for variability across the postsecondary curriculum.* CAST Professional Publishing.

Landrum, R. E., & Mulcock, S. D. (2007). Use of pre- and postcourse surveys to predict student outcomes. *Teaching of Psychology*, *34*(3), 163–166.

Langley, G., Moen, R., Nolan, K., Nolan, T., & Norman, C. (2009). *The improvement guide: A practical approach to enhancing organizational performance* (2nd ed.). Jossey-Bass.

Larson, M. (2023, January 30). *What is specifications grading?* Center for Transformative Teaching, University of Nebraska-Lincoln. https://teaching.unl.edu/resources/alternative-grading/specification-grading/

Lattuca, L., & Brown, M. (2023). Curriculum-making in higher education: A basis for teaching and learning. In M. N. Bastedo, P. G. Altbach, & P. J. Gumport (Eds.), *American higher education in the 21st Century: Social, political, and economic challenges* (pp. 68–93). John Hopkins University Press.

Lattuca, L. R., & Stark, J. S. (2009). *Shaping the college curriculum: Academic plans in context.* Jossey-Bass.

Lattuca, L. R., & Stark, J. S. (2011). *Shaping the college curriculum: Academic plans in context.* Wiley.

Laufer, M., Leiser, A., Deacon, B., Perrin de Brichambaut, P., Fecher, B., Kobsda, C., & Hesse, F. (2021). Digital higher education: A divider or bridge builder? Leadership perspectives on edtech in a COVID-19 reality. *International Journal of Educational Technology in Higher Education*, *18*, Article 51. https://doi.org/10.1186/s41239-021-00287-6

Laursen, S. L., & Rasmussen, C. (2019). I on the prize: Inquiry approaches in undergraduate mathematics. *International Journal of Research in Undergraduate Mathematics Education*, *5*, 129–146.

Lavi, R., Shwartz, G., & Dori, Y. J. (2019). Metacognition in chemistry education: A literature review. *Israel Journal of Chemistry*, *59*(6–7), 583–597.

Lawrie, G. A., Schultz, M., Bailey, C. H., & Dargaville, B. L. (2019). Personal journeys of teachers: An investigation of the development of teacher professional knowledge and skill by expert tertiary chemistry teachers. *Chemistry Education Research and Practice*, *20*(1), 132–145. https://doi.org/10.1039/C8RP00187A

Lawson, C. A., & Fong, C. J. (2024). Undergraduate Latina/o/x motivation and STEM persistence intentions: Moderating influences of community cultural wealth. *Journal of Latinx Psychology*, *12*(2), 101–117. https://doi.org/10.1037/lat0000243

LeBouef, S., & Dworkin, J. (2021). First-generation college students and family support: A critical review of empirical research literature. *Education Sciences*, *11*(6), 294.

Ledesma, M. C., & Fránquiz, M. E. (2015). Introduction: Reflections on Latinas/os, affirmative action, and education. *Association of Mexican American Educators Journal*, *9*(1), 1–7.

Lee, J., Fernandez, F., Ro, H. K., & Suh, H. (2022). Does dual enrollment influence high school graduation, college enrollment, choice, and persistence? *Research in Higher Education*, *63*(5), 825–848.

Lee, J. J. (2007). The shaping of the departmental culture: Measuring the relative influences of the institution and discipline. *Journal of Higher Education Policy and Management*, *29*(1), 41–55.

Lee, M., Volpe Horii, C., Austin, E. A., Avery, L., DeSanctis, M., Finkelstein, N., Miller, E., & Schaal, B. (2023). An instructional-workforce framework for coordinated change in undergraduate education. *Change: The Magazine of Higher Learning*, *55*(1), 54–63. https://doi.org/10.1080/00091383.2023.2151809

Lee, R., & Ahtone, T. (2020, March 30). Land-grab universities. *High Country News*. https://www.hcn.org/issues/52-4/indigenous-affairs-education-land-grab-universities/

Leijon, M., Nordmo, I., Tieva, Å., & Troelsen, R. (2022). Formal learning spaces in higher education—A systematic review. *Teaching in Higher Education*, *29*(6), 1460–1481. https://doi.org/10.1080/13562517.2022.2066469

LeMahieu, P. G., Grunow, A., Baker, L., Nordstrum, L. E., & Gomez, L. M. (2017). Networked improvement communities: The discipline of improvement science meets the power of networks. *Quality Assurance in Education*, *25*(1), 5–25.

Lemke, J. L., & Sabelli, N. H. (2008). Complex systems and educational change: Towards a new research agenda. *Educational Philosophy & Theory*, *40*(1), 118–129. https://doi.org/10.1111/j.1469-5812.2007.00401.x

Lenning, O. T., Hill, D. M., Saunders, K. P., Stokes, A., & Solan, A. (2013). *Powerful learning communities: A guide to developing student, faculty, and professional learning communities to improve student success and organizational effectiveness* (1st ed.). Routledge. https://doi.org/10.4324/9781003446385

Leslie, S.-J., Cimpian, A., Meyer, M., & Freeland, E. (2015). Expectations of brilliance underlie gender distributions across academic disciplines. *Science*, *347*(6219), 262–265. https://doi.org/10.1126/science.1261375

Lester, J. (2010). Women in male-dominated career and technical education programs at community colleges: Barriers to participation and success. *Journal of Women and Minorities in Science and Engineering*, *16*(1), 55–66. https://doi.org/10.1615/JWomenMinorScienEng.v16.i1.40

Lester, J., Struthers, B., & Yamanaka, A. (2017). Unwelcoming classroom climates: The role of gender microaggressions in CTE. *New Directions for Community Colleges*, *2017*(178), 67–77. https://doi.org/10.1002/cc.20254

Lester, J., Yamanaka, A., & Struthers, B. (2016). Gender microaggressions and learning environments: The role of physical space in teaching pedagogy and communication. *Community College Journal of Research and Practice*, *40*(11), 909–926. https://doi.org/10.1080/10668926.2015.1133333

Levy, R. (2019, January 14). VITAL faculty: A growing workforce in colleges and universities. *MAA Values*. Mathematical Association of America. https://www.mathvalues.org/masterblog/vital-faculty

Lewis, D. (2020). Student anxiety in standards-based grading in mathematics courses. *Innovative Higher Education*, *45*, 153–164.

Li, H., & Xia, X. (2024). Grades as signals of comparative advantage: How letter grades affect major choices. *Journal of Economic Behavior & Organization*, *227*, 106717.

Li, H., Yu, J., Luo, Y., & Guo, C. (2023). Inclusion and equity: Experiences and dilemmas of disability resource centers at world-class universities. *International Journal of Chinese Education*, *12*(1). https://doi.org/10.1177/2212585X231161859

Li, Y., & Singh, C. (2023). Sense of belonging is an important predictor of introductory physics students' academic performance. *Physical Review Physics Education Research*, *19*(2), 020137. https://doi.org/10.1103/PhysRevPhysEducRes.19.020137

Liera, R. (2023). Expanding faculty members' zone of proximal development to enact collective agency for racial equity in faculty hiring. *The Journal of Higher Education*, *94*(6), 766–791.

Liera, R., & Desir, S. (2023, July). Taking equity-mindedness to the next level: The equity-minded organization. *Frontiers in Education*, *8*, 1199174.

Lim, J., & Richardson, J. C. (2021). Predictive effects of undergraduate students' perceptions of social, cognitive, and teaching presence on affective learning outcomes according to disciplines. *Computers & Education*, *161*, 104063.

Limeri, L. B., Carter, N. T., Lyra, F., Martin, J., Mastronardo, H., Patel, J., & Dolan, E. L. (2023). Undergraduate lay theories of abilities: Mindset, universality, and brilliance beliefs uniquely predict undergraduate educational outcomes. *CBE—Life Sciences Education*, *22*(4), Article 40. https://doi.org/10.1187/cbe.22-12-0250

Lindsay, J., Hughes, K., Dougherty, S. M., Reese, K., & Joshi, M. (2024). *What we know about the impact of career and technical education: A systematic review of the research.*

Linn, M. C., Palmer, E., Baranger, A., Gerard, E., & Stone, E. (2015). Undergraduate research experiences: Impacts and opportunities. *Science*, *347*(6222), 1261757.

Livers, S. D., Harbour, K. E., & Sullivan, P. L. (2024). (Up)grading: A (re)humanizing assessment process with a focus on feedback. *Education Sciences*, *14*(6), 646.

Logel, C., Iserman, E. C., Davies, P. G., Quinn, D. M., & Spencer, S. J. (2009). The perils of double consciousness: The role of thought suppression in stereotype threat. *Journal of Experimental Social Psychology*, *45*(2), 299–312. https://doi.org/10.1016/j.jesp.2008.07.016

Logue, A. W., Douglas, D., & Watanabe-Rose, M. (2019). Corequisite mathematics remediation: Results over time and in different contexts. *Educational Evaluation and Policy Analysis*, *41*(3), 294–315. https://doi.org/10.3102/0162373719848777

Lombardi, D., Shipley, T. F., Bailey, J. M., Bretones, P. S., Prather, E. E., Ballen, C. J., Knight, J. K., Smith, M. K., Stowe, R. L., Cooper, M. M., Prince, M., Atit, K., Uttal, D. H., LaDue, N. D., McNeal, P. M., Ryker, K., St. John, K., van der Hoeven Kraft, K. J., & Dockter, J. L. (2021). The curious construct of active learning. *Psychological Science in the Public Interest*, *22*(1), 8–43. https://doi.org/10.1177/1529100620973974

Lopatto, D. (2003). The essential features of undergraduate research. *Council on Undergraduate Research Quarterly*, *24*, 139–142.

Lopez, J. D. (2021). Giving back as an educational outcome for postsecondary Indigenous students. In J. W. Tippeconnic III & M. J. Tippeconnic Fox (Eds.), *On Indian ground: The Southwest* (pp. 177–190). Information Age Publishing.

Lovecchio, K., & Dundes, L. (2002). Premed survival: Understanding the culling process in premedical undergraduate education. *Academic Medicine*, *77*(7), 719–724.

Lovell, E. D. (2014). College students who are parents need equitable services for retention. *Journal of College Student Retention: Research, Theory & Practice*, *16*(2), 188–202. https://doi.org/10.2190/CS.16.2.b

Luke, A., Woods, A., & Weir, K. (Eds.). (2012). *Curriculum, syllabus design and equity.* Routledge.

Lund, T. J., & Stains, M. (2015). The importance of context: An exploration of factors influencing the adoption of student-centered teaching among chemistry, biology, and physics faculty. *International Journal of STEM Education*, *2*, Article 13. https://doi.org/10.1186/s40594-015-0026-8

Lunn, S., Ross, M., Hazari, Z., Weiss, M. A., Georgiopoulos, M., & Christensen, K. (2021). How do educational experiences predict computing identity? *ACM Transactions on Computing Education*, *22*(2), 1–28. https://doi.org/10.1145/3470653

Lyle, K. B., Bego, C. R., Hopkins, R. F., Hieb, J. L., & Ralston, P. A. (2020). How the amount and spacing of retrieval practice affect the short-and-long-term retention of mathematics knowledge. *Educational Psychology Review*, *32*(1), 277–295.

Lytle, A., & Shin, J. E. L. (2023). Self and professors' incremental beliefs as predictors of STEM engagement among undergraduate students. *International Journal of Science and Mathematics Education*, *21*(3), 1013–1029. https://doi.org/10.1007/s10763-022-10272-8

Mack, K. (2021). Expand the space, expand the bravery: A practicum for building safe brave spaces within STEM faculty professional development programs. In K. Winter & A. Bramberger (Eds.), *Re-conceptualizing safe spaces: Supporting inclusive education* (pp. 79–90). Emerald Publishing Limited.

MacNell, L., Driscoll, A., & Hunt, A. N. (2015). What's in a name: Exposing gender bias in student ratings of teaching. *Innovative Higher Education*, *40*(4), 291–303. https://doi.org/10.1007/s10755-014-9313-4

Mahmud, S. (Ed.). (2024). *Academic integrity in the age of artificial intelligence*. IGI Global.

Main, J. B., Dang, T., Johnson, B., Shi, Q., Guariniello, C., & Delaurentis, D. (2023, June). *Why students choose STEM: A study of high school factors that influence college STEM major choice*. ASEE Conferences.

Makela, J. P., Ruud, C. M., Bennett, S., & Bragg, D. D. (2012, March). *Investigating applied baccalaureate degree pathways in technician education*. Office of Community College Research and Leadership, University of Illinois at Urbana-Champaign.

Malachowski, M. R., Ambos, E. L., Karukstis, K. K., Kinzie, J. L., & Osborn, J. M. (Eds.). (2024). *Transforming academic culture and curriculum: Integrating and scaffolding research throughout undergraduate education*. Taylor & Francis.

Malcom-Piqueux, L. (2020, October). [Transformation in the U.S. higher education system: Implications for racial equity]. Commissioned paper for the Symposium on Imagining the Future of Undergraduate STEM Education. https://www.nationalacademies.org/event/10-21-2020/imagining-the-future-of-undergraduate-stem-education-symposium

Malespina, A., & Singh, C. (2023). Gender gaps in grades versus grade penalties: Why grade anomalies may be more detrimental for women aspiring for careers in biological sciences. *International Journal of STEM Education*, *10*(1), 13. https://stemeducationjournal.springeropen.com/articles/10.1186/s40594-023-00399-7

Maltese, A. V., Harsh, J. A., & Svetina, D. (2015). Data visualization literacy: Investigating data interpretation along the novice—expert continuum. *Journal of College Science Teaching*, *45*(1), 84–90. https://www.jstor.org/stable/43631889

Manduca, C. A., Iverson, E. R., Luxenberg, M., Macdonald, R. H., McConnell, D. A., Mogk, D. W., & Tewksbury, B. J. (2017). Improving undergraduate STEM education: The efficacy of discipline-based professional development. *Science Advances*, *3*(2), e1600193.

Mangels, J. A., Butterfield, B., Lamb, J., Good, C. D., & Dweck, C. S. (2006). Why do beliefs about intelligence influence learning success? A social cognitive neuroscience model. *Social Cognitive and Affective Neuroscience*, *1*, 75–86.

Marbach-Ad, G., Egan, L. C., & Thompson, K. V. (2016). A disciplinary teaching and learning center: Applying pedagogical content knowledge to faculty development. In G. C. Weaver, W. D. Burgess, A. L. Childress, & L. Slakey (Eds.), *Transforming institutions: Undergraduate STEM education for the 21st century* (pp. 297–311). Purdue University Press.

Marbach-Ad, G., Hunt, C., & Thompson, K. V. (2019). Exploring the values undergraduate students attribute to cross-disciplinary skills needed for the workplace: An analysis of five STEM disciplines. *Journal of Science Education and Technology*, *28*(5), 452–469.

Marcelo, C., & Yot-Domínguez, C. (2019). From chalk to keyboard in higher education classrooms: Changes and coherence when integrating technological knowledge into pedagogical content knowledge. *Journal of Further and Higher Education*, *43*(7), 975–988. https://doi.org/10.1080/0309877X.2018.1429584

Marco-Bujosa, L. M., Joy, L., & Sorrentino, R. (2021). Nevertheless, she persisted: A comparison of male and female experiences in community college STEM programs. *Community College Journal of Research and Practice*, *45*(8), 541–559. https://doi.org/10.1080/10668926.2020.1727382

Margalef, L., & Roblin, N. P. (2018). Unpacking the roles of the facilitator in higher education professional learning communities. In *Teacher learning through teacher teams* (pp. 41–58). Routledge.

Marín-Spiotta, E., Barnes, R. T., Berhe, A. A., Hastings, M. G., Mattheis, A., Schneider, B., & Williams, B. M. (2020). Hostile climates are barriers to diversifying the geosciences. *Advances in Geosciences*, *53*, 117–127. https://doi.org/10.5194/adgeo-53-117-2020

Marín-Spiotta, E., Diaz-Vallejo, E. J., Barnes, R. T., Mattheis, A., Schneider, B., Berhe, A. A., Hastings, M. G., Williams, B. M., & Magley, V. (2023). Exclusionary behaviors reinforce historical biases and contribute to loss of talent in the Earth sciences. *Earth's Future*, *11*(3), e2022EF002912. https://doi.org/10.1029/2022EF002912

Markowitz, D. M., Laha, R., Perone, B. P., Pea, R. D., & Bailenson, J. N. (2018). Immersive virtual reality field trips facilitate learning about climate change. *Frontiers in Psychology*, *9*. https://doi.org/10.3389/fpsyg.2018.02364

Marsh, C. C., Marsh, J., & Chesnutt, K. (2022). Exploring OER as a mediator for equity gaps in student course success rates for introductory biology courses in the NCCCS. *NC Community College Journal of Teaching Innovation*, *1*(1), 6–17.

Marshall, A. M., Piatek, J. L., Williams, D. A., Gallant, E., Thatcher, S., Elardo, S., Williams, A. J., Collins, T., & Arroyo, Y. (2022). Flexible fieldwork. *Nature Reviews Earth & Environment*, *3*(12), 811.

Martin, D. B. (2000). *Mathematics success and failure among African-American youth: The roles of sociohistorical context, community forces, school influence, and individual agency*. Routledge.

Martin, M. T., Belikov, O., Hilton, J., Wiley, D., & Fischer, L. (2017). Analysis of student and faculty perceptions of textbook costs in higher education. *Open Praxis*, *9*(1), 79–91.

Martin, T. L., McNair, L. D., & Paretti, M. C. (2015). *Comparative dimensions of disciplinary culture*. ASEE.

Martinez, A. E., Gehrtz, J., Rasmussen, C., LaTona-Tequida, T., & Vroom, K. (2022). Course coordinator orientations toward their work and opportunities for professional development. *Innovative Higher Education*, *47*(2), 327–346. https://doi.org/10.1007/s10755-021-09579-1

Martinez, M. A., Valle, F., Cortez, L. J., Ponjuan, L., & Sáenz, V. B. (2017). Context is key: School leaders' approaches in creating and maintaining dual enrollment opportunities in South Texas. *Leadership and Policy in Schools*, *17*(4), 516–540. https://doi.org/10.1080/15700763.2017.1326149

Massey, M. D. B., Arif, S., Embuldeniya, S., Nanglu, K., & Bielawski, J. (2022). Ten simple rules for succeeding as an underrepresented STEM undergraduate. *PLoS Computational Biology*, *18*(6), e1010101. https://doi.org/10.1371/journal.pcbi.1010101

Master, A., & Meltzoff, A. N. (2020). Cultural stereotypes and sense of belonging contribute to gender gaps in STEM. *International Journal of Gender, Science and Technology*, *12*(1), 152–198. http://orcid.org/0000-0001-6708-6353

Mathieu, R. D., Austin, A. E., Barnicle, K. A., Campa, H., III, & McLinn, C. M. (2020). The center for the integration of research, teaching, and learning: A national-scale network to prepare stem future faculty. *New Directions for Teaching and Learning*, *2020*(163), 45–53.

Matthews, A. (2022). *Changing perceptions of career and technical education (CTE): Bridging the soft skills gap with high quality CTE*. St. John's University.

Matthews, K. E. (2017). Five propositions for genuine students as partners practice. *International Journal for Students as Partners*, *1*(2), 1–9.

Matz, R., Koester, B., Fiorini, S., Grom, G., Shepard, L., Stangor, C., Weiner, B., & Mckay, T. (2017). Patterns of gendered performance differences in large introductory courses at five research universities. *AERA Open*, *3*, 233285841774375. https://journals.sagepub.com/doi/10.1177/2332858417743754

Matz, R. L., Fata-Hartley, C. L., Posey, L. A., Laverty, J. T., Underwood, S. M., Carmel, J. H., Herrington, D. G., Stowe, R. L., Caballero, M. D., Ebert-May, D., & Cooper, M. M. (2018). Evaluating the extent of a large-scale transformation in gateway science courses. *Science Advances, 4*(10), 11. https://doi.org/10.1126/sciadv.aau0554

Mayer, R. E., & Alexander, P. A. (Eds.). (2011). *Handbook of research on learning and instruction*. Routledge.

Mazur, E. (1997). *Peer instruction: A user's manual*. Prentice Hall.

Mazur, E., & Watkins, J. (2010). Just-in-time teaching and peer instruction. In *Just in time teaching* (pp. 39–62). Routledge.

Mazuzan, G. T. (1994). *The National Science Foundation: A brief history*. National Science Foundation. https://www.nsf.gov/about/history/nsf50/nsf8816.jsp

McAnuff-Gumbs, M., & Verbeck, K. (2013). Toward a model of multi-level professional learning communities to guide the training and practice of literacy coaches. In H. H. Yang, & S. Wang (Eds.), *Cases on online learning communities and beyond: Investigations and applications* (pp. 361–402). IGI Global.

McConnell, D. A., Chapman, L., Czajka, C. D., Jones, J. P., Ryker, K. D., & Wiggen, J. (2017). Instructional utility and learning efficacy of common active learning strategies. *Journal of Geoscience Education, 65*(4), 604–625. https://doi.org/10.5408/17-249.1

McDowell, L. D. (2019). The roles of motivation and metacognition in producing self-regulated learners of college physical science: A review of empirical studies. *International Journal of Science Education, 41*(17), 2524–2541. https://doi.org/10.1080/09500693.2019.1689584

McFarland, D. A., & Rodan, S. (2009). Organization by design: Supply- and demand-side models of mathematics course taking. *Sociology of Education, 82*(4), 315–343.

McGee, E. O. (2020). *Black, brown, bruised: How racialized STEM educations stifles innovation*. Harvard Education Press.

McGinty, M., & Bang, M. (2016). Narratives of dynamic lands: Science education, indigenous knowledge and possible futures. *Cultural Studies of Science Education, 11*(2), 471–475. https://doi.org/10.1007/s11422-015-9685-5

McKnelly, K. J., Morris, M. A., & Mang, S. A. (2021). Redesigning a "writing for chemists" course using specifications grading. *Journal of Chemical Education, 98*(4), 1201–1207. https://doi.org/10.1021/acs.jchemed.0c00859

McLean, K. C., Koepf, I. M., & Lilgendahl, J. P. (2022). Identity development and major choice among underrepresented students interested in STEM majors: A longitudinal qualitative analysis. *Emerging Adulthood, 10*(2), 386–401. https://doi.org/10.1177/21676968211015549

McMurtrie, B., & Supiano, B. (2021). The future of teaching: How the classroom is being transformed. *The Chronicle of Higher Education*.

McNair, J. C. (2016). #WeNeedMirrorsAndWindows: Diverse classroom libraries for K–6 students. *The Reading Teacher, 70*(3), 375–381. https://doi.org/10.1002/trtr.1516

McNair, T. B., Albertine, S., McDonald, N., Major, T., Jr., & Cooper, M. A. (2022). *Becoming a student-ready college: A new culture of leadership for student success*. John Wiley & Sons.

McNair, T. B., Bensimon, E. M., & Malcom-Piqueux, L. (2020). *From equity talk to equity walk: Expanding practitioner knowledge for racial justice in higher education*. John Wiley & Sons.

Mead, C., Buxner, S., Bruce, G., Taylor, W., Semken, S., & Anbar, A. D. (2019). Immersive, interactive virtual field trips promote science learning. *Journal of Geoscience Education, 67*(2), 131–142. https://doi.org/10.1080/10899995.2019.1565285

Meaders, C. L., Toth, E. S., Lane, A. K., Shuman, J. K., Couch, B. A., Stains, M., Stetzer, M. R., Vinson, E., & Smith, M. K., (2019). "What will I experience in my college STEM courses?" An investigation of student predictions about instructional practices in introductory courses. *CBE—Life Sciences Education, 18*(4), Article 60. https://doi.org/10.1187/cbe.19-05-0084

Medin, D. L., & Bang, M. (2014). *Who's asking?: Native science, Western science, and science education.* MIT Press.

Melidona, D., & Wright, C. E. (2023). *Undergraduate military learners: Exploring differences between military learners' experiences in higher education* [Issue brief]. American Council on Education. https://www.acenet.edu/Documents/Undergraduate-Military-Learners.pdf

Mensah, F. M., & Jackson, I. (2018). Whiteness as property in science teacher education. *Teachers College Record, 120*(1), 1–38. https://doi.org/10.1177/016146811812000108

Meraz, A. M. (2022). *California community colleges' journey toward racial equity: Understanding the process of addressing systemic racism.* [Doctoral dissertation, Kansas State University]. https://hdl.handle.net/2097/42234

Mercader, C., & Gairín, J. (2020). University teachers' perception of barriers to the use of digital technologies: The importance of the academic discipline. *International Journal of Educational Technology in Higher Education, 17*(1), 4.

Mercer-Mapstone, L., Dvorakova, S. L., Matthews, K. E., Abbot, S., Cheng, B., Felten, P., Knorr, K., Marquis, E., Shammas, R., & Swaim, K. (2017). A systematic literature review of students as partners in higher education. *International Journal for Students as Partners.*

Metcalf, H., Russell, D., & Hill, C. (2018). Broadening the science of broadening participation in STEM through critical mixed methodologies and intersectionality frameworks. *American Behavioral Scientist, 62*(5), 580–599. https://doi.org/10.1177/0002764218768872

Meuler, M., Lee, J., Foutch, K., Al-Khayat, N., Boukouzis, K., Christensen, P., Crooks, C., Hassanain, L. M., Karimi, P., Kim, G. V., Randall, A., Redford, I. K., Socko, R., & Theobald, E. J. (2023). Biology in a social context: A comprehensive analysis of humanization in introductory biology textbooks. *Frontiers in Education, 8*, 1165239.

Micari, M., & Pazos, P. (2012). Connecting to the professor: Impact of the student–faculty relationship in a highly challenging course. *College Teaching, 60*(2), 41–47 https://www.tandfonline.com/doi/abs/10.1080/87567555.2011.627576

Michaels, C., & Liu, L. (2020). Differences in Academic achievements among high school graduates' from four career and technical education (CTE) program areas. *International Journal of Technology in Teaching and Learning, 15*(2), 109–135.

Michela, J. L., Noori, H., & Jha, S. (1996). The dynamics of continuous improvement. *International Journal of Quality Science, 1*(1), 19–47.

Miller, E. R., & Fairweather, J. S. (2016). The role of cultural change in large-scale STEM reform: The experience of the AAU Undergraduate STEM Education Initiative. In G. C. Weaver, W. D. Burgess, A. L. Childress, & L. Slakey (Eds.), *Transforming institutions: Undergraduate STEM education for the 21st century* (pp. 48–66). Purdue University Press.

Miller, S., Kerr, J. E., & Handelsman, J. (2022). AJEDI in science: Leveraging instructor communities to create antiracist curricula. *Journal of Microbiology & Biology Education, 23*(1), e00248-21. https://doi.org/10.1128/jmbe.00248-21

Mintz, S. (2024). *The learning-centered university: Making college a more developmental, transformational, and equitable experience.* Johns Hopkins University Press.

Mishra, P., & Koehler, M. J. (2006). Technological pedagogical content knowledge: A framework for teacher knowledge. *Teachers College Record, 108*(6), 1017–1054. https://journals.sagepub.com/doi/pdf/10.1111/j.1467-9620.2006.00684.x

Misra, J., Kuvaeva, A., O'Meara, K., Culpepper, D. K., & Jaeger, A. (2021). Gendered and racialized perceptions of faculty workloads. *Gender and Society*, *35*(3), 358–394.

Mitchell, C., & Sickney, L. (2019). *Sustainable improvement: Building learning communities that endure*. Brill.

Mitchell, K. M. W., & Martin, J. (2018). Gender bias in student evaluations. *Political Science & Politics*, *51*(3), 648–652. https://doi.org/10.1017/S104909651800001X

Mitchell, M., Leachman, M., & Saenz, M. (2019, October 24). *State higher education funding cuts have pushed costs to students, worsened inequality*. Center on Budget and Policy Priorities. https://www.cbpp.org/sites/default/files/atoms/files/10-24-19sfp.pdf

Mitic, R. R., Zhou, E., & Okahana, H. (2023). Socializing future community college faculty doctoral professional development and career preparation. *Community College Journal of Research and Practice*, 1–17. https://doi.org/10.1080/10668926.2023.2256238

Mitsea, E., & Drigas, A. (2019). A journey into the metacognitive learning strategies. *International Journal of Online & Biomedical Engineering*, *15*(14).

Miyake, A., Kost-Smith, L. E., Finkelstein, N. D., Pollock, S. J., Cohen, G. L., & Ito, T. A. (2010). Reducing the gender achievement gap in college science: A classroom study of values affirmation. *Science*, *330*(6008), 1234–1237. https://doi.org/10.1126/science.1195996

Mogk, D. W. (1993). Undergraduate research experiences as preparation for graduate study in geology. *Journal of Geological Education*, *41*(2), 126–128. https://doi.org/10.5408/0022-1368-41.2.126

Mogk, D. W., & Goodwin, C. (2012, April 1). Learning in the field: Synthesis of research on thinking and learning in the geosciences. In K. A. Kastens, & C. A. Manduca (Eds.), *Earth and mind II: A synthesis of research on thinking and learning in the geosciences* (pp. 131–163). Geological Society of America. https://doi.org/10.1130/2012.2486(24)

Molinaro, M., Finkelstein, N., Hogan, K., Mendoza, N., & Sathy, V. (2020). Scholarly teaching for all, research for some: On the roles of research and scholarship of education in the disciplines. *Change: The Magazine of Higher Learning*, *52*(5), 17–24. https://doi.org/10.1080/00091383.2020.1807875

Moll, L., Amanti, C., Neff, D., & Gonzalez, N. (1992). Funds of knowledge for teaching: Using a qualitative approach to connect homes and classrooms. *Qualitative Issues in Educational Research*, *31*(2), 132–141. https://doi.org/10.1080/00405849209543534

Moll, L. C. (2019). Elaborating funds of knowledge: Community-oriented practices in international contexts. *Literacy Research: Theory, Method, and Practice*, *68*(1), 130–138. https://doi.org/10.1177/2381336919870805

Moll, L. C., & Diaz, S. (1987). Change as the goal of educational research. *Anthropology & Education Quarterly*, *18*(4), 300–311. https://doi.org/10.1525/aeq.1987.18.4.04x0021u

Momsen, J., Offerdahl, E., Kryjevskaia, M., Montplaisir, L., Anderson, E., Grosz, N., & Brewe, E. (2013). Using assessments to investigate and compare the nature of learning in undergraduate science courses. *CBE—Life Sciences Education*, *12*(2), 239–249. https://doi.org/10.1187/cbe.12-08-0130

Morales, N., Bisbee O'Connell, K., McNulty, S., Berkowitz, A., Bowser, G., Giamellaro, M., & Miriti, M. N. (2020). Promoting inclusion in ecological field experiences: Examining and overcoming barriers to a professional rite of passage. *Bulletin of the Ecological Society of America*, *101*(4), e01742. https://doi.org/https://doi.org/10.1002/bes2.1742

Morcke, A. M., Dornan, T., & Eika, B. (2013). Outcome (competency) based education: An exploration of its origins, theoretical basis, and empirical evidence. *Advances in Health Sciences Education*, *18*, 851–863.

Mordacq, J. C., Drane, D. L., Swarat, S. L., & Lo, S. M. (2017). Development of course-based undergraduate research experiences using a design-based approach. *Journal of College Science Teaching*, *46*(4).

Moreno, S. E., & Mueller, C. (1999). Success and diversity: The transition through first-year calculus in the university. *American Journal of Education, 108*(1), 30–57.

Morey, A. I., Bezuk, N., & Chiero, R. (1997). Preservice teacher preparation in the United States. *Peabody Journal of Education*, *72*(1), 4–24.

Morris, R., Perry, T., & Wardle, L. (2021). Formative assessment and feedback for learning in higher education: A systematic review. *Review of Education*, *9*(3), e3292.

Morrison, C. D. (2014). From 'sage on the stage' to 'guide on the side': A good start. *International Journal for the Scholarship of Teaching and Learning*, *8*(1), Article 4. https://doi.org/10.20429/ijsotl.2014.080104

Morton, T. R., Agee, W., Ashad-Bishop, K. C., Banks, L. D., Barnett, Z. C., Bramlett, I. D., Brown, B., Gassmann, W., Grayson, K., Hollowell, G. P., Kaggwa, R., Kandlikar, G. S., Love, M., McCoy, W. N., Melton, M. A., Miles, M. L., Quinlan, C. L., Roby, R. S., Rorie, C. J., Russo-Tait, T., Wardin, A. M., & Woodson, A. N. (2023). Re-envisioning the culture of undergraduate biology education to foster Black student success: A clarion call. *CBE—Life Sciences Education*, *22*(4), es5. https://doi.org/10.1187/cbe.22-09-0175

Morton, T. R., & Parsons, E. C. (2018). #BlackGirlMagic: The identity conceptualization of Black women in undergraduate STEM education. *Science Education*, *102*(6), 1363–1393. https://doi.org/10.1002/sce.21477

Moses, R. P., & Cobb, C., Jr. (2001). Organizing algebra: The need to voice a demand. *Social Policy*, *31*(4), 4.

Mosher, S., & Keane, C. M. (Eds.). (2021). *Vision and change in the geosciences: The future of undergraduate education*. American Geosciences Institute.

Mountjoy, J. (2022). Community colleges and upward mobility. *American Economic Review*, *112*(8), 2580–2630.

Mowreader, A. (2023, April 19). Academic success tip: Rebrand office hours. *Inside Higher Ed*. https://www.insidehighered.com/news/student-success/academic-life/2023/04/19/academic-success-tip-rebrand-office-hours

___. (2024, January 16). Report: 4 ways to promote rural college student enrollment, completion. *Inside Higher Ed*. https://www.insidehighered.com/news/student-success/academic-life/2024/01/16/four-challenges-rural-college-completion-persistence#:~:text=Nationally%2C%2029%20percent%20of%20young,U.S.%20Department%20of%20Education%20data

Muenks, K., Canning, E. A., LaCosse, J., Green, D. J., Zirkel, S., Garcia, J. A., & Murphy, M. C. (2020). Does my professor think my ability can change? Students' perceptions of their STEM professors' mindset beliefs predict their psychological vulnerability, engagement, and performance in class. *Journal of Experimental Psychology: General*, *149*(11), 2119–2144. https://doi.org/10.1037/xge0000763

Muenks, K., Kroeper, K. M., Canning, E. A., & Murphy, M. C. (2024). Instructor mindset beliefs and behaviors: How do students and instructors perceive them? *Social Psychology of Education*, 27(6), 2883–2899.

Murphy, M. C. (2024). *Cultures of growth: How the new science of mindset can transform individuals, teams, and organizations*. Simon & Schuster.

Murphy, M. C., Gopalan, M., Carter, E. R., Emerson, K. T., Bottoms, B. L., & Walton, G. M. (2020). A customized belonging intervention improves retention of socially disadvantaged students at a broad-access university. *Science Advances*, 6(29), eaba4677. https://doi.org/10.1126/sciadv.aba4677

Murphy, M. C., Steele, C. M., & Gross, J. J. (2007). Signaling threat: How situational cues affect women in math, science, and engineering settings. *Psychological Science*, *18*(10), 879–885. https://doi.org/10.1111/j.1467-9280.2007.01995

Murphy, M. C., & Taylor, V. J. (2012). The role of situational cues in signaling and maintaining stereotype threat. In M. Inzlicht & T. Schmader (Eds.), *Stereotype threat: Theory, process, and application* (pp. 16–33). Oxford Academic.

Murzi, H., Martin, T. L., McNair, L. D., & Paretti, M. C. (2016). *A longitudinal study of the dimensions of disciplinary culture to enhance innovation and retention among engineering students.*

Murzi, H., Ulloa, B. C. R., Gamboa, F., Woods, J. C., Guerra, M. A., Soto, K. D. M., & Azar, R. H. (2021, July). Cultural dimensions in academic disciplines, a comparison between Ecuador and the United States of America. In *2021 ASEE Virtual Annual Conference Content Access.*

Muscanell, N. (2024). *The teaching and learning workforce in higher education, 2024.* EDUCASE. https://www.educause.edu/ecar/research-publications/2024/the-teaching-and-learning-workforce-in-higher-education-2024/introduction-and-key-findings

Nachman, B. R. (2024). "What do we have to do?" Community college CTE faculty perceptions, preparedness, and propositions in supporting disabled students' employment opportunities. *Community College Review*, 00915521231222273.

Nasir, N. I. S., Lee, C. D., Pea, R., & McKinney de Royston, M. (2020). *Handbook of the cultural foundations of learning.* Taylor & Francis.

National Academies of Sciences, Engineering, and Medicine. (2016). *Barriers and opportunities for two-year and four-year STEM degrees: Systemic change to support students' diverse pathways.* The National Academies Press. https://doi.org/10.17226/21739

___. (2017a). *Service-learning in undergraduate geosciences: Proceedings of a workshop.* The National Academies Press. https://doi.org/10.17226/24621

___. (2017b). *Undergraduate research experiences for STEM students: Successes, challenges, and opportunities.* The National Academies Press. https://doi.org/10.17226/24622

___. (2018). *How people learn II: Learners, contexts, and cultures.* The National Academies Press. https://doi.org/10.17226/24783

___. (2019c). *Minority Serving Institutions: America's underutilized resource for strengthening the STEM workforce.* The National Academies Press. https://doi.org/10.17226/25257

___. (2019a). *Monitoring educational equity.* The National Academies Press. https://doi.org/10.17226/25389

___. (2019b). *The science of effective mentorship in STEMM.* The National Academies Press. https://doi.org/10.17226/25568

___. (2020). *Recognizing and evaluating science teaching in higher education: Proceedings of a workshop—in brief.* The National Academies Press. https://doi.org/10.17226/25685

___. (2021). *Undergraduate and graduate STEM students' experiences during COVID-19: Proceedings of a virtual workshop series.* The National Academies Press. https://doi.org/10.1017226/26024

___. (2022). *Defense research capacity at historically Black colleges and universities and other minority institutions: Transitioning from good intentions to measurable outcomes.* The National Academies Press. https://doi.org/10.17226/26399

___. (2023). *Advancing antiracism, diversity, equity, and inclusion in STEMM organizations: Beyond broadening participation.* The National Academies Press. https://doi.org/10.17226/26803

___. (2024a). *Equity in K-12 STEM education: Framing decisions for the future.* The National Academies Press. https://doi.org/10.17226/26859

___. (2024b). *A plan to promote defense research at Minority-Serving Institutions.* The National Academies Press. https://doi.org/10.17226/27838

___. (2024c). *Graduate students as part of the instructional workforce for undergraduate STEM education.* The National Academies Press. https://www.nationalacademies.org/event/43862_10-2024_graduate-students-as-part-of-the-instructional-workforce-for-undergraduate-stem-education

National Association of College and University Business Officers (NACUBO). (2024a). *Resources.* https://nacubostudentsuccess.org/resources/

___. (2024b, July 8). *Charting the future: NACUBO's blueprint for student-centered strategic finance*. https://www.nacubo.org/Publications/The-Solutions-Exchange/Charting-the-Future-NACUBOs-Blueprint-for-Student-Centered-Strategic-Finance

___. (2024c, July 8). *NACUBO Student Success Hub highlights financial links to equitable student outcomes*. https://www.nacubo.org/Press-Releases/2024/NACUBO-Student-Success-Hub-Highlights-Financial-Links-to-Equitable-Student-Outcomes

National Center for Education Statistics (NCES). (n.d.a). About CTE statistics. https://nces.ed.gov/surveys/ctes/about.asp

___. (n.d.b). Fast facts. https://nces.ed.gov/fastfacts/display.asp?id=61

___. (n. d.c). *Trend generator*. https://nces.ed.gov/ipeds/TrendGenerator/app/build-table/8/35?cid=5#:~:text=Financial%20Aid%3A%20What%20is%20the,is%20based%20on%205%2C519%20institutions

___. (2019). Table 2-6: Disability status of undergraduate students, by age, institution type, financial aid, and enrollment status: 2016. *Women, minorities, and persons with disabilities in science and engineering*. https://ncses.nsf.gov/pubs/nsf19304/data

___. (2022, December). *Integrated Postsecondary Education Data System (IPEDS), Digest of Education Statistics 2022*, Table 303.70.

___. (2023a). Characteristics of postsecondary students. *Condition of Education*. U.S. Department of Education, Institute of Education Sciences. https://nces.ed.gov/programs/coe/indicator/csb/postsecondary-students

___. (2023b). Table 304.15. Total fall enrollment in public degree-granting postsecondary institutions, by state or jurisdiction: Selected years, 1970 through 2022. *Digest of Education Statistics*. https://nces.ed.gov/programs/digest/d23/tables/dt23_304.15.asp

___. (2023c). Table 304.20. Total fall enrollment in private degree-granting postsecondary institutions, by state or jurisdiction: Selected years, 1970 through 2022. *Digest of Education Statistics*. https://nces.ed.gov/programs/digest/d23/tables/dt23_304.20.asp

___. (2023d). Table 311.10. Number and percentage distribution of students enrolled in postsecondary institutions, by level, disability status, and selected student characteristics: Academic year 2019–20. *Digest of Education Statistics*. U.S. Department of Education, Institute of Education Sciences. https://nces.ed.gov/programs/digest/d22/tables/dt22_311.10.asp

___. (2023e). Table 316.80. Percentage of degree-granting postsecondary institutions with a tenure system and percentage of full-time faculty with tenure at these institutions, by control and level of institution and selected characteristics of faculty: Selected academic years, 1993-94 through 2022-23. *Digest of Education Statistics*. https://nces.ed.gov/programs/digest/d23/tables/dt23_316.80.asp

___. (2024a). *Characteristics of postsecondary faculty*. https://nces.ed.gov/programs/coe/indicator/csc/postsecondary-faculty

___. (2024b). Immediate College Enrollment Rate. Condition of Education. U.S. Department of Education, Institute of Education Sciences. https://nces.ed.gov/programs/coe/indicator/cpa

___. (2024c). *Postsecondary outcomes for nontraditional and traditional undergraduate students. Condition of Education*. U.S. Department of Education, Institute of Education Sciences. https://nces.ed.gov/programs/coe/indicator/ctu#:~:text=See%20Digest%20of%20Education%20Statistics,30%20percent%20in%202009%E2%80%9310

National Center for Science and Engineering Statistics (NCSES). (2023a). *Diversity and STEM: Women, minorities, and persons with disabilities 2023* (Special Report NSF 23-315). National Science Foundation. https://ncses.nsf.gov/wmpd

___. (2023b). *Survey of Graduate Students and Postdoctorates in Science and Engineering: Fall 2021*. National Science Foundation. https://ncses.nsf.gov/pubs/nsf23312

___. (2023c). Table 318.45. Number and percentage distribution of science, technology, engineering, and mathematics (STEM) degrees/certificates conferred by postsecondary institutions, by race/ethnicity, level of degree/certificate, and sex of student: Academic years 2012-13 through 2021-22. *Digest of Education Statistics*. https://nces.ed.gov/programs/digest/d23/tables/dt23_318.45.asp

National Institute on Scientific Teaching. (n.d.). https://www.nisthub.org/

National Research Council (NRC). (2000). How people learn: Brain, mind, experience, and school: Expanded edition. In J. D. Bransford, A. L. Brown, & R. R. Cocking (Eds.). Committee on Developments in the Science of Learning Research and Educational Practice, Commission on Behavioral and Social Sciences and Education, National Research Council. The National Academies Press. https://doi.org/10.17226/9853

___. (2001). *Classroom assessment and the national science education standards.* The National Academies Press. https://doi.org/10.17226/9847

___. (2003). *BIO2010: Transforming undergraduate education for future research biologists.* The National Academies Press. https://doi.org/10.17226/10497

___. (2012a). *A framework for K-12 science education: Practices, crosscutting concepts, and core ideas.* The National Academies Press. https://doi.org/10.17226/13165

___. (2012b). *Discipline-based education research: Understanding and improving learning in undergraduate science and engineering.* The National Academies Press. https://doi.org/10.17226/13362

___. (2015). *Reaching students: What research says about effective instruction in undergraduate science and engineering.* The National Academies Press. https://doi.org/10.17226/18687

National Science Foundation Act of 1950, Pub. L. No. 81-507, 64 Stat. 149 (1950).

___. (2023). *NSF's NCSES releases report on diversity trends in STEM workforce and education.* https://new.nsf.gov/news/diversity-and-stem-2023

National Science Foundation, & National Center for Science and Engineering Statistics. (2019). *Women, minorities, and persons with disabilities in science and engineering: 2019* (Special Report NSF 19-304). National Science Foundation. https://www.nsf.gov/statistics/wmpd/

National Student Clearinghouse Research Center. (2023). Transfer and progress. https://nscresearchcenter.org/transfer-and-progress/

___. (2024). *Current term enrollment estimates: Spring 2024.* https://nscresearchcenter.org/current-term-enrollment-estimates/

Neiles, K. Y., & Arnett, K. (2021). Backward design of chemistry laboratories: A primer. *Journal of Chemical Education*, *98*(9), 2829–2839. https://doi.org/10.1021/acs.jchemed.1c00443

Neisler, J., & Means, B. (2021). *Teaching practices of faculty adopting adaptive courseware.* Digital Promise Global.

Nespor, J. (2012). Making lectures visible: Redesigning in nutrition. In *Technology and the Politics of Instruction* (pp. 94–106). Routledge.

Newell, M. J., & Ulrich, P. N. (2022). Gains in scientific identity, scientific self-efficacy, and career intent distinguish upper-level CUREs from traditional experiences in the classroom. *Journal of Microbiology & Biology Education*, *23*(3), e00051–e00022. https://doi.org/10.1128/jmbe.00051-22

Ngai, C., Corbo, J. C., Falkenberg, K. L., Geanious, C., Pawlak, A., Pilgrim, M. E. Quan, G. M., Reinholz, D. L., Smith, C., & Wise, S. B. (2020). *Facilitating change in higher education: The Departmental Action Team Model.* Glitter Canyon Press.

Nguyen, A., & Lewis, C. M. (2020, February). Competitive enrollment policies in computing departments negatively predict first-year students' sense of belonging, self-efficacy, and perception of department. In *Proceedings of the 51st ACM Technical Symposium on Computer Science Education* (pp. 685–691).

Nicole, D., & Selvaretnam, G. (2021). Making internal feedback explicit: Harnessing the comparisons students make during two-stage exams. *Assessment & Evaluation in Higher Education*, *47*(4), 507–522. https://doi.org/10.1080/02602938.2021.1934653

Nilson, L. B. (2015). *Specifications grading: Restoring rigor, motivating students, and saving faculty time.* Stylus Publishing, LLC.

Nilson, L. B., & Stanny, C. J. (2023). *Specifications grading: Restoring rigor, motivating students, and saving faculty time*. Routledge.

Nix, S., & Perez-Felkner, L. (2019). Difficulty orientations, gender, and race/ethnicity: An intersectional analysis of pathways to STEM degrees. *Social Sciences*, *8*(2), 43. https://doi.org/10.3390/socsci8020043

Noell, S. L., Rios Buza, M., Roth, E. B., Young, J. L., & Drummond, M. J. (2023). A bridge to specifications grading in second semester general chemistry. *Journal of Chemical Education*, *100*(6), 2159–2165.

Norman, J. B., Fuesting, M. A., Geerling, D. M., Chen, J. M., Gable, S. L., & Diekman, A. B. (2022). To pursue or not to pursue STEM? Faculty behavior enhances student involvement in STEM roles by signaling role-specific support. *Social Psychological and Personality Science, 13*(2), 583–594.

Novak, G. M., Patterson, E. T., Gavrin, A. D., & Christian, W. (1999). *Just-in-time teaching blending active learning with web technology.*

Nowell, L., Ovie, G., Berenson, C., Kenny, N., & Hayden, K. A. (2018). Professional learning and development of postdoctoral scholars: A systematic review of the literature. *Education Research International*, *2018*, 1–16. https://doi.org/10.1155/2018/5950739

O'Connell, K., Hoke, K., Berkowitz, A., Branchaw, J., & Storksdieck, M. (2021). Undergraduate learning in the field: Designing experiences, assessing outcomes, and exploring future opportunities. *Journal of Geoscience Education*, *69*(4), 387–400. https://doi.org/10.1080/10899995.2020.1779567

O'Connell, K., Hoke, K. L., Giamellaro, M., Berkowitz, A. R., & Branchaw, J. (2022). A tool for designing and studying student-centered undergraduate field experiences: The UFERN model. *BioScience*, *72*(2), 189–200. https://doi.org/10.1093/biosci/biab112

O'Donnell, C. T., & Blankenship, C. (2018). Status frustration among college students: The relationship between socioeconomic status and undergraduate performance. *Deviant Behavior*, *39*(6), 679–693.

Odom, S., Bosso, H., Bowling, S., Brownell, S., Cotner, S., Creech, C., Drake, A. G., Eddy, S., Fagbodun, S., Hebert, S., James, A. C., Just, J., Juliana, J. R., Shuster, M., Thompson, S. K., Whittington, R., Wills, B. D., Wilson, A. E., Zamudio, K. R., Zhong, M., & Ballen, C. J. (2021). Meta-analysis of gender performance gaps in undergraduate natural science courses. *CBE—Life Sciences Education*, *20*(3), Article 40. https://doi.org/10.1187/cbe.20-11-0260

Oh, H. (2020). *Academic help seeking of undergraduate STEM students: A basic psychological needs theory perspective* [Doctoral dissertation, Purdue University].

O'Leary, E. S., Shapiro, C., Toma, S., Sayson, H. W., Levis-Fitzgerald, M., Johnson, T., & Sork, V. L. (2020). Creating inclusive classrooms by engaging STEM faculty in culturally responsive teaching workshops. *International Journal of STEM Education*, *7*, 1–15. https://doi.org/10.1186/s40594-020-00230-7

Oleson, A., & Hora, M. T. (2014). Teaching the way they were taught? Revisiting the sources of teaching knowledge and the role of prior experience in shaping faculty teaching practices. *Higher Education*, *68*, 29–45.

O'Meara, K., Templeton, L. L., White-Lewis, D. K., Culpepper, D., & Anderson, J. (2023). The safest bet: Identifying and assessing risk in faculty selection. *American Educational Research Journal*, *60*(2), 330–366. https://doi.org/10.3102/00028312221150438

O'Neill, T., Finau-Faumuina, B. M., & Ford, T. U. L. (2023). Toward decolonizing STEM: Centering place and sense of place for community-based problem-solving. *Journal of Research in Science Teaching*, *60*(8), 1755–1785. https://doi.org/10.1002/tea.21858

Orakcı, Ş. (2021). Exploring the relationships between cognitive flexibility, learner autonomy, and reflective thinking. *Thinking Skills and Creativity*, *41*, 100838.

Organisation for Economic Co-operation and Development. (2019). An OECD Learning Framework 2030. *The Future of Education and Labor*, 23–35.

Orndorf, H. C., Waterman, M., Lange, D., Kavin, D., Johnston, S. C., & Jenkins, K. P. (2022). Opening the pathway: An example of universal design for learning as a guide to inclusive teaching practices. *CBE—Life Sciences Education*, *21*(2), Article 28. https://doi.org/10.1187/cbe.21-09-0239

Ortiz-Rodríguez, J. C., Brinkman, H., Nglankong, L., Enderle, B., & Velázquez, J. M. (2021). Promoting inclusive and culturally responsive teaching using co-classes for general chemistry. *Journal of Chemical Education*, *99*(1), 162–170. https://doi.org/10.1021/acs.jchemed.1c00339

Ortquist-Ahrens, L., & Torosyan, R. (2009). The role of the facilitator in faculty learning communities: Paving the way for growth, productivity, and collegiality. *Learning Communities Journal*, *1*(1).

O'Sullivan, P., Voegele, D. C. J., Buchan, T., Dottin, R., Goin Kono, K., Hamideh, M., Howard, W., Todd, J., Kruse, S., de Gruyter, J., & Berg, K. (2020). Adaptive courseware implementation: Investigating alignment, course redesign, and the student experience. *Curriculum and Instruction Faculty Publications and Presentations*, *74*. https://pdxscholar.library.pdx.edu/ci_fac/74/

Osler, J. E., & Mansaray, M. (2014). A model for determining teaching efficacy through the use of qualitative single subject design, student learning outcomes and associative statistics. *Journal on School Educational Technology*, *10*(1), 22–35.

Overall, J. U., & Marsh, H. W. (1979). Midterm feedback from students: Its relationship to instructional improvement and students' cognitive and affective outcomes. *Journal of Educational Psychology*, *71*(6), 856–865. https://doi.org/10.1037/0022-0663.71.6.856

Packard, B. W. L., Gagnon, J. L., LaBello, O., Jeffers, K., & Lynn, E. (2011). Women's experiences in the STEM community college transfer pathway. *Journal of Women and Minorities in Science and Engineering*, *17*(2), 129–147. https://doi.org/10.1615/JWomenMinorScienEng.2011002470

Packard, B. W. L., Gagnon, J. L., & Senas, A. J. (2012). Navigating community college transfer in science, technical, engineering, and mathematics fields. *Community College Journal of Research and Practice*, *36*(9), 670–683. https://doi.org/10.1080/10668926.2010.495570

Page-Reeves, J., Marin, A., Moffett, M., DeerInWater, K., & Medin, D. (2019). Wayfinding as a concept for understanding success among Native Americans in STEM: "Learning how to map through life." *Cultural Studies of Science Education*, *14*, 177–197. https://doi.org/10.1007/s11422-017-9849-6

Pajares, F. (1996). Self-efficacy beliefs in academic settings. *Review of Educational Research*, *66*(4), 543–578.

Palmer, M. S., Bach, D. J., & Streifer, A. C. (2014). Measuring the promise: A learning-focused syllabus rubric. *To Improve the Academy*, *33*(1), 14–36. https://doi.org/10.1002/tia2.20004

Palmer, M. S., Gravett, E. O., & LaFleur, J. (2018). Measuring transparency: A learning-focused assignment rubric. *To Improve the Academy*, *37*(2), 173–187. https://doi.org/10.1002/tia2.20083

Palmer, M. S., Wheeler, L. B., & Aneece, I. (2016). Does the document matter? The evolving role of syllabi in higher education. *Change: The Magazine of Higher Learning*, *48*(4), 36–47. https://doi.org/10.1080/00091383.2016.1198186

Palmer, R. T., Davis, R. J., & Thompson, T. (2010). Theory meets practice: HBCU initiatives that promote academic success among African Americans in STEM. *Journal of College Student Development*, *51*(4), 440–443. https://doi.org/10.1353/csd.0.0146

Palmer, R. T., Maramba, D. C., & Gasman, M. (Eds.). (2013). *Fostering success of ethnic and racial minorities in STEM: The role of minority serving institutions*. Routledge.

Park, E. S., Ngo, F., & Melguizo, T. (2021). The role of math misalignment in the community college STEM pathway. *Research in Higher Education, 62*(4), 403–447. https://doi.org/10.1007/s11162-020-09602-y

Park, S., Hironaka, S., Carver, P., & Nordstrum, L. (2013). *Continuous improvement in education.* Carnegie Foundation for the Advancement of Teaching. https://carnegiefoundation.org/wp-content/uploads/2014/09/carnegie-foundation_continuous-improvement_2013.05.pdf

Park, S. M. (1996). Research, teaching, and service: Why shouldn't women's work count? *The Journal of Higher Education*, *67*(1), 46–84.

Partridge, M. A., Schaller, T. K., Berry, R. L., & Routon, P. W. (2021). The economic benefit from tuition savings for dual enrollment students in Georgia. *Journal of School Choice*, *15*(4), 655–667.

Peck, F. (2020). Towards anti-deficit education in undergraduate mathematics education: How deficit perspectives work to structure inequality and what can be done about it. *PRIMUS*, *31*(9), 940–961. https://doi.org/10.1080/10511970.2020.1781721

Peffer, M. E., & Ramezani, N. (2019). Assessing epistemological beliefs of experts and novices via practices in authentic science inquiry. *International Journal of STEM Education*, 6, Article 3, 1–23. https://doi.org/10.1186/s40594-018-0157-9

Pensky, J., Richardson, C., Serrano, A., Gorski, G., Price, A. N., & Zimmer, M. (2021). Disrupt and demystify the unwritten rules of graduate school. *Nature Geoscience*, *14*(8), 538–539. https://doi.org/10.1038/s41561-021-00799-w

Perea, B. (2020). Using smaller credentials to build flexible degree completion and career pathways. In N. Maxwell & S. Gallagher (Eds.), *New directions for community colleges*, (Vol. 189, pp. 23–37). Wiley.

Perez, C., & Verdin, D. (2022, August). Mastery learning in undergraduate engineering courses: A systematic review. In *2022 ASEE Annual Conference & Exposition*.

Pérez, L. F., & Johnston, S. C. (2023). [Creating disability-friendly and inclusive accessible spaces in higher education]. Commissioned paper prepared for the National Academies of Sciences, Engineering, and Medicine. Committee on Beyond Compliance: Promoting the Success of People with Disabilities in the STEM Workforce. https://nap.nationalacademies.org/resource/27245/Johnston_and_Perez_Creating_Disability-Friendly_and_Inclusive_Accessible_Spaces_in_Higher_Education.pdf

Perez, R. J., Motshubi, R., & Rodriguez, S. L. (2023). (Mis)alignment of challenges and strategies in promoting inclusive racial climates in STEM graduate departments. *AERA Open*, *9*, 23328584231168639.

Petcovic, H. L., Stokes, A., & Caulkins, J. L. (2014). Geoscientists' perceptions of the value of undergraduate field education. *GSA Today*, *24*(7), 4–10. https://doi.org/10.1130/GSATG196A.1

Petersen, C. I., Baepler, P., Beitz, A., Ching, P., Gorman, K. S., Neudauer, C. L., Rozaitis, W., Walker, J. D., & Wingert, D. (2020). The tyranny of content: "Content coverage" as a barrier to evidence-based teaching approaches and ways to overcome it. *CBE—Life Sciences Education*, *19*(2), Article 17. https://doi.org/10.1187/cbe.19-04-0079

Pfund, C., Miller, S., Brenner, K., Bruns, P., Chang, A., Ebert-May, D., Fagen, A. P., Gentile, A., Gossens, S., Khan, I. M., Labov, J. B., Pribbenow, C. M., Susman M., Tong, L., Wright, R., Yuan, R. T., Wood, W. B., & Handelsman, J. (2009). Summer institute to improve university science teaching. *Science*, *324*(5926), 470–471. https://doi.org/10.1126/science.1170015

Philip, T. M., & Azevedo, F. S. (2017). Everyday science learning and equity: Mapping the contested terrain. *Science Education*, *101*(4), 526–532. https://doi.org/10.1002/sce.21286

Philip, T. M., Bang, M., & Jackson, K. (2018). Articulating the "how," the "for what," the "for whom," and the "with whom" in concert: A call to broaden the benchmarks of our scholarship. *Cognition and Instruction*, *36*(2), 83–88. https://doi.org/10.1080/07370008.2018.1413530

Picard, R. W., Papert, S., Bender, W., Blumberg, B., Breazeal, C., Cavallo, D., Machover, D., Resnick, M., Roy, D., & Strohecker, C. (2004). Affective learning—A manifesto. *BT Technology Journal*, *22*(4), 253–269.

Pietri, E. S., Drawbaugh, M. L., Lewis, A. N., & Johnson, I. R. (2019). Who encourages Latina women to feel a sense of identity-safety in STEM environments? *Journal of Experimental Social Psychology*, *84*, Article 103827. https://doi.org/10.1016/j.jesp.2019.103827

Piloto, C. (2023, March 13). The gender gap in STEM: Still gaping in 2023. *MIT Professional Education*. https://professionalprograms.mit.edu/blog/leadership/the-gender-gap-in-stem/

POD Network. (n.d.). *Occasional report. Defining what matters: Guidelines for comprehensive Center for Teaching and Learning (CTL) evaluation*. https://podnetwork.org/content/uploads/POD_CTL_Evaluation_Guidelines__2018_.pdf

Poole, J. L., & Germain, L. J. (2022). Tool 4: Beyond Title IX—pursuing full participation through Plan, Do Study, Act (PDSA). In *Leadership at the intersection of gender and race in healthcare and science* (pp. 226–241). Routledge.

Portner, H. (2005). *Teacher mentoring and induction: The state of the art and beyond*. Corwin Press.

Posselt, J., Hernandez, T. E., Villarreal, C. D., Rodgers, A. J., & Irwin, L. N. (2020). Evaluation and decision making in higher education: Toward equitable repertoires of faculty practice. In J. C. Smart (Ed.), *Higher education: Handbook of theory and research* (Vol. 35, pp. 1–63).

Posselt, J. R., & Nuñez, A.-M. (2022). Learning in the wild: Fieldwork, gender, and the social construction of disciplinary culture. *The Journal of Higher Education*, *93*(2), 163–194. https://doi.org/10.1080/00221546.2021.1971505

Postsecondary National Policy Institute. (2024). *Tribal Colleges and Universities*. https://pnpi.org/wp-content/uploads/2024/07/TCU_FactSheet_May24.pdf

Prince, M., Felder, R., & Brent, R. (2020). Active student engagement in online STEM classes: Approaches and recommendations. *Advances in Engineering Education*, *8*(4), 1–25.

Psaromiligkos, Y., Orfanidou, M., Kytagias, C., & Zafiri, E. (2011). Mining log data for the analysis of learners' behaviour in web-based learning management systems. *Operational Research*, *11*, 187–200.

Pullias Center for Higher Education. (n.d.). The Delphi Project on the changing faculty and student success. https://pullias.usc.edu/project/the-delphi-project-on-the-changing-faculty-and-student-success/

Qaqish, O., Grant, C. S., & Bowles, T. (2020). Success factors that shape Black male transfer and academic experiences in engineering. *Community College Journal of Research and Practice*, *44*(10–12), 885–898. https://doi.org/10.1080/10668926.2020.1771628

Queiruga-Dios, M., Santos Sánchez, M. J., Queiruga-Dios, M. Á., Acosta Castellanos, P. M., & Queiruga-Dios, A. (2021). Assessment methods for service-learning projects in engineering in higher education: A systematic review. *Frontiers in Psychology*, *12*, 629231. https://doi.org/10.3389/fpsyg.2021.629231

Quijano, A. (2000). Coloniality of power and eurocentrism in Latin America. *International Sociology*, *15*(2), 215–232. https://doi.org/10.1177/0268580900015002005

Rabelo, A., Rodrigues, M. W., Nobre, C., Isotani, S., & Zárate, L. (2024). Educational data mining and learning analytics: A review of educational management in e-learning. *Information Discovery and Delivery*, *52*(2), 149–163.

Rademacher, L., Burmeister, K. C., Ryker, K., Atchison, C. L., Egger, A. E., Shipley, T. F., & Tikoff, B. (2021). *The lasting impacts of the COVID pandemic on teaching and learning without the field.* Geological Society of America Annual Meeting, Portland, OR, USA. https://doi.org/10.1130/abs/2021AM-368918

Rader, E., Love, R., Reano, D., Dousay, T. A., & Wingerter, N. (2021). Pandemic Minecrafting: An analysis of the perceptions of and lessons learned from a gamified virtual geology field camp. *Geoscience Communication*, *4*(4), 475–492. https://doi.org/10.5194/gc-4-475-2021

Rainey, K., Dancy, M., Mickelson, R., Stearns, E., & Moller, S. (2018). Race and gender differences in how sense of belonging influences decisions to major in STEM. *International Journal of STEM Education*, *5*, Article 10. https://doi.org/10.1186/s40594-018-0115-6

___. (2019). A descriptive study of race and gender differences in how instructional style and perceived professor care influence decisions to major in STEM. *International Journal of STEM Education, 6*, Article 6. https://doi.org/10.1186/s40594-019-0159-2

Ralph, V. R., Scharlott, L. J., Schafer, A. G. L., Deshaye, M. Y., Becker, N. M., & Stowe, R. L. (2022). Advancing equity in STEM: The impact assessment design has on who succeeds in undergraduate introductory chemistry. *JACS Au*, *2*(8), 1869–1880. https://doi.org/10.1021/jacsau.2c00221

Ramos, H. V., Cobian, K. P., Srinivasan, J., Christie, C. A., Crespi, C. M., & Seeman, T. (2024). Investigating the relationship between participation in the building infrastructure leading to diversity (BUILD) initiative and intent to pursue a science career: A cross-sectional analysis. *Evaluation and Program Planning*, *102*, 102380. https://doi.org/10.1016/j.evalprogplan.2023.102380

Ramsey, L. R., Betz, D. E., & Sekaquaptewa, D. (2013). The effects of an academic environment intervention on science identification among women in STEM. *Social Psychology of Education*, *16*(3), 377–397. https://doi.org/10.1007/s11218-013-9218-6

Ream, R. K., Lewis, J. L., Echeverria, B., & Page, R. N. (2014). Trust matters: Distinction and diversity in undergraduate science education. *Teachers College Record*, *116*(4), 1–50.

Reed, A. (2023). Micro-credentials and the role of evidence: Increasing the potential for learner-centeredness, inclusivity and an expansive model of assessment and credentialing. *International Journal of Information and Learning Technology*, *40*(5), 401–412.

Rehabilitation Act of 1973, Pub. L. No. 93-112, 87 Stat. 355 (1973), codified as amended at 29 U.S.C. § 794 et seq.

Rehrey, G., Shepard, L., Hostetter, C., Reynolds, A., & Groth, D. (2019). Engaging faculty in learning analytics: Agents of institutional culture change. *Journal of Learning Analytics*, *6*(2), 86–94.

Reinholz, D. L. (2023). *Equitable and engaging mathematics teaching: A guide to disrupting hierarchies in the classroom*. Mathematical Association of America Press.

Reinholz, D. L., Ngai, C., Quan, G., Pilgrim, M. E., Corbo, J. C., & Finkelstein, N. (2019). Fostering sustainable improvements in science education: An analysis through four frames. *Science Education*, *103*(5), 1125–1150.

Reinholz, D. L., Pilgrim, M. E., Stone-Johnstone, A., Falkenberg, K., Geanious, C., Ngai, C., & Corbo, J. C. & Wise, S. B. (2021a). Focus on outcomes: Fostering systemic departmental improvements. *To Improve the Academy: A Journal of Educational Development, 40*(2). https://doi.org/10.3998/tia.154

Reinholz, D. L., Ridgway, S., Sukumar, P. T., & Shah, N. (2023). Visualizing inequity: How STEM educators interpret data visualizations to make judgments about racial inequity. *SN Social Sciences*, *3*, Article 76. https://doi.org/10.1007/s43545-023-00664-0

Reinholz, D. L., Stone-Johnstone, A., & Shah, N. (2020). Walking the walk: Using classroom analytics to support instructors to address implicit bias in teaching. *International Journal for Academic Development*, *25*(3), 259–272. https://doi.org/10.1080/1360144X.2019.1692211

Reinholz, D. L., White, I., & Andrews, T. (2021b). Change theory in STEM higher education: A systematic review. *International Journal of STEM Education*, *8*, Article 37. https://doi.org/10.1186/s40594-021-00291-2

Renaissance. (n.d.). *Student agency*. https://www.renaissance.com/edword/student-agency/

Rendon, L. I. (1994). Validating culturally diverse students: Toward a new model of learning and student development. *Innovative Higher Education*, *19*(1), 33–51.

Renninger, K. A., & Hidi, S. E. (2019). *The Cambridge handbook of motivation and learning*. Cambridge University Press.

Reynolds, H. L., & Kearns, K. D. (2017). A planning tool for incorporating backward design, active learning, and authentic assessment in the college classroom. *College Teaching*, *65*(1), 17–27. https://doi.org/10.1080/87567555.2016.1222575

Reynolds, J., & Cruise, S. (2020). Factors that influence persistence among undergraduate students: An analysis of the impact of socioeconomic status and first-generation students. *Interchange*, *51*(2), 199–206.

Riegle-Crumb, C. (2006). The path through math: Course sequences and academic performance at the intersection of race-ethnicity and gender. *American Journal of Education*, *113*(1), 101–122. https://doi.org/10.1086/506495

Riegle-Crumb, C., King, B., & Irizarry, Y. (2019). Does STEM stand out? Examining racial/ethnic gaps in persistence across postsecondary fields. *Educational Researcher*, *48*(3), 133–144. https://doi.org/10.3102/0013189X19831006

Riihimaki, C. A., & Viskupic, K. (2019). Motivators and inhibitors to change: Why and how geoscience faculty modify their course content and teaching methods. *Journal of Geoscience Education*, *68*(2), 115–132. https://doi.org/10.1080/10899995.2019.1628590

Rincón, B. E., Fernández, É., & Dueñas, M. C. (2020). Anchoring comunidad: How first-and continuing-generation Latinx students in STEM engage community cultural wealth. *International Journal of Qualitative Studies in Education*, *33*(8), 840–854. https://doi.org/10.1080/09518398.2020.1735567

Roberts, M. T. (2016). *Syllabus review guide*. Center for Urban Education, University of Southern California. https://cue-equitytools.usc.edu/

Rockinson-Szapkiw, A., & Wendt, J. L. (2020). The benefits and challenges of a blended peer mentoring program for women peer mentors in science, technology, engineering, and mathematics (STEM). *International Journal of Mentoring and Coaching in Education*, *10*(1), 1–16. https://doi.org/10.1108/IJMCE-03-2020-0011

Rodríguez, G., Díez, J., Pérez, N., Baños, J. E., & Carrió, M. (2019b). Flipped classroom: Fostering creative skills in undergraduate students of health sciences. *Thinking Skills and Creativity*, *33*, 100575.

Rodriguez, S. L., & Blaney, J. M. (2021). "We're the unicorns in STEM": Understanding how academic and social experiences influence sense of belonging for Latina undergraduate students. *Journal of Diversity in Higher Education*, *14*(3), 441–455. https://doi.org/10.1037/dhe0000176

Rodriguez, S. L., Cunningham, K., & Jordan, A. (2017). What a scientist looks like: How community colleges can utilize and enhance science identity development as a means to improve success for women of color. *Community College Journal of Research and Practice*, *41*(4–5), 232–238. https://doi.org/10.1080/10668926.2016.1251354

Rodriguez, S. L., Hensen, K. A., & Espino, M. L. (2019a). Promoting STEM identity development in community colleges & across the transfer process. *Journal of Applied Research in the Community College*, *26*(2), 11–22.

Rodriguez, S. L., Perez, R. J., & Schulz, J. M. (2022). How STEM lab settings influence graduate school socialization and climate for students of color. *Journal of Diversity in Higher Education*, *15*(1), 58–72. https://doi.org/10.1037/dhe0000361

Rogers, K., Galvin, T., & Yee, S. P. (2022, February). *Active-learning strategies that suggest ingresses for math graduate student instructors' use of student-centered teaching.* Conference Proceedings in the 24th annual Conference on Research in Undergraduate Mathematics Education, Boston, MA, USA.

Rogers, K. C., & Steele, M. D. (2016). Graduate teaching assistants' enactment of reasoning-and-proving tasks in a content course for elementary teachers. *Journal for Research in Mathematics Education*, *47*(4), 372–419.

Ross, M., Capobianco, B. M., & Godwin, A. (2017). Repositioning race, gender, and role identity formation for Black women in engineering. *Journal of Women and Minorities in Science and Engineering*, *23*(1), 37–52. https://doi.org/10.1615/JWomenMinorScienEng.2017016424

Rossouw, N., & Frick, L. (2023). A conceptual framework for uncovering the hidden curriculum in private education. *Cogent Education*, *10*, Article 2191409. https://doi.org/10.1080/2331186X.2023.2191409

RTI International. (2023). *First-generation college students in 2020: Demographic characteristics and postsecondary enrollment.* https://firstgen.naspa.org/files/dmfile/15405_NASPA_FactSheet-01.pdf

Ruder, S., Brown, P. J., & Stanford, C. (2020). Developing POGIL materials: Writing and refining activities for a spectrum of content areas. *Journal on Excellence on College Teaching*, *31*(1), 189–228.

Rudolph, F. (2021). *The American college and university: A history.* Plunkett Lake Press.

Rush, B. (2023). *Disabilities in higher education: The impact of the disability resource center at Mississippi State University.* [Doctoral dissertation, 5974, Mississippi State University]. https://scholarsjunction.msstate.edu/td/5974

Russel, J. L., Bryk, A. S., Dolle, J. R., Gomez, L. M., Lemahiue, P. G., & Grunow, A. (2017). A framework for the initiation of networked improvement communities. *Teachers College Record*, *119*(5), 1–36. https://journals.sagepub.com/doi/10.1177/016146811711900501

Rutschow, E. Z., Sepanik, S., Deitch, V., Raufman, J., Dukes, D. C., & Moussa, A. (2019). *Gaining ground: Findings from the Dana Center Mathematics Pathways Impact Study.* Center for the Analysis of Postsecondary Readiness. https://academiccommons.columbia.edu/doi/10.7916/d8-bhz4-4112

Ryan, R. M. (Ed.). (2019). *The Oxford handbook of human motivation.* Oxford University Press USA.

Rybarczyk, B., Lerea, L. Lund, P. K, Whittington, D., & Dykstra, L. (2011). Postdoctoral training aligned with the academic professoriate. *BioScience*, *61*(9), 699–705. https://doi.org/10.1525/bio.2011.61.9.8

Saetermoe, C. L., Chavira, G., Khachikian, C. S., Boyns, D., & Cabello, B. (2017, December). Critical race theory as a bridge in science training: The California State University, Northridge BUILD PODER program. In *BMC Proceedings* (Vol. 11, pp. 41–55). BioMed Central.

Saitta, E., & Donnelly, J. (2022). The role and influence of the discipline-based education research (DBER) community on stem faculty development. In S. M. Linder, C. M. Lee, S. K. Stefl, & K. A. High (Eds.), *Handbook of STEM faculty development* (pp. 61–70). Information Age Publishing.

Sáiz-Manzanares, M. C., Rodríguez-Díez, J. J., Díez-Pastor, J. F., Rodríguez-Arribas, S., Marticorena-Sánchez, R., & Ji, Y. P. (2021). Monitoring of student learning in learning management systems: An application of educational data mining techniques. *Applied Sciences*, *11*(6), 2677.

Salam, M., Awang Iskander, D. N., Ibrahim, D. H. A., & Farooq, M. S. (2019). Service learning in higher education: A systematic literature review. *Asia Pacific Education Review*, *20*(4), 573–593.

Salehi, S., Berk, S. A., Brunelli, R., Cotner, S., Creech, C., Drake, A. G., Fagbodun, S., Hall, C., Hebert, S., Hewlett, J., James, A. C., Shuster, M., St Juliana, J. R., Stovall, D. B., Whittington, R., Zhong, M., & Ballen, C. J. (2021). Context matters: Social psychological factors that underlie academic performance across seven institutions. *CBE—Life Sciences Education*, *20*(4), Article 68. https://doi.org/10.1187/cbe.21-01-0012

Salehi, S., Burkholder, E., Lepage, G. P., Pollock, S., & Wieman, C. (2019a). Demographic gaps or preparation gaps?: The large impact of incoming preparation on performance of students in introductory physics. *Physical Review Physics Education Research*, *15*(2), 020114.

Salehi, S., Cotner, S., Azarin, S. M., Carlson, E. E., Driessen, M., Ferry, V. E., Harcombe, W., McGaugh, S., Wassenberg, D., Yonas, A., & Ballen, C. J. (2019b). Gender performance gaps across different assessment methods and the underlying mechanisms: The case of incoming preparation and test anxiety. *Frontiers in Education*, *4*, 107. https://doi.org/10.3389/feduc.2019.00107

Sanabria, T., & Penner, A. (2017). Weeded out? Gendered responses to failing calculus. *Social Sciences*, *6*(2), 47. https://doi.org/10.3390/socsci6020047

Sandi-Urena, S., Cooper, M. M., & Stevens, R. H. (2011). Enhancement of metacognition use and awareness by means of a collaborative intervention. *Internation Journal of Science Education*, *33*(3), 323–340.

Santangelo, J., Cadieux, M., & Zapata, S. (2021a). Developing student metacognitive skills using active learning with embedded metacognition instruction. *Journal of STEM Education: Innovations and Research*, *22*(2).

Santangelo, J., Hobbie, L., Lee, J., Pullin, M., Villa-Cuesta, E., & Hyslop, A. (2021b). The (STEM)^2 Network: A multi-institution, multidisciplinary approach to transforming undergraduate STEM education. *International Journal of STEM Education*, *8*, Article 3, 1–15. https://doi.org/10.1186/s40594-020-00262-z

Sathianathan, D. (1997, November). Faculty collaboration and course coordination in geographically dispersed campuses. In *Proceedings Frontiers in Education 1997 27th Annual Conference: Teaching and Learning in an Era of Change* (Vol. 1, pp. 34–37). IEEE.

Sathy, V., & Moore, Q. (2020). Who benefits from the flipped classroom?: Quasi-experimental findings on student learning, engagement, course perceptions, and interest in statistics. In *Teaching statistics and quantitative methods in the 21st century* (pp. 197–216). Routledge.

Savaria, M. C., & Monteiro, K. A. (2017). A critical discourse analysis of engineering course syllabi and recommendations for increasing engagement among women in STEM. *Journal of STEM Education: Innovations and Research*, *18*(1).

Sawyer, R. K. (Ed.). (2005). *The Cambridge handbook of the learning sciences*. Cambridge University Press.

Schaller, T. K., Routon, P. W., Partridge, M. A., & Berry, R. (2023). A systematic review and meta-analysis of dual enrollment research. *Journal of College Student Retention: Research, Theory & Practice*, 15210251231170331.

Schinske, J., & Tanner, K. (2014). Teaching more by grading less (or differently). *CBE—Life Sciences Education*, *13*(2), 159–166. https://doi.org/10.1187/cbe.cbe-14-03-0054

Schinske, J. N., Perkins, H., Snyder, A., & Wyer, M. (2016). Scientist spotlight homework assignments shift students' stereotypes of scientists and enhance science identity in a diverse introductory science class. *CBE Life Sciences Education*, *15*(3), Article 47. https://doi.org/10.1187/cbe.16-01-0002

Schmader, T., & Johns, M. (2003). Converging evidence that stereotype threat reduces working memory capacity. *Journal of Personality and Social Psychology*, *85*(3), 440–452. https://doi.org/10.1037/0022-3514.85.3.440

Schmidt, E., Vik, R., Brubaker, B. W., Abdulahad, S. S., Soto-Olson, D. K., Monjure, T. A., Battle, C. H., & Jayarickramaraja, J. (2020). Increasing student interest and self-efficacy in STEM by offering a service-learning chemistry course in New Orleans. *Journal of Chemical Education*, 97(11), 4008–4018. https://doi.org/10.1021/acs.jchemed.9b01140

Schneider, J., & Hutt, E. (2013). Making the grade: A history of the A-F marking scheme. *Journal of Curriculum Studies*, 46(2), 201–224. https://doi.org/10.1080/00220272.2013.790480

Schreffler, J., Vasquez, E., III, Chini, J., & James, W. (2019). Universal design for learning in postsecondary STEM education for students with disabilities: A systematic literature review. *International Journal of STEM Education*, 6(1), 1–10.

Schunk, D. H. (1989). Self-efficacy and achievement behaviors. *Educational Psychology Review*, 1, 173–208.

Schwab, K., Moseley, B., & Dustin, D. (2018). Grading grades as a measure of student learning. *SCHOLE: A Journal of Leisure Studies and Recreation Education*, 33(2), 87–95. https://doi.org/10.1080/1937156X.2018.1513276

Schwartz, D. L., & Bransford, J. D. (1998). A time for telling. *Cognition and Instruction*, 16(4), 475–522.

Schweitzer, J., Groeger, L., & Sobel, L. (2016). The design thinking mindset: An assessment of what we know and what we see in practice. *Journal of Design, Business & Society*, 2(1), 71–94. https://doi.org/10.1386/dbs.2.1.71_1.

Scileppi, J. A. (1988). *A systems view of education: A model for change*. University Press of America.

Scott Coker, J. (2017). Student-designed experiments: A pedagogical design for introductory science labs. *Journal of College Science Teaching*, 46(5), 14–19.

Seagren, A. T., Creswell, J. W., & Wheeler, D. W. (1993). *The department chair: New roles, responsibilities, and challenges*. ERIC Clearinghouse on Higher Education, George Washington University, School of Education and Human Development.

Sekaquaptewa, D., & Thompson, M. (2003). Solo status, stereotype threat, and performance expectancies: Their effects on women's performance. *Journal of Experimental Social Psychology*, 39(1), 68–74. https://doi.org/10.1016/S0022-1031(02)00508-5

Sellers, V. B., & Villanueva, I. (2021). *What strategies do diverse women in engineering use to cope with situational hidden curriculum?* [Virtual conference session]. Paper presented at 2021 ASEE Virtual Annual Conference Content Access, Virtual Conference. https://doi.org/10.18260/1-2--38051

Senior, R. M., Bartholomew, P., Soor, A., Shepperd, D., Bartholomew, N., & Senior, C. (2018). "The rules of engagement": Student engagement and motivation to improve the quality of undergraduate learning. *Frontiers in Education*, 3, Article 32. https://doi.org/10.3389/feduc.2018.00032

Seok, S., DaCosta, B., & Hodges, R. (2018). A systematic review of empirically based universal design for learning: Implementation and effectiveness of universal design in education for students with and without disabilities at the postsecondary level. *Open Journal of Social Sciences*, 6(05), 171.

Servicemen's Readjustment Act of 1944, Pub. L. No. 78-346, 58 Stat. 284 (1944), codified as amended at 38 U.S.C. § 2001 et seq.

Settles, I. H., Jones, M. K., Buchanan, N. T., & Dotson, K. (2021). Epistemic exclusion: Scholar(ly) devaluation that marginalizes faculty of color. *Journal of Diversity in Higher Education*, 14(4), 493–507. https://doi.org/10.1037/dhe0000174

Sexton, M. W., & Sharma, V. (2021). Building equitable research experiences at a two-year community college. *Perspectives on Undergraduate Research & Mentoring*, 10(1). https://www.elon.edu/u/academics/undergraduate-research/purm/purm-10-1/

Seymour, E., & Hewitt, N. M. (1997). *Talking about leaving: Why undergraduates leave the sciences*. Westview Press.

Seymour, E., & A. -B. Hunter (Eds.). (2019). *Talking about leaving revisited: Persistence, relocation, and loss in undergraduate STEM education* (pp. 197–243). Springer International Publishing. https://doi.org/10.1007/978-3-030-25304-2_7

Seyranian, V., Madva, A., Duong, N., Abramzon, N., Tibbetts, Y., & Harackiewicz, J. M. (2018). The longitudinal effects of STEM identity and gender on flourishing and achievement in college physics. *International Journal of STEM Education, 5*, Article 40. https://doi.org/10.1186/s40594-018-0137-0

Shafer, G. W., Viskupic, K., & Egger, A. E. (2023). Critical workforce skills for bachelor-level geoscientists: An analysis of geoscience job advertisements. *Geosphere, 19*(2), 628–644. https://doi.org/10.1130/ges02581.1

Shakman, K., Wogan, D., Rodriguez, S., Boyce, J., & Shaver, D. (2020). *Continuous improvement in education: A toolkit for schools and districts* (REL 2021-014). U.S. Department of Education, Institute of Education Sciences, National Center for Education Evaluation and Regional Assistance, Regional Educational Laboratory Northeast & Islands. https://ies.ed.gov/ncee/edlabs

Shapiro, D. T., & Tang, Z. (2019). The national student clearinghouse: Leveraging administrative data for postsecondary improvement. *New Directions for Institutional Research, 2019*(181), 117–131.

Sherman, D. K., Hartson, K. A., Binning, K. R., Purdie-Vaughns, V., Garcia, J., Taborsky-Barba, S., Tomassetti, S., Nussbaum, A. D., & Cohen, G. L. (2013). Deflecting the trajectory and changing the narrative: How self-affirmation affects academic performance and motivation under identity threat. *Journal of Personality and Social Psychology, 104*(4), 591–618. https://doi.org/10/1037/a0031495

Sherman, D. K., Lokhande, M., Müller, T., & Cohen, G. L. (2021) Self-affirmation interventions. In G. M. Walton & A. J. Crum (Eds.). *Handbook of wise interventions: How social psychology can help people change* (pp. 63–99). Guilford Press.

Shortlidge, E. E., & Eddy, S. L. (2018). The trade-off between graduate student research and teaching: A myth?. *PLoS One, 13*(6), e0199576. https://doi.org/10.1371/journal.pone.0199576

Shukla, S. Y., Theobald, E. J., Abraham, J. K., & Price, R. M. (2022). Reframing educational outcomes: Moving beyond achievement gaps. *CBE—Life Sciences Education, 21*(2), es2. https://doi/org/10.1187/cbe.21-05-0130

Shulman, L. (1986). Paradigms and research programs in the study of teaching: A contemporary perspective. In M. C. Whittrock (Ed.), *Handbook of research in teaching* (3rd ed., pp. 3–26). Macmillan.

Simonsmeier, B. A., Flaig, M., Deiglmayr, A., Schalk, L., & Schneider, M. (2022). Domain-specific prior knowledge and learning: A meta-analysis. *Educational Psychologist, 57*(1), 31–54.

Simpson, A., & Bouhafa, Y. (2020). Youths' and adults' identity in STEM: A systemic literature review. *Journal for STEM Education Research, 3*(9), 167–194. https://doi.org/10.1007/s41979-020-00034-y

Singer, A., Montgomery, G., & Schmoll, S. (2020). How to foster the formation of STEM identity: Studying diversity in an authentic learning environment. *International Journal of STEM Education, 7*, 1–12.

Singh, J., & Singh, H. (2015). Continuous improvement philosophy—literature review and directions. *Benchmarking: An International Journal, 22*(1), 75–119.

Slattery, J. M., & Carlson, J. F. (2005). Preparing an effective syllabus: Current best practices. *College Teaching, 53*(4), 159–164. https://doi.org/10.3200/CTCH.53.4.159-164

Slim, A., Kozlick, J., Heileman, G. L., & Abdallah, C. T. (2014, July). The complexity of university curricula according to course cruciality. In *Proceedings—2014 Eighth International Conference on Complex, Intelligent and Software Intensive Systems, CISIS 2014* (pp. 242–248). Institute of Electrical and Electronics Engineers. https://doi.org/10.1109/CISIS.2014.34

Smart, J. C., Feldman, K. A., & Ethington, C. A. (2000). *Academic disciplines: Holland's theory and the study of college students and faculty*. Vanderbilt University Press.

Smith, K. A. (1996). Cooperative learning: Making "groupwork" work. In *T. E. Sutherland & C. C. Bonwell (Eds.), Using active learning in college classes: A range of options for faculty* (pp. 71–82). Jossey-Bass.

Smith, L. T. (2021). *Decolonizing methodologies: Research and Indigenous peoples*. Bloomsbury.

Smith, M. K., Jones, F. H., Gilbert, S. L., & Wieman, C. E. (2013). The Classroom Observation Protocol for Undergraduate STEM (COPUS): A new instrument to characterize university STEM classroom practices. *CBE—Life Sciences Education*, *12*(4), 618–627. https://doi.org/10.1187/cbe.13-08-0154

Smith, M. K., Wood, W. B., Adams, W. K., Wieman, C., Knight, J. K., Guild, N., & Su, T. T. (2009). Why peer discussion improves student performance on in-class concept questions. *Science*, *323*(5910), 122–124. https://doi.org/10.1126/science.1165919

Snyder, B. R. (1971). *The hidden curriculum*. Alfred A. Knopf.

Solanki, S., McPartlan, P., Xu, D., & Sato, B. K. (2019). Success with EASE: Who benefits from STEM learning community? *PLoS One, 14(3),* e0213827. https://doi.org/10.1371/journal.pone.0213827

Soliz, A. (2023). Career and technical education at community colleges: A review of the literature. *AERA Open*, *9*. https://doi.org/10.1177/23328584231186618

Solyom, J. A., Chin, J., McKinley Jones Brayboy, B., Poleviyuma, A., Abuwandi, S., Richmond, A., Tachine, A., Ben, C., & Bang, M. (2019). *Systems of support: What institutions of higher education can do for Indigenous communities.*

Sorcinelli, M. D. (2002). Ten principles of good practice in creating and sustaining teaching and learning centers. In *A guide to faculty development: Practical advice, examples, and resources* (pp. 9–23).

Speer, N., Gutmann, T., & Murphy, T. J. (2005). Mathematics teaching assistant preparation and development. *College Teaching*, *53*(2), 75–80. https://doi.org/10.3200/CTCH.53.2.75-80

Spencer, S. J., Logel, C., & Davies, P. G. (2016). Stereotype threat. *Annual Review of Psychology*, *67*, 415–437. https://doi.org/10.1146/annurev-psych-073115-103235

Spoon, K., LaBerge, N., Wapman, K. H., Zhang, S., Morgan, A. C., Galesic, M., Fosdick, B. K., Larremore, D. B., & Clauset, A. (2023). Gender and retention patterns among U.S. faculty. *Science Advances*, *9*(42). https://doi.org/10.1126/sciadv.adi2205

Spooren, P., Brockx, B., & Mortelmans, D. (2013). On the validity of student evaluation of teaching: The state of the art. *Review of Educational Research*, *83*(4), 598–642. https://doi.org/10.3102/0034654313496870

Spurlin, J., Rajala, S. A., & Lavelle, J. P. (Eds.). (2008). *Designing better engineering education through assessment: A practical resource for faculty and department chairs on using assessment and ABET criteria to improve student learning*. Routledge.

St. John, K., & McNeal, K. S. (2017). The strength of evidence pyramid: One approach for characterizing the strength of evidence of Geoscience Education Research (GER) community claims. *Journal of Geoscience Education*, *65*(4), 363–372. https://doi.org/10.5408/17-264.1

Stack Hankey, M., Burge, P. L., Knight, D. B., Seidel, R. W., & Skaggs, G. (2019). Community college engineering students' perceptions of classroom climate and fundamental engineering skills. *Community College Journal of Research and Practice*, *43*(7), 494–504. https://doi.org/10.1080/10668926.2018.1494063

Stains, M., Harshman, J., Barker, M. K., Chasteen, S. V., Cole, R., DeChenne-Peters, S. E., Eagan, M. K., Esson, J. M., Knight, J. K., Laski, F. A., Levis-Fitzgerald, M., Lee, C. J., Lo, S. M., McDonnell, L. M., McKay, T. A., Michelotti, N., Musgrove, A., Palmer, M. S., Plank, K. M., Rodela, T. M., Sanders, E. R., Schimpf, N. G., Schulte, P. M., Smith, M. K., Stetzer, M., Van Valkenburgh, B., Vinson, E., Weir, L. K., Wendel, P. J., Wheeler, L. B., & Young, A. M. (2018). Anatomy of STEM teaching in North American universities. *Science, 359*(6383), 1468–1470. https://doi.org/10.1126/science.aap8892

Stanberry, M. L., & Payne, W. R. (2018). Active learning in undergraduate STEM education: A review of research. In M. Shelley & S. A. Kiray (Eds.), *Research highlights in STEM education* (pp. 147–146). ISRES Publishing.

Stanich, C. A., Pelch, M. A., Theobald, E. J., & Freeman, S. (2018). A new approach to supplementary instruction narrows achievement and affect gaps for underrepresented minorities, first-generation students, and women. *Chemistry Education Research and Practice, 19*(3), 846–866. https://doi.org/10.1039/C8RP00044A

Stanton, J. D., Dye, K. M., & Johnson, M. S. (2019). Knowledge of learning makes a difference: A comparison of metacognition in introductory and senior-level biology students. *CBE—Life Sciences Education, 18*(2), Article 24. https://doi.org/10.1187/cbe.18-12-0239

Stanton, J. D., Sebesta, A. J., & Dunlosky, J. (2021). Fostering metacognition to support student learning and performance. *CBE—Life Sciences Education, 20*(2), fe3. https://doi.org/10.1187/cbe.20-12-0289

Starobin, S. S., & Laanan, F. S. (2008). Broadening female participation in science, technology, engineering, and mathematics: Experiences at community colleges. *New Directions for Community Colleges, 2008*(142), 37–46. https://doi.org/10.1002/cc.323

Starobin, S. S., Smith, D. J., & Santos Laanan, F. (2016). Deconstructing the transfer student capital: Intersect between social and cultural capital among female transfer students in STEM fields. *Community College Journal of Research and Practice, 40*(12), 1040–1057. https://doi.org/10.1080/10668926.2016.1204964

Starr, C. R., Hunter, L., Dunkin, R., Honig, S., Palomino, R., & Leaper, C. (2020). Engaging in science practices in classrooms predicts increases in undergraduates' STEM motivation, identity, and achievement: A short-term longitudinal study. *Journal of Research in Science Teaching, 57*(7), 1093–1118. https://doi.org/10.1002/tea.21623

State Higher Education Executive Officers Association (SHEEO). (2021, May 18). *New analysis finds that you get what you pay for: State higher education funding directly impacts student success.* https://sheeo.org/new-analysis-finds-that-you-get-what-you-pay-for-state-higher-education-funding-directly-impacts-student-success/

___. (2022). *State effort and capacity to fund higher education: FY 2019 and 2020.* https://shef.sheeo.org/wp-content/uploads/2022/06/SHEEO_SHEF_FY20_State_Effort_Report.pdf

Steele, C. M. (1997). A threat in the air: How stereotypes affect intellectual identity and performance. *American Psychologist, 52*(6), 613–629. https://doi.org/10.1037/0003-066X.52.6.613

Steele, C. M., & Aronson, J. (1995). Stereotype threat and the intellectual test performance of African Americans. *Journal of Personality and Social Psychology, 69*(5), 797–811. https://doi.org/10.1037/0022-3514.69.5.797

Steele, C. M., Spencer, S. J., & Aronson, J. (2002). Contending with group image: The psychology of stereotype and social identity threat. *Advances in Experimental Social Psychology, 34*, 379–440. https://doi.org/10.1016/S0065-2601(02)80009-0

Steele-Johnson, D., & Leas, K. (2013). Importance of race, gender, and personality in predicting academic performance. *Journal of Applied Social Psychology, 43*(8), 1736–1744.

Steer, D., Iverson, E. R., Egger, A. E., Kastens, K. A., Manduca, C. A., & McConnell, D. (2019). The InTeGrate materials development rubric: A framework and process for developing curricular materials that meet ambitious goals. In D. Sosselin, A. Egger, & J. Taber (Eds.), *Interdisciplinary teaching about earth and the environment for a sustainable future* (pp. 25–43). AESS Interdisciplinary Environmental Studies and Sciences Series. Springer, Cham. https://doi.org/10.1007/978-3-030-03273-9_2

Stein, W. J. (1999). Tribal colleges: 1968–1998. In K. C. Swisher & J. W. Tippeconnic III (Eds.), *Next steps: Research and practice to advance Indian education* (pp. 259–270). Appalachia Educational Laboratory.

Stenalt, M. H., & Lassesen, B. (2021). Does student agency benefit student learning? A systematic review of higher education research. *Assessment & Evaluation in Higher Education*, *47*(5), 653–669. https://doi.org/10.1080/02602938.2021.1967874

Stephens, N. M., Fryberg, S. A., Markus, H. R., Johnson, C. S., & Covarrubius, R. (2012). Unseen disadvantage: How American universities' focus on independence undermines the academic performance of first-generation college students. *Journal of Personality and Social Psychology*, *102*(6), 1178–1197. https://doi.org/10.1037/a0027143

Stephens-Martinez, K., & Railling, B. (2019, February). How can we make office hours better? In *Proceedings of the 50th ACM Technical Symposium on Computer Science Education* (pp. 1247–1247). https://doi.org/10.1145/3287324.3293741

Stevens, M. L., Armstrong, E. A., & Arum, R. (2008). Sieve, incubator, temple, hub: Theoretical advances in the sociology of higher education. *Annual Review of Sociology*, *34*, 127–151.

Stewart-Rozema, J. & Pratts, C. (2023, December 18). International student enrollment statistics. *BestColleges*. https://www.bestcolleges.com/research/international-student-enrollment-statistics/

Stokes, A., & Boyle, A. P. (2009). The undergraduate geoscience fieldwork experience: Influencing factors and implications for learning. In S. J. Whitmeyer, D. W. Mogk, & E. J. Pyle (Eds.), *Field geology education: Historical perspectives and modern approaches* (pp. 291–311). Geological Society of America. https://doi.org/10.1130/2009.2461(23)

Stokes, A., Feig, A. D., Atchison, C. L., & Gilley, B. (2019). Making geoscience fieldwork inclusive and accessible for students with disabilities. *Geosphere*, *15*(6), 1809–1825. https://doi.org/10.1130/ges02006.1

Stoll, L., Bolam, R., McMahon, A., Wallace, M., & Thomas, S. (2006). Professional learning communities: A review of the literature. *Journal of Educational Change*, *7*(4), 221–258.

Stommel, J. (2024). Ungrading: An introduction. *Pedagogy*, *24*(3), 327–340.

Stout, J. G., Dasgupta, N., Hunsinger, M., & McManus, M. A. (2011). STEMing the tide: Using ingroup experts to inoculate women's self-concept in science, technology, engineering, and mathematics (STEM). *Journal of Personality and Social Psychology*, *100*(2), 255–270. https://doi.org/10.1037/a0021385

Stratton, T. D., & Elam, C. L. (2014). A holistic review of the medical school admission process: Examining correlates of academic underperformance. *Medical Education Online*, *19*(1), 22919.

Strayhorn, T. L. (2018). *College students' sense of belonging: A key to educational success for all students*. Routledge.

Strayhorn, T. L., Williams, M. S., Tillman-Kelly, D. L., & Dorimé-Williams, M. (2013). STEMming the tide: Psychological factors influencing racial and ethnic minority students' success in STEM at community colleges. In R. T. Palmer & J. L. Wood (Eds.), *Community colleges and STEM: Examining underrepresented racial and ethnic minorities* (pp. 91–100). Routledge.

Strohl, J., Nyhof, E., & Morris, C. (2024). *Progress interrupted: Evaluating a decade of demographic change at selective and open-access institutions prior to the end of race-conscious affirmative action*. Center on Education and the Workforce, Georgetown University. https://cew.georgetown.edu/cew-reports/progressinterrupted/

Student Experience Project.(2022a, July 13). *Community of practice handbook*. https://studentexperienceproject.org/handbook/

___. (2022b). *Increasing equity in college student experience: Findings from a national collaborative*. https://s45004.pcdn.co/wp-content/uploads/Increasing-Equity-in-Student-Experience-Findings-from-a-National-Collaborative.pdf

Swing, R. L., Jones, D., & Ross, L. E. (2016). *The AIR National Survey of Institutional Research Offices*. Association for Institutional Research. http://www.airweb.org/nationalsurvey.

Tagg, J. (2012). Why does the faculty resist change? *Change: The Magazine of Higher Learning*, *44*(1), 6–15. https://doi.org/10.1080/00091383.2012.635987

Talbot, R. M., Hartley, L., Marzetta, K., & S. Wee, B. (2015). Transforming undergraduate science education with learning assistants: Student satisfaction in large-enrollment courses. *Journal of College Science Teaching*, *44*(5), 24–30.

Tankard, M. E., & Paluck, E. L. (2016). Norm perception as a vehicle for social change. *Social Issues and Policy Review*, *10*(1), 181–211. https://doi.org/10.1111/sipr.12022

Tanner, K., & Allen, D. (2007). Cultural competence in the college biology classroom. *CBE—Life Sciences Education*, *6*(4), 251–258. https://doi.org/10.1187/cbe.07-09-0086

Tanner, K. D. (2012). Promoting student metacognition. *CBE—Life Sciences Education, 11*(2), 113–120.

Tatapudy, S., Potter, R., Bostrom, L., Colgan, A., Self, C. J., Smith, J., Xu, S., & Theobald, E. J. (2024). Visualizing inequities: A step toward equitable student outcomes. *CBE—Life Sciences Education*, *23*(4), es9. https://doi.org/10.1187/cbe.24-02-0086

Taylor, D. G., & Frechette, M. (2022). The impact of workload, productivity, and social support on burnout among marketing faculty during the COVID-19 pandemic. *Journal of Marketing Education*, *44*(2), 134–148.

Taylor, J. L., & Jain, D. (2017). The multiple dimensions of transfer: Examining the transfer function in American higher education. *Community College Review*, *45*(4), 273–293. https://doi.org/10.1177/0091552117725177

Taylor, L. D., Jr. (2020). Neoliberal consequence: Data-driven decision making and the subversion of student success efforts. *The Review of Higher Education*, *43*(4), 1069–1097. https://dx.doi.org/10.1353/rhe.2020.0031

Teasdale, R., Ryker, K., & Bitting, K. (2019). Training graduate teaching assistants in the geosciences: Our practices vs. perceived needs. *Journal of Geoscience Education*, *67*(1), 64–82. https://doi.org/10.1080/10899995.2018.1542476

Temponi, C. (2005). Continuous improvement framework: Implications for academia. *Quality Assurance in Education*, *13*(1), 17–36.

Teshera-Levye, J., Atchison, T., Callis-Duehl, K., Gould, T., Lichti, D., Scemama, J. L., & Vance-Chalcraft, H. D. (2023). Transfer-bound community college students' biology identity and perception of teaching. *Journal of Microbiology & Biology Education*, *24*(3), e00116-23. https://doi.org/10.1128/jmbe.0016-23

Thacker, I., Seyranian, V., Madva, A., Duong, N. T., & Beardsley, P. (2022). Social connectedness in physical isolation: Online teaching practices that support underrepresented undergraduate students' feelings of belonging and engagement in STEM. *Education Sciences*, *12*(2), 61. https://doi.org/10.3390/educsci12020061

Tharayil, S., Borrego, M., Prince, M., Nguyen, K. A., Shekhar, P., Finelli, C. J., & Waters, C. (2018). Strategies to mitigate student resistance to active learning. *International Journal of STEM Education*, *5*, 1–16.

The First Morrill Act of 1862, 7 U.S.C. 301 et seq. (1862). https://uscode.house.gov/view.xhtml?req=morrill+act+1862&f=treesort&fq=true&num=0&hl=true&edition=prelim&granuleId=USC-prelim-title7-section301

The Second Morrill Act of 1890, Pub. L. No. 51-841, 26 Stat. 417 (1890), codified as amended at 7 U.S.C. § 321 et seq. https://uscode.house.gov/view.xhtml?req=second+morrill+act+1890&f=treesort&fq=true&num=0&hl=true&edition=prelim&granuleId=USC-prelim-title7-section301

Theobald, E. J., Eddy, S. L., Grunspan, D. Z., Wiggins, B. L., & Crowe, A. J. (2017). Student perception of group dynamics predicts individual performance: Comfort and equity matter. *PLoS One*, *12*(7), e0181336.

Theobald, E. J., Hill, M. J., Tran, E., Agrawal, S., Arroyo, E. N., Behling, S., Chambwe, N., Cintron, D. L., Cooper, J. D., Dunster, G., Grummer, J. A., Hennessey, K., Hsiao, J., Iranon, N., Jones, L., II, Jordt, H., Keller, M., Lacey, M. E., Littlefield, C. E., Lowe, A., Newman, S., Okolo, V., Olroyd, S., Peecook, B. R., Pickett, S. B., Slager, D. L., Caviedes-Solis, I. W., Stanchak, K. E., Sundaravardan, V., Valdebenito, C., Williams, C. R., Zinsli, K., & Freeman, S. (2020). Active learning narrows achievement gaps for underrepresented students in undergraduate science, technology, engineering, and math. *Proceedings of the National Academy of Sciences*, *117*(12), 6476–6483. https://doi.org/10.1073/pnas.1916903117

Thiele, T., Singleton, A., Pope, D., & Stanistreet, D. (2014). Predicting students' academic performance based on school and socio-demographic characteristics. *Studies in Higher Education*, *41*(8), 1424–1446. https://doi.org/10.1080/03075079.2014.974528

Thiry, H. (2019a). What enables persistence? In E. Seymour & A.-B. Hunter (Eds.), *Talking about leaving revisited: Persistence, relocation, and loss in undergraduate STEM education* (pp. 399–436). Springer Cham. https://doi.org/10.1007/978-3-030-25304-2_12

Thiry, H. (2019b). Issues with high school preparation and transition to college. In E. Seymour & A.-B. Hunter (Eds.), *Talking about leaving revisited: Persistence, relocation, and loss in undergraduate STEM education* (pp. 137–147). Springer. https://doi.org/10.1007/978-3-030-25304-2_5

Thiry, H., & Laursen, S. L. (2011). The role of student-advisor interactions in apprenticing undergraduate researchers into a scientific community of practice. *Journal of Science Education and Technology*, *20*, 771–784. https://doi.org/10.1007/s10956-010-9271-2

Thiry, H., & Weston, T. J. (2019). Choosing STEM majors. In E. Seymour & A.-B. Hunter (Eds.), *Talking about leaving revisited: Persistence, relocation, and loss in undergraduate STEM education* (pp. 115–136). Springer. https://doi.org/10.1007/978-3-030-25304-2_5

Thiry, H., Zahner, D. H., Weston, T., Harper, R., & Loshbaugh, H. (2023). How can universities support STEM transfer students? A framework for strategic planning and action. *Change: The Magazine of Higher Learning*, *55*(4), 11–22.

Thorp, H., & Goldstein, B. (2018). *Our higher calling: Rebuilding the partnership between America and its colleges and universities*. The University of North Carolina Press.

Thorp, H., & Goldstein, B. (2024, March 11). With confidence in higher ed plummeting, colleges must recommit to teaching. *Inside Higher Ed*. https://www.insidehighered.com/opinion/views/2024/03/11/rebuild-public-confidence-focus-teaching-opinion

Tiede, H. J. (2015). *University reform: The founding of the American Association of University Professors*. John Hopkins University Press.

Tierney, W. G., & Lanford, M. (2018). Institutional culture in higher education. In R. N. Teixeria, J. C. Shin, A. Amaral, E. Balbachevsky, A. Bernasconi, E. Choi, H. De Wit, G. Goatsellec, F. Hunter, B. M. Kehm, M. Klemenčič, P. Langa, A. Magalhâes, G. Mohamedbhai, T. Nokkala, L. Rumbley, B. Stensaker, L. Unangst, J. Valimaa, & R. Yang (Eds.), *Encyclopedia of international higher education systems and institutions* (pp. 1–7). Springer.

Tijsma, G., Hilverda, F., Scheffelaar, A., Alders, S., Schoonmade, L., Blignaut, N., & Zweekhorst, M. (2020). Becoming productive 21st century citizens: A systematic review uncovering design principles for integrating community service learning into higher education courses. *Educational Research*, *62*(4), 390–413. https://doi.org/10.1007/s12564-019-09580-6

Title IX of the Education Amendments of 1972, Pub. L. No. 92-318, 86 Stat. 235 (1972), codified as amended at 20 U.S.C. § 1681 et seq.

Toldson, I. A. (2019). Cultivating STEM talent at minority serving institutions: Challenges and opportunities to broaden participation in STEM at historically Black colleges and universities. In L. L. Winfield, G. Thomas, L. M. Watkins, & K. S. Wilson-Kennedy (Eds.), *Growing diverse STEM communities: Methodology, impact, and evidence* (pp. 1–8). https://doi.org/10.1021/bk-2019-1328

Toledo, S., & Dubias, J. M. (2017). A learner-centered grading method focused on reaching proficiency with course learning outcomes. *Journal of Chemical Education*, *94*(8), 1043–1050.

Tomasik, J. H., Cottone, K. E., Heethuis, M. T., & Mueller, A. (2013). Development and preliminary impacts of the implementation of an authentic research-based experiment in general chemistry. *Journal of Chemical Education*, *90*(9), 1155–1161, https://doi.org/10.1021/ed300328p

Tomkin, J. H., Beilstein, S. O., Morphew, J. W., & Herman, G. L. (2019). Evidence that communities of practice are associated with active learning in large STEM lectures. *International Journal of STEM Education*, *6*, Article 1. https://doi.org/10.1186/s40594-018-0154-z

Tomovic, M. M. (1994). Undergraduate research—prerequisite for successful lifelong learning. *American Society for Engineering Education Annual Conference Proceedings*, *1*, 1469–1470

Totonchi, D. A., Perez, T., Lee, Y. K., Robinson, K. A., & Linnenbrink-Garcia, L. (2021). The role of stereotype threat in ethnically minoritized students' science motivation: A four-year longitudinal study of achievement and persistence in STEM. *Contemporary Educational Psychology*, *67*, Article 102015. https://doi.org/10.1016/j.cedpsych.2021.102015

Towns, M. H. (2010). Developing learning objectives and assessment plans at a variety of institutions: Examples and case studies. *Journal of Chemical Education*, *87*(1), 91–96. https://doi.org/10.1021/ed8000039

Townsley, M., & Schmid, D. (2020). Alternative grading practices: An entry point for faculty in competency-based education. *The Journal of Competency-Based Education*, *5*(3), *e01219*. https://doi.org/10.1002/cbe2.1219

Transforming Higher Education Multidimensional Evaluation of Teaching. (n.d.). Tools for evaluation. https://teval.net/?tools_for_evaluation

Traweek, S. (1993). An introduction to cultural and social studies of sciences and technologies. *Culture, Medicine, and Psychiatry*, *17*, 3–25. https://doi.org/10.1007/BF01380596

Tripp, B., Cozzens, S., Hrycyk, C., Tanner, K. D., & Schinske, J. N. (2024). Content coverage as persistent exclusionary practice: Investigating perspectives of health professionals on the influence of undergraduate coursework. *CBE—Life Sciences Education*, *23*(1), Article 5.

Trujillo, G., & Tanner, K. D. (2014). Considering the role of affect in learning: Monitoring students' self efficacy, sense of belonging, and science identity. *CBE—Life Sciences Education*, *13*(1), 6–15. https://doi.org/10.1187/cbe.13-12-0241

Tsoi, M. Y., Anzovino, M. E., Erickson, A. H., Forringer, E. R., Henary, E., Lively, A., Morton, M. S., Perell-Gerson, K. L., Perrine, S., Villanueva, O., Whitney, M., & Woodbridge, C. M. (2019). Variations in implementation of specifications grading in STEM courses. *Georgia Journal of Science*, *77*(2), Article 10. https://digitalcommons.gaacademy.org/gjs/vol77/iss2/10

Turner, N., & Farooqi, M. (2017). Campus climate survey paints grim picture of students' emotional safety, sense of belonging at American University. *The Eagle*. https://www.theeagleonline.com/article/2017/10/american-university-campus-climate-survey-shows-lack-of-emotional-safety-sense-of-belonging-among-students-of-color

Turner, S., & Bound, J. (2002). Closing the gap or widening the divide: The effects of the GI Bill and World War II on the educational outcomes of black Americans. *The Journal of Economic History*, *63*(1), 145–177.

Turochy E., Ballesteros, L., Nelson, T. N. T., Perez, M., Estes, K., Poleacovschi, C., Doran, E., & Yuen, T. (2023). Stereotypes and stereotype threats experienced by Latinx undergraduate engineering students. *International Journal of Engineering Education*, *39*(5), 1181–1195.

Tuthill, M. C., & Berestecky, J. M. (2017). Integrating undergraduate research at two-year colleges. *Journal of College Science Teaching*, *46*(4). https://doi.org/10.2505/4/jcst17_046_04_12

Twombly, S., & Townsend, B. K. (2008). Community college faculty what we know and need to know. *Community College Review*, *36*(1), 5–24. https://doi.org/10.1177/0091552108319538

University of California, Davis. (n.d.). Know your students. https://cee.ucdavis.edu/know-your-students

University of California, Santa Barbara. (n.d.). Data dashboards. https://otl.ucsb.edu/data-dashboards

University of Nebraska-Lincoln. (n.d.). Course insights. https://analytics.unl.edu/

University System of Georgia. (n.d.). *Board of regents policy manual: 3.3 curriculum*. https://www.usg.edu/policymanual/section3/C338

Upadhyay, B., Atwood, E., & Tharu, B. (2020). Actions for sociopolitical consciousness in a high school science class: A case study of ninth grade class with predominantly indigenous students. *Journal of Research in Science Teaching*, *57*(7), 1119–1147. https://doi.org/10.1002/tea.21626

Urban Institute. (2024). *Student-parent families at the center*. https://www.urban.org/projects/student-parent-families-center

U.S. Department of Education (ED). (2023). Upward bound program. https://www.ed.gov/grants-and-programs/grants-higher-education/trio/upward-bound-program

___. (2024a). Ronald E. McNair Postbaccalaureate Achievement Program. https://www2.ed.gov/programs/triomcnair/index.html

___. (2024b). TRIO home page. https://www.ed.gov/grants-and-programs/grants-higher-education/trio-home-page

U.S. Department of Health and Human Services. (2024). *Building Infrastructure Leading to Diversity (BUILD) initiative*. National Institute of General Medical Sciences. https://www.nigms.nih.gov/training/dpc/Pages/build.aspx

Uttamchandani, S. (2018). Equity in the learning sciences: Recent themes and pathways. In J. Kay & R. Luckin (Eds.), *Rethinking learning in the digital age: Making the learning sciences count, 13th International Conference of the Learning Sciences (ICLS) 2018, Volume 1*. International Society of the Learning Sciences. https://doi.dx.org/10.22318/cscl2018.480

van Barneveld, A., & DeWaard, H. (2021). Preclass surveys to inform course design. In *Designing courses with digital technologies* (pp. 149–153). Routledge.

Van Dusen, B., Nissen, J., Talbot, R. M., Huvard, H., & Shultz, M. (2021). A QuantCrit investigation of society's educational debts due to racism and sexism in chemistry student learning. *Journal of Chemical Education*, *99*(1), 25–34.

Van Noy, M., Trimble, M., Jenkins, D., Barnett, E., & Wachen, J. (2016). Guided pathways to careers: Four dimensions of structure in community college career-technical programs. *Community College Review*, *44*(4), 263–285. https://doi.org/10.1177/0091552116652939

Van Noy, M., & Zeidenberg, M. (2014). [Hidden STEM knowledge producers: Community colleges' multiple contributions to STEM education and workforce development]. Commissioned paper prepared for the Committee on Barriers and Opportunities in Completing 1- and 4-Year STEM Degrees, National Academy of Sciences.

___. (2017). Community college pathways to STEM workforce: What are they, who follows them, and how? In D. J. Smith & S. Sarobin (Eds.), *Preparing a STEM workforce through career-technical education: New directions for community colleges* (No. 178, pp. 9–22). Jossey Bass.

Van Vliet, E. A., Winnips, J. C., & Brouwer, N. (2015). Flipped-class pedagogy enhances student metacognition and collaborative-learning strategies in higher education but effect does not persist. *CBE—Life Sciences Education*, *14*(3), Article 26.

Vega, Y., & Meaders, C. L. (2023). Have you heard about this? An exploration of instructor communication about campus resources to students in biology courses. *Journal of Research in Science, Mathematics, and Technology Education*, 6(2), 41–64.

Velasco, T., Fink, J., Bedoya, M., & Jenkins, D. (2024). *Tracking transfer four year institutional effectiveness in broadening bachelor's degree attainment.* CCRC. https://ccrc.tc.columbia.edu/media/k2/attachments/tracking-transfer-four-year-institutional-effectiveness.pdf

Vélez-Ibáñez, C. G., & Greenberg, J. B. (1992). Formation and transformation of funds of knowledge among U.S. Mexican households. *Anthropology & Education Quarterly*, *23*(4), 313–335. https://doi.org/10.1525/aeq.1992.23.4.05x1582v

Vermunt, J. D. (1996). Metacognitive, cognitive, and affective aspects of learning styles and strategies: A phenomenographic analysis. *Higher Education*, *31*(1), 25–50. https://doi.org/10.1007/BF00129106

Vescio, V., Ross, D., & Adams, A. (2008). A review of research on the impact of professional learning communities on teaching practice and student learning. *Teaching and Teacher Education*, *24*(1), 80–91.

Vican, S., Friedman, A., & Andreasen, R. (2020). Metrics, money, and managerialism: Faculty experiences in competing logics in higher education. *The Journal of Higher Education*, *91*(1), 139–164. https://doi.org/10.1080/00221546.2019.1615332

Villa, E. Q., Kephart, K., Gates, A. Q., Thiry, H., & Hug, S. (2013). Affinity research groups in practice: Apprenticing students in research. *Journal of Engineering Education, 102*(3), 444–466. https://doi.org/10.1002/jee.20016

Villalobos, C., Garza, G., Setayesh, S., Fernandez, L., Balogh, A., Serbin, K. S., & Huber, T. J. (2024). Our never-ending pathway to innovate calculus 1: Course coordination and active learning to specifications grading and growth mindset. *PRIMUS*, 1–17. https://doi.org/10.1080/10511970.2024.2352874

Villalobos, C., Kim, H. W., Huber, T. J., Knobel, R., Setayesh, S., Sasidharan, L., Galstyan, A., & Balogh, A. (2021). Coordinating STEM core courses for student success. *Primus*, *31*(3-5), 316–329. https://doi.org/10.1080/10511970.2020.1793855

Villanueva, I., Gelles, L. A., Di Stefano, M., Smith, B., Tull, R. G., Lord, S. M., Benson, L., Hunt, A. T., Riley, D. M., & Ryan, G. W. (2018). *What does hidden curriculum in engineering look like and how can it be explored?* Paper presented at 2018 ASEE Annual Conference & Exposition, Salt Lake City, Utah, USA. https://doi.org/10.18260/1-2--31234

Villanueva Alarcón, I., & Muñoz, J. A. (2024). Exploring the hidden realities of Latinx/e contingent faculty in STEM. *Journal of Latinos and Education*, *23*(2), 905–913. https://doi.org/10.1080/15348431.2023.2175683

Vito, M., Ramirez, M., & Gunder, A. (2024). [Bridging innovation and access: Academic innovation to advance student success in undergraduate STEM education]. Commissioned paper prepared for the Committee on Equitable and Effective Teaching in Undergraduate STEM Education: A Framework for Insitutions, Educators, and Disciplines. The National Academies Press.

Vogel, S., & Schwabe, L. (2016). Learning and memory under stress: Implications for the classroom. *npj Science of Learning*, *1*, Article 16011. https://doi.org/10.1038/npjscilearn.2016.11

Voigt, M. (2022). A quantitative exploration of queer-spectrum students' experiences in introductory undergraduate mathematics courses. *PLoS One, 17*(10), e0275325.

___. (July 2024). Identifying queer discourses and navigational strategies in mathematics for undergraduate STEM students. *Frontiers in Education*, *9*, p. 1442806.

von Hoene, L. M. (2020). From orientations to outcomes: Articulating a comprehensive and systematic approach to preparing future higher education instructors. *New Directions for Teaching and Learning*, *2020*(163), 13–23. https://doi.org/10.1002/tl.20406

Wafubwa, R. N., & Csíkos, C. (2022). Impact of formative assessment instructional approach on students' mathematics achievement and their metacognitive awareness. *International Journal of Instruction*, *15*(2), 119–138.

Walling, C. L. (2023). *Bridging the gap for contingent faculty: An analysis of the professional development and growth resources used in public universities across Michigan* [Doctoral dissertation, University of Toledo].

Walton Family Foundation. (2023, December 5). Majority of Gen Z interested in STEM, but schools struggle to provide adequate support. https://www.waltonfamilyfoundation.org/about-us/newsroom/majority-of-gen-z-interested-in-stem-but-schools-struggle-to-provide-adequate-support

Walton, G. M., & Cohen, G. L. (2011). A brief social-belonging intervention improves academic and health outcomes of minority students. *Science*, *331*(6023), 1447–1451. https://doi.org/10.1126/science.1198364

Walton, G. M., Murphy, M. C., & Ryan, A. M. (2015). Stereotype threat in organizations: Implications for equity and performance. *Annual Review of Organizational Psychology and Organizational Behavior*, 2(1), 523–550. https://doi.org/10.1146/annurev-orgpsych-032414-111322

Walton, G. M., Murphy, M. C., Logel, C., Yeager, D. S., Goyer, J. P., Brady, S. T., Emerson, K. T. U., Paunesku, D., Fotuhi, O., Blodorn, A., Boucher, K. L., Carter, E. R., Gopalan, M., Henderson, A., Kroeper, K. M., Murdock-Perriera, L. A., Reeves, S. L., Ablorh, T. T., Ansari, S., Chen, S., ... Krol, N. (2023). Where and with whom does a brief social-belonging intervention promote progress in college? *Science*, *380*(6644), 499–505. https://doi.org/10.1126/science.ade4420

Walvoord, B. E., & Anderson, V. J. (2010). *Effective grading: A tool for learning and assessment in college*. John Wiley & Sons.

Wang, M. C., Haertel, G. D., & Walberg, H. J. (1990). What influences learning? A content analysis of review literature. *Journal of Educational Research*, *84*(1), 30–43. https://doi.org/10.1080/00220671.1990.10885988

Wang, X. (2013a). Baccalaureate expectations of community college students: Socio-demographic, motivational, and contextual influences. *Teachers College Record*, *115*(4), 1–39. https://doi.org/10.1177/016146811311500402

___. (2013b). Modeling entrance into STEM fields of study among students beginning at community colleges and four-year institutions. *Research in Higher Education, 54*, 664–692. https://doi.org/10.1007/s11162-013-9291-x

___. (2015). Pathway to a baccalaureate in STEM fields: Are community colleges a viable route and does early STEM momentum matter? *Educational Evaluation and Policy Analysis*, *37*(3), 376–393. https://doi.org/10.3102/0162373714552561

___. (2017). Toward a holistic theoretical model of momentum for community college student success. In M. Paulsen (Ed.), *Higher education: Handbook of theory and research* (Vol. 32, pp. 259–308). Springer.

___. (2020). *On my own: The challenge and promise of building equitable STEM transfer pathways*. Harvard Education Press.

Wang, X., Chan, H. Y., Soffa, S. J., & Nachman, B. R. (2017a). A nuanced look at women in STEM fields at two-year colleges: Factors that shape female students' transfer intent. *Frontiers in Psychology*, *8*. https://doi.org/10.3389/fpsyg.2017.00146

Wang, X., Sun, N., & Wickersham, K. (2017b). Turning math remediation into "homeroom": Contextualization as a motivational environment for community college students in remedial math. *The Review of Higher Education*, *40*(3), 427–464. https://doi.org/10.1353/rhe.2017.0014

Wang, X., Wickersham, K., Lee, S. Y., Lor, N. B., Gaskew, A., & Prevost, A. (2020). The road to becoming a scientist: A mixed-methods investigation of supports and barriers experienced by first-year community college students. *Teachers College Record*, *122*(2), 1–50. https://doi.org/10.1177/016146812012200208

Wang, Y., Apkarian, N., Dancy, M. H., Henderson, C., Johnson, E., Raker, J. R., & Stains, M. (2024). A national snapshot of introductory chemistry instructors and their instructional practices. *Journal of Chemical Education*, *101*(4), 1457–1468. https://doi.org/10.1021/acs.jchemed.4c00040

Wapman, K. H., Zhang, S., Clauset, A., & Larremore, D. B. (2022). Quantifying hierarchy and dynamics in US faculty hiring and retention. *Nature*, *610*, 120–127. https://doi.org/10.1038/s41586-022-05222-x

Ward, C., Topham, T., Dixon, H., Peterson, A., Rieder, J., Duffin, B., & Coburn, J. (2024). Culturally inclusive STEM learning: Mentored internships for Native American undergraduates at a tribal college and a university. *Journal of Diversity in Higher Education*, *17*(3), 443–455. https://doi.org/10.1037/dhe0000413

Watson, C. N., Duran, P., Castillo, A., Fuller, E., Potvin, G., & Kramer, L. (2023). The supportive role of active learning in a calculus course on low precalculus proficiency students. *International Journal of Mathematical Education in Science and Technology*, 1–22. https://doi.org/10.1080/0020739X.2023.2255189

Weaver, G. C., Austin, A. E., Greenhoot, A. F., & Finkelstein, N. D. (2020). Establishing a better approach for evaluating teaching: The TEval Project. *Change: The Magazine of Higher Learning*, *52*(3), 25–31. https://doi.org/10.1080/00091383.2020.1745575

Webb, D. J., & Paul, C. A. (2023). Attributing equity gaps to course structure in introductory physics. *Physical Review Physics Education Research*, *19*(2), 020126. https://doi.org/10.1103/PhysRevPhysEducRes.19.020126

Webster-Wright, A. (2009). Reframing professional development through understanding authentic professional learning. *Review of Educational Research*, *79*(2), 702–739. https://doi.org/10.3102/0034654308330970

Weeden, K. A., Gelbgiser, D., & Morgan, S. L. (2020). Pipeline dreams: Occupational plans and gender differences in STEM major persistence and completion. *Sociology of Education*, *93*(4), 297–314. https://doi.org/10.1177/0038040720928484

Wei, C. A., & Woodin, T. (2011). Undergraduate research experiences in biology: Alternatives to the apprenticeship model. *CBE—Life Sciences Education*, *10*(2), 123–131. https://doi.org/10.1187/cbe.11-03-0028

Wei, X., Christiano, E. R., Yu, J. W., Blackorby, J., Shattuck, P., & Newman, L. A. (2014). Postsecondary pathways and persistence for STEM versus non-STEM majors: Among college students with an autism spectrum disorder. *Journal of Autism and Developmental Disorders*, *44*, 1159–1167.

Weinstein, C. E., Husman, J., & Dierking, D. R., (2000). Self-regulation interventions with a focus on learning strategies. In M. Boekaerts, P. R. Pintrich, & M. Zeidner (Eds.), *Handbook of self-regulation* (pp. 727–747). Academic Press.

Wells, R. S., Chen, L., Bettencourt, G. M., & Haas, S. (2023). Reconsidering rural-nonrural college enrollment gaps: The role of socioeconomic status in geographies of opportunity. *Research in Higher Education*, *64*(8), 1089–1112.

Wells, R. S., Manly, C. A., Kommers, S., & Kimball, E. (2019). Narrowed gaps and persistent challenges: Examining rural-nonrural disparities in postsecondary outcomes over time. *American Journal of Education*, *126*(1), 1–31.

Wenger, E. (1999). *Communities of practice: Learning, meaning, and identity.* Cambridge University Press.

Wenger, E., McDermott, R., & Snyder, W. M. (2002). *Cultivating communities of practice: A guide to managing knowledge.* Harvard Business Review Press.

Wenger, E., & Nückles, M. (2015). Knowledge acquisition or participation in communities of practice? Academics' metaphors of teaching and learning at the university. *Studies in Higher Education*, *40*(4), 624–643.

Werth, A., West, C. G., Lewandowski, H. J. (2022). Impacts on student learning, confidence, and affect in a remote, large-enrollment, course-based undergraduate research experience in physics. *Physical Review Physics Education Research*, *18*, 010129. https://doi.org/10.1103/PhysRevPhysEducRes.18.010129

West, T. M. (2019). A survey of college students with learning disabilities and attention deficit hyperactivity disorder to identify their relationship and use of college disability resource centers. *All Graduate Plan B and other Reports*. Utah State University. https://digitalcommons.usu.edu/gradreports/1395

Weston, T. J., Seymour, E., Koch, A. K., & Drake, B. M. (2019). Weed-out classes and their consequences. In E. Seymour & A.-B. Hunter (Eds.), *Talking about leaving revisited: Persistence, relocation, and loss in undergraduate STEM education* (pp. 197–243). Springer International Publishing. https://doi.org/10.1007/978-3-030-25304-2_7

Wheeler, L. B., & Bach, D. (2021). Understanding the impact of educational development interventions on classroom instruction and student success. *International Journal for Academic Development, 26*(1), 24–40.

Whitcomb, K. M., Cwik, S., & Singh, C. (2021). Not all disadvantages are equal: Racial/ethnic minority students have largest disadvantage among demographic groups in both STEM and non-STEM GPA. *AERA Open*, *7*, 23328584211059824. https://journals.sagepub.com/doi/10.1177/23328584211059823

White, J. W., & Lowenthal, P. R. (2011). Minority college students and tacit "codes of power": Developing academic discourses and identities. *Review of Higher Education: Journal of the Association for the Study of Higher Education*, *34*(2), 283–318. https://doi.org/10.1353/rhe.2010.0028

White, K. N., Vincent-Layton, K., & Villarreal, B. (2020). Equitable and inclusive practices designed to reduce equity gaps in undergraduate chemistry courses. *Journal of Chemical Education*, *98*(2), 330–339. https://doi.org/10.1021/acs.jchemed.0c01094

White, M. M., Olson, S. J., & Canning, E. A. (2024). Disentangling the impact of instructor mindset and demeanor on student experiences. *Motivation Science*.

The White House. (2024, May 16). *The economics of HBCUs*. https://www.whitehouse.gov/cea/written-materials/2024/05/16/the-economics-of-hbcus/#:~:text=Although%20they%20make%20up%20less,degrees%20earned%20by%20Black%20students

Whitehead, A. (2018). Examining influence of family, friends, and educators on first-year college student selection STEM major selection. *Journal of Mason Graduate Research*, *5*(2), 58–84.

Wickersham, K., & Wang, X. (2016). What's life got to do with it? The role of life experiences in shaping female community college students' transfer intent in STEM fields of study. *Community College Journal of Research and Practice*, *40*(12), 1001–1012. https://doi.org/10.1080/10668926.2016.1211039

Wickersham, K. R. (2020). Where to go from here? Toward a model of 2-year college students' postsecondary pathway selection. *Community College Review*, *48*(2), 107–132. https://doi.org/10.1177/0091552119880941

Wieman, C. (2017). *Improving how universities teach science: Lessons from the science education initiative*. Harvard University Press.

Wieman, C. E., Rieger, G. W., & Heiner, C. E. (2014). Physics exams that promote collaborative learning. *The Physics Teacher*, *52*(1), 51–53.

Wiggins, G. P., & McTighe, J. (2005). *Understanding by design*. Association for Supervision and Curriculum Development.

Wilder, C. S. (2013). *Ebony and ivy: Race, slavery, and the troubled history of America's universities*. Bloomsbury Press.

Williams, A. (2021). *Using an assets-based approach to explore Black women's pursuit and persistence in undergraduate STEM majors* [Doctoral dissertation, George Mason University].

Williams, A., & Perry, A. (2020). *Prioritizing equity in dual enrollment* [Policy brief]. Equitable Transitions through Pandemic Disruptions. Education Commission of the States.

Williams, M., Apkarian, N., Uhing, K., Martinez, A. E., Rasmussen, C., & Smith, W. M. (2022). In the driver's seat: Course coordinators as change agents for active learning in university Precalculus to Calculus 2. *International Journal of Research in Undergraduate Mathematics Education*, *8*(1), 121–148. https://doi.org/10.1007/s40753-021-00153-w

Winget, M., & Persky, A. M. (2022, December) A practical review of mastery learning. American *Journal of Pharmaceutical Education*, *86*(10). https://doi.org/10.5688/ajpe8906

Wingfield, A. H. (2024). Faculty of color and the changing university. In *Conditionally accepted: Navigating higher education from the margins* (pp. 165–168). University of Texas Press.

Winkelmes, M.-A. (2019). Introduction: The story of TILT and its emerging uses in higher education. In M.-A. Winkelmes, A. Boye, & S. Tapp, (Eds.), *Transparent design in higher education teaching and leadership: A guide to implementing the transparency framework institution-wide to improve learning and retention* (pp. 1–14). Stylus Publishing.

Winkelmes, M. A., Boye, A., & Tapp, S. (Eds.). (2019). *Transparent design in higher education teaching and leadership: A guide to implementing the transparency framework institution-wide to improve learning and retention*. Taylor & Francis.

Winstone, N. E., & Boud, D. (2020). The need to disentangle assessment and feedback in higher education. *Studies in Higher Education*, *47*(3), 657–667.

Winter, J., & Cotton, D. (2012). Making the hidden curriculum visible: Sustainability literacy in higher education. *Environmental Education Research*, *18*(6), 783–796.

Winter, K., Kent, J., & Bradshaw, R. (2018). *Preparing future faculty: A framework for program design and evaluation at the university level*. Council of Graduate Schools.

Wofford, A. M., & Gutzwa, J. A. (2022). Funds of science identity: Toward an asset-based framework for undergraduate STEM research and praxis. *Journal of Women and Minorities in Science and Engineering*, *28*(3), 59–81. https://doi.org/10.1615/JWomenMinorScienEng.2022036454

Wolfe, P. (2006). Settler colonialism and the elimination of the native. *Journal of Genocide Research*, *8*(4), 387–409. https://doi.org/10.1080/14623520601056240

Wolniak, G. C., & Engberg, M. E. (2019). Do "high-impact" college experiences affect early career outcomes? *The Review of Higher Education*, *42*(3), 825–858.

Wolniak, G. C., George, C. E., & Nelson, G. R. (2018). The emerging differential tuition era among US public universities. In *Under pressure* (pp. 191–214). Brill.

Won, S., & Chang, Y. (2024). Antecedents and consequences of academic help-seeking in online STEM learning. *Frontiers in Psychology*, *15*, 1438299.

Woolf, K., McManus, I. C., Gill, D., & Dacre, J. (2009). The effect of a brief social intervention on the examination results of UK medical students: A cluster randomised controlled trial. *BMC Medical Education*, *9*, Article 35. https://doi.org/10.1186/1472-6920-9-35

Wright, C. D., Eddy, S. L., Wenderoth, M. P., Abshire, E., Blankenbiller, M., & Brownell, S. E. (2016). Cognitive difficulty and format of exams predicts gender and socioeconomic gaps in exam performance of students in introductory biology courses. *CBE—Life Sciences Education*, *15*(2), Article 23. https://www.lifescied.org/doi/10.1187/cbe.15-12-0246

Wright, M. C. (2023). *Centers for teaching and learning: The new landscape in higher education*. Johns Hopkins University Press.

Wright-Kim, J. (2022). The impact of offering baccalaureate degrees on institutional enrollment in community colleges. *Community College Review, 51*(1), 3–29. https://doi.org/10.1177/00915521221125500

Wu, J., Cropps, T., Phillips, C. M. L., Boyle, S., & Pearson, Y. E. (2023). Applicant qualifications and characteristics in STEM faculty hiring: An analysis of faculty and administrator perspectives. *International Journal of STEM Education, 10*, Article 41. https://doi.org/10.1186/s40594-023-00431-w

Xie, Y., Fang, M., & Shauman, K. (2015). STEM education. *Annual Review of Sociology, 41*(1), 331–357. https://www.annualreviews.org/content/journals/10.1146/annurev-soc-071312-145659

Xu, C., & Lastrapes, R. E. (2022). Impact of STEM sense of belonging on career interest: The role of STEM attitudes. *Journal of Career Development, 49*(6), 1215–1229.

Yao, C., Follmer Greenhoot, A., Mack, K., Myrick, C., Poolaw, J., Powell, L., & Yarger, L. (2023, October). Humanizing STEM education: An ecological systems framework for educating the whole student. *Frontiers in Education, 8*, p. 1175871.

Yeager, D. S., & Dweck, C. S. (2012). Mindsets that promote resilience: When students believe that personal characteristics can be developed. *Educational Psychologist, 47*(4), 302–314. https://doi.org/10.1080/00461520.2012.722805

Yee, M. (2019). Why 'safe spaces' are important for mental health—especially on college campuses. *Healthline*. https://www.healthline.com/health/mental-health/safe-spaces-college#1

Yee, S. P., Deshler, J., Rogers, K. C., Petrulis, R., Potvin, C. D., & Sweeney, J. (2021). Bridging the gap between observation protocols and formative feedback. *Journal of Mathematics Teacher Education, 25*(2), 217–245. https://doi.org/10.1007/s10857-020-09485-x

Yee, S. P., Hauk, S., Lopez Gonzalez, T., & Wang, J. (2023a). College mathematics instructor professional development providers: Who are they? *School Science and Mathematics, 123*(2), 39–41. https://doi.org/10.1111/ssm.12571

Yee, S. P., Papalia, N., Deshler, J., Rogers, K. C., Lamarche, A., & Petrulis, R. (2023b). Graduate student instructor peer-mentoring: Design and impact. *Problems, Resources, and Issues in Mathematics Undergraduate Studies (PRIMUS), 34*(7), 693–713. https://doi.org/10.1080/10511970.2023.2241459

Yee, S. P., Rogers, K. C., Miller, E., & Galvin, T. (2022). Collegiate mathematics observation protocols: Current characteristics and desired foci. *International Journal of Research in Undergraduate Mathematics Education, 10*, 318–249. https://doi.org/10.1007/s40753-022-00199-4

Yee, S. P., Wang, J., Hauk, S., & Lopez Gonzalez, T. (2023c). Providers of professional development for novice college mathematics instructors: Perspectives and values about teaching and learning. In S. Cook, B. Katz, and D. Moore-Russo (Eds.), *Proceedings of the 25th Annual Conference on Research in Undergraduate Mathematics Education* (pp. 420–428). Omaha, Nebraska, USA.

Yik, B. J., Raker, J. R., Apkarian, N., Stains, M., Henderson, C., Dancy, M. H., & Johnson, E. (2022). Evaluating the impact of malleable factors on percent time lecturing in gateway chemistry, mathematics, and physics courses. *International Journal of STEM Education, 9*, Article 15. https://doi.org/10.1186/s40594-022-00333-3

Yother, T. L., Dubikovsky, S., Ropp, T., Thom, J. M., Wang, P. H., Hagovsky, T. C., Davis, J. M., & Barnes, D. (2022). Identification of core competencies for bachelor of science degrees in aeronautical engineering technology. *Journal of Engineering Technology, 39*(1), 42–55.

Yuen, V. (2020). *The $78 billion community college funding shortfall.* Center for American Progress. https://www.americanprogress.org/wp-content/uploads/sites/2/2020/10/Community-College-Shortfall6.pdf

Zhang, C., Kuncel, N. R., & Sackett, P. R. (2020). The process of attrition in pre-medical studies: A large-scale analysis across 102 schools. *PLoS One, 15*(12), e0243546.

Zhang, Y. L. (2022). Early academic momentum: Factors contributing to community college transfer students' STEM degree attainment. *Journal of College Student Retention: Research, Theory & Practice*, *23*(4), 873–902.

Zimmerman, B. J. (2000). Self-efficacy: An essential motive to learn. *Contemporary Educational Psychology*, *25*(1), 82–91.

Zimmerman, J. (2020). *The amateur hour: A history of college teaching in America.* Johns Hopkins University Press.

Zinth, J. D. (2014). *Increasing student access and success in dual enrollment programs: 13 model state-level policy components.* Education Commission of the States.

___. (2019, August). 50-state comparison: Dual/concurrent enrollment policies 2019. https://reports.ecs.org/comparisons/dual-concurrent-enrollment-2019

Ziori, E., & Dienes, Z. (2008). How does prior knowledge affect implicit and explicit concept learning? *Quarterly Journal of Experimental Psychology*, *61*(4), 601–624.

Zydney, A. L., Bennett, J. S., Shahid, A., & Bauer, K. W. (2002). Impact of undergraduate research experience in engineering. *Journal of Engineering Education*, *91*(2), 151–157. https://doi.org/10.1002/j.2168-9830.2002.tb00687.x

Appendix A

Public Comments on Draft Report and Committee Response

METHODOLOGY

The Committee recognized that obtaining feedback from a broad range of stakeholders and experts would be crucial for the framework's success. For this reason, the Board on Science Education solicited feedback on a discussion draft of this report via

- **A publicly available online questionnaire** that was open for seven and a half weeks. It featured scaled-choice (close-ended) and open-ended questions about the framework, open-ended questions about supporting equitable and effective teaching, and screening and demographic questions. The survey recorded 115 respondents with 111 maximum responses for any one question. Not all respondents answered every question.
- **Feedback at two meetings** (a December 2023 hybrid public input session[1] and a December 2023 meeting of members of the Roundtable on Systemic Change in Undergraduate STEM Education[2]).

[1] The agenda and recordings from the December 5–6, 2023 meeting are available at https://www.nationalacademies.org/event/40702_12-2023_equitable-and-effective-teaching-in-undergraduate-stem-education-a-framework-for-institutions-educators-and-disciplines-meeting-5-and-public-input-session

[2] More information about the Roundtable on Systematic Change in Undergraduate STEM Education is available at https://www.nationalacademies.org/our-work/roundtable-on-systemic-change-in-undergraduate-stem-education

- **Organizational submissions** (17 groups and individuals within organizations [listed in Table A-1] that provide or advocate for undergraduate STEM education submitted comments).

Given the response rates and representation across institution types, roles, and respondent demographics, disaggregating any subgroup with statistical significance was difficult. However, this analysis did use disaggregation to identify broad themes.

The analysis of the open-ended responses on the questionnaire, meeting summaries, and organizational submissions took this approach:

1. Each response was coded in a matrix, organized by survey question and thematic categories.
2. Category responses were reviewed to discover prominent themes within categories.
3. Categories and themes were identified by survey question (e.g., What's missing from Principle 3?).
4. Top overarching themes for the draft report, framework, and principles for systemic change in undergraduate science, technology, engineering, and mathematics (STEM) education were identified and synthesized across all questions.

Overall, the public feedback was positive, with no significant requests for changes to the content or organization of the Principles for Equitable and Effective Teaching, although there were suggestions to improve the draft.

This summary of the public input on the discussion draft includes five overarching themes, broad themes for principles and practices, suggested actions for departments and institutions, and recommendations for strengthening the Principles for Equitable and Effective Teaching in undergraduate STEM education. It also includes the Committee's responses based on the feedback received.

FIVE OVERARCHING THEMES

1. **Offer More Contextualization.** Respondents asked for more emphasis on the critical importance of equitable and effective STEM education in the broader global context, both at the macro level and for individual students. They wanted more discussion about the current state of equity and effectiveness in undergraduate STEM teaching. They indicated a need to incorporate varied perspectives and partnerships (including with students) to improve teaching.

2. **Improve the Framework.** Respondents offered suggestions to improve the framework to achieve the goal of equitable and effective STEM education:
    - **Go beyond the classroom.** To drive meaningful change, take a bolder and broader approach to address out-of-classroom challenges, rather than focusing solely on classroom-dominant solutions.
    - **Make the Principles for Equitable and Effective Teaching actionable—and provide examples.** Convey what is realistic and attainable. Frame the Principles with clear context, supported by evidence-based theories, and include thorough references and illustrative examples. Provide more clarification on existing effective efforts, identify the stakeholders responsible for specific practices, and ensure the language is accessible to non-education stakeholders. Respondents repeatedly emphasized the need to illustrate concepts and practices with concrete examples of implementation across modalities and institution types, particularly for faculty; responsibilities of stakeholders at all levels; and ideas for how the examples can be scaled.
    - **Integrate the evidence.** Better connect the evidence and citations with the practices in the framework, rather than as a separate section. Survey respondents offered suggestions for more evidence and suggested that evidence must better represent diverse schools.
    - **Convey the interconnectedness of the Principles.** Acknowledge that the Principles do not operate in isolation and often overlap with each other. For example, integrate the messages about belonging to messages about engaging in disciplinary learning.
3. **Address the Broader Ecosystem.** Across all forms of public input, respondents indicated that it is imperative to address the broader ecosystem (including K–12, the workforce, disciplinary organizations, and nongovernment organizations):
    - **Emphasize institutions and departments.** Highlight the role of institutional and departmental policies in implementing equitable and effective teaching. Acknowledge that classroom practices alone will not adequately address this challenge. Clarify institutional and departmental responsibilities more broadly across the disciplines, while still reflecting discipline-specific needs.
    - **Connect to K–12 education.** Consider the connection to K–12 education (including Next Generation Science

Standards [NGSS]) and partner with K–12 systems to provide guidance on how to address gaps in prior knowledge and recruit more students into STEM.
- **Increase focus on community colleges and career and technical education.** Expand discussion on connections with community colleges, particularly the emerging role of community college prerequisite work, and the relevance of career and technical education.
- **Broaden organizational recommendations.** Involve professional societies in enacting the recommendations and encourage federal agencies and accrediting associations to update standards that incentivize equitable and effective teaching practices.

4. **Focus on Faculty.** Respondents overwhelmingly emphasized the critical role of faculty in addressing equitable and effective STEM education. They suggested adding a faculty-specific principle that calls for directly supporting and providing professional development for all faculty types, informed by broader and more representative faculty input:
   - **Broaden the traditional concept of faculty.** Include teaching assistants, adjunct, and non-tenure-track instructors.
   - **Align faculty incentives.** Create a stronger alignment between equitable and effective teaching and career advancement. Reform teaching evaluations incorporated in review, promotion, and tenure decisions.
   - **Emphasize effective faculty professional development and support.** Consider enriching professional development and other opportunities (e.g., mentors), and include self-reflection and explicit instruction on equitable and effective teaching across all modes of instruction (including laboratory opportunities). Emphasize how student and faculty success are intertwined.
   - **Consider workload and resources.** Pay attention to faculty workload and increase faculty buy-in by ensuring they have the time, resources, and professional learning to support effective implementation. This is critical—and will require clear instructional guidance for institutions.
5. **Coordinate Curriculum Reform.** Respondents stressed a need for curricular reform, with student input, that emphasizes accessible and effective active learning with real-world opportunities. They suggested explicitly recognizing that core STEM content, skills, and knowledge are necessary for STEM success and that equitable and effective teaching should not sacrifice rigor:

- **Address discipline-specific concerns.** Make interdisciplinary connections, but attend to discipline-specific issues, particularly requirements to address the leaky STEM pipeline, such as math reform.
- **Personalize learning.** Maintain high standards while emphasizing the need for pedagogical approaches that personalize learning to accommodate diverse needs. Incorporate progressive, evidence-based instructional techniques. Consider, but do not overemphasize, demographic identifiers.
- **Make more real-world and workforce connections.** Add more overt links to the workforce and to real-world experiences and opportunities, including experiential and lifelong learning. Emphasize the importance of instructional labs for active learning and of ensuring quality instruction in all types of environments.

Committee Response

The final report offers more contextualization to demonstrate where the Principles for Equitable and Effective Teaching fit into the overall system of higher education. It includes a chapter on using the Principles to improve learning experiences (Chapter 5). The evidence for the Principles is no longer separated out in a separate section (Chapter 4) and additional language has been added about the interconnections between the principles. Additional material is added about the current state of undergraduate STEM education (Chapters 2 and 3). Additional examples of have been added as has material on community colleges and career and technical education, including discussion of transfer pathways.

Multiple recommendations are included that focus on faculty and other types of instructors. They call for directly supporting and providing professional development for all types of instructors. The definition of instructors used in the report has been explained to be clear that it includes VITAL and tenure track educators. Recommendations also call for academic units and institutions to provide professional learning and development and to support instructors in other ways including by rewarding efforts to improve teaching (and to improve how teaching is evaluated).

Extensive portions of the final report discuss the role of departments and institutions in implementing equitable and effective teaching and clearly state that classroom practices alone will not adequately address this challenge (Chapters 6–9). Recommendations for funders and disciplinary societies have been included.

BROAD THEMES FOR PRINCIPLES AND PRACTICES

Examples and Guidance Needed. The public input indicated a need for more examples of how to implement concepts and practices effectively across modalities and institution types. Some respondents expressed concern that the practices across *Principle 3: Affective and social dimensions* and *Principle 6: Flexibility and responsiveness* may be challenging in asynchronous learning environments.

High-Priority Actions. Respondents suggested several high-priority actions, with diverse environments and stakeholders in mind. Their message: Avoid one-size-fits-all approaches. Stay flexible while advocating for change. Call for critical funding and support. Specifically:

- **Stress development and support for all faculty types, including adjunct and non-tenure-track instructors.** Emphasize effective and equitable instructional practices, clarify institutional expectations for career success, foster professional learning communities, share resources, and assign instructors to courses with intentionality.
- **Emphasize student supports and opportunities.** Stress the need for a coordinated and comprehensive approach to holistic student support (e.g., academic, financial, health, and beyond) and the importance of understanding diverse prior experiences and flexibility to accommodate cultural differences and various learning needs.
- **Attend to pedagogy and curriculum.** Conduct ongoing curriculum reviews at the course, departmental, and institutional levels to address inequitable practices, such as "weed-out classes." Some respondents highlighted math requirements as a barrier to success in STEM and recommended greater connection with and access to workforce/research opportunities. Some advocated for a broader examination of instruction, beyond STEM majors, and incorporating practices like peer learning and critical thinking, which are not discipline specific.
- **Consider accountability.** Vary accountability measures, such as institutional coordination and faculty collaboration for assessment development and improved faculty evaluation. Assess and align accountability from classrooms to institutions, which involves multiple measures and a flexible data system that allows disaggregation based on diverse and evolving subgroup definitions.
- **Take a systems approach.** Examine efforts comprehensively, both within and beyond the institution, considering broader community involvement. Align goals and efforts across the entire learner-to-earner continuum, beginning in K–12. Avoid operating in isolation; instead, institutions should actively seek partnership and input from students, faculty, nonprofits, and other institutions to enhance collaboration and broaden their impact.

Committee Response

More examples of how to use the Principles for Equitable and Effective Teaching effectively in a variety of modalities and institution types are now provided in Chapter 5. VITAL as well as tenure-track faculty are explicitly included in the report. The need for attention to curriculum structures and pathways is now discussed, including weed-out classes and math requirements. Assessment is discussed on various levels as is the role and use of data systems and the importance of disaggregation.

SUGGESTED ACTIONS FOR DEPARTMENTS AND INSTITUTIONS

Many respondents offered similar suggestions for institutions and departments and call for a greater alignment of efforts. They recommended clearly defining the roles of stakeholders and specifying responsibilities, striking a balance between shared responsibility and individual academic freedom.

In general, the public input cautions that the framework puts too much reliance on faculty. Organizational submissions emphasized the need to explicitly call for institutional changes at all levels and hold institutions accountable for nurturing a culture of equitable and effective teaching.

Departmental Actions

Departmental actions that were suggested by respondents included

- **Bolster faculty development** with quality, sustained professional learning for all faculty. Encourage faculty participation and buy-in with incentives and alignment to accountability practices. Build faculty community and interdisciplinary collaboration.
- **Incorporate accountability** by tying faculty evaluations to review, promotion, and tenure decisions that reflect equitable and effective teaching. Articulate and align learning, course, and department outcomes and ensure that outcomes are measured, analyzed, and actionable.
- **Emphasize effective leadership and departmental operations**, including reflection and communication about departmental policies, practices, and resources to enhance equity. Emphasize the importance of diverse hiring and promotion, intentional faculty assignment, and workloads aligned with goals.
- **Scrutinize pedagogy and curriculum** to enhance equity and include culturally relevant lessons and guidance on equitable syllabi, instruction, and classroom norms. Highlight real-world connections

with a balanced and engaging curriculum and address barriers (e.g., whether math is an important gatekeeper across STEM disciplines). Make evidence-based efforts to standardize sections and courses to ensure continuity between professors and reduce duplicative efforts, where appropriate. Include broad perspectives in developing and reviewing curriculum, (e.g., alumni, students, faculty) and consider the outcomes for all students (STEM majors and beyond).

- **Provide whole-student support**, including advising, peer mentors, tutoring for prerequisite/foundational courses, and corequisite support. Approach each student as an individual and focus on the student-teacher relationship.

Committee Response

The report now includes the importance of sustained faculty development and the role of evaluations and rewards in accountability and promotion. The role of departments and other academic units in supporting and encouraging attention to policies and practices that support equitable and effective teaching is included. The need for them to analyze pedagogy and curriculum is also included.

Institutional Actions

Institutional actions that were suggested by respondents included

- **Create incentives and broaden accountability.** Offer robust faculty support and development for cultivating equitable and effective instructional practices, including aligning review, promotion, and tenure decisions with the integration of these Principles and ensuring thorough evaluation of course outcomes. Acknowledge and reward exemplary and equitable teaching practices and extend these efforts to non-tenure-track faculty, including adjuncts. Factor in faculty support and workload considerations throughout these initiatives.
- **Optimize operations.** Remove obstacles for departments and faculty to achieve effective and equitable teaching, which involves incentives, accountability, and resources (funding and time). Ensure that departments, faculty, and students have access to comprehensive support services and institutional policies promote equity and visibly demonstrate the priority of effective and equitable teaching (via aligned policies and accountability measures). Improve the connection to K–12 education via outreach and support.
- **Strengthen communications, engagement, and leadership.** Improve

strategies to articulate a shared and coherent commitment to equitable and effective teaching, considering diverse perspectives from departmental leadership, faculty, and students, while actively involving leaders at all levels of the institution. Some respondents suggested that it is important to hold upper administrators accountable for a commitment to academic excellence.

- **Foster cross-disciplinary and interdisciplinary collaboration.** Prioritize a broad STEM foundation for all students and cultivate cross-disciplinary collaboration among faculty. Focus on building a strong interdisciplinary community committed to equity, with the goal of breaking down institutional silos and promoting collaboration both within and outside STEM disciplines.

Committee Response

The report discusses the important role of institutions and institutional leaders in setting priorities and influencing culture around instruction and student-centered approaches. It discusses the need to offer instructors support to improve their teaching and also the importance of holding people accountable for teaching (Chapter 10).

SUBMISSIONS FROM ORGANIZATIONS AND INDIVIDUALS

TABLE A-1 Submissions from Organizations and Individuals

Organizations and Individuals	Description
Accelerating Systemic Change Network	Members of the working group on Aligning Incentives with Systemic Change
American Physical Society (APS) Programs Department	Comments do not represent the APS position
American Society for Biochemistry and Molecular Biology	Membership organization
Howard Hughes Medical Institute Inclusive Excellence 3 Learning Community Cluster 2	120+ undergraduate STEM educators, administrators, and staff in 14 universities and colleges. Comments represent the opinion of members, not the institute.
National Science Teaching Association Post-Secondary Science Teaching Committee	Faculty from a variety of higher education institutions (community colleges, four-year public colleges and universities, R1 research institutions, and more)

continued

TABLE A-1 Continued

Organizations and Individuals	Description
National Association of Geoscience Teachers	Association of college and university faculty, K–12 teachers, informal educators, graduate and undergraduate students, and geoscience and education professionals.
Portland Community College Center for Teaching and Learning Excellence (CTLE)	Five faculty/staff and two CTLE facilitators
Laura J. Bottomley, Director of Engineering Education at the North Carolina State University	Individual
Clare Carlson and four chemistry education researchers	Michigan State University
James D. DeKloe, Professor of Biological Science, Biotechnology, and Biomanufacturing, Solano Community College	Individual
Douglas K. Duncan, emeritus faculty member in the Department of Astrophysical and Planetary Sciences at the University of Colorado, Boulder	Individual
Nicole LaDue, Geoscience Education Researcher at Northern Illinois University	Individual
Sarah Kinnison, Associate Director of Program Development at Achieving the Dream	Individual, editorial comments
Bruce Nappi, retired educator and engineer	Individual
William (Bill) Penuel, Professor of Learning Sciences and Human Development at the University of Colorado Boulder	Individual, professor in the School of Education and Institute of Cognitive Science
Frank Thorne, Mathematics Professor at the University of South Carolina	Individual
Dave Ucko, President of Museums+*more*	Individual, previously of the National Science Foundation; included overview of Personalized Undergraduate & Lifelong Learning (PULL) STEM Center

Appendix B

Biographies of Committee Members and Staff

COMMITTEE MEMBERS

ARCHIE HOLMES (*Chair*) is the executive vice chancellor for academic affairs at The University of Texas (UT) System and is a professor in the Chandra Family Department of Electrical and Computer Engineering at UT Austin. Throughout his career, he has served as a professor in the Department of Electrical and Computer Engineering at the University of Virginia, vice provost for academic affairs, and vice provost for educational innovation and interdisciplinary studies and associate provost. Among his many accomplishments at the University of Virginia, Holmes led efforts to better integrate academic advising, career advising, and personal development and provide opportunities for students to enhance their education via experiential learning opportunities. At both UT Austin and the University of Virginia, he led or served on numerous committees and task forces related to academic advising, curriculum reform, and student and faculty recruiting. Holmes has received numerous awards for his teaching and advising activities. At UT Austin, he received the Texas Excellence Teaching Award in Engineering and the Gordon T. Lepley IV Endowed Memorial Teaching Award. Holmes received his B.S. and Ph.D. degrees both in electrical engineering from The University of Texas at Austin and The University of California at Santa Barbara, respectively.

TRACIE M. ADDY is the founding director of the Institute for Teaching, Innovation, & Inclusive Pedagogy at Rutgers University-New Brunswick. Until recently she was associate dean of teaching and learning and director of the Center for the Integration of Teaching, Learning, and Scholarship at Lafayette College. She is an invited speaker and facilitator of professional development opportunities for instructors nationally, as well as a scholar in teaching and learning. Addy publishes scholarship of various types such as op-eds, research articles, and learning activities. She is co-author of the books *What Inclusive Instructors Do: Principles and Practices for Excellence in College Teaching* and *Enhancing Inclusive Instruction: Student Perspectives and Practical Approaches for Advancing Equity in Higher Education*. Addy received her Ph.D. in science education from North Carolina State University.

HILLARY BARRON is an assistant professor of biology at Bemidji State University. Her research focuses on creating equitable and culturally responsive science learning opportunities for students. Barron works with faculty and teaching assistants in academic biology to create teaching strategies that center culturally relevant pedagogy, funds of knowledge, and social justice science issues. Her framework for this work, Culturally Responsive Undergraduate Science Education, is a novel approach to biology education. Barron is a descendant of the White Earth Band of Ojibwe and works to support the many Indigenous students at Bemidji State. She received her Ph.D. in science education from the University of Minnesota.

MICHAEL DENNIN is a professor of physics and astronomy and vice provost for teaching and learning at the University of California, Irvine (UCI). He is dedicated to public outreach in the area of science—teaching a number of Massive Open Online Courses, as well as translating educational research into practical applications throughout the university. Dennin also initiated an academic support program, called the Student Successes Initiatives Unit, dedicated to helping first-generation college, low-income, former foster youth, and/or disabled students succeed at UCI. This unit is positioned to help students successfully transition in order to maximize their college experiences so that they can thrive at UCI. He is a recipient of UCI's Senate awards in all three categories: Distinguished Mid-Career Award for Service, Distinguished Faculty Award for Teaching, and Distinguished Assistant Professor Award for Research. Dennin received his M.S. and Ph.D. in physics from the University of California, Santa Barbara.

ERIN E. DORAN is an associate professor in the Department of Educational Leadership and Foundations at the University of Texas at El Paso (UTEP). She is also a Research Affiliate for the Diana Natalicio Institute for Hispanic Student Success at UTEP. Her research focuses on the success of Latinx students, especially in Hispanic Serving Institutions (HSIs) and community colleges. In addition, she studies faculty and culturally relevant pedagogy. Her experience teaching as an adjunct at community colleges influenced her choice of research field. She also has experience working in academic affairs at an HSI. She was named a faculty Fellow of the American Association of Hispanics in Higher Education in 2020. She holds an Ed.D. from the University of Texas at San Antonio in Educational Leadership.

ANNE EGGER is a professor of geological sciences and science and mathematics education at Central Washington University. She also serves as the executive director of the National Association of Geoscience Teachers. Egger's work focuses on professional development for college and university faculty to implement evidence-based and inclusive teaching strategies, with a particular emphasis on science courses for future K–12 teachers. She was elected a fellow of the Geological Society of America, fellow of the American Association for the Advancement of Science, and she served on the National Academies of Sciences, Engineering, and Medicine's Committee on Science Investigations and Engineering Design Experiences in Grades 6-12, which produced the consensus report *Science and Engineering for Grades 6-12: Investigation and Design at the Center*. Egger earned her undergraduate degree from Yale University and received her M.S. and Ph.D. degrees in geological and environmental sciences from Stanford University.

MARCO MOLINARO is the executive director for educational effectiveness and analytics at the University of Maryland, College Park. Prior to coming to Maryland, he served as assistant vice provost for educational effectiveness at the University of California, Davis (UCD), and is the founding director of the Center for Educational Effectiveness. Molinaro has educational experience creating and leading applications of academic analytics, technology for instruction, scientific visualization and simulation, as well as curriculum development and evaluation. His most recent work focuses on student equity and inclusion through (a) being co-primary investigator (PI) of the Howard Hughes Medical Institute Inclusive Excellence project MIDAS, to ensure that all STEM students have the opportunity to pursue and excel in science, technology, engineering, and medicine (STEM) fields through the efforts of dedicated and informed instructors utilizing evidence-based instructional practices; (b) acting as the UCD campus PI for the Sloan Equity & Inclusion in STEM Introductory Courses collaborative and co-leading the 10 institution based Structures working group focused on establishing structures and cataloging narratives that best support lasting change in the instruction of foundational STEM courses; and (c) serving as chair of the Analytics Sub-Committee and Advisory Board member of the American Association for the Advancement of Science STEM Equity Achievement Change initiative aimed at ensuring that the full range of talent can be recruited and retained in STEM. Molinaro has served on National Academy of Sciences, Association of Public and Land-Grant Universities, and numerous National Science Foundation (NSF) grant-related committees and received funding from the NSF, National Institutes of Health, and various private foundations such as the Gates Foundation, Intel, the Helmsley Trust and Howard Hughes Medical Institute. Molinaro received his Ph.D. in biophysical chemistry from the University of California, Berkeley.

MARY MURPHY is a professor in the Department of Psychological and Brain Sciences at Indiana University. She is also the primary investigator of the Mind and Identity in Context Lab at Indiana University and Founder of the Equity Accelerator. Murphy's research focuses on developing and testing theories about how people's social identities and group memberships interact with the contexts they encounter to affect their thoughts, feelings, behaviors, physiology, and motivation. She also examines the particular concerns the situational cues engender among underrepresented groups, with an eye toward intervention. Murphy's research has been funded by the Spencer Foundation, Raikes Foundation, and the National Science Foundation and has been profiled in *The New York Times*, *Forbes*, *Harvard Business Review*, *Scientific American*, and NPR, among other outlets. She received her Ph.D. in social psychology at Stanford University.

JOSEPHINE D. PINO is currently instructor of biology at Portland Community College (PCC). Previously, she served as PCC instructor/department chair of bioscience technology, instructor of biotechnology and biology at the Community College of Rhode Island, and instructor of biology/coordinator of biotechnology at Shoreline Community College. Pino was an original co-primary investigator of the Northeast Biomanufacturing Center & Collaborative and Rhode Island EPSCOR grants. She served as PCC coordinator for BUILD-EXITO and liaison to the Community College Undergraduate Research Initiative. She chaired the PCC Educational Advisory Council for 5 years and her ongoing college service focuses on diverse ways of achieving equitable student success through cross-functional collaboration and inclusive teaching. Pino received the National Institute for Staff and Organizational Development's Excellence Award and the National Association of Biology Teachers Two-Year College Biology Teaching Award. She earned an M.S. in marine biology from Scripps Institution of Oceanography and received a second M.S. in biology from the University of Utah.

MELONIE W. SEXTON is a professor of psychology at Valencia College. She is also the College's Coordinator of Undergraduate Research. In these roles, Sexton introduces first- and second-year students to critical thinking, inquiry-based learning, and research practices. Prior to coming to Valencia, she was an academic adviser at Miami Dade College and Vanderbilt

University. During her tenure as an adviser, Sexton assisted first-time in college students in developing their academic pathways. Since starting at Valencia, she has worked with students to create a scientific approach to learning, but she has also designed several professional development opportunities for faculty and staff to engage in this work. Her expertise even extends beyond the college; Sexton is a board member of the TRiO Alumni Faculty Network, a member for the Society of Experiential Education (SEE)'s Research and Scholarship Committee, and peer reviewer for multiple research journals. She recently won the Rising Leader award for her diversity, equity, and inclusion work in the SEE's certification workshop. Sexton holds a Ph.D. in psychology from Vanderbilt University.

ELLI J. THEOBALD is an assistant professor of Biology at the University of Washington. Prior to her current position, she was a teaching professor of Biology in the same department after completing a postdoc in discipline-based education research. Theobald's working commitment to educational equity and student success was born when she worked as a middle school and high school teacher. Currently, the heart of her research program revolves around how to be a better teacher, with particular emphasis on how to achieve equity in college-level science, technology, engineering, and medicine (STEM) classes. Theobald uses quantitative and sometimes qualitative approaches to (a) describe inequities in student outcomes from, experiences in, and perceptions of STEM classes; (b) identify instructor and systemic practices that disrupt inequities; and (c) scale equitable practices to all classes in all STEM disciplines. She recently won the University of Washington's Distinguished Teaching Award and has been nominated twice to serve on National Academies of Sciences, Engineering, and Medicine committees (this committee: Equitable and Effective Teaching in Undergraduate STEM Education; and Advancing Anti-racism, Diversity, Equity, and Inclusion in STEM Organizations). Theobald received her B.A. in biology from Colby College, her M.A. in teaching from Alliant University, and her Ph.D. in ecology from the University of Washington.

CRISTINA VILLALOBOS is the Myles and Sylvia Aaronson Endowed Professor in the School of Mathematical and Statistical Sciences at the University of Texas Rio Grande Valley (UTRGV). Currently, she serves as Interim Dean of the Honors College and is the founding director of the Center of Excellence in STEM Education, which provides resources for the academic and professional development of faculty and students, especially increasing the numbers of underrepresented students attaining science, technology, engineering, and mathematics (STEM) degrees. From 2019 to 2024, Villalobos served as Associate Dean for Strategic Initiatives and Institutional Effectiveness in the College of Sciences. Villalobos' research areas lie in optimization, optimal control, and STEM education where she and her colleagues explore the mathematics identity of Calculus students in an alternative grading system. She served as Interim Director of the mathematics school, transitioning the school through the first two years (2015–2017) of UTRGV and increasing the numbers of Latino and women faculty. Villalobos' recognitions at the national level for mentoring and STEM leadership can be summarized with the 2020 Presidential Award for Excellence in Science, Mathematics, and Engineering Mentoring. She is also a recipient of the University of Texas System Board of Regents' Outstanding Teaching Award, the Society for Advancement of Chicanos/Hispanics & Native Americans in Science Distinguished Undergraduate Institution Mentor Award and the Presidential Award, and the Richard A. Tapia Achievement Award for Scientific Scholarship, Civic Science, and Diversifying Computing. Villalobos is a Fellow of the American Mathematical Society; a Ford Foundation Pre-doctoral fellow; and Sloan Foundation fellow. She received her B.S in mathematics from the University of Texas at Austin and her Ph.D. in computational and applied mathematics from Rice University.

GABRIELA WEAVER is the assistant dean and professor of chemistry at the University of Massachusetts, Amherst. She previously served as vice provost for faculty development, and director of the Institute for Teaching Excellence and Faculty Development. Weaver was elected a fellow of the American Association for the Advancement of Science for distinguished contributions to transforming science education at the undergraduate level. She served as director of a National Science Foundation-funded multi-institutional project Center for Authentic Science Practice in Education, dedicated to involving first- and second-year undergraduate students in course-based undergraduate research experiences. Weaver's research interests include educational practices that increase student success and the institutionalization of such practices through the transformation of cultures and processes in higher education. She has contributed to the work of the Board on Science Education at the National Academies of Sciences, Engineering, and Medicine in the past as a member of consensus study committee for Developing Indicators for Undergraduate STEM Education and on the organizing committee for a convocation on Integrating Discovery-Based Research into the Undergraduate Curriculum, as well as having been invited to provide papers or presentations for other consensus studies. Weaver received her Ph.D. in chemical physics from the University of Colorado, Boulder.

JOHN L. WILLIAMS is an associate professor of biology at Albany State University, where he currently serves as the chair of the Natural Sciences Department. His professional expertise is in science, technology, engineering, and medicine (STEM) student development and pre-professional preparation in the areas of medicine, pharmacy, and dentistry. Williams is also the director of STEM Strategic Partnerships and Initiatives, where he is tasked with developing and strengthening key institutional and community partnerships, primarily within the medical, health, and research fields. He was selected as a Center for Advancement in STEM Leadership fellow, and he has gained leadership experience in academic affairs through the Albany State University Provost fellowship. Through these activities, Williams has implemented several key Presidential and institutional initiatives that focus on student success in the sciences. He was also selected as Albany State University's Educator/Teacher of the Year due to his innovation in teaching. Williams is a graduate of Florida State University, where he received his Ph.D. in cell/molecular biology.

SEAN P. YEE is an associate professor of mathematics education at the University of South Carolina (USC) and the co-director of the Center for Science Education. He taught secondary school mathematics for eight years and guided preservice teachers in Ohio and California before joining USC to focus on pedagogy courses for mathematics graduate student instructors. Yee's research on mentoring, induction, and professional development (PD) for college mathematics instructors emphasizes generating communities of practice around student-centered instructional methods such as active-learning strategies. His research also includes problem solving, problem posing, conceptual metaphor theory, mathematical proof education, and graduate student instructor pedagogical education. Yee's national proceedings, publications, and external funding have focused on PD for novice science, technology, engineering, and medicine educators, established for the purpose of equitable access to evidence-based teaching practices. His honors include an Association of Mathematics Teacher Educators, Service, Teaching, and Research fellowship, a USC Innovative Teaching McCausland fellowship, being elected to the Board of Directors for the School Science and Mathematics Association, and associate editor for multiple journals. Yee received his Ph.D. from Kent State University in mathematics curriculum and instruction.

STAFF BIOS

KERRY BRENNER is a senior program officer with the Board on Science Education at the National Academies of Sciences, Engineering, and Medicine. She leads the Roundtable on Systemic Change in Undergraduate STEM Education and the Equitable and Effective Undergraduate STEM Teaching study that produced this report. She was co-study director for the Disrupting Ableism workshop series on people with disabilities in the STEM workforce and the Call to Action for Science Education project. She was also the study director for the Symposium on Imagining the Future of Undergraduate STEM Education, Undergraduate Research Experiences for STEM Students and Science and Engineering for Grades 6-12: Investigation and Design at the Center. She earned a bachelor's degree from Wesleyan University and a Ph.D. in molecular biology from Princeton University.

JANET GAO is a program officer with the Board on Science Education at the National Academies of Sciences, Engineering, and Medicine. She has been an active scholar-practitioner in the field of postsecondary education research, policy, and administration, and has taught students at many different levels. In Board on Science Education, she supports and coordinates work for a variety of K–12 and Higher Education projects, including events related to the Symposium on Imagining the Future of Undergraduate STEM Education, the Roundtable on Systemic Change in Undergraduate STEM Education, the Call to Action for Science Education, Foundations of Data Science for Students in Grades K–12. She has worked on three consensus studies including Equity in PreK–12 STEM Education, Assessing NASA Science Activation 2.0, and the current report on Supporting Equitable and Effective Teaching. She holds a doctoral degree from the George Washington University with a specialization in higher and international education and a master's degree in intercultural communication from the University of Pennsylvania.

LUCY OLIVEROS is a senior program assistant with the Board on Science Education at the National Academies of Sciences, Engineering, and Medicine. She supports the consensus study on Equitable and Effective Teaching in Undergraduate STEM Education; the consensus study on the Committee to Assess NASA Science Activation 2.0, and was newly added to the planning committee staff for the Convocation on the Status of Informal Science and Engineering Education. She earned her bachelor's degree in social welfare from The University of California, Berkeley.

HEIDI SCHWEINGRUBER is the director of the Board on Science Education at the National Academies of Sciences, Engineering, and Medicine. She oversees a portfolio of work that includes K–12 science education, informal science education, and higher education. Schweingruber joined the staff of the board in 2004 as a senior program officer. In this role, she directed or co-directed several projects including the study that resulted in the report A Framework for K-12 Science Education (2012), the blueprint for the Next Generation Science Standards. Most recently, she co-directed the study that produced the report Call to Action for Science Education: Building Opportunity for the Future (2021). Schweingruber is a nationally recognized leader in leveraging research findings to catalyze improvements in science and STEM education policy and practice. She holds a Ph.D. in psychology and anthropology, and a certificate in culture and cognition from the University of Michigan.